PRAYING THE PSALMS IN CHRIST

READING THE SCRIPTURES

Gary A. Anderson, Matthew Levering, and Robert Louis Wilken

series editors

PRAYING 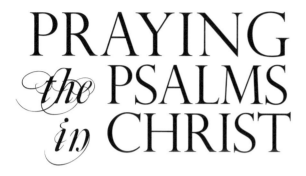 the PSALMS in CHRIST

LAURENCE KRIEGSHAUSER, O.S.B.

University of Notre Dame Press
Notre Dame, Indiana

BS
1430.54
.K75
2009

Library of Congress Cataloging-in-Publication Data

Kriegshauser, Laurence.
Praying the Psalms in Christ / Laurence Kriegshauser.
    p.   cm. — (Reading the Scriptures)
Includes bibliographical references and indexes.
ISBN-13: 978-0-268-03320-0 (pbk. : alk. paper)
ISBN-10: 0-268-03320-X (pbk. : alk. paper)
1. Bible. O.T. Psalms—Devotional use.   2. Bible. O.T. Psalms—Criticism,
interpretation, etc.   3. Jesus Christ.   I. Title.
BS1430.54.K75   2009
223'.207—dc22

                                                      2009001154

∼ To my mother and to Abbot Luke

CONTENTS

ACKNOWLEDGMENTS

I am grateful to the following who in various ways made this work possible: Abbot Thomas Frerking, O.S.B., Ralph Wright, O.S.B., Ambrose Bennett, O.S.B., the Passionist Nuns of Ellisville, Missouri, the Saint Anselm Parish prayer group, Dom Bernard McElligott of Ampleforth Abbey, Professor Frank O'Malley of the University of Notre Dame, Dominique Barthélemy, O.P., of the University of Fribourg, Katie Lehman and Barbara Hanrahan of the University of Notre Dame Press, Dr. Thomas Moran, Jordan Cherrick, Reverend Mr. Gerry Quinn, Nick White, and Joseph Marrs.

~ Psallite sapienter. Ps 47:8

INTRODUCTION

> The excellence of Christian prayer lies in this, that it shares in the very love of the only-begotten Son for the Father and in that prayer which the Son put into words in his earthly life and which still continues unceasingly in the name of the whole human race and for its salvation, throughout the universal Church and in all its members. (*GILH* 7)

With these words from the *General Instruction for the Liturgy of the Hours,* the Church proclaims the dignity of Christian prayer: it is a share in the prayer of the Incarnate Son of God himself. The Gospels show Christ frequently in prayer. He needed to commune with his heavenly Father to find wisdom and strength for his saving ministry and to entrust himself and his mission to the Father's guidance. It was his prayer that animated his sacrificial offering of himself to the Father (Heb 5:7). But at an even deeper level, as the eternal Son of God he was always in intimate communion with the Father from whom he proceeded and whom he loved with an infinite love. The love of the Father for the Son and of the Son for the Father is a third and distinct person, the Holy Spirit, who is the bond between the Father and the Son. The prayer of the Son on earth was a human participation in this trinitarian love, and the Church teaches that Christians who are baptized in Christ are drawn into this ineffable prayer of the Son to the Father: they are privileged to participate in it. Even when we cannot put this prayer into words or concepts, the Spirit of Christ is praying in us the prayer of the Son "with unutterable groanings" (Rom 8:26). It is the Christian's task to allow the Spirit to produce this prayer in us, so that we say with Christ, "Abba, Father" (Rom 8:15–17).

1

Eucharist and Liturgy of the Hours

The principal Christian prayer is the Eucharist, in which we are invited to offer to the Father the very sacrifice of the Son on Calvary. As Christ offers himself to the Father in our midst, we let ourselves be taken up into his offering, giving to the Father both the Sacred Body and Blood of his Son and our own selves incorporated into him. The single, once-for-all sacrifice of the Son on behalf of the whole human race is not repeated but is realized again, made present in our time and place. The offering of the Son to the Father did not cease at his death but endures forever: the Son continually offers to the Father the Body that was slain and is now risen. In the measure in which we can join in this truly cosmic sacrifice we are purified of sin and made holy. The Eucharist perfects our transformation in Christ.

From apostolic times Christians gathered for prayers outside the Eucharist as well. They practiced with new meaning the prayers offered in Judaism at certain times of the day. They prayed in the morning, seeing in the rising sun a symbol of the Lord who rose on Easter morning. They prayed in the evening, recalling the Lord's Supper and his Crucifixion both of which occurred toward the end of the day. Prayers celebrated at regular hours became a kind of sacramental fulfilment of the Lord's injunction to "Pray always" (Luke 18:1; cf. 1 Thess 5:17), and the common vocal prayer was meant to sustain an interior prayer that would continue through the whole of the day.

Liturgy of the Hours and Psalms

Where were the first disciples to find words to formulate the ineffable prayer of the Son to the Father? Christ himself gave the example in praying the psalms of Israel. On the cross he uttered both the psalmist's cry, "My God, my God, why have you abandoned me?" (Matt 27:46 = Ps 22:2) and the prayer of trust, "Into your hands I commend my spirit" (Luke 23:46 = Ps 31:6). He applied passages from the psalms to himself: "The stone which the builders rejected has become the corner stone" (Matt 21:42 = Ps 118:22); "The Lord's revelation to my master: 'Sit on my right.

I will put your foes beneath your feet'" (Matt 22:43–45, 26:64 = Ps 110:1); "My friend in whom I trusted, who ate my bread, has raised his heel against me" (John 13:18 = Ps 41:10); "Now my soul is troubled" (John 12:27 = Ps 42:7); "They hated me without cause" (John 15:25 = Ps 35:19, 69:5). After his resurrection he showed the apostles how the psalms were fulfilled in him, particularly in his suffering, death, and rising (cf. Luke 24:44–47).

The apostles and evangelists followed suit in finding Christ in the psalms. Particularly in the events of his Passion they found the psalms fulfilled: "They divide my clothing among them; they cast lots for my robe" (John 19:24 = Ps 22:19); "For food they gave me poison; in my thirst they gave me vinegar to drink" (Matt 27:34, 48 = Ps 69:22), and so forth. Saint Peter found a prophecy of his resurrection from the dead in Psalm 15: "Even my body will rest in safety, for you will not leave my soul among the dead nor let your beloved know decay. You will show me the path of life, the fullness of joy in your presence, at your right hand happiness forever" (Acts 2:26–28, 31 = Ps 16:9–11). For Saint Paul Psalm 8:7, "You put all things under his feet," was to be applied to Christ (1 Cor 15:26–28, Eph 1:22–23). Three times the author of Revelation applies to the risen Christ Psalm 2:9: "With a rod of iron you will break them" (Rev 2:27, 12:5, 19:15). Not only did Christians see Christ in the psalms; in praying the psalms they explicitly related certain verses to the events of his death and resurrection (see Acts 4:24–30 with respect to Ps 2:1–2). The psalms were as much part of early Christian prayer as they were part of the prayer of Jesus (cf. Mark 14:26, 1 Cor 14:26, Eph 5:19, Col 3:16, Jas 5:13).

By the beginning of the third century psalmody was a regular part of the daily hours of prayer. Psalms were commented on by bishops and catechists. Already Tertullian had heard in the psalms the voice of Christ: "Nearly all the psalms bear the person of Christ, that is, they represent Christ uttering words to the Father. Notice also the Spirit speaking as a third person about the Father and the Son."[1] It was Saint Augustine who

---

1. "[O]mnes paene psalmi Christi personam sustinent: Filium ad Patrem, id est Christum ad Deum verba facientem repraesentant. Animadverte etiam Spiritum loquentem ex tertia persona de Patre et Filio" (*Adversus Praxean* XI, 5–7 in Salmon, *Les "Tituli Psalmorum,"* 53 n. 23; all translations mine).

most consistently propounded the Christian application of the psalms. For him the psalm was the "voice of the whole Christ, head and members," that is, the prayer of Christ in his Body the Church. His vision is magisterially expressed in the great beginning of the exposition on Psalm 85:

> God could have granted no greater gift to human beings than to cause his Word, through whom he created all things, to be their head, and to fit them to him as his members. He was thus to be both Son of God and Son of Man, one God with the Father, one human being with us. The consequence is that when we speak to God in prayer we do not separate the Son from God and when the body of the Son prays it does not separate its head from itself. The one sole savior of his body is our Lord Jesus Christ, the Son of God, who prays for us, prays in us, and is prayed to by us. He prays for us as our priest, he prays in us as our head, and he is prayed to by us as our God. Accordingly we must recognize our voices in him, and his accents in ourselves. . . .

He further counsels his listeners, "Say nothing apart from [Christ], as he says nothing apart from you."[2] And so if the psalm prays, "Out of the depths I call to you, O Lord," it is Christ in his Passion praying along with Christ in his suffering members throughout the world right now. If it prays, "I will praise you among the nations," it is the risen Christ praising the Father in the Church spread throughout the world. In the words of Jean Corbon:

---

2. *Enarrationes in Psalmos* 85.1. A recent study summarizes Augustine's approach as follows:

> Neither the narrow life span of the individual pray-er nor the limited history of Israel, but only the time-transcending subject of the *whole Christ* could entirely embrace and perfectly assimilate the individual and collective experiences condensed in the psalms, from lamenting *de profundis* to jubilant *Alleluia,* and so unite pilgrimage and war, exile and temple, cult-criticism and priestly sacrifice, royal dignity and levitical ministry, sickness and ecstasy, betrayal and brotherly concord that their spiritually-interpreted reality became the expression of a single life that endures from the morning of creation to the last day to reach fulfilment in eternity. (Fiedrowicz, *Psalmus Vox Totius Christi,* 425–26; my translation)

[T]he prayer of the Hours consists chiefly of the prayer which Jesus himself used in his mortal condition: the psalms. In this single book of the Old Testament the entire economy of salvation became prayer, and now this love-inspired plan has been fulfilled in Jesus. When the church prays, the liturgy that "fulfills" this love-inspired plan is expressed through these same psalms. In them the Spirit repeats with the Bride the wonderful deeds of her Lord. (*Wellspring of Worship,* 127)

The present commentary will offer suggestions about how the psalms can become the vehicles of Christ's prayer in his Body the Church.

Aspects of the Psalms

In making the psalms his own Christ gave them their definitive meaning. They are the prayers of the man-God who is also the Son of God. He became incarnate, so to speak, in them. For this reason a Christian understanding of the psalms cannot neglect any dimension of these prayers that contributed to their original meaning, since that is the meaning taken up into the prayer of Christ. In any study of the Scriptures it is necessary to begin with the literal meaning of the passage in its historical context. For the Book of Psalms this includes an understanding of the genre or category of each psalm, its internal structure and emotional tensions, imagery, rhythm, and poetic devices such as parallelism and chiasmus, and asyndeton and consonance, by which meaning is enhanced or reinforced. The commentary will occasionally note how these various literary devices enrich the experience of the poetry; clearly only selected examples can be noted.

In the last quarter century research has centered on a previously unrecognized dimension of the Book of Psalms, its interconnectedness. Psalms are seen to have been deliberately placed so as to reflect and complement each other. In particular, greater attention is being paid to the division of the psalms into five "books," each ending with a doxology. These are Book One, Psalms 3–41; Book Two, Psalms 42–72; Book Three, Psalms 73–89; Book Four, Psalms 90–106; Book Five, Psalms 107–150. Within these units are found smaller collections such as the "Songs of Ascents" (Pss 120–134), collections of psalms attributed to David (first collection, Pss 3–41; second collection Pss 51–65; third collection Pss 138–145), psalms attributed to the "sons of Korah" (Pss 42–49; 84–85; 87–88), or to Asaph (Pss 50; 73–83), etc. Word links between adjacent or nearby psalms in the various groups encourage the reader to see these psalms in relation to each other. In this way the psalms "comment on" each other. No one psalm stands in isolation, but each is to be seen as a partial aspect of a larger whole. That is to say that the complexity of the relations between God and man can be suggested only by a reading of the whole psalter, just as all the parts of a novel are necessary for the whole. This commentary draws particularly on the work of Erich Zenger and Frank-Lothar Hossfeld[3] to highlight the significance of the positioning of each psalm in relation to the smaller collections of psalms and to the Book of Psalms as a whole. These interconnections will be part of the meaning that is taken up into the Christian praying of the psalm.

Often a verse of the Psalms is illuminated by a passage from another part of the Old Testament. Such parallels are indicated in the commentary, and the reader is encouraged to look up the parallel passages and reflect on the light they throw on the psalm. It may be necessary to read a few verses before the cited passage in order to understand the context, possibly with the help of explanatory footnotes, as in the Jerusalem Bible. Such a leisurely and meditative reflection on the links within the word of God can gradually point us toward the profound mystery beyond all words.

But it is the New Testament parallel passages that give the Christian dimension to the psalms. These passages point to the Christian relevance of the Old Testament prayers, bringing them to a new fullness of meaning. Throughout the Old Testament and in the Psalms in particular, God is portrayed as in love with his people. He created them, made them his own, rescued them from bondage, bound himself to them with a covenant, worked wonders for them; gave them a land, victory over enemies, kings and prophets, a temple in which he would dwell; and continually appealed to them to accept his lordship. Just as continually, his people refused his love, preventing him from being able to give them the fullness of peace he intended for them. The two sides of this God-man rela-

---

3. Hossfeld and Zenger, *Die Psalmen*, vol. 1, *Psalm 1–50*; vol. 2, *Psalm 51–100* (Würzburg: Echter Verlag, 1993, 2002).

tionship are the warp and woof of the psalms. God longs for man; man longs for God but feels held back by sin or hostile forces. The impasse was only resolved when God sent his Son: the Incarnate Son of God would be the first human being to respond with wholehearted obedience to the loving will of the Father. Jesus's vocation was to show God's love for man in human flesh and to persevere in showing that love even when it was rejected and crucified. Because Jesus clung to the Father's will even to death, he successfully fulfilled the task of man, and there was no reason that death should keep him in its power (cf. Acts 2:23–24). In raising him from the dead the Father reconciled all humankind to himself, taking away their sin (2 Cor 5:18–19). The risen Christ is our way to the Father (John 14:6, Heb 10:20), the mediator between God and man (1 Tim 2:5–6). When Christians accept Jesus as their Lord they receive the forgiveness of their sins and stand in the Father's presence in the risen Son, calling God Father. And when they pray the psalms together on earth it is the saving love of Christ for the Father that they put into words: such is the import of the passage cited at the beginning of this introduction. They offer to the Father the one prayer by which the world was saved, participating in the remaking of the world. At the same time they are introduced into the heart of the dialogue between the Father and the Son in the bosom of the Trinity: they are drawn into the inner life of God.

Thus when a psalm speaks of God's love (*ḥesed*) for his people, the Christian means the love shown in his sending of his Son to die for us. When it speaks of God's dwelling among his people in the temple, the Christian means the Body of Christ, his Church. When it speaks of liberation from Egypt or defeat of enemies, the Christian means the liberation from sin won by Christ. When the psalm cries out in anguish, the Christian hears the voice of Christ offering his pain to the Father as propitiation for our sins, and he prays in the name of the suffering body of Christ on earth still bearing the cross on its pilgrim journey. In making suggestions about how to pray the psalms from within the Christian mystery, it is hoped that this commentary may stimulate Christians to find their own correspondences between the psalms and the mystery of Christ as presented in the New Testament.

As we continue to pray the psalms in Christ, allowing more and more his Spirit to possess us, we find that the psalms are expressing our

own emotions. They channel our longing, our sorrow, our joy, our grati-
tude, our love into the full expression of the humanity of Christ. Even
our anger becomes transmuted into zeal for the coming of the kingdom.
In this way the psalms have an educatory function as was noted by the
early monastic writers. For Saint Athanasius the psalms were a "mirror"
in which the one praying finds his own self and emotions:

> And the one who hears is deeply moved, as though he himself were
> speaking, and is affected by the words of the songs, as if they were his
> own songs.... Each sings them as if they were written about himself....
> Then the things spoken are such that he lifts them up to God as if he
> were acting and speaking them from himself.... Each psalm is both
> spoken and composed by the Spirit so that in these same words ... the
> stirrings of our souls might be grasped, and all of them be said as con-
> cerning us, and they issue from us as our own words, as a reminder of the
> emotions in us, and a chastening of our life. (*Letter to Marcellinus* 11–12)

In the next century John Cassian wrote in a similar vein:

> Nourished by continual feeding on the psalms and appropriating all
> their emotions as his own, he will begin to sing them in such a way that
> in profound compunction of heart he will produce them not as com-
> posed by a prophet but as if uttered by himself as his own prayer, or at
> least he will consider them to have been directed to his own person and
> will recognize that their sentiments were not only realized formerly
> through or in the prophet but are carried out and fulfilled today in him-
> self. (Conference X, 11; my translation)[4]

Athanasius went even further in attributing a kind of "Christ therapy"
to the psalms. God composed these prayers as a pattern of the humanity

---

4. "Quorum iugi pascuo vegetatus omnes quoque psalmorum adfectus in se re-
cipiens ita incipiet decantare, ut eos non tamquam a propheta conpositos, sed velut a
se editos quasi orationem propriam profunda cordis conpunicitione depromat vel
certe ad suam personam aestimet eos fuisse directos, eorumque sententias non tunc
tantummodo per prophetam aut in propheta fuisse conpletas, sed in se cotidie geri in-
plerique cognoscat."

of Christ "before his sojourn in our midst, so that just as he provided the model of the earthly and heavenly man in his own person, so also from the Psalms he who wants to do so can learn the emotions and dispositions of the souls, finding in them also the therapy and correction suited for each emotion" (*Letter to Marcellinus* 13). Through the psalms we can experience our own feelings as the feelings of Christ and vice versa. Our feelings become purified, liberated of anything selfish. "So the psalms have been formed like a sculptor's tools for the true overseer who, like a craftsman, is carving our souls to the divine likeness" (Gregory of Nyssa, *On the Inscriptions* II, 137).

FEATURES OF THE COMMENTARY

The reader will notice at the head of each commentary a single word. These words are meant not as titles or summaries of the psalms, but as indications of something distinct about them. Sometimes the word is an image more developed in one psalm than in any other (e.g., "tree" in Ps 1); other times the word is used in a striking way in the psalm (e.g., "apple" for Ps 17) or as a motif (e.g., "poor" in Ps 9-10); still other times the word alludes to an item found in the psalm (e.g., "sickbed" in Ps 6, "theophany" in Ps 18). These choices are personal and may stimulate the reader to find his or her own "key word" that will designate the uniqueness of a psalm.

The commentary is based on the Hebrew text of the psalms as found in the *Biblia Hebraica* and follows the current trend in scholarship to respect this Masoretic text without alteration or emendation. The attempt to render the literal sense of the Hebrew may yield awkward English, but it has the advantage of giving the reader the force, and often roughness, of the original poem, even at the cost of elegance. Stylistic variations in word order, as in chiastic expressions, are difficult to reproduce in English, but as they are features of Hebrew poetry the reader has a right to know where they occur. It is hoped that some awareness of these features may deepen a reader's praying of a psalm even if the official translation of these prayers does not reproduce them. The Grail translation, which is the most widely used version in the Liturgy of the Hours in the English-speaking world, has the merit of general accuracy, singability, and rhythm;

it can easily be prayed even when one is aware that it cannot reproduce all the subtleties of the original Hebrew. The reader might find it helpful to have at hand a copy of the Grail translation as he or she peruses the commentaries on individual psalms.

The Greek translation, the Septuagint (LXX), is occasionally consulted to throw light on a psalm. Most often, however, the commentary takes the form of a literal translation of the Hebrew text, generally in the third person so that the author's comments can blend with the text. When it was felt necessary to give a literal rendering of passages in the second or first person, the translation is provided within quotation marks. Quotation marks are also used around individual words that have a theological significance or that have important parallels in other verses of the Psalms or other biblical books, these parallels being indicated in parentheses.[5]

A particular feature of the commentary is the effort to translate a Hebrew word with the same English word each time it appears in a psalm. In this way words having a certain theological "weight," such as *ḥesed* (covenant love), *yš* (save), *bāṭaḥ* (trust), are preserved as are distinctions between synonyms that may have slightly different nuances, as in the rich vocabulary for verbs of rejoicing or nouns for anger or sin. Again the price for literal accuracy will be a loss of elegance, but the reader will have the advantage of knowing which Hebrew concept or poetic device is present in a given verse. At the end of the book is a table of English renderings of selected Hebrew words as translated in this commentary. Certain other translation choices require special comment. The divine name, YHWH, which appears over 680 times in the Book of Psalms, is sometimes rendered "Yahweh," but generally "The Lord." The title *ʾādôn* is regularly rendered "Master." The word *nefeš* is translated by the traditional "soul," although it originally meant "throat," the channel of breath, and is sometimes likely to have this meaning.[6] The important word *ḥesed* is rendered "covenant love" or simply "love."

---

5. For quotations from Scripture other than the Psalms, I rely on the Jerusalem Bible, the RSV, or my own translation.

6. See the helpful discussion by Robert Alter in the introduction to his translation of the Psalms, *The Book of Psalms* (New York: W.W. Norton, 2007), 32–33.

An attempt is made in the commentary to read the psalms as a book, in which each psalm makes a new contribution to the work as a whole. This means that themes are slowly developed, later psalms adding nuances to themes introduced in earlier ones. For this reason references to other psalms tend to look backward not forward, that is, to psalms already discussed rather than to psalms appearing later in the book. Like the reading of a novel, the continuous reading of the psalms is a cumulative experience. The first appearance of a theme will be discussed in its place, and later appearances will refer back to the earlier ones for clarification and enrichment. Only upon completing a reading of the Book of Psalms does one gain a grasp of the whole.

CHRISTIAN AND JEWISH READING OF THE PSALMS

The psalms are given to us by Judaism. They are the voice of a humanity befriended by God. If Christians see this humanity as taken up into Jesus, they are paying the utmost tribute to these Jewish prayers. The Church inherits the Hebrew Scriptures as a treasure of divine revelation; it does not reject them but venerates every last iota of them. Christians cannot afford to bypass the Hebrew Scriptures in trying to understand the One who is their fulfilment. While our Jewish brothers and sisters cannot be expected to read the psalms through the lens of Christ, we Christians will not read the psalms divorced from their Jewish roots. It is to be hoped that the Church's growing awareness of the interlocking of the two Testaments will lead to a greater mutual appreciation between our two faiths. Christians see a "potentiality of meaning" in the Jewish Scriptures that does not abolish the original meaning of those texts for the Jews themselves (*Jewish People and Their Sacred Scriptures*, 64).

~ The Psalms are a vast temple in which God is worshipped. Each individual psalm is like a room in the temple, full of God's presence but not exhausting it. Praising God in one psalm we hear echoes of songs from other rooms. The psalms in their totality are the "script" for the people of God, themselves a temple wherein God is worshipped, so that in the singing of the psalms the two temples come together. Our task is to open ourselves to the risen Christ who prays within us, whose Spirit guides our prayer. Because the ongoing psalmody of the Church on earth is a participation in the action by which all men and women are reconciled to God, no other action of the Church, apart from the Eucharist from which it flows, surpasses it in efficacy (*Sacrosanctum Concilium* 7).

Let us conclude with the great passage on the Liturgy of the Hours from Pius XII's encyclical *Mediator Dei,* the document that renewed the Church's understanding of the liturgy as the prayer of Christ (1947). The present book is simply an attempt to draw out the implications of this paragraph for each of the 150 prayers in the Book of Psalms.

> The Word of God, when He assumed a human nature, introduced into this land of exile the hymn that in heaven is sung throughout all ages. He unites the whole community of mankind with Himself and associates it with Him in singing this divine canticle of praise. We have to confess humbly that 'we do not know what prayer to offer, to pray as we ought'; but 'the Spirit himself intercedes for us, with groans beyond all utterance,' and Christ Himself beseeches the Father through His Spirit in us. (144)

Let us then study the psalms as the language spoken to the Father by the humanity redeemed in Christ.

～ PSALM 1   tree

The first psalm establishes an important principle: success in life comes from an absorption in the revealed will of God. The psalm is less a prayer than a statement of a spiritual truth, or rather the uttering of it becomes a praise of the truth it expresses. The psalm begins with a "beatitude," a statement of who is happy, of which there are twenty-six in the psalter. The first requirement for happiness is a refusal to walk according to the plans of the "wicked" who have no interest in God's will (v. 1), a refusal to stand on the way of sinners who act against God, a refusal to sit in the abode of scoffers. Amid the bewildering array of lifestyles a man must be careful where he derives his principles of behavior. He must reject attractive but deadly formulas for happiness and instead delight in the revelation of Israel's God committed to writing in the Torah. In that book he finds that he is a member of a people specially chosen and loved by the Creator, a God who has given his people a land and a promise of life, and who has invited them freely to affirm his rights over all life. The Law includes all the great deeds the Lord has done for Israel and also the commands that delineate how men may please him to receive the fullness of his gifts. His will is a gracious will: he loves all that he has made and invites the men and women made in his image (Gen 1:26–27) to share in that love. The man who will be happy is the one who delights in the word that reveals the loving plan of God and murmurs it to himself day and night (v. 2). Men are invited to delight in the Lord's revealed plan and keep it constantly present to mind and lips.

What is the result of this ongoing converse with the word of God? One becomes firmly rooted in existence like a tree by water channels that bears its fruit in its time and whose leaves never fade; all that such a man does prospers (v. 3). The man firmly rooted in God is Jesus, whose food was to do his Father's will (John 4:34) and who did always what pleased the Father (John 8:29). He continually sought time with the Father in prayer (Luke 5:16, 6:12, 9:18, 28, 11:1, 22:41) and thought of his mission as the fulfilling of the Father's plan expressed in the Old Testament (Luke 24:44–47). His love for the Father was shown in perfect obedience to the Father's command (John 14:31), as a result of which he was raised to an everlasting life (Phil 2:9, Rom 6:9, 1 Pet 3:18). In his manhood he is eternally rooted in the Father and bears the fruit of everlasting life for all who accept him.

But this man is himself the incarnate Word of the Father (John 1:1, 14), and as such, a source of living water springing up to eternal life for those who are thirsty (John 4:14). This water is identified by Saint John with the Holy Spirit poured out from Christ's body (John 7:37–39), like the spirit poured out on the thirsty soil to give life to abundant plants (Isa 44:3–4). The word Christ spoke and the Word he was[1] are spirit and life (John 6:63). The Christian who drinks in this water bears much fruit in Christ (John 15:5, 8, 16), bears the fruits of the Holy Spirit (Gal 5:22–23). By accepting the Spirit of the risen Jesus, the believer is incorporated into him, lives with his life. He cannot help but prosper because he lives with a divine life.

The wicked have no roots because their wickedness consists precisely in cutting themselves off from the giver of life; they are ephemeral, lacking substance, blown away like chaff in the wind (v. 4; cf. Luke 3:17). When men are judged on their basic choices, the wicked will not be left standing, nor sinners in the gathering of the just (v. 5), the counterpart of the group of scoffers (v. 1). For the Lord "knows" the way of the just (as he does not "know" those who sin, Matt 7:23, 25:12): their lives of conformity to his will are totally transparent, while the way of the wicked vanishes (v. 6). The Church is the assembly of all those who, delighting in the revealed will of God, bear the fruit of eternal life in Christ.

The psalmist has borrowed from two books of Scripture outside the Psalms, Joshua and Jeremiah. On the threshold of the land of Canaan, the Lord instructs Joshua to "murmur" the "book of the Law day and night" that he might "prosper in all [his] ways" (Jos 1:8). Thus both the second and third sections of the Hebrew Scriptures, the Prophets (Greater and Lesser) and the Writings (beginning with the Book of Psalms), begin

---

1. "Jesus himself is the living 'fulfillment' of the law inasmuch as he fulfills its authentic meaning by the total gift of himself: he himself becomes a living and personal law, who invites people to follow him; through the Spirit he gives the grace to share his own life and love and provides the strength to bear witness to that love in personal choices and actions" (John Paul II, *Veritatis Splendor* 15).

by hearkening back to the first section, the Law or Torah. The image of the fruitful tree by running waters is taken from the prophet Jeremiah (Jer 17:7–8) where it is applied to the man who puts his trust in the Lord, a theme that undergirds the entire psalter. Continual converse with the law of the Lord and trust in him are but two aspects of a single willingness to draw life from him.

∾ PSALM 2   son

If in Psalm 1 man is rooted in God, in Psalm 2 he is a son of God. If nations and peoples, kings and princes rebel against God and his representative on earth, it is because they do not understand the unbreakable bond between Israel's God and his anointed king. God is the one who "sits in the heavens" (v. 4) and who has "begotten" the king as his son on the "day" of the king's coronation (v. 7). Speaking through the prophet Nathan, God had said of David's son, "I will be a father to him and he a son to me" (2 Sam 7:14). No other Israelite could boast of having God as his father like the reigning son of David. The king's vocation was to administer on earth the justice of Yahweh himself (see esp. Ps 72). He would make the law of Yahweh obeyed on earth, with Yahweh there to support him in this task. The king had the right of "asking" for a worldwide rule and his father would grant what he asked, smashing all opposition (vv. 8–9). For a short time David and his son Solomon did enjoy a rule over Israel's neighboring kingdoms (cf. 2 Sam 8:1–14).

Such a "son of David" was Jesus Christ (cf. Matt 20:30, 21:9, Rom 1:3, Acts 13:23). As son of David he was son of God like each one of the kings of Judah. But divinity radiated from his person as it had from no other king. He performed actions that only God could perform (Mark 1:27, 4:39–41), his words carried a divine authority (John 8:26–28, 18:6). He spoke what he had seen with his Father before he came into the world (John 8:38). His being reflected that of his Father (Heb 1:3). He was Son of God for all eternity before becoming incarnate as a son of David. He knew the innermost secrets of the Father: there was nothing the Father did not show him (John 5:20). In short, he was the equal of his Father, distinct from his Father but the same God. While the son of David had become an adopted son of God on the "day" of his coronation, Jesus has been Son of God by nature from all eternity. He is the reflection of the Father's essence who appeared in human form. Jesus thus adds a totally unexpected meaning to the term "son" of God in our psalm: this descendant of David has shared God's nature for all eternity.

The son enjoys an unparalleled intimacy with the Father. Whatever he asks is granted, in particular the spread of salvation to the ends of the earth. Through Christ God establishes his kingship over the world (1 Cor 15:28). But Christ wishes to share his divine sonship with men. Through baptism those who accept him become sons of God (Gal 3:26–27), brothers of Christ (Rom 8:29, John 20:17), members of his Body (1 Cor 12:27). Christ has become the firstborn of many brethren. Insofar as we are "in him" we are "sons in the Son" (*Gaudium et spes* 22). We have the right to say with the psalmist-king: "The Lord said to me, 'You are my son; it is I who have begotten you this day'" (v. 7). We share in the very relationship the divine Son of God has with his Father (*Catechism of the Catholic Church* 2780). We have all the privileges of the son in the house (cf. Heb 3:6): absolute assurance of our Father's love and protection, intimate fellowship and communion, mutual knowledge, resemblance, sharing of concerns, cooperation in a single mission in the world. All these aspects of the father-son relationship will be developed in the psalms.

The son of God in our psalm is associated with a place: God's holy mountain, Zion, the mountain on which Jerusalem and the temple were built. God's rule radiates from this place. His king reigns from the very place where God dwells among men. For Christians this place is the Body of Christ, the earthly members of which form his Church. Christ's reign extends from this body to incorporate all nations and peoples. Beginning with the very next psalm, the psalms will often "localize" God's presence on Mount Zion, which for Christians designates the temple that is the Body of Christ, the Church, with its divinely ordained ministries. As the baptismal ritual puts it, we call God Father in the midst of the Church. God establishes his rule on earth through the people who believe in him and form a temple of living stones.

The revelation of the king as son of God emerges in Psalm 2 in an atmosphere of contention. The psalmist is amazed that the nations rage and the races murmur empty things against God's rule through his king. The opening verse illustrates synonymous parallelism in a chiastic (reverse) order: the initial "Why" matches the final "empty things," the verbs come second and second from the end, and the noun subjects meet in the middle. The verb "murmur" found in Psalm 1:2 is now used in a pejorative sense. From the outset the psalms display dynamic tensions among themselves, patterns of unity in contrast. Verse 2 introduces kings of the earth and rulers taking their stand and conspiring against the Lord and his messiah. The activity of the rebels culminates in the cry, "Let us sunder their fetters; let us throw from us their bonds" (v. 3).

But the speaker sees beyond the present crisis to abiding realities. The earthly drama is watched from above by the creator of the world, who "laughs" at the folly of man's rebellion (cf. Pss 59:9, 37:13); the Master derides them (v. 4). The laughter quickly becomes anger, which is how man experiences the holiness of God when it is rejected. God does not wish to "terrify" (v. 5) man but to save him (1 Tim 2:4, John 3:17) by giving him life (John 10:10, Isa 55:3). Rejection of the gift deprives one of that life and so is experienced as a thwarting of one's deepest longing. God's anger is simply man's experience of the consequences of his own rejection of divine goodness. "'Wrath' does not refer precisely to an emotion in God, but denotes the situation created by human defiance of the divine will" (Byrne, *Romans,* 302). The "anger of God" against sin is good news (Rom 1:18) because it destroys man's refusal to receive the divine love. Jesus manifested anger at the hardness of heart of the Pharisees (cf. Mark 3:5–6) because it prevented him from being able to save them and others. As the "revolt" scene in the opening of the psalm culminated in a speech, so God's anger finds expression in words: "It is I who have set my king on Zion my holy mountain" (v. 6). The verse breaks the psalm's pattern of synonymous parallelism: the second half of the line adds new information to the first rather than echo it.

At the heart of the psalm is the citation by the king of the Lord's oracle, beginning with verse 7: "My son are you, I today have begotten you." There follow the Lord's promises to grant him the "nations" (cf. v. 1) as an inheritance and as his property the ends of the earth (v. 8), and to eliminate all resistance (v. 9). The six words of verse 9 are artfully arranged: verbs at beginning ("you will shatter them") and end ("you will dash in pieces") surround adverbial phrases, one expressing the victor's instrument ("with a rod of iron"), the other a comparison for the vanquished ("like a potter's vessel"). The Book of Revelation applies the verse to the victorious Christ (Rev 12:5, 19:15, reading with the LXX "rule" for "shatter"), who shares his rule with his loyal disciples (Rev 2:26–28).

In the light of this revelation of the king's divine sonship, the speaker advises the rebel kings and rulers (lit. "judges") to recognize the sovereignty of Israel's God and his messiah (v. 10, chiasmus). They are to "serve the Lord with fear," fear not that God will punish them but that they might reject his love. Such a fear of the Lord is entirely compatible with "rejoic[ing] with trembling" (v. 11). After a disputed two-word phrase ("Kiss the son") the final verse (12) alludes both to the opening of the psalm (cf. "anger," v. 5) and to the end of Psalm 1 ("vanish on the way"). The concluding beatitude, which makes an inclusion with Psalm 1:1, introduces the theme of "taking refuge" in God, a major theme in Book One (Pss 3–41).

The first two psalms lay the foundation for the intimacy between man and God developed in the rest of the psalms. Neither psalm is addressed directly to God, and neither is really a prayer. The first emphasizes man's willingness to receive life from God, the second the divine initiative in the establishment of his kingdom.

∿ PSALM 3   thousands

The first psalm to address God directly introduces the theme of trust, though the word itself is not used. Innumerable are the psalmist's oppressors, innumerable those who "rise against" him and claim that there is no salvation for him in God (vv. 2–3). The psalmist has recourse to the divine name (vv. 2, 4), confessing the Lord as both a "shield" (cf. Gen 15:1) around him and one "who lifts up [his] head" in victory (v. 4). As in Psalm 2 the speaker sees an invisible savior behind an overwhelming present crisis.

The psalmist develops his confession of trust in three additional verses, speaking of God now in the third person. The first act of trust is to "call aloud to the Lord"; instantaneously the Lord "answers." The pairs "call/answer" and "hear/prayer," frequent in the psalter, remind us of Jesus's teaching, "Ask and you shall receive" (Matt 7:7–11, John 16:23–24). In this case it is "from his holy mountain" that God answers the cry: wherever the psalmist may be, it is from God's dwelling on earth that he will answer—the same Mount Zion on which God has established his king (v. 5; Ps 2:6). For Christians the temple is the Body of Christ, the Church, through which comes every saving grace that we receive. Whenever Christ in his suffering members calls to the Father for help, it is from the Body of Christ that salvation comes. So certain is this help that the psalmist can lie down and sleep (v. 6) without fear in the midst of "thousands" of enemies (v. 7) and be certain of waking because the Lord "upholds" him (v. 6). Divine power radiates from Zion across any distance (cf. Jonah 2:3, 8).

Having portrayed his plight and expressed his trust, the psalmist voices his petition to the Lord, the first in the psalter and an example of the prayer alluded to in verse 5. For God to "arise" (v. 8a; cf. v. 2) is for him to act, to intervene in the human situation. The verb was part of the ark ritual: Yahweh, seated invisible on the cherubs above the ark, was summoned to arise as the Israelites broke camp in the desert (cf. Num 10:33–35). His active presence would scatter Israel's enemies. Here the verb is paired with the more frequent "save" (yšʿ) a word designating God's most characteristic act and used in its verb or noun forms 134 times in the psalter. "To save" is the specialty of Israel's God, a fact of which the oppressors are ignorant (v. 3). The word yšʿ is the root of the name Jesus whose mission was to save (Matt 1:21, Luke 19:10, John 3:17). The Jesus who prayed to the one who could "save him from death" (Heb 5:7), who was mocked on the cross as unable to save (Matt 27:39–42), is the very one in whose name alone we can be saved (Acts 4:12).

In a reminiscence of the messiah's actions (Ps 2:9) the speaker envisions God striking his enemies (first use of this common word) on the cheek (v. 8b) and breaking the teeth of the "wicked," as the enemies are now designated (cf. Ps 1:1, 4–6). It is of the essence of wickedness to deny that God saves (v. 3). The psalmist counters this blasphemy with his succinct act of faith: "To Yahweh belongs salvation" (v. 9), to which he adds a petition for God's blessing on the whole people.

The psalm puts into words the confident trust of the man rooted in God's torah (Ps 1) and enjoying the status of God's son (Ps 2). Alone against thousands he is invincible and victorious. Besieged he sleeps in peace. This is the faith of a Paul: "the Lord will rescue me from all evil attempts on me, and bring me safely to his heavenly kingdom" (2 Tim 4:18).

With its reference to "waking" the psalm is assigned by Saint Benedict to the beginning of the night office. It is an appropriate prayer to be prayed on Holy Saturday as the Church waits for Christ to "wake" from death on Easter morning. An ancient "psalm title"[2] reads, "The psalm shows that Christ slept in the sleep of death for us and rose again" (Salmon, Les "Tituli Psalmorum," 138).

∿ PSALM 4   corn

The speaker makes his own spiritual life transparent to his neighbors that they might know where true happiness is found. He admonishes the "sons of men" to desist from loving emptiness (cf. Ps 2:1) and seeking falsehood (v. 3) and imagines "many" (cf. Ps 3:2–3) asking, "Who will show us good things? For the light from your face has fled from us, O Lord" (v. 7). Although the speaker himself is in distress (v. 2), his "glory [cf. Ps 3:4] disgraced" by those he addresses (v. 3a), he asks the Lord to have mercy on him and to hear his prayer (v. 2; cf. Ps 3:5); he expresses his trust in this Lord (vv. 4, 9), testifies before the hearers to the joy the Lord has given him (v. 8), and recommends behaviors that will win the same blessings for them (vv. 5–6). He thus appears as a "wounded healer" who out of his own need becomes a source of strength for others. The psalm is appropriate in the mouth of Christ from both points of view: Christ needed to be saved from death by his Father (see on Ps 3:8a), while at the same time proclaiming to men where peace and joy were to be found (John 14:27, 15:11, 16:24).

The speaker's thoughts do not follow a linear development but move back and forth between addressing God (vv. 2, 7b, lament; vv. 8–9, trust) and addressing men (vv. 3–6). Even the address to men moves from chastisement to personal testimony to recommendation. The long meter (generally 4 + 4) is explained by the need to complete one of these distinct thoughts in the span of a single verse. The contrasting modes are epitomized in the opening verse, where a past action of God ("from distress you released me," lit. "in narrowness you made a broad space for me") is inserted between the imperatives calling for present hearing. The

---

2. Psalms in ancient Latin manuscripts often carry "titles" giving suggestions for the Christian praying of a psalm. These should not be confused with the "titles" or "superscriptions" that are part of the Hebrew text of many psalms. See Glossary of Terms for the latter.

apparent "jerkiness" of thought is unified by the psalmist's undeviating orientation toward Yahweh, the "God of [his] justice" (v. 2).

What advice can the speaker give to those seeking good? First, to recognize that Yahweh grants favors to (or does wonders for) his devoted one and that Yahweh hears the psalmist's prayer (v. 4). Verse 4 thus combines an objective fact with a personal testimony. Such a God should be approached with "trembling" (as with those who heard of Yahweh's deeds at the Red Sea, Exod 15:14; cf. Isa 64:1, Jer 33:9) since one's life depends on his favor. For that reason the hearers must be careful "not to sin." They should speak (reflect) in their hearts on their beds and be still (v. 5). They should offer to Yahweh sacrifices that represent just behavior, and above all, they should "trust in the Lord." This is the first occurrence of the word that expresses the heart of the psalmist's attitude and is akin to what the New Testament means by "believe." It is a handing oneself over to the Lord, a reliance on his power and love, and a conviction that God is "for us." It is the act that enables God to give a joy "greater than the times when grain [corn in British English] and wine abound" (v. 8; for verb see Ps 3:2) and a peace that permits the psalmist both to lie down and to sleep, for the Lord alone has made him dwell in security (v. 9; cf. Ps 3:6).

Contemporary man is still asking, "Who will make us see good things?" Our psalm suggests that Christians who are not afraid to let their need for God be seen can reveal to the world the true source of joy and peace in the heart. Prayerful calling on the Lord for "mercy" (v. 2), a prayer springing from deep trust, provides for man a "safety" (v. 9, a word formed from the root "trust" of v. 6) that none of today's false gods can give. Our psalmist is not unlike the Saul who after his conversion went around with the apostles "preaching boldly in the name of the Lord" (Acts 9:28) and who found his strength precisely in his weakness (2 Cor 12:9–10). The speaker of Psalm 4 is fulfilling the injunction of Saint Peter: "Always have your answer ready for people who ask you the reason for the hope that you all have" (1 Pet 3:15).

⌁ PSALM 5   access

Psalm 5 reveals the moral rectitude that is required in God's presence. The psalmist finds himself at the house of God, bowing down before the holy place (v. 8). He proclaims at length what was suggested in Psalm 1:5, that intimate union with Israel's God requires a conformity of will and action with that God. It would be impossible to be united with God while flouting his will: that would be for God to be divided against himself. Jesus ate with sinners to win them from sin, not to condone sin. The principle is laid down in verse 5: "For you are not a God who delights in wickedness; evil does not sojourn with you." It is the principle enunciated by Saint Paul: "Virtue is no companion for crime. Light and darkness have nothing in common. Christ is not the ally of Beliar, nor has a believer anything to share with an unbeliever. The temple of God has no common ground with idols . . ." (2 Cor 6:14–16). The psalmist then details behaviors that are incompatible with dwelling in God's house. Boasters cannot stand before him, he hates all evildoers (v. 6; cf. Jdt 5:17, ". . . they have a God who hates wickedness"). He destroys the speakers of falsehood (cf. Ps 4:3), and the man of bloodshed and deceit he loathes (v. 7, chiasmus). The emphasis is on words and deeds that destroy the social fabric.

But through the abundance (cf. Pss 3:2–3, 4:7–8) of God's covenant love—the first use in the psalms of the noun *ḥesed,* the Lord's enduring attachment to his people through the covenant—the psalmist can enter the house of God, and he shows the appropriate attitude, prostrating himself toward God's holy temple with fear (v. 8). This is the same fear recommended to the rebellious nations in Psalm 2:11, the taking account of the primacy of the transcendent God. It is very different from the human or earthly fear from which God delivers his faithful (cf. Ps 3:7). Entry into the presence of God requires a readiness to undergo the purification from sin, which God in his mercy effects. For this reason the Roman Rite of the Mass begins with an acknowledgement of sins and a plea for mercy.

This beautiful verse 8 is like an island in the middle of the psalm. On either side, at the end of verse 7 and the beginning of verse 9, occurs the divine name Yahweh, like the wall that banishes sin from the sanctuary where God dwells with his people. Beyond the divine name on both sides we encounter sin. Verses 5–7 listed sins that exclude from Yahweh's company; verses 9–11 reveal adversaries whose flattering words cover ruinous intent. Their sin has inner ("belly," "throat," "counsels") and verbal ("mouth" and "tongue") elements and is at root a rebellion and a defiance of God (v. 11). In a few vivid verses the psalmist has covered the three faculties of sin: thought, word, and deed, a threesome often met in the psalms. But these three verses are combined with petitions. "Lord, lead me in your justice [cf. Ps 4:2, 6] in the face of my adversaries; make straight before me your way" (v. 9). Guidance on the path of justice must be God's; this justice is not man's achievement. God is asked to declare the enemies guilty, in the abundance (cf. v. 8) of their rebellions to repudiate them (v. 11). The holiness of God must radiate from the temple to convert the hearts and minds of sinful men. With Christ we pray that the rebellion in the heart of man may be broken so that all may welcome his salvation (cf. 1 Cor 5:4–5). It is the conversion of sinners, not their death, that God wants (Ezek 33:11).

On either side of the descriptions of behavior incompatible with God's presence we have an introduction and a conclusion to the prayer. The opening verse (v. 2) is arranged chiastically around the divine name: "To my words give ear, Lord; pay attention to my meditation." A second verse (v. 3) renews the plea in different words with two other titles of the Lord in the center: "Attend to the voice of my cry for help, my king and my God, for to you I pray." Both titles reveal that the psalmist is placing himself under a God who has care of him, unlike his enemies who "defy" God (v. 11). In the following verse (4) the psalmist accompanies his prayer with a gesture: he is preparing a morning sacrifice while he watches for the divine answer. The suggestion of sacrifice prepares us for the reference to the temple later on in the psalm.

Matching the groaning and pleading of the introduction are the joy and confidence of the conclusion. Transcending his own situation, the psalmist declares that all who "take refuge" in Yahweh (cf. Ps 2:12) "will be glad" (cf. Ps 4:8; this verb and its noun equivalent will be used sixty-eight times in the psalter), implying that his surrender to the holiness of God in the temple was a kind of hiding in God's protection. A second verb of rejoicing, found thirty-seven times in the Psalms, follows: "They will shout with joy forever." Yahweh "screens" them from attack as the curtain in the tabernacle screened the ark (Exod 40:21). Yet again in this long verse 12 comes a synonym (found four times in the psalter) for rejoicing: "they will be joyful in you, those who love your name." Fear of the Lord, taking refuge in him, and loving his name are all aspects of the attitude that puts the transcendent above self. The term "name" of the Lord will be found over one hundred times in the psalter. Men cannot know God, but God has revealed the name by which they can call upon him and that embodies all that he has been and done for Israel, just as the name of a loved human being contains all that the person is. The "name" both veils and reveals God, leaving his mysterious self intact but making possible a contact with him. Yahweh's name is his mystery available to men.

Why this joy? The final verse gives the reason, as in the body of a hymn (cf. Pss 33, 96, 117, etc.). "For you bless the just man, Lord; with favor as with a large shield you encircle him" (v. 13). As in the opening verse the sacred name appears in the middle, representing the secure center where the psalmist finds refuge. "Just" is the term for those who live in conformity with God's will and so abide in his presence (cf. Ps 1:6). The favor of the Lord is the best military protection.

∼ Psalm 6   sickbed

The speaker is sick unto death (v. 6), and his suffering is poignantly described. He is frail, his bones are in terror (v. 3) as is his soul (possibly "throat"); he can hold out no longer (v. 4). He is exhausted with his groaning (like Baruch, Jer 45:3), floods the whole night his cot, with tears makes his couch melt (v. 7). His eye is wasted from grief and dimmed in the midst of foes (v. 8).

These laments are embedded among seven petitions, which the psalmist seems to gasp out. Sickness and death are not part of God's plan: they were brought into the world by man (Gen 3:16–19). One who suffers them knows himself part of a race that in refusing divine love has blocked God's offer of life. As we saw in Psalm 2, this "anger" of God is simply the way man experiences God's love when he has rejected it. For the psalmist to ask that God not reprove him in anger or chastise him in fury (v. 2) is to ask that the psalmist himself be healed of his rejection of God or his participation in it. He asks for mercy (cf. Ps 4:2) and healing (v. 3), that God "return" to him, "deliver" his soul like plunder, and "save" him "through his covenant love" (v. 5; cf. Ps 5:8). The love that brought the psalmist into God's presence in Psalm 5 is now invoked to "save" (cf. Ps 3:8, 9) the psalmist from extinction, so that he may fulfill his life's purpose in remembering and thanking the Lord (v. 6). For Saint Paul, too, saving is the act of God's love: "God loved us with so much love that he was generous with his mercy: when we were dead through our sins, he brought us to life with Christ—it is through grace that you have been saved . . ." (Eph 2:4–5). God's plan will only be successful if the creature reflects back to him the Creator's glory.

So sure is the psalmist of the nexus between the divine *ḥesed* and the act of salvation that he finds the strength to banish "all who do evil" (cf. Ps 5:6) for the Lord has heard the sound of his weeping (v. 9). The evildoers might be the "foes" mentioned at the end of the lament (cf. v. 8). They are all those who infect the psalmist with the notion that God does not love and cannot save (cf. Pss 3:3, 4:7, 5:7, 11), thus compounding the speaker's own awareness of having rejected love. The psalmist repudiates lifestyles not grounded on the divine mercy. An inner light or actual healing has convinced him that the Lord has heard his plea (cf. Ps 4:2); the Lord his prayer will receive (v. 10, chiasmus). The psalmist's enemies will "turn back and be utterly terrified," as he was in body and soul (cf. vv. 3–4); they will turn back and be suddenly shamed (v. 11). God cannot allow the one who calls on him to see corruption.

The risen Christ prays this psalm in his suffering members who already know by faith his triumph over death and Sheol. He raised the sick from their beds (Matt 8:14–15, 9:2, 6–7). He saved others from death: the daughter of Jairus, the son of the widow of Nain, and Lazarus. He saved the human race from death by passing through death and removing its sting (1 Cor 15:55). The one who suffers is also the one who hears the sick man's prayer and saves him. His death saves from death.

∾ Psalm 7   judge

The speaker of this psalm is glad that God is a judge because the evil that threatens his life on earth will be annihilated. God is a "just judge" who vindicates the falsely charged and permits men to destroy themselves by their free choice of evil. The psalmist takes refuge (cf. Ps 5:12) in Yahweh and pleads to be "saved" (Ps 6:5) from pursuers (v. 2), whom he compares to a lion ready to tear him to pieces and drag him off to eat (v. 3; psalms often compare enemies to wild animals, e.g., Ps 22:13–14, 17).

Repeating his opening cry, "Lord, my God," the psalmist calls down punishments on himself if his palms have done the wrong he is accused of (v. 4), if he has rendered evil to one who was at peace with him (like Saul, 1 Sam 24:18) or plundered (cf. same verb in Ps 6:5) his foe without cause (v. 5). The appropriate punishment would be for the enemy to pursue (cf. v. 2) and overtake him, trample his life to the ground, and lay his honor (or "glory," cf. Pss 3:4, 4:3) in the dust (v. 6). The speaker wants only the triumph of divine justice.

Since it is not he but his pursuers who are at fault, God must "arise" (cf. on Ps 3:8) in the "anger" that dissolves the evil in man (cf. on Ps 2:5) and that will neutralize the "rage" of the "foes" (Ps 6:8). It is as if God is asleep and must "rouse himself" on the psalmist's behalf (like Jesus in the storm, Mark 4:39), since he has commanded judgment (following the Hebrew of v. 7). Surrounded by the gathering of races, he must "return on high" above them (v. 8). The Lord who gives judgment on the peoples will judge the psalmist according to his justice and perfection (v. 9). The Christian can only pray this prayer in Christ, who by giving us a share in his own victory over sin has become "our righteousness and sanctification" (1 Cor 1:30). It is the blood of Christ that pleads for our redemption and sanctifies us (Rom 5:9, Heb 10:29, 12:24, 13:12, 1 John 1:7, Rev 1:5). By faith the Christian appropriates the holiness won for him by the blood of the Lamb, so that the Father sees us clothed in white robes washed in that blood (Rev 7:14), "clothed in Christ" (Gal 3:27).[3] In Christ and through Christ we ask that the justice that is in Christ be extended to the whole human race, so that "the evil of the wicked come to an end" and the just man be firmly established (v. 10). Only God can do this because only he can test the "hearts and kidneys" (cf. Jer 11:20, 17:10) where the secret choices of man are made. He is the "just God" (cf. John 17:25). But the Father has also given all judgment to his Son (John 5:22, 27, 30) who in his turn is the "just judge" (2 Tim 4:8) who "scrutinizes hearts and kidneys" (Rev 2:23). We meet again the double role of Christ in the psalms: the one who is judged is also the one who judges, man and God, who holds the universe together in himself.

The psalmist's evocation of the just judge now inspires an extended lesson on divine judgment. He speaks no longer to God but to men. The unusual expression "My shield [cf. Ps 3:8] is over God" means that "God stands beside the speaker and holds the shield over himself and his protected one" (Hossfeld and Zenger, *Die Psalmen*, 1:74; all transla-

---

3. Here are two Latin titles for Psalm 7: *Ecclesia ad Christum loquitur et Christus de Juda* (The Church speaks to Christ and Christ speaks of Judas); *Iste psalmus ad Christi humanitatem pertinet, quia per id quod factus est humilis, secundum suam justitiam veritatemque se expetit judicari* (Christ humbled himself to become a man so that there might be truly a man who could ask to be judged according to his justice and truth) (Salmon, *Les "Tituli Psalmorum,"* 100, 154).

tions mine), for he "saves the upright of heart" (v. 11). He is a just judge and a God who punishes every day (v. 12, often corrected in translation). If God does not turn back from his task of judging, he will sharpen the wicked man's sword; he has stretched and aimed the wicked man's bow (v. 13), drawing up his own deadly weapons against him, making his arrows burning (v. 14; these two verses often corrected). Conceiving injustice and pregnant with toil (cf. Isa 59:4), such a man gives birth to lies (v. 15; cf. Job 15:35; 2 + 2 + 2 meter), as a rotten tree bears rotten fruit (Matt 12:33). A final metaphor drawn from hunting shows how a man is destroyed by his own evil: "A pit he excavated and dug, and he will fall into the grave he made" (v. 16; cf. Qoh 10:8, Sir 27:25–27, Prov 5:22). We have already seen how a man's choice against God is a choice against the source of his own life and therefore a choice for death. Such an organic connection between sin and death Gerhard von Rad has called the "immanent nemesis" of sin (cited in Kraus *Psalmen,* 1:62). The principle is finely summarized in the chiastic line: "There returns his toil on his own head, and on his skull his violence descends" (v. 17). God turns the wicked man's weapons against him by allowing his evil choices to bear their natural fruit: he respects the man's free choice. His "just judging" is woven into the fabric of his creation.

The psalmist emerges from this dark reflection, from which the name of Yahweh has been conspicuously absent, with a burst of thanks (cf. Ps 6:6) for the Lord's justice, vowing to make music to the name (cf. Ps 5:12) of the Lord Most High (v. 18). This is what will be accomplished in the following psalm.

◇ PSALM 8   man

From the depths of personal need the psalmist lifts his gaze to the splendor of Yahweh himself in this first hymn of the psalter. He speaks in the name of the community, addressing "Lord, our Master." The "how" of chagrin (Ps 3) becomes the "how" of amazement: "How splendid is your name through all the earth; you have placed your majesty above the heavens" (v. 2). The majesty of Yahweh, Israel's covenant God, is visible throughout his creation, particularly, as the psalm will show, in the dignity of man as ruler of that creation. The psalm alludes to the Priestly account of creation (Gen 1) in its portrayal of man as lord over creatures. The psalmist reverses the order of Genesis in listing first the animals of the sixth day, "sheep and cattle, all of them" and the wild beasts of the field (v. 8), then those of the fifth day, birds of the sky and fish of the sea, the latter pictured "passing through the paths of the seas" to complement the original evocation of the heavenly bodies and to indicate that even the watery chaos is subject to man's dominion (v. 9). Even the fourth day of creation is alluded to in the psalmist's being ravished by "the moon and stars" (v. 4), which seem to be so much more worthy of God's "remembering" and "noting" than man (v. 5). The heavens may be the "work of [God's] fingers" (v. 4), but man is the ruler over the works of God's hands; all have been placed under his feet (v. 7; cf. Sir 17:2, 4). His dignity is "little less than a god's"; he is "crowned with glory and splendor" (v. 6). He is lord of creation, whose task is to make the earth produce and develop its full potential, to foster life (Gen 1:28, 2:15). Man is God's agent for bringing creation to its fulfilment. His dignity as God's coworker is the greatest manifestation of the divine splendor on earth. Man is the way God's name is "splendid through all the earth."

The clear logic of the psalm seems disturbed by verse 3: "From the mouths of infants and sucklings, you have founded a bulwark because of your foes to put to rest the enemy and avenger." The "infants and sucklings" are like man in that they seem powerless in relation to God's more spectacular wonders, but by acknowledging God as their lord they become the bulwark or strength of creation. Man's greatness consists precisely in being dependent on his creator to receive dominion. God has "chosen the weak to confound the strong" (1 Cor 1:27–28). By becoming like a little child one is "great in the kingdom of heaven" (Matt 18:1–4). It was children who recognized the Messiah when he entered his temple in Jerusalem (Matt 21:15–16). As for the presence of "foes" in this verse, they might be leftovers from the previous psalms (cf. Pss 6:8, 7:5, 7) in which man's "glory and splendor" were under attack. Praise of God's name is the ultimate defense against the foes of man (a theme to be met with in the penultimate psalm of the Book of Psalms), who are foes also of God insofar as they seek a lordship apart from their dependence on the Creator.

Christ is the perfect man in whom God's plan is fulfilled, the new Adam who through his obedience repairs the damage done by the disobedience of the first Adam (Rom 5:18–19). By grabbing for authority (determining what was good and what was evil, cf. Gen 3:5–6), Adam lost his dominion over creation and became its slave. By freely becoming a slave in human form (Phil 2:6–7), the Son of God restored man's rightful dependence on God so that all things are now "under his feet" (Eph 1:22–23). It is in Christ that man is clothed with glory and splendor (Heb 2:8–9). The Church's task is to extend to every corner of creation the victory won in principle by Christ. When the opening verse is repeated at the end of the psalm, the line about God's majesty in the heavens (v. 2c) is omitted; through man God's splendor is now found on earth.

~ PSALM 9   poor

From a succinct, tightly reasoned psalm we move to one much more diffuse. Each pair of verses begins with a successive letter of the Hebrew alphabet, a format in which the logic of ideas is second to the need to find words beginning with the requisite letter. There are nine such psalms in the psalter. Although the psalm is alphabetical, its length and subject matter caused it to be split in the Hebrew text into two psalms, 9 and 10, whereas in the Septuagint (Greek translation) it is presented as one. The style and content of the two halves of the psalm justify treatment of them separately, but it is also important to consider the psalm as a whole. The first half consists primarily of praise of God as judge of nations and repeats a number of words. The second half contains one of the longest descriptions of the machinations of the psalmist's enemy. Both halves have connections with Psalm 7, which introduces the concept of Yahweh as judge of the nations but also portrays the hounding of the psalmist by more local enemies. The more general utterances about the justice of God in the first section are complemented by the vivid descriptions of enemy wiles in the second. The name of Yahweh, abundant in the first section, is missing from the great central section of Psalm 10, a phenomenon noted also in Psalm 7.

The controlling image of Psalm 9 is that of Yahweh "seated on the throne, judging with justice" (v. 5b; cf. v. 8), bringing about the psalmist's judgment and verdict (v. 5a). From his dwelling in Zion (v. 12) God judges the world with justice, gives judgment for the races uprightly (v. 9, anticipation of Pss 96:13 and 98:9), rebuking the nations, destroying the wicked (vv. 6a, and vv. 18, 20, 21; cf. Zeph 3:8, Joel 4:2, 12) and blotting out their name (v. 6b), uprooting the "enemy's" cities so their memory vanishes (v. 7; cf. the "annihilation" of all the powers hostile to

God by the risen Lord, 1 Cor 15:24). As in Psalm 7, the Lord's judgment means that "the nations are sunk in the grave they have made; in the net they laid their feet are caught" (v. 16, chiasmus). By the action of his own palms the wicked man is snared (v. 17) and destined for Sheol (v. 18, where the wicked are paralleled with the "nations forgetful of God"). Only in verse 4 ("may they stumble and vanish before you") and verse 14 ("have mercy on me," as in Pss 4:2, 6:3) is a personal enemy of the psalmist indicated: his own plea for being raised (lit. "exalted") from the "gates of death" does not play a significant part in the psalm. On the other hand he calls attention to the group of those for whom Yahweh has special judicial care: the wretched (v. 10), those who "know [his] name" and search for him (v. 11), the "poor" (v. 13, the word, which in its two forms, *ʿănāwîm* and *ʿănîyim*, will become the leitmotif of the psalm), the "needy." These folk will "trust" in the Lord, knowing he does not abandon those who seek him but is their "high refuge" (twice in v. 10), as one who "searches out" bloodshed, "remembering" and "not forgetting" their outcry (vv. 13, 19) or letting their hope vanish forever (v. 19).

These notations on Yahweh's judgments on behalf of the poor are interspersed with the psalmist's desire to thank the Lord (v. 2), to "be glad and be joyful" in him (v. 3; cf. Ps 5:12 for these two verbs) and to "make music" to his "name" (vv. 3, 12), the name proclaimed as "splendid" throughout the earth in Psalm 8. While the psalmist proclaims Yahweh's "wonders" (vv. 2, 15), he tells his hearers to publish the Lord's doings among the peoples (v. 12). He makes a final reference to himself in the promise to "rejoice ecstatically" (Ps 2:11) in God's "salvation at the gates of the daughter of Zion" (v. 15). His opening promise of thanksgiving is matched by two concluding verses of petition, asking that God "arise" (cf. Pss 3:8, 7:7) and prevent "mere men" (same word as in Ps 8:5) from prevailing so that they may know their mortal status (vv. 20–21). The petition for justice forms a transition to the second half of the poem in which the vicious activity of the arrogant will be graphically described.

For the Christian, Christ is both the poor man (2 Cor 8:9) pleading for justice and the judge who will judge the world with his truth (John 5:27, 30, 2 Cor 5:10). He prays this psalm in the midst of his people and at the same time establishes divine justice in the world. We ask in him that his justice be established.

~ PSALM 10   (continuation of Psalm 9)

The second half of Psalm 9-10 exhibits more unity than the first but presents a more corrupted text, particularly in verses 4–11. The petitions at the end of Psalm 9 provide a good transition to the description of the "times of distress" (v. 1; cf. Ps 9:10) in Psalm 10. The just judge of the world now seems to stand "far off" and "be secret" while the "wicked" man (vv. 2–4, 13, 15; cf. Ps 9:17) hounds the "poor." Verses 2–7 characterize the inner attitude of the wicked: his pride, scheming (v. 2), flaunting of desires, grasping, and above all his disdain for God (v. 3), who for him does not really exist, who does not search out or punish crimes (v. 4), whose judgments do not matter (v. 5; cf. also v. 13). This man snorts at his foes and is quite sure that he will "not totter"; his ways always succeed (v. 6). Such an attitude is lived out in the speech and behaviors mentioned in verse 7: cursing, deceit (cf. Ps 5:7), oppression, toil, and injustice (cf. Ps 7:15).

Verses 8–11 draw a vivid picture of the wicked man in action against the poor. He sits in ambush in courtyards, from his hiding place kills the innocent (cf. the sin of Cain, Gen 4:8), his eyes spying on the unfortunate (v. 8). He lies in ambush in hiding like a lion (cf. Ps 7:3) in his thicket (same word as "hut"), to seize the poor man (v. 9a). In a scarcely noticeable change of image (v. 9b) he becomes a hunter seizing the poor man as he draws his net. He lowers himself and crouches, and the unfortunate man (Hebrew emendation) falls beneath his force (v. 10). Once again we are reminded that such sinister behavior is rooted in the rejection of God, in the mind that says, "God forgets; he hides his face; he will never see" (v. 11; cf. Isa 29:15). The multiplication of clauses with asyndeton and the repetition of certain roots (e.g., "hide," "ambush," "seize") convey the cruel and relentless persistence of the godless against the weak.

With verse 12 the psalmist renews the petition of Psalm 9:20, asking God to "arise" and act and *not* to "forget" the poor (cf. v. 11, Ps 9:19), to show that he *does* search out (v. 13; cf. v. 4), that he sees the [evil] toil and looks on the grief, for the helpless one is abandoned to Yahweh, "helper of the orphan" (v. 14). Yahweh is called on to break the arm of the wicked, to "search out" his wickedness (v. 15) and so prove him wrong about divine judgment (cf. vv. 4, 13). The psalmist's concern is that the "wickedness" of the man be utterly annihilated, not that the man himself be destroyed.

The final three verses break into praise, as the speaker proclaims that the just God can see to the removal from the earth of all the evil of the wicked. Because Yahweh is an everlasting king, the nations will vanish (v. 16; cf. Ps 9:6 etc.) from his earth (in the sense indicated above). The "desire" (same word used of the wicked man, v. 3) of the poor is heard by the Lord who strengthens their heart (v. 17), who judges for the orphan and the downtrodden (cf. Ps 9:10) so that they might never again be in dread on earth (v. 18; translation disputed). Even the wicked man's scheming, so vividly rendered in verses 1–11, is obliterated by the God who "judges" (Ps 9:9, 20) for the weak. Mortal man cannot prevail against this God (Pss 9:20, 10:18).

One may see in this psalm Christ as both "innocent [cf. v. 8] poor man" and "judge." The very one whom the godless man seeks to exterminate becomes the one who eliminates the godless, or more exactly, eliminates godlessness from his kingdom. In Christ we experience both the wretchedness of exploitation by evil powers and the definitive victory over these powers (Mark 10:33–34; Luke 24:26–27). From his sacrificed and risen body comes justice on earth.

Despite expressions of praise and petition the dominant tone of Psalm 9-10 is discursive. The long meter contributes to this impression of a lesson in theodicy. Many of the lines are in 4 + 4 meter, and more than half of the verses contain at least one four-beat colon. Although half of the lines address God in the second person, even these leave the impression of talking more about God than to him. The reflective/narrative mode supersedes the hymnic element.

∼ PSALM 11   throne

Psalm 11 follows a pattern similar to that of Psalm 7: after an initial portrayal of his distress, the psalmist pulls aside a veil to reveal behind the contemporary scene a God who is just and abiding and active. The center of the psalm is the throne on which the Lord sits gazing on the whole world, assessing the conformity or non-conformity of each human heart with his will (v. 4). Those who choose justice will "gaze on" his face (v. 7; cf. Rev 22:4, 1 John 3:2); those who violate the rights of others, the "lovers of violence" (v. 5; cf. Ps 7:17, Amos 3:10, Mic 6:12, Zeph 1:9) will experience the torture of absence from him, described in vivid language as a rain of fiery coals and sulfur, a raging whirlwind (v. 6ab; cf. the destruction of Sodom and Gomorrah, Gen 19:24, Luke 17:29); such is the "share of their cup" (v. 6c).

The just man is faced with attacks from the wicked who wield bow and arrows (v. 2; cf. Ps 7:13–14), with the demolishing of the "pillars" of society (v. 3), and worst of all with the advice of people who counsel him to "flee to your mountain like a bird" (v. 1; cf. Judg 6:2, 1 Sam 13:6). He responds to the latter that his "refuge" is not mountains but the Lord (cf. Pss 2:12, 7:2).

Behind the earthly chaos and injustice is a God who is just. He resides in the "holy place" that is his temple, yet at the same time his throne is "in heaven" (v. 4a). The God who dwells in Jerusalem is eternal judge of mankind, and conversely the judge of all has taken up residence in the midst of his people. The first two cola of verse 4 strongly imply the principle of incarnation. Throughout the Bible the infinite God is reaching out to mankind, wishing to find a home among them from which he can exercise his merciful plan to give life. An early stage of that earthly dwelling was the Jerusalem temple, but this has been replaced by the temple that is the body of the Son of God (John 2:19–21), in whom dwells the fullness of divinity (Col 2:9). Through baptism Christians are incorporated into this body and become its members (1 Cor 12:27). The God enthroned above the heavens exercises his sovereign justice through his Church, the Body of his Son. He "gazes" on men (v. 4b), "testing" the authenticity of the just man (v. 5; cf. Ps 7:10), unable to save the "lovers of violence" because he "loves justice" (v. 7). Those who accept his lordship reign with him (Rev 3:21).

The Christian must live with his eyes focused "beyond the veil" (Heb 6:19), where Christ is seated at the right hand of God (Col 3:1–2), governing the earth, "drawing all things to himself" (John 12:32). In the midst of his trials the Christian is conscious of being already a part of that risen body: "the life you have is hidden with Christ in God" (Col 3:3, Eph 2:19–22, 1 Pet 2:5). The present psalm is not a prayer addressed to God but a robust act of faith uttered in the presence of men of weak faith; in this it is similar to Psalm 4. The many echoes of earlier psalms do not prevent Psalm 11 from having a unique focus. It is a fresh variation on a theme that contributes its own new theological perspective, that of the throne of God as the reference point for all human creatures. This is the throne of God from which proceed all the judgments of the Book of

Revelation (Rev 4; 20:11–12), which serves as the focus of the heavenly liturgy (Rev 5:13–14, 7:9–12, 14:3, 19:4) and which is also the throne of the Lamb (Rev 22:1, 3).

The final verse (7) summarizes the psalm by using earlier words in a fresh application. The God who tested the just (cf. v. 5) is now himself "just"; the "upright" who were targeted by the arrows of the wicked (cf. v. 2) will now "gaze" on God's face as he "gazes" on the world (cf. v. 4).

The psalm exhibits no regular meter.

∼ Psalm 12   words

At the center of the psalm is an oracle from Yahweh. In view of the despoiling of the "poor" and the groan of the needy, as if answering the plea of Psalms 3:8, 7:7, 9:20 and 10:12, God promises to "arise" now (cf. Isa 33:10) to accomplish the "salvation" they sigh for (v. 6). These "promises" of the Lord are to be trusted, in a world where the devoted man has disappeared, where faithfulness has come to an end among the sons of men (v. 2). The Lord's promises are pure promises, like silver smelted in the crucible (word uncertain), refined seven times (v. 7). What he promises he will perform. Worthless, however, are the words men speak to their friend (Prov 26:28); "with flattering lips they speak in doubleness of heart" (v. 3; cf. the double weights and ephahs of Deut 25:13–14, Prov 20:10, 23). Their tongue speaks "great things" (v. 4) as they say: "With our tongues we prevail, our lips are our own: who is master over us?" (v. 5). They do not subordinate themselves to a truth outside themselves. They recall the false monks described at the beginning of the *Rule of Saint Benedict*: "What they like is what they call holy" (*RB* 1:9). Their words are for themselves; the Lord's words (v. 6) are for others. Among men like this no one can be relied on and the weak are at the mercy of the powerful. The psalmist asks the Lord to cut off the flattering lips of men and the tongue speaking great things (v. 4) and to implement his promise to save (v. 2a). May he guard the poor and protect them forever from "this generation" (v. 8; cf. Gen 7:1, Matt 11:16, Mark 8:12), where the wicked strut about and foulness is exalted among the "sons of men" (v. 9; cf. v. 2, Ps 11:4).

Among the many words that bombard us today, we seek those that are authentic, words on which we can base our lives. The words of Jesus are reliable because they were spoken with authority and backed up by deeds (Mark 1:27, Matt 7:29, John 7:46). He practiced what he preached (Matt 5:39–40 with 26:52–54; Matt 6:10 with 26:42; Luke 11:4 with 23:34; John 15:13 with 10:17). His words are a treasure because they give life (John 6:63). Indeed he himself is the Word spoken by the Father who contains all that the Father is (John 1:1, Heb 1:2–3). He is the revelation spoken by the Father to men (John 1:18), the Word made flesh (John 1:14). His are the words that the disciples believed (John 6:68–69), which made them like their Master (cf. Acts 7:60) and sustained them in death. Such men allowed the word sown in their hearts to bear abundant fruit (Luke 8:15). The words of Jesus are "saving" words (cf. Ps 12:2, 6) as his very name indicates (Matt 1:21).

The psalm begins and ends with direct address of the Lord; verses 4–5 and 7 speak of him in the third person, and the Lord himself speaks in the central oracle (v. 6). Long meter (the four-beat line) prevails in the poem.

∼ PSALM 13   how long

Psalm 13 is a classic and concise individual lament. For a long time God has forgotten the psalmist (against Ps 9:13, 19), hiding his face from him (cf. Pss 4:7, 10:11–12). He asks if this will last "forever" (v. 2). He is reduced to making his own brooding "plans" (cf. Sir 30:21), which leave sorrow in his heart all day long; some "enemy" is "exalted" (cf. Ps 12:9) over him (v. 3). The four "how longs" of these two verses have their echo in the cries of the souls of the martyrs who were killed for witnessing to "the word of God" (cf. Ps 12!): "Holy, faithful Master, how long before you judge and avenge our blood on the inhabitants of the earth?" (Rev 6:9–10). It is the cry of all those in anguish down the ages who cannot understand why God's definitive judgment on sin is postponed. The delay in judgment only encourages the wicked to keep sinning (cf. Qoh 8:11). Why does God tolerate the wicked? The Lord's answer in the parable of the weeds among the wheat (Matt 13:24–30, 36–43) was not available to the Hebrews of the Old Testament. It was a matter of urgency that God demonstrate his justice on earth before the wicked succeeded in destroying the good. Still today the people of God ask how long they will suffer physical, mental, moral, and social evils before their endurance and trust evaporate. Important to remember is that "God will not let you be tried beyond your strength, and with any trial will give you a way out of it and the strength to bear it" (1 Cor 10:13). Man's "how long" is the longing of the Mystical Body of Christ for final liberation and transformation.

After the lament comes petition. Three imperatives are addressed to the Lord: "Look, answer me, enlighten my eyes" (v. 4a): the psalmist needs to see a way out of his daily (cf. v. 3) gloom (cf. Lam 5:17). These imperatives are matched by three clauses destined to motivate Yahweh to act: if he does not the psalmist will sleep in death (cf. Ps 9:14), his enemy will say, "I have finished him," his oppressors will "rejoice ecstatically" when he "totters" (vv. 4b–5). The quotation of the enemy's words echoes that of the arrogant speakers in the previous psalm.

The turning point comes in the first line of verse 6, in which the psalmist formulates an act of trust that has been implicit in his bringing his troubles before God. The concise formulation says all that needs to be said and prepares the final assurance that God will save. "But I . . . ," he says, recalling what his heart knows, "in your covenant love . . .'"— in that generous and mighty attachment that brought his people out of Egypt and made them his own—"put my trust," that is, he relies on that love because it cannot fail to save. Saving is its specialty (see on Ps 6:5), and so the heart that was full of sorrow (v. 3) will "rejoice ecstatically" (cf. v. 5) in this salvation (v. 6b).

In this short line (v. 6a) the speaker expresses the two ingredients necessary for salvation: God's initiative and man's response. God's love impels him to save, man has only to accept this saving love. This is biblical faith: a conviction that God is "for" his creature (Rom 8:31–32) with a willingness to "lean" on him that involves a surrender to his guidance. This is the faith Jesus looked for, without which he could not save (Mark 6:5–6, John 3:18, 36, Rom 1:16, 3:28, 5:1–2, Gal 2:16, 20). It is all that is asked of a person, his "Yes" to the offer of salvation, and it opens the door to the gift of the Holy Spirit with his power for keeping the commandments (cf. Gal 5:6). Saint John shows how faith admits God's life, his Spirit, into the soul, in whose power we keep the commandment of love: "His commandments are these: that we believe in the name of his Son Jesus Christ and that we love one another as he told us to. Whoever keeps his commandments lives in God and God in him. We know that he lives in us by the Spirit that he has given us" (1 John 4:23–24).

Such faith in God, such deep trust in the person of God, in his identity as committed love, animates the whole psalter. It often explains, as in Psalm 13, the abrupt transition from lament to praise, a transition operated by the engaging of the psalmist's trust. That is why the key words for the psalmist's attitude or stance are "trust" and "take refuge," along with "poor" to express the awareness of his need for a higher power. It is one of the unique features of Old Testament psalmody that despite many features it shares with other ancient Near Eastern prayers, it alone knows that its God is trustworthy and not fickle.

The act of trust is often, as here (v. 6a), the shortest section of an individual lament, despite its power to change the psalmist's sorrow into joy. It leads here directly into the vow of praise, by which the psalmist declares his intention to make music "to the Lord" (the only line of the psalm not addressed directly to God) for rendering good (v. 6c, mistakenly given in the Grail as 7a; cf. Ps 7:5 for another use of this verb). The Greek version fills out the vow of praise with a line from the end of Psalm 7: "I will sing psalms to the name of the Lord the Most High" (v. 7; cf. LXX Ps 7:18b).

Although the psalm is short, the long four-beat line prevails.

∿ PSALM 14   fool

The psalm shares with Psalm 12 the conviction that loyal and truthful men have vanished from society (Ps 12:2), which is dominated by the "fool" who does not acknowledge a God to whom he is responsible for his actions. Men who deny God in their hearts are ruined and abhorrent in their doings (v. 1; cf. Ps 10:4, 11, 13, Ps 12:5). The speaker then views the human condition as seen by God (v. 2). Yahweh "looks down" from heaven on the "sons of men" (cf. Pss 11:4, 12:2, 9), as he looked down on Sodom and Gomorrah (Gen 18:16), to see if anyone is understanding and searches for God. The answer comes in four short cola (v. 3): "All have turned aside [cf. Deut 11:16, Jer 5:23], together they are corrupt [a word used of spoiled fruit or milk], no one does good, not even one." Saint Paul will see in this global critique a sign of the human race's need for redemption, of its inability to produce the full justice God seeks (Rom 3:10–12). This universal condemnation is good news, a "happy fault" (the *Exsultet*) because it calls forth a divine redeemer (Rom 3:23–25, 7:21–25).

Returning to the human perspective, the psalmist asks, "Will they know, those who do evil? They eat my people as though they ate bread;

the Lord they do not call on" (v. 4). Again the lack of "knowledge" of God leads to immoral behavior (cf. Hos 4:1–2, Jer 5:4–6), here presented as cannibalism (cf. Mic 3:3, Prov 30:14, Ps 27:2, Gal 5:15), the practice of pagans (Jer 10:25 = Ps 79:6–7). In this verse "calling on" God is the natural corollary of acknowledging his dominion over human affairs. Prayer is the life-breath of faith.

In the second half of the psalm emerges a group of people exempt from the universal corruption lamented in the first half. They have been suggested in the "my people" of verse 4; in verse 5 they are called the "just generation" (cf. Ps 12:8) and the "poor" (cf. Ps 12:6, Ps 9-10 passim). Since God is seen to be with the just, their "devourers" tremble with terror. Though they shame the poor man's "plan" (cf. Ps 13:3), the Lord is his refuge (v. 6). Human iniquity cannot separate the poor from his God (Rom 8:35, 39). The psalm reveals an ineluctable divine order behind social chaos, as in the three previous psalms, although in Psalm 14 the speaker is more an observer than a victim. This wisdom psalm does not become a prayer until the final long verse (4 + 4 + 4 meter), in which the psalmist prays that Israel's "salvation" might emerge "from Zion" (v. 7). The psalm thus echoes Psalm 3 (see 3:5, 8–9) in expecting the Lord to exercise his saving power for Israel from the holy mountain where he dwells (cf. also Ps 11:4). The two psalms stand as the beginning and end of the first subsection of Book One, the first mini-collection in the psalter, with Psalm 8 as the hymnic center. The theme of salvation also echoes Psalm 12:2, 6 and Psalm 13:6. Such a salvation will constitute a "change of fortune" for God's people (cf. Deut 30:3, Amos 9:14), the occasion for Israel's ecstatic rejoicing (cf. Ps 13:6) and gladness (cf. Pss 4:8, 5:12, 9:3). Verse 7 is thus a fitting conclusion not only for this psalm but for this mini-collection, Psalms 3–14. It lifts to the national level the hopes of the poor for salvation to come from Mount Zion.

Christ is the one just man. His dwelling on earth, the Church, is a refuge for the poor (cf. Isa 14:32). In him we become just (Jer 5:1, Rom 3:22, 28, 4:24–25).

∼ PSALM 15   admittance

Psalm 5 has shown that dwelling with the Lord requires moral purity. Now a whole psalm is devoted to that topic. It asks who can "sojourn" (v. 1; cf. Ps 5:5, Gen 21:23, 34, Isa 33:14) in the Lord's "tent" (ancient name for the temple deriving from the desert period when the ark of God was housed in a tent) and dwell on his "holy mountain" (Zion; cf. Pss 2:6, 3:5).

The remainder of the psalm outlines the sort of behavior that conforms to God's will and being, since union with God means willing what he wills, loving what he loves. A man must have toward himself, the world, and his neighbor the same attitude God has, that is, an attitude of affirmation, reverence, and dedication (Deut 10:18–19). As the psalm expresses it, a man must "walk" (act) blamelessly (Prov 28:18), "do" justice (instead of evil, Pss 5:6, 14:4), and speak faithfully in his heart (v. 2).

The heart is the organ of spiritual experience. It is the seat of gladness (Ps 4:8), uprightness (Ps 7:11), thanksgiving (Ps 9:2), decisions about God (Ps 10:6, 11, 13, Ps 14:1), strength (Ps 10:17), duplicity (Ps 12:3), sorrow (Ps 13:3), joy (Ps 13:6). To utter truth in the heart is to acknowledge one's identity as a child of God with all the dignity and responsibility that status implies. It is to live as one's true self, a creature of a good God who provides his children with all the strength they need for responding to his love with their "whole heart" (Matt 22:37). To speak the truth from the heart is to acknowledge that one is a redeemed sinner with the capacity to forgive as God forgives (Matt 18:35, Eph 4:32). The heart is the place of the fundamental choices. If it is "pure" in its acknowledging of the truth (Matt 5:8), it becomes an organ of the Spirit of God (Rom 5:5). From the honest heart proceed all the actions by which a man treats his neighbor with respect: not slandering with his "tongue" (cf. Pss 10:7, 12:4–5), not causing harm to his "friend" (cf. Ps 12:3) or taking up a reproach against him (v. 3).

The subject of the sentence in verse 3 changes at the beginning of verse 4: "The despicable man in his eyes is rejected, but he honors those who fear the Lord; if he swears to his own detriment, he does not go back on his word" (for the latter see Lev 5:4). These three practices reflect a more group mentality and remind us that one is saved as a member of a people. Christians align themselves with other Christians and eschew the lifestyle, if not the company, of evildoers. Finally the man who dwells with God avoids two principal ways of taking advantage of others (v. 5ab): charging interest on a loan (Lev 25:37, Ezek 18:8, 13) and taking bribes against the innocent (Exod 23:8, Deut 27:25).

The qualities have proceeded from interior choices through treatment of the neighbor to social attitudes and finally to non-abuse of power. Remarkable is the immediate connection between one's choice of "justice" in the heart and one's treatment of his fellow man. In the words of Saint Anthony of Egypt: "Our life and our death is with our neighbor. If we gain our brother, we have gained God, but if we scandalize our brother, we have sinned against Christ" (*Sayings of the Desert Fathers,* Anthony 9). In Saint Paul and Saint James the entire law is summed up in the commandment, "Love your neighbor as yourself" (Rom 13:9–10, Gal 5:14, Jas 2:8), and Jesus himself gave as his new commandment, "Love one another as I have loved you" (John 13:34, 15:12, 17). There can be no union with God that bypasses union with the neighbor (1 John 4:20–21).

To show this kind of love from a pure heart (1 Pet 1:22, 1 Tim 1:5) is possible only with the grace of God who must "create" this heart (Ps 51:12, Ezek 36:26). In praying Psalm 15 the Christian is praising God that in Christ a man has conformed totally to the will of God, loving his neighbor as God does even to giving his life. Further, the Christian prays that the grace of the Holy Spirit will conform his own heart and behavior to Christ's. We celebrate that the grace of God can make us saints worthy to dwell in the house of God.

Psalms 14 and 15 complement each other. The one shows man to be universally corrupt, while the other assumes men will "do justice." It is the righteous Christ who joins the two. The righteousness we were unable to achieve on our own has been achieved in him and imparted to us by his Spirit. In that Spirit we can obey the commandment of brotherly love.

Psalm 15 ends on a surprising note. Having heard the qualities for admission to the temple, we might expect a closing like: Such is the man who dwells with the Lord. But the conclusion points in a new direction. Not only will this man dwell in the Lord's presence, he will "not totter" forever (v. 5c; cf. Prov 10:30, 12:3). He has found true stability on the mountain of the Lord, that is, in the Lord himself. His permanence is assured. This is now the third use of the verb "[not] totter" (Pss 10:6, 13:5), and it will be found three more times in the next few psalms (16:8, 17:5, 21:8), enough to count as a "mini-theme" linking together the prayers of this second subsection of Book One (Pss 15–24). The *Rule of the Master,* predecessor of the *Rule of Saint Benedict,* links this final line with the conclusion of the Sermon on the Mount: the house built on the words of Jesus "did not fall: it was founded on a rock" (Matt 7:24–25; *RM* Theme sequence, 31–34). The theme of God as a rock will soon emerge in the psalter (Ps 18:3).

~ PSALM 16   portion

Psalm 16 might be interpreted as an expansion of the last line of the preceding psalm: it develops the experience of "not tottering" in the Lord. The word itself is used in verse 8. The psalmist expresses at length what delight the Lord's presence brings him in body and spirit.

The Lord is first of all the "portion" that is his share (v. 5). The word recalls the portion of a sacrifice given to an individual but even more the portion allotted to each of the twelve tribes of Israel. Only Levi did not receive a portion of land, for the Lord had declared, "It is I who will be your portion and your inheritance among the sons of Israel" (Num 18:20). The Levites, the priestly tribe, would "live on foods offered to the Lord and on his dues" (Deut 18:1). Our psalmist is applying the Levite privilege to himself: he experiences the Lord as his allotted portion of livelihood. Next, the Lord is his "cup," the drink given him to drain or to make his own, his fate (cf. Ps 11:6; Matt 26:39, Mark 10:38, John 18:11). Third, the Lord holds firmly the psalmist's "lot" or destiny. Fourth, he envisions his allotment as a pleasant estate marked out by measuring cords (v. 6). Finally, his "inheritance" is most agreeable, since it is the Lord himself (cf. Num 18:20, Deut 10:9, 18:2, Jos 13:14, 33, 18:7; cf. also Acts 20:32, 1 Pet 1:4).

The psalmist is not completely passive in his enjoyment of the Lord: he "blesses" the Lord, keeps him always in mind (vv. 7–8). But even these responses are occasions for telling more of what the Lord means to him. Yahweh gives him counsel, working through his "kidneys" (cf. Ps 7:10), which chasten him even at night. The speaker's experience is at once mental and bodily. The Lord is at his right side keeping him from tottering (v. 8b). Therefore his heart is glad and his honor (lit. "glory," cf. Pss 4:3, 7:6) rejoices ecstatically (v. 9; see same two verbs in Ps 14:7); even his flesh will dwell (cf. Ps 15:1) in security (cf. Ps 4:9).

From third person speech the psalmist returns to direct address of the Lord in the final two verses. Not only will the Lord not abandon the speaker's soul to the underworld nor allow his devoted one to see the grave (v. 10); he will acquaint him with the "path of life," "the fullness of gladness" (cf. John 15:11, 16:24, 17:13) before the Lord's face, pleasant things (cf. v. 6) at the Lord's right hand forever (v. 11). Saint Peter on Pentecost morning saw these words literally fulfilled in the resurrection of

Christ from the dead (Acts 2:24–32). The intimacy with God won by Christ's resurrection is passed on to all who accept the Easter good news.

The body of the psalm is introduced by four verses in which the psalmist distinguishes himself from worshippers of other gods. He takes refuge in the Lord, having nothing good outside of him (v. 2). The text of verses 3–4 is corrupt, but the speaker seems to be associating himself with the "holy ones" in the land (priests?; cf. on v. 5) in whom God delights (v. 3). Those who run after other [gods] suffer many wounds, but he abjures the offering of any blood-libations to pagan gods, refusing to take "their names" (the gods or those men for whom as priest he is offering sacrifice) on his lips. His profession of loyalty is thus a prelude to his confession of what the Lord is to him. In the light of this progression of thought the first word of the psalm seems out of place: it is the only petition in the psalm, a prayer for God to "guard" the speaker, a petition immediately giving way to a lengthy statement of trust.

∼ Psalm 17 apple

Several factors make this a murky psalm. First are the sinister descriptions of the movements of the enemy, who is compared to a lion crouched in hiding (v. 12), hungry for prey (cf. Pss 7:3, 10:8–10). Second is the "night" atmosphere (vv. 3, 15) together with the image of hiding "in the shadow" of wings (v. 8). Third is the textual corruption of several verses (cf. Pss 3–5, 10–12, 14), which makes translation conjectural. Last is the "crowding" of the verses: several have more than two cola, one (v. 14) as many as six, with the number of beats varying from two to four without regular pattern. Yet out of the murkiness emerges a strong experience of intimacy with God, culminating in the vision of the Lord's face in the morning.

"Hear, O Lord, justice," opens the psalmist. The cry is followed by two cola asking for God's attention to his lamentation and prayer (a common pairing, cf. 1 Kgs 8:28b, Jer 7:16), and a final colon matching the opening: "There is no deceit [cf. Pss 5:7, 10:7] on my lips" (v. 1; cf. Pss 12:3–5, 16:4). The psalmist deserves to be heard because of his innocence (cf. Ps 7:4–6). From the Lord's "face" (cf. Ps 16:11) will proceed judgment, whose eyes "gaze" on uprightness (v. 2; cf. Ps 11:4). Four cola in verse 3 confess the Lord's "testing" of the heart and visiting at night (cf. Ps 16:7), his "smelting" (cf. Jer 6:27–30, 9:6, Prov 17:3) and finding no impurity, for the speaker has intended not to transgress with his mouth. In the midst of men's actions, in accordance with the word from God's "lips" he guards himself from the paths of the lawbreaker (v. 4). His footsteps hold fast to God's "tracks" (Prov 2:9, 4:11, 5:6), his steps have "not tottered" (v. 5; cf. Ps 15:5). Among the paths of men he has threaded the path to God.

As in Psalm 7, petitions follow the assertion of innocence. They begin with the "call/answer" and "hear/prayer" themes (v. 6; cf. Pss 3:5, 4:2, 4, 6:10). Verse 7 is a dense line of only six words in Hebrew: "Show your wonderful love, savior of those who take refuge from those who rise against your right hand" (cf. Ps 16:11). God will manifest his *hesed* by saving (cf. Ps 6:5) those who "take refuge" in him (Pss 2:12, 5:12, 7:2, 11:1, 14:6, 16:1). The speaker asks God to guard him (cf. Ps 16:1) as if he were protecting the pupil of his own eyeball from attack (cf. Deut 32:10) and in the shadow of his wings to hide him (v. 8, chiasmus). This is the first use of a favorite image for the Lord's sheltering protection, an image that gives concreteness to the "refuge" theme. The image of wings may be drawn from Egyptian representations of gods sheltering their young with wings (cf. Jesus's lament over Jerusalem, Matt 23:37) or from the wings of the golden cherubs stretched out over the ark, upon which the Lord was enthroned (cf. Exod 25:20, 1 Kgs 8:7). In either case the image is a striking expression of the protective intimacy to which the Lord draws man. The verse is appropriately used at Compline, the Church's night prayer.

The speaker must now describe the activities of the wicked from which he seeks protection. They despoil him; his enemies encompass him (v. 9). They have shut up their hearts (lit. "fat") while their mouths speak with pride (v. 10; cf. Ps 10:2). With their steps now they surround him, they "set their eyes" to bring him to the ground—eyes used for a very different purpose from the Lord's eyes (v. 11; cf. v. 2). Their hostile advances are concretized in the simile of the lion yearning to tear in pieces (cf. Ps 7:3), the young lion crouched in hiding (v. 12; cf. Ps 10:8–9).

With the now familiar "Arise, Lord" (v. 13; cf. Pss 3:8, 7:7, 9:20, 10:12) the speaker renews his petitions, this time not for his defense but for the Lord's offense against the wicked. May the Lord advance to meet him, to force him to his knees, bringing the psalmist to safety with his sword and with his hand from men of the world whose portion is in this life

(v. 14a). But God will fill the bellies of those whom he shelters; their sons will be "filled" and leave what is left to their offspring (14b).

Because of his "justice" (inclusion with v. 1) the psalmist is assured of "gazing on [the] face" of God (v. 15; cf. v. 2, Ps 11:7). He for his part will be "filled" (cf. v. 14) on waking with the Lord's "form" (cf. Num 12:8), as with the light of the sun. Thus a new dimension is given to the call for the Lord to "arise" (v. 13). As the hymn for Sunday Lauds puts it, the daily rising of the sun scatters the burglars and waylayers of the night (cf. Job 24:14–16) just as the risen Christ puts to flight the minions of Satan.

A less obvious feature of the psalm is the number of body parts mentioned: for the psalmist, lips, heart, mouth, belly, steps; for Yahweh, face, eyes, lips, ear, hand, wings; for the enemy, mouth, eyes, steps. The psalmist's religion is grounded in bodily experience, and he boldly employs bodily terms for God to make real his sense of intimacy with him. The conclusion of the psalm is a good preparation for the description of heaven at the end of the Book of Revelation: "The throne of God and of the Lamb will be in its place in the city; his servants will worship him, they will see him face to face, and his name will be written on their foreheads. It will never be night again and they will not need lamplight or sunlight, because the Lord God will be shining on them" (Rev 22:3–5).

Christ is the one who takes refuge in the shadow of his Father's wings and also the one who invites us to shelter under his wings. His mighty power exercised through his humanity transforms us into his likeness so that we can see him and his Father's face.

∿ Psalm 18   theophany

The speaker is a military leader: his foes are other nations whom he subdues (vv. 44–46, 48). A final verse applies the psalm to David, the anointed king, and to his sons (v. 51). The psalm falls into two clearly defined parts connected with a lengthy suture. The first part (vv. 2–20) describes a saving theophany in earthquake and storm, in the course of which Yahweh plucks the speaker from overwhelming destruction. The speaker here is largely passive; the work of salvation is entirely the Lord's. In the second part (vv. 29–50) Yahweh's saving help takes the form of empowering the speaker to inflict defeat on his enemies. Both parts attribute victory to the grace of God, one focusing on God's help without man's effort, the other on God's help empowering man to act.

The psalmist picks up the "call/hear" theme of Psalm 17:6, knowing that when he "calls" he will be "saved" from his enemies by the Lord who is worthy of praise (v. 4; for "hearing" see v. 7). The whole psalm is a praising account of that "salvation." The first account begins with chiastic parallelism: "They encompassed me, the cords of death, and the rivers of vileness menaced me" (v. 5); the first half of the verse is found also in Psalm 116:3. A second verse is in the reverse chiastic parallelism (beginning with noun): "The cords of Sheol surrounded me; they advanced on me, the snares of death" (v. 6). The psalmist felt submerged by the primitive chaos. In his distress, like Jonah he called to the Lord and to his God cried for help; from his temple (cf. Ps 11:4) God heard his voice, whose cry came to his ears. (v. 7; Jonah 2:3–6 shares much of the vocabulary of Ps 18:5–7). For the psalmist, the Lord's help comes through his dwelling on earth, for Christians the Body of Christ, the Church.

In response to the speaker's prayer the earth heaved and quaked, and the foundations of the mountains trembled, for the Lord was wrathful toward them. Volcanic phenomena—smoke, fire, burning coals— emanated from his person (v. 9; cf. the theophany on Sinai, Exod 19:16–18). He inclined the heavens and came down (v. 10, against v. 7), a thick gloom (as at Sinai, Exod 20:21, Deut 4:11, 1 Kgs 8:12, Ps 97:2) under his feet. He rode on a winged animal like the storm god Baal on his chariot, and he soared on the wings of the wind (v. 11), shrouded in the darkness of watery clouds (v. 12). From a gleam before him clouds passed over, emitting hail and burning coals (v. 13). He thundered in the heavens, the Lord; the Most High sounded his voice (v. 14; cf. Pss 29:3, 96:11, 98:7, Job 37:4, 40:9). He shot his arrows and scattered them, and these many lightnings caused havoc (v. 15). Revealed were the stream-channels of the waters, and exposed the foundations (cf. v. 8) of the world at the Lord's rebuke, at the breath of the spirit of his anger (v. 16). The purpose of the violent manifestation of Yahweh is the rescue of his king: "He sends from on high, he takes me, he pulls me from the many waters" (v. 17, the only verse not in past tense in this first part). He rescued the psalmist from the strong enemy and from those who hated him, for they were sturdier than he (v. 18). They advanced against him on the day of disaster, but the Lord was his support (v. 19), leading him into a broad space (v. 20).

Natural phenomena of storm and wind, earthquake and volcano are instruments of the Lord's wrath against the enemies of the one who loves him. They either emanate from his person or cloak him or serve as his weapons. They both hide and reveal him. The prevailing three-beat meter conveys a sense of advancing relentlessness.

The clause, "He pulls me from the many [cf. Pss 3:2–3, 93:4] waters" (v. 17b) is a classic metaphorical profession of faith, which reminds us of the Lord's saving of Peter (Matt 14:31). From the beginning of the Bible God combats chaos to bring life out of it. He saved Noah from the Flood. He saved his people from the waters of the Red Sea while drowning their pursuers. He raises Jesus from Sheol (Acts 2:27) and through baptism plucks us from the dominion of sin and death (Rom 6:3–4). The Christian can recite this line exultantly, for all his greatest foes are destroyed. The following verses (18–19) express the same truth without imagery. Verse 20a is the counterpart of verse 7: the constriction of the psalmist's distress has been replaced with a "broadness" (cf. Ps 4:4); the second half of the verse (20b), in giving the reason for the Lord's deliverance ("he delighted in me"), introduces the suture (vv. 21–28) between the two accounts of salvation.

The saving action of the Lord is grounded in the king's "justice": "because my hands were clean he rewarded me" (v. 21). Again we see the theme introduced in Psalm 1: the Lord can help only those who are aligned with his will. The king, in particular, was obliged to love and obey the law.

> When he is seated on his royal throne he must write a copy of this Law on a scroll for his own use at the dictation of the levitical priests. It must never leave him and he must read it every day of his life and learn to fear Yahweh his God by keeping all the words of this Law and observing these laws. So his heart will not look down on his brothers and he will swerve neither right nor left from these commandments. If he does this, he will have long days on his throne, he and his sons, in Israel. (Deut 17:18–20)

Our psalmist guarded the Lord's ways, not acting wickedly against his God (v. 22). For all the Lord's judgments were before him [in his mind], and his statutes he does not desert (v. 23) in order to remain blameless with him and guard himself from iniquity (v. 24). He closes this first section of the suture with a return to its opening verse: the Lord repaid him for his justice; the cleanness of his hands was before the Lord's eyes (v. 25).

In the second half of the suture the speaker presents his own experience as an example of a general law: the Lord responds to people according to their actions, blameless (vv. 26–27a) or perverted (v. 27b; cf. Prov 11:20, 17:20). His specialty is to "save the people that are poor" and "bring down the eyes that are exalted" (v. 28; cf. the Magnificat, Luke 1:52; 1 Sam 2:7–8). Here the righteous king is assimilated to the "poor of Yahweh" (ʿănāwîm) whose wealth consists in conforming their lives to him (cf. Pss 9:13, 10:17, 12:6).

In verse 29 the speaker enters on the second account of his salvation. The Lord lights his lamp, enlightening his darkness (v. 29), enabling him to run over ridges and leap over barriers (v. 30). Before getting down to detail, the speaker praises the God whose way is blameless (v. 31; cf. v. 24), whose promise is "smelted" (cf. Ps 12:7), the "shield" (Ps 3:4) for "all who take refuge in him" (Pss 2:12, 5:12, and esp. Ps 17:7). The verse looks back not only to previous psalms but to the themes of "shield" and "refuge" at the beginning of this one (v. 3), as does the following verse (32) confessing God as "rock."

With verse 33 the speaker enters in earnest on the second account of salvation. Having rescued him in his helplessness, the Lord girded him with vigor and made his way blameless. The psalmist multiplies the ways the Lord strengthened him: making his feet like those of a doe, on the high places making him stand (v. 34), teaching his hands for battle, and his arms have bent a bow of bronze (v. 35). The speaker directly addresses God, who has given him a shield (cf. v. 31) of salvation, whose right hand (cf. Ps 17:7) has supported him and whose "answer" (as in 2 Sam 22:36) made him great (v. 36), made wide room for his steps under him, and his ankles did not waver (v. 37). The God who was so intimately woven with his manifestations in nature in the first part is now intimately woven with the body and destiny of the king.

Thus strengthened by the Lord the speaker moved into action, pursuing his enemies and overtaking them, not returning till they were finished off (v. 38). He smote them so they could not rise; they fell beneath his feet (v. 39). The Lord "girded him with vigor for battle" (cf. v. 33), made those who rose against him bow beneath him (v. 40), made his enemies turn their backs on him, and those who hated him he silenced (v. 41). They cried and there was no savior, and the Lord did not answer (v. 42). He ground them like dust before the wind, like mud in the streets he swept them away (v. 43, chiasmus). The speaker returns to direct address: "You brought me to safety from the quarrels of the people, put me at the head of the nations; a people I did not know served me" (v. 44; for the fourth time in the section a third (or first) person statement interrupts the flow of "you" statements, cf. vv. 35b, 37b, 41b). At the hearing of the ear they listen to him, foreigners cower before him (v. 45); they fade away (cf. Ps 1:3) and come trembling from their enclosures (v. 46; verb tenses shift in vv. 33–46). With the help of the Lord the king has penetrated even to the secret hiding places of the enemy nations and entirely subjugated them.

The first account of salvation was preceded by a splendid introduction in which the psalmist confesses that he loves (lit. "has compassion for," sometimes corrected to "exalts") the Lord, whom he describes with eight epithets signifying strength and protection (vv. 2–3). Several of these, all in verse 3, are alluded to in the course of the psalm: "the one who brings me to safety" (cf. v. 44), "the rock where I take refuge" (cf. vv. 31, 32), "my shield" (cf. vv. 31, 36), "my horn of salvation" (cf. vv. 4, 28, 37, 42). Three of these themes return in the song of praise that concludes the psalm: "The Lord lives; blessed is my rock, exalted the God of my salvation . . . who brings me to safety from my enemies" (vv. 47, 49a). God has given the psalmist vengeance and subdued peoples beneath him (v. 48), exalting him above his attackers and rescuing him from the man of violence (v. 49b). The king will thank the Lord among the nations and make music to his name (v. 50). A concluding verse sees the whole psalm as testimony to God's gifts of "salvation" and *ḥesed* to David and his sons forever (v. 51). The king's love for the Lord is his response to the Lord's saving love for him.

The psalm is found *in toto* near the end of 2 Samuel 22 where it serves as a kind of testament of David to posterity. David is thus the emblem of the "poor" man, the "servant" of the Lord (v. 1), who in taking refuge in the Lord finds himself raised above all his foes.

∼ PSALM 19   sun

Most of Psalm 19 is starkly declarative, explaining with enthusiasm how man knows God but only at the end involving the speaker personally. In this it stands out from the surrounding psalms, in which the speakers are deeply engaged with God. The psalm expresses the wonder of creation and the Law as utterances by which God speaks to man, but does not explicitly praise him. It is composed with such poetic art that the speaker would have it be pleasing to God; in this way it is an implicit song of praise.

The heavens are "recounting" the glory of God, and the work of his hands the firmament (subject) reveals (v. 2, chiasmus). The splendor of the heavens witnesses to the glory of the God who made them. One day "pours forth speech" to the next, night (cf. Ps 17:3) to night announces knowledge (v. 3). Yet all these communications are silent: no speech, no words, no voice are heard by man (v. 4), even though through all the earth goes forth their "voice" (common emendation of obscure Hebrew: "measuring-line") and to the ends of the world their "utterances" (common word in Job, only here and Ps 139:4 in the Psalms) (v. 5a). The knowledge of the creator communicated by the splendor of the heavens needs an interpreter if man is to perceive it.

The principal resident of the heavens, the sun, is personified as a "champion" for whom God has placed a tent in the sky (v. 5b), and who emerges like a "bridegroom" from his "wedding chamber" (*huppāh*, cf. Joel 2:16, Isa 4:5), "rejoicing" to run his path (v. 6). From the end of the heavens is his emerging, and his circuit is to their end; nothing is hidden from his heat (v. 7). The description conveys the radiant energy of the sun, the joy associated with its light, and its life-giving potency. Yet vigorous as the sun is, testifying to the power of the one who made it, it does not speak.

The revelation of God that man did not hear from the heavens has been given to Israel in the Law. God chose Israel to hear the word of his love, to know his saving deeds, and to be a covenant partner by recognizing his sovereignty. The Law gave Israel a privileged knowledge of the mind of God. For this reason it was called "blameless" (cf. Ps 18:31): nothing was lacking to it, in it God disclosed all man needed to know (v. 8a). As in Psalm 119 the speaker uses several synonyms for the Law in extolling its virtues: "testimony," "precepts," "command," "fear of the Lord" (the global attitude of taking the commandments seriously), "judgments" (vv. 8–10). These are faithful, upright, pure, enduring, and just. Their effect on man is beneficent: they "restore" his soul, "make wise the simple" (latter word frequent in Proverbs, cf. Prov 1:4), "gladden the heart," "give light to the eyes" (cf. Ps 18:29). They are more coveted than gold, much pure gold, and sweeter than the richest honey, honey dripping from the comb (v. 11). They are these things because they satisfy man's appetite for God, showing what God has done for him and how he can enjoy the kind of communion with God described in Psalm 16.

At this point the speaker expresses his own rapport with the Law (v. 12): as the Lord's "servant" (cf. Ps 18:1, Hebrew superscript), he is admonished by the Law, finding "great profit" in "guarding" it (cf. Ps 18:22), for which he needs divine help. Infractions who can discern? From hidden ones may the Lord declare him exempt (v. 13), withholding him from proud men—may they not rule over him; then he will be blameless, innocent of serious rebellion (v. 14). The psalmist ends by consecrating his poem to the Lord: "May they be pleasing [lit. "pleasure"], the declarations of my mouth, the meditation of my heart before you, my rock [cf. Ps 18:3, 47] and my redeemer" (v. 15). The God who created the heavens and the sun in all their glory is the intimate companion of the one who observes his Law.

The Law of Moses stipulated how man might be pleasing to God but did not confer the power to carry it out. That is why Jesus came to "satisfy the Law's just demands" (Rom 8:3–4). His response of obedience to the Father's will fulfilled the purpose of the Law (Matt 5:17–18), rendering mankind now pleasing to God. In so doing he gave new meaning to the term "law": it now refers to the "supreme law of love" (Jas 2:8, Rom 13:10, 1 John 3:23–24), love of man even unto death (John 15:12–13), the "new commandment" of fraternal charity (John 13:34), for which all the precepts of the Old Testament Law were a preparation. This is the law that Christ hymns in Psalm 19, the Law that he himself observed and empowers us to observe. The psalm praises the law of God at its profoundest level, which is the law of self-giving love. Its concluding petitions show that the very power to keep the law is God's gift to us and must be prayed for. Christ praises the law that he himself embodied and fulfilled in his life, death on the cross, and resurrection. Through faith Christians make their own this righteousness of Christ. In them too the Law's "just demands" are fulfilled (Rom 8:4) because the Spirit of Christ pronounces Christ's Yes to the Father in us (Rom 8:14–17).

If the Law of God is the revelation of who God is and what he asks of man, then it is also a light, like Jesus the Word, "enlightening every man" (John 1:9). Jesus embodies God's revelation of himself and so is the light of the world (John 8:12), the true "sun of justice" (Mal 3:20) who in fulfilling the Father's will reconciles humanity to the Father. All that the first part of our psalm says about the sun is an image of the light of Christ, the spouse of humanity. Law of God and light coalesce in him: "What is being carried out in your lives as it was in his, is a new commandment; because the night is over and the real light is already shining. Anyone who claims to be in the light but hates his brother is still in the dark. But anyone who loves his brother is living in the light and need not be afraid of stumbling . . ." (1 John 2:8–11).

It is possible to see in the psalm three stages of revelation: the revelation in nature, the revelation in the Law of Moses, and the revelation in Christ implied in the petition for divine help in fidelity to the Law. The first section is written predominantly in long lines of four beats, the second (except for v. 11) in the 3 + 2 *qinah* meter, and the third in lines mainly of three beats. The three stages are thus clearly profiled by the varying meters.

∼ PSALM 20   name

Psalm 19 was the center of the group of Psalms 15–24. The psalms that follow match in reverse order the first four psalms of the group: the two royal psalms, 20 and 21, mirror Psalm 18, the lament Psalm 22 mirrors Psalm 17, the trust song Psalm 23 mirrors Psalm 16, and the entrance song Psalm 24 mirrors Psalm 15. Word links between Psalms 19 and 18 ("servant," "my rock," "give light," "pure," "blameless," "judgments," etc.) invite us to see in the speaker of Psalm 19 David or the ideal king committed to observing the Lord's Law. That would be one more link with Christ, the son of David, in whom the Law was fulfilled.

Psalm 20 is a prayer for victory of the king in battle. First, the community makes a series of petitions that the king's prayers be heard; then in a single verse an individual speaker, perhaps the king himself, expresses confidence (v. 7); next the community in turn expresses its faith in the Lord (vv. 8–9), and the psalm ends with a summarizing petition of the community.

The first five verses contain ten verbs in volitional mode; except in verse 2 the verbs are chiastically placed at the beginning and end of each verse, and the verses display clear synonymous parallelism. Thus in verse 2 "Yahweh" is parallel to "the name of the God of Jacob." Here as in two later verses (vv. 6, 8) the "name" of God is treated as a subsistent person, protecting the king. There is something alive about the "name" of God because it was revealed to Israel that they might call upon it and engage the saving power it represented. May Yahweh send help and may he support (cf. Ps 18:36) the king from the holy place on Mount Zion (v. 3), where he has offered oblations and holocausts (v. 4) for the success of every plan of his heart (v. 5). May the people shout for joy at his "salvation" under the "banner" of the "name" of their God; may the Lord fulfill all his requests (v. 6).

Verse 7 is distinguished by a change to the first person singular and the disappearance of the synonymous or indeed any parallelism. An individual speaker, perhaps the king himself, expresses the certainty "now" that the Lord will "save" his anointed one (cf. Ps 18:51), "answering" not now from the temple but from his "holy heaven" with the saving mighty deeds of his right hand (cf. Ps 18:36).

The community in turn professes that "these to chariots and these to horses, but we to the name of the Lord our God give acknowledgment" (v. 8). The name of Israel's God is stronger (cf. 1 Sam 17:45) than the chariots and horses on which others depend (cf. Deut 17:16, Mic 5:9, Prov 21:31). For Christians that name is Jesus. Christian monks early discovered that there is no more powerful weapon against evil and temptation than the utterance of this sacred name. A writer in the *Philokalia* expresses the common teaching:

> When you notice thoughts arising and accosting you, do not look at them, even if they are not bad; but keeping the mind firmly in the heart, call to Lord Jesus and you will soon sweep away the thoughts and drive out the instigator—the demons—invisibly scorching and flogging them with this Divine Name. Thus teaches John of the Ladder, saying: with the name of Jesus flog the foes, for there is no surer weapon against them, either on earth or in heaven. (*Writings from the Philokalia*, 85)

According to the *Catechism of the Catholic Church,*

> The name "Jesus" contains all: God and man and the whole economy of creation and salvation. To pray "Jesus" is to invoke him and to call him within us. His name is the only one that contains the presence it signifies. Jesus is the risen One, and whoever invokes the name of Jesus is welcoming the Son of God who loved him and who gave himself up for him. (2666)

Saint Bernard, too, described the power of the name of Jesus in his Sermons on the Song of Songs:

> Your disputations and your conferences remain flat to me unless they ring with the name of Jesus. Jesus is honey to the mouth, sweet song to the ear, joyful delight to the heart. But it is also a medicine. Is someone sad among us? Let Jesus come into his heart and from there leap to his lips. . . . Has someone lapsed into sin? into despair? . . . If he invokes the name of life he will be revitalized at once. (Sermon 15)

To "call on the name of the Lord" is to enable the Lord to exercise in our lives the divine salvation, which the name signifies (Acts 2:21, 3:16, 4:12, 30). That invocation of his name is always answered, since he and his Father grant what we pray for in his name (John 14:13–14, 15:16, 16:23–24).

While those who relied on the strength of creatures fell to their knees and collapsed (a possible reference to the collapse of the ruthless Assyrian empire), the speakers of the psalm rose and stood tall (v. 9).

A final verse summarizes the prayer, first with the single imperative in the psalm: "O Lord, save the king," then with a return to the third person wish: "May he answer us on the day we call" (v. 10; for the "call/answer" duality see Pss 3:5, 4:2, 17:6). The expression "answer on the day" thus forms an inclusion with verse 2 designating the theme of the psalm. The predominance of the theme "save/salvation" (mentioned four times) links the psalm closely with Psalm 18, the thanksgiving of the king for the Lord's salvation (mentioned seven times). The Christian praying the psalm knows that God has saved his Christ by raising him from the dead and making him savior of his people.

It is easy to ask the Father to hear the prayers (and sacrifice) of Christ—for example, the prayer he offered the night before he died: that all may be one, that all may be kept from evil and consecrated in the truth, that we may be with him and see his glory, that the Father's love for the Son may be in us and the Son himself in us (John 17:15, 17, 22–23, 24, 26). These great intentions of the Son have already been heard and granted by the Father, but their working out on earth requires our constant making Christ's prayer our own. Nations still have not heard of him; nations that have known him have forgotten him. There is too much suffering, too much lack of peace in the world for us to cease asking the Father to hear the prayer of the Son. And curiously, if our prayer is a calling on the divine name that is Jesus, we are by that very word allying ourselves with the prayer of Jesus, which is always heard; we are, as it were, calling down Jesus on the world. This is "asking the Father in the name" of Jesus. Let us not forget that the holy name *Yēšûaʿ* comes from the root meaning "save" (*yšʿ*). Jesus is the embodiment of salvation. He prays for it, he won it, he is it. The world waits for him.

⌁ PSALM 21   crown

The community that prayed for the king's victory in Psalm 20 now praises God for the king's joy at the answering of his prayer. Key word-links connect the two psalms: "king," "salvation," "heart," "ask." While Psalm 20 referred to God almost entirely in the third person, Psalm 21 addresses him directly. The exception is a middle verse that separates the two parts of the psalm. The first part contains several long (four-beat) lines, the second part is in 3 + 3 meter.

"Lord, in your strength the king is glad, and in your salvation how ecstatically he rejoices" (v. 2). The speaker mentions first the Lord's gifts and then the king's reaction to the gifts. Christ exults in the Father's raising him from the dead for the salvation of mankind. God has given him the "desire of his heart" (v. 3), which was that all men be saved (1 Tim 2:3–6) and be with him forever (John 17:24); the prayer of his lips God has not denied. God "advanced before him" with blessings of goodness (v. 4), placing on his head a crown of "fine gold" (cf. Ps 19:11). Life he asked from God who gave it to him, length of days forever (v. 5). Jesus "asked" that his followers receive a share in the eternal life he himself received from the Father (cf. John 17:2, 6:57, 5:26). "Great is his glory" in the salvation of God (v. 6), who has laid on him the "majesty and splendor" in which he himself is robed (Ps 104:1; cf. Ps 96:6, John 17:5, 24). God has made him an eternal blessing (cf. v. 4), making him glad with the gladness of his face (v. 7, inclusion with v. 2). We receive some glimpse of the joy of Jesus in his Father through the Holy Spirit in his prayer recorded in Luke 10:21. This joy was a reflection of the eschatological joy of the Son with the Father after his resurrection, the joy of heaven "shared by all the people" (Luke 2:10).

The center of the psalm speaks of both God and king in the third person: "For the king trusts in the Lord, and through the covenant love of the Most High he will not totter" (v. 8). The king is the epitome of the Israelite of the previous psalms who by relying not on his own strength (Ps 10:6) but on the Lord's *ḥesed* (Ps 13:6) becomes firm and secure (cf. esp. Pss 13:5, 14:5, 16:8).

The second part of the psalm was originally addressed to the king. The addition of four words in verse 10, "At the time of your face [manifestation], Lord, in its anger . . . ," redirects these verses to the Lord, for whom they might seem more appropriate since they describe the fiery extermination of the enemies. But given Christ's share in the glory of the Father (cf. on v. 6 above), it is appropriate to attribute these divine actions both to God and to the king. His hand will find all his enemies, his right hand find those who hate him (v. 9), gripping them like a fiery furnace; it swallows them up and fire devours them (v. 10). Their offspring he destroys from the earth and their seed from the sons of men (v. 11). Though they intended evil against him, the plots they planned did not succeed (v. 12). The king will make them turn their shoulder (retreat), stretching his bowstrings against them (v. 13).

As in Psalm 18, a first part tells of God's gifts to the king, and a second of the king's activity made possible by those gifts.

In a concluding verse (14) the community calls on the Lord to be exalted in his "power" (inclusion with v. 2); they will sing and make music for his mighty deeds (cf. Ps 20:7).

∼ PSALM 22   abandonment

Psalm 22 was destined for Christ not just by the details that announce his Passion (cf. vv. 2, 9, 19) but for the scope of the psalmist's suffering and its significance. The individual lament achieves here a solemnity and a breadth that we have not yet seen in the psalter and will scarcely see again.

The opening cry reveals the deepest possible distress: "My God, my God . . ." The speaker is aware of an intimate relationship with this God who has helped him in the past, in whom he has trusted, to whom he has prayed. He has personally appropriated the covenant term, "Our God" (cf. Jos 24:17–18, 24, Lev 26:12, Exod 6:7), knowing himself partner in an inviolable covenant relationship. He doubles the cry in anguish at his abandonment (against Ps 9:11) by this God: part of himself has been torn away. What he is suffering makes no sense, hence the "Why?", echoed down the ages by all who cannot reconcile their acute pain with the goodness and fair promises of their God. The God whom other psalms will call "near" (Pss 34:19, 73:28, 119:151, 145:18) has become "far" from the psalmist's salvation and from his "roaring" (v. 2). The first half of the verse focuses on the psalmist's desolation, the second on God's distance: he has become an invisible point in a remote distance. Verse 3 flatly challenges the call/answer duality we have often seen (e.g., Ps 3:5): this time the psalmist's God has *not* answered his call in the day, and the night affords no stillness.

Verses 4–6 develop the covenant idea implicit in the opening cry. The holy God, seated on Israel's "praises," always "brought to safety" (cf. Ps 18:3, 44, 49) the "fathers" who "trusted" (the key word for the psalmist's basic religious attitude; cf. Pss 13:6, 21:8) in him. Not to have "freed" them when they "cried" (as in Exod 2:23, Judg 3:9, 15, 6:7, 1 Sam 12:8) would have been to "shame" them by rendering their trust misplaced. The psalmist speaks as a member of "Israel," drawing on Israel's faith as he heard it expressed in the liturgy.

But now he feels excluded from "the people" and even from humanity, a "worm" rather than a man, the reproach of men and despised by the people (v. 7). Up to now the psalmist has had enemies, even "thousands" (Ps 3:7), but never the whole people or the whole human race. The one figure to be universally rejected would be Israel's and the world's Messiah, hated by enemies, abandoned by friends, annihilated as the vilest of creatures. Christians pray this psalm not with an unhealthy sense of worthlessness but in solidarity with their rejected Lord, who gives them a share in his Passion as in his victory, but also with awareness that their own sin was the cause of the Savior's suffering. The adult Catholic must both feel his invaluable worth as a child of God and acknowledge his share in the refusal of God's love.

All who see the psalmist deride him, curl their lips, shake their head (v. 8). Their taunt calls in question the psalmist's trust (v. 9): "Let him roll his concern [LXX and Matt 27:43 render in past tense] onto the Lord, he will bring him to safety [cf. v. 5]; he will rescue him since he [the Lord] delights in him" (= Ps 18:20b). Indeed it was the Lord who drew him from the womb, entrusting him to his mother's breasts (v. 10); on the Lord was he cast from birth; "From my mother's womb you have been my God" (v. 11; cf. v. 2). Having recalled the Lord's deliverance of the "fathers," he now does the same for his own personal history. The first section ends with a brief petition reiterating the opening theme of God's "distance": "Do not be far from me, for distress is near; there is no helper" (v. 12; cf. v. 2).

The first lament has focused on the absence of God; now a second fuller lament evokes the ferocity of the enemies and the psalmist's disintegration. "They surround me, many bulls; strong bulls of Bashan circle me [v. 13, chiasmus]. They open against me their mouths—a lion [cf. Ps 17:12, 1 Pet 5:8] tearing and roaring" (v. 14; cf. v. 2). Like water he is poured out and all his bones are dislocated; his heart has become like wax, dissolved in the middle of his entrails (v. 15). Dried up like a potsherd is his power, and his tongue clings (cf. Lam 4:4) to his palate (cf. John 19:28?), and in the dust of death the Lord has laid him (v. 16). For surrounding him are dogs (cf. Ps 59:7); a gathering of wrongdoers surrounds him (third synonym in five verses for this action). The final line of verse 17, "like a lion, my hands and my feet," seems a later addition. He can count all his bones; those who look on him gloat over him (v. 18). He is treated as already dead by those who cast lots for his clothes (v. 19; cf. Matt 27:35, Mark 15:24, Luke 23:34, John 19:24). This half-dead body, beset by a pack of savages (cf. v. 17), abandoned by God, is what the Messiah, the Word made flesh, is reduced to (cf. Matt 27:46, Mark 15:34). No other psalm evokes so deeply the desolation, brutality, isolation, and contempt that would afflict God's favored one.

The psalmist musters his last strength to invoke the Lord (v. 20), renewing the plea, "Do not be far off" (cf. v. 12), invoking God as "my strength" (in a word used only here in the Bible) to hasten to the "help" that is nowhere else forthcoming (cf. v. 12). Specifically he wants to be "rescued" from sword and dog (v. 21), "saved" from the mouth of the lion and the horns of oxen (v. 22), the three animals of the lament mentioned now in reverse order.

Verse 22 ends with the word "you have answered me" (*'ănîtānî*), sometimes emended to "my wretchedness" (*'ăniyyātî*) as object of "save" since the verb seems abrupt. If the Hebrew text is correct, the speaker would be expressing the sudden and spectacular answering of his prayer. Immediately the psalm rings with "praise" (cf. vv. 23, 24, 27, noun in v. 26; cf. also v. 4) and the psalmist is surrounded by an "assembly" of "brothers" to whom he recounts the "name" of the Lord (v. 23). One cannot but think of the Easter appearances of Jesus to the disciples whom he now calls "my brothers" (John 20:17, Matt 28:10, Heb 2:11–12). His death has washed away their sins and made them into his family. The psalmist calls on the devout "fearers of the Lord" to second his praise, on all the descendants of Jacob to glorify him, and on all the descendants of Israel to be in awe of him (v. 24). "For" (conjunction used in hymn genre to introduce reasons for praise) the Lord did not "despise" (cf. v. 7) or detest the wretchedness of the poor one (cf. Pss 18:28, 12:6) nor hide his face from him, but when he cried for help the Lord heard (v. 25). To the Lord is his praise in the large assembly; his vows he will pay before those who fear God (v. 26; cf. v. 24). The poor will eat [of his sacrificial offerings] and be filled. These "searchers for God" (cf. Pss 9:11, 14:2) will praise him, their hearts will live forever (v. 27; cf. Ps 21:5). Remarkable is the complete silence of the speaker with respect to his own restoration and the defeat of the murderous attackers. His experience is entirely one of reintegration into the community of praise.

With verse 28 the horizon opens to the future, as it had earlier to the past (vv. 4–6) and transcends even the bounds of Israel. All the ends of the earth will remember and return to the Lord, all the clans of the nations falling prostrate before him (v. 28). For to the Lord belongs kingship, and he rules the nations (v. 29). Not just the local poor but the "well-fed" of the earth will eat and prostrate themselves; before him will bow all who go down to the dust (v. 30ab). The bold idea that even the dead might praise the Lord led a later author to add a qualification: "When a man no longer lives, his descendants will take up the service of praise" (vv. 30c–31a). Praise of the Master will be recounted for generations (v. 31b). They will come and tell God's "justice" to people still to be born, for God has acted (v. 32).

The abandoned, contemned one has become the center of praise to the Lord for all nations and times. His focus is not on himself but on the universal recognition of the Lord's kingship. That is why the psalm is ideally suited to Christian praise, in which the insulted and destitute Lord gathers his brothers and sisters around him to praise the name and justice of the one who raised him from the dead. Such was already the vision of the Letter to the Hebrews (Heb 2:10–13).

The sharp contrast between the two parts of the psalm is mirrored in the change of meter. The measured 3 + 3 meter of the earlier part gives way in the final section to an accumulation of cola of different lengths: verses 24, 25, 26, 28, and 30 each contain at least one four-beat colon; several verses have three or more cola. The change of meter reinforces the change of mood.

∾ Psalm 23   shepherd

As in the previous psalm the speaker shows from the very start that he has personally appropriated Israel's faith in the covenant God (see on Ps 22:2, "My God"). Yahweh is his personal shepherd, even if he is apart from the flock (of which there is no mention). Yahweh "guides" (v. 2) and "leads" (v. 3) him as he guided and led his people out of Egypt (Exod 15:13), as he "guides" the mother ewes that symbolize the people returning from Babylon (Isa 40:11) to springs of water (Isa 49:10) and as he "led" his people like a flock through the desert (Pss 77:21, 78:14, 53). He sees that his sheep "lacks" nothing (v. 1), as he did for his people on their forty-year trek (Deut 2:7, Neh 9:21) and promised to do in Canaan (Deut 8:9). In particular he finds "meadows" (v. 2) as he once did for his wandering people (Exod 15:13) and will do again after their exile to Babylon (Jer 23:3), meadows of "fresh vegetation" (cf. the pleasing images in Deut 32:2, 2 Sam 23:4, Job 38:27, Isa 66:14). Here he makes the sheep "lie down," as he promises to do in the great prophecy about the shepherds of Israel, Ezekiel 34:14–15. The waters he provides are waters of "rest" (v. 2), a term the Lord used of the promised land of Israel (Ps 95:11).

Yahweh will "restore" the speaker's "soul" (cf. Ps 22:21) as he restores to the fold the stray sheep (Ezek 34:16), leading him on tracks of "justice," a word that suggests both correct paths to a destination and righteous behavior (see "pasture of justice" in Jer 31:23). In showing to the individual Israelite the attentive, solicitous care he shows the whole people, the Lord is acting according to that "name" (v. 3) of his that contains his identity as a God of love (cf. Pss 22:23, 20:2, 6, 8, Exod 34:5–6). Thus nearly every word in the first two verses of the psalm roots the psalmist's experience in the history of Israel, which he would have often heard recounted and celebrated in the liturgy. The Christian too must make his own and live by the story of Christ's death and resurrection into which he has been inserted by his baptism.

The sheep metaphor continues into verse 4 as the psalmist moves into direct speech to the Lord. Even should the psalmist traverse the valley of the "shadow of death" (cf. Isa 9:1), he would fear no evil (unlike Israel on the threshold of Canaan, Deut 1:21, 27–29), for the Lord is "with" him, comforting him with his shepherd's "crook" (cf. Mic 7:14) and staff. "Comforting" was to be the great action of the Lord as he led his people from Babylon across the desert after the Exile (cf. Isa 49:9–13; also Jer 31:10–13). The care given to the individual member of God's "flock" prepares for Jesus's parables about the lost sheep (Luke 15:4–5) or the sheep fallen down a hole on the sabbath (Matt 12:11–12). God's care for his people extends to each individual in the group.

Still addressing the Lord, the psalmist abandons the sheep metaphor for that of a banquet (v. 5) given for him in the "house of the Lord" (v. 6). The same individual care will be given to the guest as to the sheep, this time in the form of a "table prepared," anointing of the head, an overflowing cup of wine. Since this favor is shown "in the presence of foes," it is probably the partaking of a communion sacrifice offered in the temple after the psalmist received a favorable judgment, echoing the sacrificial meal shared by the speaker of the previous psalm with the poor (Ps 22:26–27). The enjoyment of the meal is a sign that the psalmist enjoys the favor of God, whose "goodness and love" are personified as "following" him all the days of his life, just as the shepherd's care was expressed in the twin metaphors of crook and staff (v. 4).

With verse 6 the psalmist returns to the third person speech about God with which he began. The resulting "sandwich" structure of the psalm is in tension with the two-part division based on the sheep and banquet metaphors. While the sheep metaphor focuses on the journey and the temple banquet on the goal, each metaphor also contains the other: the shepherd provides pasture and drink, the host through his attributes "follows" his guest. But the final word of the psalm has to do with the dwelling "for length of days" in the house of the Lord, the goal of all God's guidance on earth. The divine name is used at the beginning and the end of the psalm, holding the prayer together like a clamp.

Psalm 23 is the most quoted and most memorized of the psalms. It gives simple but striking and unforgettable images of God's lavish care on the individual, who has no other obligation than to receive the care: there is no word of repayment for righteous behavior (cf. Ps 18:21–25), of calling on the Lord (Ps 4:4), of being poor (Pss 18:28, 12:6), or even of trust (Ps 13:6), although the prayer is rightly classified as a psalm of trust.

It expresses the truth that everything about our salvation is God's work: we can only consent to be the "lost" ones who need guidance, the sick who need healing (Mark 2:17), the hungry who will be fed (Luke 6:21). All is grace.

The complementary psalm in the group, Psalms 15–24, Psalm 16, relies less on extended metaphors and more on literal language to express the intimacy of the individual with God. For this reason it reaches a profounder level of the human person but not in so memorable a way. The psalmist's "kidneys" and gaze, his "right hand" and his "glory," his "flesh" and "soul" are encompassed by the Lord's presence, which produces a fullness of life and joy. Psalm 23 relies more on visual and spatial imagery to create a context of protection. The two trust psalms share only the one significant word "cup," used quite differently in Psalms 16:5 and 23:5.

Christ is both sheep (John 1:29, 36, Rev 5:6, 1 Pet 1:19) and shepherd (John 10:11, 14–15, Heb 13:20, 1 Pet 2:25). The paradox is expressed succinctly in Revelation 7:17: "The Lamb who is at the throne will be their shepherd and will lead them to springs of living water." In a mysterious way the one who submits freely to the Father's will becomes the one who leads his brothers to salvation (Heb 2:10–12).

∼ PSALM 24   gates

The final psalm in this second subsection of Book One matches the opening Psalm 15, in treating the qualifications for entry into the temple of the Lord. Here, however, the subject is treated more briefly and in the context of an actual procession into the temple. It is this procession that unifies the disparate "pieces" of the short psalm; hence the psalm is assigned to the category of "liturgy."

Israel worships its Lord as creator and, therefore, possessor of the world. The Lord's are the earth and all that fills it, the world and those who dwell in it (v. 1), for "on the seas he founded it, and on the rivers he established it" (v. 2). Creation, for the ancient people of the Near East, consisted in establishing a firm place upon or amid the swirling waters of primeval chaos, conceived in non-Israelite mythology as a rival god to the Creator. Since it is this creator God who is worshipped in Israel's temple, the worshippers, after singing his praises, ask what is required for them to dwell in his presence. It is here that is met the parallel with Psalm 15.

Both passages begin by asking "who" can dwell on (Ps 15) or climb (Ps 24) the Lord's "mountain" (v. 3a); who can rise in his "holy" place (v. 3b). The answer in Psalm 24 is given in a single verse (4): one whose palms are innocent and whose heart is clean; to this general reference to outer and inner conformity with the will of God are added two clauses excluding specifically the one who "lifts up his soul to worthless things" (idols?, false gods?) and the one who "swears deceitfully." A similar movement from personal to public morality was noted in Psalm 15. As in that psalm the speaker concludes somewhat unexpectedly by giving rewards of right behavior: blessing from the Lord and "justice" from the "God of his salvation" (v. 5). There follows a curious summarizing comment: "Such is the generation of those who search for him, those who seek your face, O Jacob" (v. 6). To "seek God" is to seek his presence in his temple and to seek to accomplish his will; it designates the quality of genuine worshippers of Yahweh (cf. Pss 9:11, 14:2, 22:27). What is surprising is the second half of verse 6 where the object of the second verb for "seek" is not God but the face of Jacob. The phrase is often emended to "seek the face of the God of Jacob," but it is possible that the psalmist has in mind gentile nations seeking out Israel as the home of the true God and his Law (cf. Zech 2:15). Norbert Lohfink believes the verse has in mind pagans converted from idols to the recognition of the true God; the following psalm, Psalm 25, would be the petition of one such pagan to be taught the Law of Yahweh (cf. Isa 2:1–3; Lohfink and Zenger, *God of Israel,* 61–62).

After this species of entrance rite, the procession calls on the gates of the temple to open to permit the entrance of the "king of glory" (v. 7). The psalmist can apply this title to Israel's God because, as seen above, this God is creator of the world. All peoples are therefore subject to him. While other nations might refer to their god as "king" of other gods or of other peoples, Israel's covenant God was the only god and the maker of all that exists. "Glory" was the visible manifestation of his royal power. On certain feasts this Lord, who was "seated on the cherubs" (2 Sam 6:2) above the ark as on a throne, would reenter his temple in triumph as once he entered Jerusalem under David (2 Sam 6:12–17) and later entered the temple Solomon built for him (1 Kgs 8:1–13). The ark would be taken to the bottom of the temple Mount and carried in procession up the mountain to songs of praise and jubilation. On reaching the temple, the bearers of the ark and other worshippers would summon the gates of the temple to "lift [their] heads" (i.e., lintels) and its "eternal doors" to "be lifted" to admit the king on his throne.

From inside would come the voice of priest or minister asking the identity of this king (v. 8a). At first he is identified as "Yahweh, powerful and a champion, Yahweh a champion in battle" (v. 8b), since it was through the might of Yahweh that Israel conquered the inhabitants of Canaan and took possession of it. A second time the procession cries for the opening of the gates (v. 9), this time identifying the king of glory by his traditional name, "the Lord of hosts — he is the king of glory" (v. 10). This title appears first in 1 Samuel 1:3 where it is associated with the ark (cf. Isa 6:3–5). It was a favorite term for Yahweh as Lord not only of Israel's armies but also of the hosts of heaven, the stars and "all the cosmic forces, cf. Gen 2:1, under God's command" (*Jerusalem Bible,* OT, 345 n. b). It is thus an appropriate term for designating the God of creation evoked at the beginning of the psalm and the God of the covenant who settled his people in the land of Canaan. In the Lofhink hypothesis, the final two cola of the psalm amount to a confession of faith on the part of the converted pagans.

When Christians pray Psalm 24, they praise the Creator who comes to dwell with us in his Son and the Son who purifies mankind from sin to make us worthy to dwell with the Father (cf. 1 John 2:1–2). With profound insight John Keble and William Hall conclude their hymn "Blest are the pure in heart" by identifying the temple of God with the heart that is pure: "Give us a pure and lowly heart, / A temple meet for thee."

∾ PSALM 25   way

The speaker of the psalm knows that the paths of the Lord are all "love and faithfulness" (v. 10) and that he has not always walked in them. He asks for both forgiveness of his sins and a deeper knowledge of the Lord's "way" (cf. vv. 4, 8, 9, 12). Although his reflections are organized by the demands of the alphabetical structure, each verse beginning with a new letter of the Hebrew alphabet, the psalm also exhibits another structure. The Lord is addressed directly in verses 1–7 and 16–22 and in the central verse 11. On either side of the central verse God is spoken of in the third person (vv. 8–10, 12–15). The central verse expresses the core of the psalmist's prayer: it is a plea that the Lord "forgive" his many offenses in accordance with his "name," since that name connotes generous, unmerited loving condescension, the *ḥesed* (cf. vv. 6–7) that chose Israel out of all the peoples of the earth to make them his own (Deut 7:6–9). This is the first of only four occurrences of the root "forgive" in the Psalms. It is associated with the Lord's revelation to Moses on Mount Sinai of his attributes of love and faithfulness (Exod 34:6–9) and is a recurring theme of Solomon's prayer at the dedication of the temple (1 Kgs 8:30, 34, 36, 39, 50; cf. 2 Chr 7:14), of Jeremiah's later preaching (Jer 31:34, 33:8, 36:3, 50:20; cf. also Isa 55:7), and of the priestly law of sacrifice for sin (Lev 4:20, 26, 31, 35, 5:10, 13, 16, 18, 26, 19:22, Num 15:25, 26, 28). It is in the New Testament that the theme will find its fulfilment.

In choosing a word for sin (*ʿāwôn*, v. 11) that means "a disposition not standing in harmony with the will of God" (Gerhard Köhler, *TheolAT* 3rd ed. cited in Kraus, *Psalmen,* 1:255; all translations mine), the psalmist indicates that his sin is not only great but deep. The other words for sin in the psalm identify sin as a "missing of the mark" (*ḥaṭṭāʾt,* vv. 7, 8, 18) and as "rebellion" (*pešaʿ,* v. 7; see on Ps 32:1–2). The presence of these three terms in different parts justifies identifying the psalm as a plea for forgiveness, but otherwise sin does not have a high profile in the psalm, which is not numbered among the "penitential" psalms. Its overall tenor and tone give it a wisdom character: it is a loving meditation of a "poor one" on the mercy promised by God's law. We can imagine Christ praying it on behalf of a sinful humanity to a Father whose love he knows from within. He himself is the pardon he asks for (Luke 23:34, Col 1:13–14, Eph 1:7, 4:32).

The psalmist's opening prayer seems an allusion to the previous psalm: he "lifts up his soul" not to false gods (Ps 24:4) but to the Lord (v. 1), whom he identifies (v. 2) as "my God" (phrase omitted in the Grail). The "faithfulness" of this God (vv. 5, 10) ensures that the speaker can "trust" him and not be ashamed. "Enemies," about whom we hear no more until verse 19, will not be joyful (cf. Pss 5:12, 9:3) over him. Indeed none who "wait for" the Lord (first appearance of this theme in the psalter; see also v. 5) will be shamed; shamed are only the "faithless" (v. 3, chiasmus; cf. Prov 11:3) and base. The psalmist asks to be "taught" the Lord's "ways/

paths" (v. 4) and to be made to walk in his faithfulness (v. 5; cf. Isa 30:21), for the Lord is the "God of [his] salvation" (cf. Ps 24:5), whose "compassion and *ḥesed*" are "from of old" (v. 6). These the Lord should "remember" not the sins of the speaker's youth (cf. Jer 31:19, Job 13:26) and his rebellions, and this "for the sake of [his] goodness" (v. 7; latter phrase transferred by Grail to end of v. 5). The heart of the psalmist's trust is the conviction that the Lord will act in accordance with the goodness of his nature.

Switching to third person speech the psalmist continues his reflection on the Lord's goodness and willingness to "instruct sinners in the way" (v. 8). It is the "poor," those who acknowledge their need for God, whom he guides in judgment and teaches his way (v. 9; cf. vv. 4–5). All his paths are "covenant love and faithfulness," available to any who observe his "covenant" (v. 10; see Exod 34:10, 27–28 in context of Exod 34:6–9, and see above on v. 11) and testimonies. After the central petition for forgiveness of sin the speaker resumes third person speech, now focusing more on the human partner of the covenant, who "fears the Lord" (vv. 12, 14; cf. Ps 22:24, 26), is instructed on the path he should choose, abides in "good things" (v. 13), wins an inheritance of land for his offspring (cf. Ps 37 passim), is part of the Lord's "circle" (cf. Amos 3:7, Jer 23:18, Prov 3:32), and receives deeper knowledge of the covenant (v. 14). Within this intimate relationship the psalmist keeps his eyes on the Lord who releases his feet from the net (v. 15). The center of the psalm thus focuses on the intimacy with the Lord that the poor enjoy in the covenant.

The speaker returns to the petition mode of verses 4–7 and 11, asking now for deliverance from (mainly) external difficulties. Just as his eyes are on the Lord (cf. v. 15), may the Lord turn to him in his aloneness (cf. Ps 22:21) and poverty (v. 16; cf. v. 9) and have mercy (cf. Pss 4:2, 6:3, 9:14), expanding a heart constricted by distress (v. 17; cf. Ps 4:2), releasing him from hardships, affliction, toil (cf. Deut 26:7 for this last pair), and sins (v. 18), as well as from the violence and hatred of many (cf. Ps 3:2) enemies (v. 19). He asks the Lord to keep and rescue him (v. 20) as one who "takes refuge" in him (cf. Pss 16:1, 17:7, 18:3), a phrase parallel to the verb "trust" at the beginning of the psalm. "Perfection and uprightness" (cf. 1 Kgs 9:4, Job 1:1) will protect him, since he has waited for the Lord (v. 21; cf. vv. 3, 5), trusting, that is, in the Lord's grace and not in himself. Such is the teaching of Saint Paul (Rom 3:24–26) and Saint John (1 John 1:8–2:2, 3:5–9). It is through redemption by Christ that the Christian is both sinner and righteous, and so it is not surprising that our psalm ends with a plea that the whole nation of Israel be "ransomed" from all its distresses caused by sin (v. 22).

∼ PSALM 26   innocence

Psalm 26 expresses the joy of righteousness in the presence of the Lord. As we saw in Psalm 5, there is no union with God without moral purity. The psalmist expresses what it is like to experience this moral righteousness in the presence of Israel's God in the Temple. He does not tell us the source of his righteousness, he is not bragging as if it were a result of his own effort. His focus is on the nexus between holiness and union with God. For the Christian this righteousness is the gift of God in Jesus Christ; everything the psalmist says refers to that righteousness.

The psalmist "loves" the habitation of God's house (v. 8), that is, the temple, the Body of the risen Christ, head and members, the place where God's "glory" dwells (1 Kgs 8:11, John 1:14, 2:12, 19–22, 17:24; cf. Ps 24:7–10). The temple provides him access to God. In it he "washes [his] palms in innocence" (cf. Ps 24:4) as a sign of the removal and rejection of sin (v. 6). He circles the altar to indicate a revolving of his life around the Lord. At the same time he gives voice to "thanksgiving" (v. 7), proclaiming all the Lord's "wonders" (cf. Ps 9:2), his great deeds on behalf of Israel and of the psalmist himself.

Corresponding to this love for the Lord, which fills the center of the psalm, is a detestation of sin. From the beginning the psalmist exposes himself to the judgment of God (cf. Ps 7:9), wishing to be judged as having "walked in perfection" (v. 1; cf. Ps 25:21, Prov 10:9, 19:1, 20:7), not wavering in "trust" (cf. Ps 25:2). He asks to be "tested" (cf. Ps 7:10) and "tried" (v. 2), that his "kidneys [cf. Pss 7:10, 16:7] and heart" be smelted (cf. Pss 12:7, 17:3). He wishes utter conformity to the Lord in both inner being and outer behavior and asks the Lord to ensure it. For God's *ḥesed* and *'ĕmet* (love and faithfulness) have been the constant guides of his mind (lit. "eyes," cf. Ps 25:15) and action (v. 3; the two attributes stand at the beginning and end of the verse, cf. Ps 25:5–6, 10). To maintain this moral conformity to the Lord he has had to abjure "sitting" (cf. Ps 1:1) with "worthless men" (cf. Pss 12:3, 24:4) and going about with the secretive (v. 4) so as not to be swayed by their lifestyle. He "hates" the assembly of the wrongdoers as much as he "loves" (v. 8) the presence of the Lord, and with the wicked does not sit (v. 5; cf. v. 4).

But the psalmist knows that his union with the Lord is God's gift: he must plead that his soul not be gathered with "sinners," or his life with men of blood (v. 9); these groups would be analogous to those mentioned in verses 4–5. In their hands is plotting, their right hand is full of bribes (v. 10; cf. Ps 15:5, Exod 23:8, Isa 1:23, Prov 17:23). The psalmist sets himself against this behavior (v. 11), repeating what he said at the beginning but now in the present tense: "But I in perfection walk; ransom me [cf. Ps 25:22] and have mercy on me" (cf. Ps 25:16). The verse combines both the love for moral righteousness and the need for divine redemption and forgiveness. The many echoes of Psalm 25 are found again in the final verse: the "foot" of the man whose feet are rescued from the snare (Ps 25:15) can stand on even ground (v. 12). The fruition of his right behavior will be his "blessing" (cf. Ps 24:5) of the Lord in the assemblies.

The righteousness of the psalmist is that won for him by Christ. It permits entrance into the temple (cf. Ps 24:3–4) and is celebrated in ritual song and gesture. It is truly the possession of the psalmist and yet must always be implored as the gift of Christ's grace.

The psalm exhibits a regular 3 + 3 meter, the only clear exceptions being verses 1, 8 (4 + 3 meter), and 11 (3 + 2 meter).

∾ Psalm 27   light

The divine name begins and ends the psalm and is found eleven more times in the body of the prayer, including at the very end of the first part and near the beginning of the second. So far only the much longer Psalms 9-10 and 18 have used the name with greater frequency, fourteen times for Psalm 9-10, and sixteen for Psalm 18. The psalmist is surrounded by the Lord's help and protection even amidst the hostility of men. An ancient title describes the psalm as "The voice of the chosen people glorying in the protection of Christ during persecutions" (Salmon, *Les "Tituli Psalmorum,"* 102). After establishing complete trust in the first part the psalmist cries out from his distress in the second, sure of being heard.

The beginning of Psalm 27 is reminiscent of the opening of Psalm 23: "*yhwh ʾôrî*" (The Lord is my light) even sounds like "*yhwh rōʿî*" (The Lord is my shepherd), and both phrases are followed soon after by a negative consequence of this confession: not "wanting" or not "fearing," the latter expressed as a question: "Whom shall I fear?" (v. 1). In what way is the Lord the psalmist's light? As with the metaphor of the shepherd, the answer can be found in Israel's experience and Scriptures. Light first becomes a major theme in the context of exile. After the dispersion of the northern kingdom by the Assyrians, Isaiah foresaw a coming salvation: "The people who walked in darkness has seen a great light; on those who live in a land of deep shadow [cf. "shadow of death" in Ps 23:4] a light has shone" (Isa 9:1). A successor of Isaiah after the Babylonian exile imagined light shining above Jerusalem while the whole world lay in darkness (Isa 60:1–3) and identified that everlasting light as the Lord himself (Isa 60:19–20). Later the wisdom writer would identify the light of the pillar of fire at the Exodus as a symbol of the Law of Yahweh through which the world would be enlightened (Wis 18:1–4). Like the writer of Psalm 23 the psalmist drew from these traditions to express his own personal experience of Yahweh as light. Light here means clarity of purpose and joy: it permits the psalmist to experience the world's meaning, it shows him the truth of divine love. It makes everything in his life meaningful in the context of the divine glory. For Christians the light is the Son of God made flesh (John 1:4–5, 9, 8:12, 9:5, 12:35–36, 46) who illumines our darkness (Eph 5:14).

The light is accompanied by "salvation": the Lord not only illumines but plucks from danger and preserves from destruction, like a fortress sheltering the psalmist's "life." For this reason he will not "dread" when wrongdoers draw near to "devour [his] flesh" (cf. Ps 14:4), for these oppressors and enemies will be the ones who "stumble and fall" (v. 2). Even an army encamped against him would not make his heart fear (v. 3; cf. Ps 3:7); if battle "rose" against him, he would still trust (cf. Pss 26:1, 25:2).

The only thing the psalmist asks for and seeks (cf. Ps 24:6) is to enjoy this light forever in the security of God's temple (v. 4). While the phrases "to dwell in the house of the Lord" and "all the days of my life" are borrowed from Psalm 23:6, what is unique in Psalm 27 is the formulation, "to gaze [cf. Pss 11:7, 17:15] on the sweetness of the Lord and to watch in his temple." The Christian beholds God from within the temple that is the Body of Christ. In fact in the new Jerusalem the Lord is both temple and light (Rev 21:22–24). For the Lord shelters the psalmist in his "hut" on the day of evil, hides him in the shelter of his "tent" (archaisms for temple), on a rock exalts him (v. 5). His head is exalted above the surrounding enemies (cf. v. 2) while the Lord's "tent" (cf. v. 5) becomes the scene of jubilant sacrifice and song and music for the Lord (v. 6). Dwelling with the Lord comprises contemplation, protection, victory, and joyful worship. Liturgy flows from the revelation and rescue bestowed by the Lord.

The psalm might have ended at that point but it is enriched by a new section in the lament mode. The triple cry, "Hear, Lord, my voice when I call; have mercy on me and answer me" (v. 7) is characteristic of the opening of a lament (cf. Pss 4:2, 17:1, 20:1, 28:2, 54:4, 55:2–3, 61:2, etc.). The security enjoyed by the psalmist in the first part of the psalm is now under attack and at the same time grounds his plea for help. Several words in this second section were used also in the first. The psalmist's "heart" (cf. v. 3) reminds him to "seek" (cf. v. 4) the Lord's face (v. 8). Petitions pile up in verse 9: "Do not hide [cf. v. 5] your face from me, do not turn away in anger your servant—you have been my help [cf. Ps 22:20], do not forsake me and do not abandon me [cf. Ps 22:2], God of my salvation" (cf. v. 1, Pss 25:5, 24:5); each pair of imperatives in this long verse is followed by an assertion of Yahweh's "being there" for the psalmist. Human parents may have abandoned him, but the Lord will gather him in (v. 10). Then follows an unexpected petition to be "instructed" in the Lord's way and led on an even path (or path of uprightness, cf. Ps 26:12) on account of the adversaries (v. 11). The psalmist has remembered that no one "sees" the Lord without moral conformity to his will (cf. Ps 24:3–6), that the Lord himself must be the guide (Pss 5:9, 23:3) on that path, and that the "adversaries," by distracting his gaze from the Lord, are a threat to that conformity—hence the need to be instructed. He asks not to be given to the "throat" of the oppressors (cf. v. 2), for lying witnesses have "risen" (v. 3) against him who "breathe out violence" (v. 12; cf. Pss 7:17, 11:5, 18:49, 25:19).

Petition and lament have been mingled in these verses. Now the psalmist ends with a verse of trust (v. 13). He "has faith" that he will "see" the goodness (cf. Ps 25:7) of the Lord in the land of the "living" (cf. vv. 1, 4). Thus the Lord's "light" and the vision of his "loveliness" are still present at the end of the poem. The speaker can even turn to his hearers and counsel them twice to "wait for the Lord" (cf. Ps 25:3, 5, 21, Hos 12:7, Isa 51:5, 25:9), separating the two imperatives with a phrase of encouragement that echoes that of Yahweh and Moses to Joshua and the people on the verge of the conquest of Canaan (Deut 31:6–7, 20, Jos 1:6–7): "Have courage and let your heart [cf. vv. 3, 8] be fortified," as they long for the vision of the Lord amid earthly conflicts (v. 14).

The psalm thus exhibits the main parts of the individual lament: trust and the vow of praise in the first section, petition and lament in the second. The result is a psalm where trust and petition/lament are more evenly balanced than in most psalms and where the long trust element precedes the lament. The first section of the psalm speaks of God in the third person, the second addresses him in the second person with a return to third person speech in the final verse, unless one understands this verse as an oracle of the Lord himself (cf. Kraus, *Psalmen*, 1:222). The 3 + 2 *qinah* meter prevails in the psalm.

Only the one who walks in the light of Christ and builds his house on the rock of his word (Matt 7:24–25) has strength for the battles that must be fought against destructive lies, whether they come from within ourselves or from the culture in which we live.

∾ PSALM 28   hands

Once again the psalmist describes his activity in the temple. In Psalm 26 he walked around the altar admiring the "dwelling of [Yahweh's] house" (Ps 26:8). In Psalm 27 he longs to watch in the "temple" (*hêkāl*, Ps 27:4) and vows to sacrifice in the Lord's "tent" (Ps 27:6). Here it is to the "Holy of Holies" (*děbîr*) itself, the inner sanctuary where resided the ark, that he "lifts up [his] hands" (v. 2). This action is accompanied by poignant and insistent prayer: he asks God his "rock" (cf. Ps 27:5) not to be deaf to him (v. 1) or be silent, but to hear the voice of his pleading when he cries for help (v. 2). If God does not respond, he will be likened to those going down to the pit—there is no hope for him.

Specifically the speaker asks not to be drawn in with wicked evildoers who speak peace with their friends but with evil (pun on *rēaʿ*, friend, and *rāʿâ*, evil) in their hearts (v. 3; cf. Jer 9:7, Luke 20:20–21), sinners in thought, word, and deed. Petitions for their punishment tumble out in succession: "Treat them according to their actions and their evil deeds; according to the work of their hands treat them [chiasmus], give them their deserts" (v. 4; cf. Lam 3:64). Rejection of the Lord can never succeed because it is a rejection of the source of life, but if the evil is not requited soon, the psalmist fears he will be swamped by it. Since the wickedness of these men is rooted in their failure to perceive the deeds of the Lord or the "work of his hands" (cf. Isa 5:12), "May he demolish them and not rebuild them" (v. 5; cf. same pair of verbs in Jer 1:10, Ezek 36:36, Mal 1:4, Job 12:14). We must pray this verse ardently for the extermination of evil from God's people, that the people themselves may be saved. Christians ask that the salvation from evil already won by Christ truly be accepted by all men and women for the establishment of a just and rightly ordered society where no one, not even the converted evildoer, is excluded or exploited.

Suddenly (v. 6) comes the change in mood we have become familiar with in individual laments: "Blessed be the Lord, for he has heard the voice of my pleading" (cf. v. 2, Ps 27:7). Christians know by faith that their prayer is already answered (Mark 11:24): God's kingdom is being established in men's hearts. The psalmist can express this confidence by calling the Lord his "strength" and his "shield" (Pss 3:4, 18:3, 31). His heart (cf. v. 3) "trusted" (cf. Ps 27:3), so he was helped; his heart exulted, so now he thanks the Lord with his "song" (v. 7; cf. Ps 27:6). The Lord is strength for society, a fortress of salvation (cf. Ps 27:1) for the anointed ruler (v. 8). In this larger social perspective the psalmist makes three petitions: that the Lord save his people, bless his inheritance (cf. Deut 32:8–9), and shepherd (cf. Ps 23:1) and lift them up forever (v. 9).

An ancient writer tells in a single sentence how to read the psalm as the prayer of the God-man: "Christ the Lord prays as man that his prayer be heard; and he gives thanks that he has been heard, asking that just as he was raised up by the power of his divinity, so the people might be saved who would believe in his name" (Salmon, Les "Tituli Psalmorum," 159).

"Hands" are a minor motif in the psalm. The psalmist's are raised in supplication, the evildoers' are engaged in mischief, and the Lord's are occupied with the work of creation and salvation. There is also a play on the word "lift": the psalmist lifts his hands and prays that Yahweh may "lift" his people. The hands of the psalmist joined with the hands of the Lord are strong enough to nullify the work of the hands of evil.

∼ PSALM 29   storm

We have arrived at the central psalm in the third subsection of Book One. The section begins and ends with the alphabetical Psalms 25 and 34, and its central psalm, like those of the first two subsections, is a hymn (cf. Pss 8, 19), in this case a powerful ancient hymn of Canaanite origin, celebrating the god of the storm. Attributes of the Canaanite gods El (high god) and Baal (storm god) have been transferred to Yahweh who manifests his glory in the power of the storm. The body of the psalm consists of seven exclamations beginning "The voice of the Lord," followed by attributes of the thunder (see the seven claps of thunder in Rev 10:3–4). The attributes can be brief (second, third, and fifth) or extended by two or more phrases. Even today the buildup of thundering phrases is a powerful evocation of the might of the God of nature.

The hymn is introduced by four cola of four beats each, the first three (vv. 1–2a) falling into the typical Canaanite pattern *abc, abd, abe,* in which the beginning of the cola are the same while the endings are different. The repeated element, "Give to the Lord," is followed successively by the addressee ("sons of gods"), the object, and a specification of the object. The term "sons of gods" betrays the pagan origin of the psalm and was understood in Judaism first as pagan gods subordinate to Yahweh and then as heavenly but not divine powers (cf. Job 1:6). To "give" him glory and strength was to recognize and confess these attributes of his: for "glory" see Psalms 19:2, 24:7–10, 26:8; for "strength" see Psalms 21:2, 28:8. The glory to be rendered to the Lord is the glory of his "name," that is, "Yahweh," the name that contains all that this God has been and done for his people. To this standard three-line pattern has been added a fourth line: "Worship the Lord in the manifestation of his holiness" (v. 2b). This manifestation is presented in the body of the hymn with the seven "thunder blasts" of the voice of the Lord.

The first "voice of the Lord" (v. 3) is "above the waters," that is, the primitive waters of chaos that had to be tamed by the creator God (cf. Gen 1:2, 6–9; Ps 24:2). In pagan mythology these waters were a rival god, but in Judaism they have been demythologized: the creator has complete reign over them. To this phrase is added another, which identifies Yahweh as the "God of glory" and the voice as the thunder (clause placed by the Grail after v. 9), and a third, which places Yahweh himself over the "many waters" (cf. Ps 93:4).

The second "voice of the Lord" (v. 4a) is "in power," the third "in splendor" (v. 4b). From these inner and outer attributes the psalm moves to the effects of the thunder on earth. The fourth "voice of the Lord" (v. 5) "breaks cedars"; an additional phrase says Yahweh himself breaks the mighty cedars of Lebanon. Further, he makes them "skip like a calf," makes Lebanon and Mount Hermon (Anti-Lebanon range) skip like young wild oxen (v. 6). The images convey power and vigor.

The fifth "voice of the Lord" (v. 7) is again brief: the thunder shoots out flashes of fire, that is, lightning. This mention of fire completes the trio of storm (wind), earthquake, and fire, which before Elijah were associated with epiphanies of Yahweh (1 Kgs 19:11–12; Isa 29:6, Ps 18:8–15). The sixth voice (v. 8) makes the desert shake; the pendant phrase specifies that Yahweh himself makes the Kadesh desert shake. The final voice (v. 9) has the most bizarre effect: it brings the doe into labor and brings their offspring to premature birth. Clearly the God present in the storm has complete power to change the normal course of nature. As a result the psalmist imagines the divine assembly (cf. v. 1) saying "Glory!" in the heavenly "temple" (cf. Ps 27:4).

It is possible that the poet is envisioning a real storm in geographical terms: it begins over the sea (v. 3), attacks the Lebanon and Hermon mountains (vv. 5–6), then strikes a Kadesh in the north or turns to the Kadesh in the southern desert.

The conclusion returns to the theme of Yahweh as seated above the flood (v. 10), this time enthroned as king (cf. "king of glory," Ps 24:7–10) forever. All of the "strength" (cf. v. 1) described in the psalm he will wield on behalf of his "people" to "bless" them (cf. Ps 28:9) with his "peace" (v. 11; cf. Ps 28:3!). In his commentary on this psalm John Paul II has well captured the paradox of the storm that brings peace: "[t]he psalmist thinks of thunder as a symbol of the divine voice, with its transcendent and unattainable mystery, that breaks into created reality in order to disturb and terrify it, but which in its innermost meaning is a word of peace and harmony. One thinks of chapter 12 of the Fourth Gospel, where the voice that responds to Jesus from heaven is perceived by the crowd as thunder (cf. John 12:28–29)" (*Psalms and Canticles*, 32).

Christ in his Body prays this psalm in exaltation of the strength and glory of the Father whose voice was heard over the waters of the Jordan at his baptism and who by his "glory" plucked him from the waters of death (Rom 6:3–4) to establish him as the firstfruits of the new creation (Rom 8:29–30, 1 Pet 3:20–22). Christians by their baptism share in this glory of the Father and the Son (Luke 9:26, 2 Cor 3:18).

∾ Psalm 30   resurrection

The psalmist gives thanks to God for healing him (v. 3) from a sickness leading to death (vv. 4, 10). This is the first mention of healing since Psalm 6 (cf. 6:3), and the psalm is the purest example of the individual thanksgiving genre we have encountered so far. As with other psalms (e.g., Pss 8, 16) there is a certain amount of introductory material (vv. 2–6) before the body of the psalm (vv. 7–13) begins. The speaker at once expresses the motif of the psalm: "I will exalt you, Lord, for you drew me up" (v. 2a). The latter verb is used for drawing a bucket from a well (cf. Exod 2:16, 19), an appropriate metaphor for drawing a soul from the "pit" (v. 4; cf. Jer 38:7, 13) of death. The second half of verse 2 has the only allusion to "enemies" in the psalm: God has not let them be "glad" over his death. Verse 3 imitates verse 2 in the change of subject between each half of the verse: "I cried to you, and you healed me." Verse 4 continues the metaphor of God "raising" the psalmist from the underworld, "giving life" when he was "going down to the pit" (cf. Ps 28:1).

As is frequent in a thanksgiving psalm, the speaker turns to those around him to teach a lesson from his experience. This he does in the form of a mini-hymn (vv. 5–6), inviting the Lord's devoted ones to make music to the Lord, to thank his holy memorial (i.e., the name that recalls his goodness and deeds). The motive for this thanks is what the psalmist has learned through his rescue from death: that the anger of God (which leads to death) is momentary (cf. Isa 54:7), while there is "life" (cf. v. 4) in his favor. The second half of verse 6 expresses the idea in metaphor: in the evening comes weeping but with morning the joyful shout.

In the body of the prayer the psalmist returns to direct speech to God to recount his near-death experience. In the experience of well-being he was sure he would never "totter" (v. 7; cf. Pss 10:6, 13:5, 15:5, 16:8, 21:8); the Lord in his "favor" (cf. v. 6) had stood him on a strong (cf. Pss 29:1, 28:7–8) mountain (v. 8). All the Lord had to do was "hide [his] face," and the psalmist became "terrified" (cf. Ps 6:3–4, 11). In verses 9–11 the psalmist expresses in the present tense the prayer he made. To the Lord he calls (cf. "cried," v. 3) and to his Master pleads for mercy (v. 9). What can the Lord gain from his "blood" (i.e., death, cf. Gen 37:26)? From the mountain he is descending (cf. v. 4) to the grave (v. 10), where dust cannot "thank" God (cf. v. 5) or manifest his faithfulness. In the Hebrew of verse 11 the speaker asks God to "hear" (cf. Ps 27:7) and "have mercy" (cf. v. 9), and to be his "helper" (cf. Pss 10:14, 27:9, 28:7). The Lord's answer to this prayer (v. 12) was to change the psalmist's "mourning" into "dancing," "sackcloth" into a robe of "gladness" (cf. v. 2). Dancing is the expression of joy brimming over at the end of trial: cf. Exodus 15:20, Judges 11:34, 1 Samuel 18:6, Jeremiah 31:13, Lamentations 5:15. At the end the psalmist resolves that his "glory" (cf. Pss 3:4, 29:9) will "make music" to God and not be still; he will "thank" the Lord forever (v. 13; note same two verbs in v. 5: the psalmist fulfills his own recommendation).

The psalm is notable for its close juxtaposition of opposites: raising and descending, life and death, anger and favor, tears and joy, evening and morning, mountain and pit, beseeching and thanking, mourning and dancing, sackcloth and gladness. The prayer thus highlights sharply the two poles of the Christian's existence: joy in the gift of life, anguish at the reality of death. Verse 4 seems ready-made to be recited by the risen Christ, who not only was raised from the brink of death but actually suffered death and went down to Sheol to liberate its captives (1 Pet 3:18–19, Matt 12:40, Acts 2:24, 31, Eph 4:9). The members of his body on earth pray this psalm with him, knowing that "this present light affliction prepares us for an eternal weight of glory" (2 Cor 4:17). Similarly the apostles' "sorrow" before his Passion "turned to joy" at his resurrection (John 16:20–22, 20:20). The resurrection of Christ is the source of unending joy for the world.

∾ PSALM 31   commend

The four principal ingredients of the individual lament—lament, petition, trust, and vow of praise—as in Psalm 28, are equally represented in this psalm but unusually distributed. Petition and trust are intermingled in verses 2–7 and followed by a brief section of praise (vv. 8–9). Verse 10 begins a long movement of lament (vv. 10–14), which passes via an expression of trust (v. 15) to a section of petition (vv. 16–19) and thence to a long conclusion of praise (vv. 20–25). A sense of intimacy with God pervades the psalm.

The psalmist has "taken refuge" in the Lord (v. 2a) as at the beginning of Psalms 7, 11, and 16. His first petition, "let me never be put to shame" (v. 2b), rises from that act of trust as in Psalm 25:20. The second petition is in positive form: "in your justice, bring me to safety" (v. 2c). Imperatives succeed each other rapidly in verse 3: incline the ear, hasten, rescue (cf. Pss 7:2, 25:20), be a rock fortress (Pss 27:1, 28:8), a stronghold (Ps 18:3), save (Pss 7:2, 22:22). The speaker is in immediate need of sheltering protection. In each of the following verses (4–7), an expression of trust is joined to a petition without the nature of the speaker's distress yet becoming clear. As "rock" (cf. Ps 18:3) and "stronghold" (cf. v. 2) and "for the sake of [his] name" may the Lord "lead" him and "guide" him (v. 4); the second half of verse 4 echoes Psalm 23:2–3. In verse 5 the petition comes first: the psalmist asks to be brought out of the "net" that has been laid for him, for the Lord is his "fortress" (cf. v. 3). In an act of supreme trust he "commends" his "spirit" into the "hands" of the Lord (v. 6), God of "faithfulness" (cf. Ps 30:10), who "has ransomed" him (either in the past or in anticipation of the future). The speaker hates those who revere worthless (cf. Ps 24:4) vanities, while he himself "trusts" in the Lord (v. 7). Thus the two key synonyms "take refuge" and "trust" enclose this unusual opening section in which petition and trust are intricately interwoven.

The psalmist will "rejoice ecstatically" (cf. Pss 13:6, 16:9) and "be glad" in the Lord's "covenant love" (not mentioned since Ps 25), shown in his seeing the psalmist's affliction, knowing the distress of his soul (v. 8), not shutting him up in the hand of the enemy (v. 9), and making his feet stand in a broad place (no longer in a rock fortress; cf. Ps 18:20).

But an appeal for mercy (cf. Pss 25:16, 26:11, 27:7, 30:11) opens a long section lamenting the psalmist's "distress" (v. 10). The second half of verse 10 is a repetition of Psalm 6:8a and adds to the wasting of "eye" that of "throat" and "belly." Verse 11 adds "bones" after indicating that the speaker's life is consumed in "sorrow" (cf. Ps 13:3) and his years in groaning (cf. Ps 6:7), and his strength wobbles because of his iniquity. The reminiscences of Psalm 6 indicate that the psalmist is experiencing physical sickness, but the mention of his own sin is new. The following verse (12) adds the element of "foes" for whom he is a "reproach" even to his neighbors, an object of "terror" to those who know him; those who see him in the street flee from him. He is forgotten in men's hearts like the dead, like a ruined (lit. "vanishing") vessel (v. 13; cf. Ps 2:9). With Jeremiah he has "heard the calumny of many" and experiences "terror on every side" (cf. Jer 20:10; second phrase also in Jer 6:25, 46:5, 49:29, Lam 2:22). All have conspired (cf. Ps 2:2) against him, plotting to take his life (v. 14). The images connote vicious rejection by society.

There is only one direction in which the psalmist can turn (v. 15; cf. John Donne's Holy Sonnet 1[4]): he renews his trust (cf. v. 7) in the Lord, confessing him as his God; his "times" (v. 16) are in God's "hand" (cf. v. 6). This trust supports a string of petitions: for rescue (cf. v. 3) from the "hand" of enemies and pursuers, for the shining of Yahweh's "face" (cf. Ps 30:8) on his "servant" (v. 17), for salvation (cf. v. 3) through God's *hesed* (cf. v. 8), for not being "shamed" in his calling on God (v. 18; cf. v. 2) but for the shaming of the wicked and their "stilling" (cf. Ps 30:13) in the underworld (cf. Ps 30:4), for the making dumb of lying lips that speak insolently against the just man in pride and contempt (v. 19). The speaker seems less interested in recovery from his physical ills than in the public elimination of the calumny against him, despite the single reference to his "iniquity" in verse 11.

Without warning the speaker erupts into praise of the "goodness" (cf. Ps 27:13) that the Lord has stored up for "those who fear him" and that he has performed for "those who take refuge in him" (cf. v. 2) in the presence of men (v. 20). He hides them in the shelter of his "face"

---

4. I dare not move my dimme eyes any way,
   Despair behind, and death before doth cast
   Such terrour, and my feeble flesh doth waste
   By sin in it, which it t'wards hell doth weigh;
   Only thou art above and when towards thee
   By thy leave I can looke, I rise againe.

(cf. v. 17) from the slanders of men and shelters them in a "hut" from quarreling tongues (v. 21), implying that the temple is the place for beholding the light of God in security, as in Psalm 27:1, 5. Applying these general statements to himself, the psalmist blesses God for showing him a wonderful love (cf. vv. 8, 17) in a fortified city (v. 22). In verse 23 he recapitulates the events of the psalm: he had said in his alarm that he was cut off from the eyes of the Lord, but the Lord heard his pleading (cf. Ps 28:6) when he cried to him for help. The Lord's "devoted ones" (cf. Ps 30:5) should love the Lord who protects the faithful (v. 24) and repays without measure those who act with pride (cf. v. 19). The psalmist concludes with an admonition drawn from Psalm 27:14 but now in the plural: "Have courage and be stout of heart, all who hope in the Lord" (v. 25).

In spite of sharing the vocabulary of trust with other psalms (take refuge, rock, fortress, stronghold, hide, shelter) and even quoting passages from other psalms and other biblical books verbatim (cf. vv. 10, 14, 25), the psalm is unique in conveying both the anguish of the person viciously rejected by society and profound surrender into the hand of God. Both extremes were perfectly realized by the Savior on the cross when he "cried out in a loud voice, 'Father, into your hands I commend my spirit'" and with those words "breathed his last" (Luke 23:46).

∼ PSALM 32   confession

A man who trusted enough to confess his sin makes a joyful discovery of the Lord's kindness and protection and shares his discovery with others.

The opening verses enunciate the theme of the prayer: "Happy is the one whose rebellion is taken away, whose sin is covered over [v. 1]. Happy the man whose iniquity the Lord does not consider against him" (v. 2a). Here appear together the three main Old Testament words for sin, which we first met dispersed in Psalm 25 and which each connote different aspects of sin: *peša'*, rebellion (cf. 25:7); *ḥăṭā'â*, a missing of the mark (cf. 25:7, 8, 18); and *'āwôn*, an inner disposition out of harmony with the divine will (cf. 25:11). The three terms are used together here and elsewhere (e.g., Ps 25:7, 8, 18) to show the full dimensions of man's rejection of God (see Exod 34:7, Lev 16:21, Pss 51:3–4, 59:4–5, 103:10–12, Job 13:23,

14:16–17). The end of verse 2 gives a hint of what human quality is needed for this sin to be removed: there must be no "deception" in a man's "spirit," that is, he must be candid about his sin. The psalmist will recount to God how he learned this lesson from his own experience.

When he kept quiet about his guilt, his "bones" (cf. Ps 31:11) became worn out as he "roared" (cf. Ps 22:2) all day [with pain] (v. 3). Day and night the Lord's "hand" (cf. Ps 31:6!) lay heavy upon him (cf. 1 Sam 5:6, 11, and a similar expression in Ezek 3:14), his tongue (vitality?) sapped by the heat of summer (v. 4). His "sin" he made known, and his "iniquity" he did not cover, saying, "I will confess my rebellions to the Lord," and the Lord "took away" the "iniquity of my sin" (v. 5). Similarly all that the Prodigal Son needed to do to enjoy his father's lavish favor was to say, "I have sinned" (Luke 15:18, 21). David, too, with these words won forgiveness for his triple sin of adultery, murder, and treachery (2 Sam 12:13) though not without suffering the consequences of his sin. Jesus began his preaching of the Gospel with the call to "repent" with a view to having one's sins forgiven through faith and baptism (Mark 1:15). "Repent" was the first requirement Saint Peter made of the crowds on Pentecost morning (Acts 2:38; see also Prov 28:13 and esp. 1 John 1:8–9). In his *Rule* for monks Saint Benedict cites verse 5 to illustrate the importance of confession of sins as a step on the ladder of humility that reaches to heaven (*RB* 7:48).

The psalmist now brims over with disconnected utterances that can be individually related to the experience he has recounted. He confesses to God that every "devoted one" (cf. Pss 30:5, 31:24) who prays earnestly in time of difficulty will never be touched by the swirling waters of chaos (v. 6; cf. Pss 18:17, 24:2, 29:3). The Lord has been the psalmist's "shelter" (cf. Pss 27:5, 31:21), "protecting" (cf. Ps 31:24) him in "distress" (Ps 31:8, 10), surrounding him with joyful shouts of safety (v. 7; cf. Ps 31:2); the terms suggest a temple venue, the rock fastness secure in the midst of tumultuous waters. Then without introduction comes an oracle of the Lord, promising to make the speaker understand and to instruct him on the way to go, giving him counsel with his eye upon him (v. 8). This is both a word the psalmist himself has received from the Lord upon being forgiven and a word he broadcasts to those around him. Speaking then on his own he addresses this group in the plural, sharing, as often in the psalms, the benefits of his experience with the devout. They must not be like horse or mule without discernment (cf. Prov 26:3, Sir 30:8), needing to be bridled and muzzled if their power is to be restrained and they can approach (v. 9, end of verse unintelligible in Hebrew). In the context of the psalm the "discernment" needed would be the confession of their own sin. In verse 10 the psalmist cites the many pains suffered by the "wicked" (cf. Ps 31:18; perhaps an allusion to his experience in vv. 3–4) and the love (cf. Ps 31:8, 17, 22) that "surrounds" (cf. v. 7), those who "trust" (cf. Pss 25:2, 26:1, 27:3, 28:7, 31:7, 15) in the Lord, as he did when he confessed his guilt. Similarly the "just" and "upright of heart" whom he calls to "be glad in the Lord" and "rejoice ecstatically" and "shout for joy" (v. 11) would be those whose justice is not a matter of keeping the law but of accepting the forgiveness of sins (cf. Rom 4:5, a passage immediately followed by a citation of the opening of our psalm: Paul argues that the just man is the one against whom God does not "reckon" his sin because of his faith, cf. also Gen 15:6). The celebration of forgiveness can only end in a shared expression of joy (cf. Luke 15:6–7, 9–10, 23–24, 32). In this way the disjointed statements in the second part of the psalm explore dimensions of the experience of forgiveness related in the first part: necessity of prayer, experience of security, celebration with the devout redeemed, the Lord's training and guidance, recommendation of discernment, the experience of divine love, the summons to joy.

The frequent word links with immediately preceding psalms show how interwoven the psalms are and how they invite us to read them as parts of a larger whole. While each psalm has its distinctive character, its allusions to neighboring psalms invite us to see our psalm against a background of the full dimensions of God's plan. The word "trust," for example, which our psalm shares with five of the preceding seven psalms, is enriched by what is said about it in each of those psalms and vice-versa. In this way a single verse can be said to include the whole psalter. This way of praying the psalms obviously grows cumulatively over time.

∼ PSALM 33   heart

Psalm 33 celebrates the joy of Israel's special relationship with the creator God. The whole earth was made by him, but only Israel is his "inheritance" (v. 12; cf. Ps 28:9) while the plans of the pagans are frustrated.

The hymn calls on the just to "shout for joy to the Lord" (cf. Ps 32:11) with "praise" (v. 1), to "thank" and "make music" to him with musical instruments (vv. 2–3) and "jubilant cry," and to "sing" him a new song (cf. on Ps 96:1). No psalm thus far has piled up so many "praise" words in so short a space. Voice and instruments combine to express the praise that is "fitting" for the upright.

The body of the hymn is introduced by the typical "for" in verse 4. The "word" of the Lord, by which the heavens were made (cf. v. 6), is "upright" because it can be relied on: all his works are done in "faithfulness" (see similar pairing of works and word in Ps 111:7). Because the Lord loves justice (cf. Ps 11:7) his covenant love fills the earth (v. 5). The very created world is penetrated with the divine love that made covenant with Israel. In the words of Erich Zenger, "All [the Lord's] activity is carried out in accordance with the right ordering established by him, the innermost principle of which is his loving kindness" (Hossfeld and Zenger, *Die Psalmen,* 1:205–206). The Lord's "word" is accompanied by his "spirit" (v. 6) in the act of creation as in Genesis 1:2, 3, 6, etc. Besides the creation of the "heavens" and their "hosts" (stars), his primordial creative act is to control the waters of chaos, gathering them into a "wall" (v. 7; cf. Exod 15:8, Jos 3:13), committing the abysses to storehouses (cf. Pss 24:2, 29:3, 10). The chaotic waters are the antithesis of "justice" and right order that permeate the Lord's creation.

New imperatives appear in verse 8, calling on the whole earth to "fear the Lord," on all who dwell in the world to be in awe of him (cf. Ps 22:24). A new "for" clause dramatizes the creation by word: "He spoke and it came to be; he commanded and it stood firm" (v. 9). The synonymous parallelism continues with a new idea: the creator God can foil the "plan" of the nations and thwart the "designs" of the peoples (v. 10), while the plan of the Lord stands (cf. v. 9) forever, the designs of his heart from age to age (v. 11). Therefore happy (cf. Ps 32:1) the nation that has him as its God, the people he chose for his inheritance (v. 12).

We now learn in what the Lord's loving plan consists: he is looking for a response from his human creatures. He "looks from heaven" on all the "sons of men" (v. 13; cf. Pss 11:4, 14:2), from the place of his dwelling scrutinizing all who dwell on the earth (v. 14), he who "forms completely their hearts [cf. v. 11] and discerns all their works" (v. 15; cf. Prov 15:11; the parallelism in the verse moves from inward to outward). No king is saved by the size of his army; a champion is not rescued by the abundance of his power (v. 16). Deceptive (lit. "lying") is the horse (cf. Ps 32:9) for salvation, and in the abundance of its vigor it cannot free (v. 17). But the eye of the Lord is on those who "fear him" (v. 18; cf. v. 8), that is, respect his lordship over creation and the "plans" inscribed in creation. Instead of imposing their will on the Lord these people "hope for" his *hesed* (cf. v. 5), which he manifests by "rescuing" their souls from death and giving them life in famine (v. 19), acts that only the creator can do. It is in recognizing his dependence on and need for the Lord that man finds life. We are now in a position to understand who are the "just" who were summoned to "shout for joy to the Lord" in the opening verse: "Those who, as the disadvantaged of the world, allow God to give them *hesed*, that is, God's royal steadfast love and favor, are the true 'righteous'" (Lohfink and Zenger, *God of Israel,* 106).

The psalm ends with a first person group expressing their desire to be the kind of people the Lord seeks. Their souls "wait patiently" on him because he is their "helper" and "shield" (v. 20). In him their "hearts" (cf. vv. 11, 15) will be glad, for in his holy name they "trust" (v. 21; cf. Pss 32:10, 31:7, 15). In the only verse addressed to the Lord (v. 22) they ask that the love that fills the earth (cf. v. 5) may be upon them as they hope in him (cf. v. 18, Ps 31:25).

The psalm, whose regular 3 + 3 meter and synonymous parallelism reflect an ordered mind, can be called theology in praise. It is a joyful summons to "all" (cf. vv. 8, 13–15) to contemplate the presence of divine order in nature and to accept the salvation and strength offered by the creator. It is the message expressed in different forms in Psalms 28:7–9 and 29:1 with 11. At the same time the psalm expresses the appropriate human response to this offer: reverent and trustful waiting on God's help. It is the "weak," those who know they are not autonomous, whom God makes strong (cf. 2 Cor 12:9–10). The extended hymnic expression of these truths is truly something "new" (cf. v. 3) in the psalter to this point. The psalm stands out from the other psalms in this third subsection (Pss 25–34) of Book One. If Psalm 29 is seen as the center of the group, Psalms 27 and 31 mirror each other as a "frame," Psalms 26 and 32 treat respectively the psalmist's innocence and his confession of sin, and Psalms 25 and 34 are both alphabetical psalms. Psalm 33 seems an anomaly, although we will see that it can be viewed as a pendant to Psalm 34. The "theological joy" of the psalm sheds its light on the other psalms in the group while lifting them onto a higher plane.

If creation is stamped with the right ordering of God and with his *ḥesed,* then it contains Christ, in whom and through whom and for whom all things were made and who holds all things in unity (Col 1:16–17). The one who became flesh is the Word through whom all things were made (John 1:1–3). After his resurrection this creation, which already contained him, is fully reconciled to God in a "new creation" (Col 1:20, 2 Cor 5:17–19, Rev 21:5). The "plans of [the Lord's] heart" stand "from age to age" because this heart has taken the world to himself to fill it with his eternal life.

Artful repetitions of simple words, "upright," "word," "works," "*ḥesed,*" "heavens," "earth," "fear," "dwell," "all," "plan," "design," "nation," "people," "stand," "heart," "much," "rescue," "soul," "hope," have stitched together the different thought patterns of the psalm. The word "trust" in the penultimate verse ties the psalm to earlier psalms in this group: Pss 25:2, 26:1, 27:3, 28:7, 31:7, 15, 32:10. The heart of God (v. 11) and the heart of man (vv. 15, 21) meet in Jesus, in whom divine love is answered by filial trust and surrender so that God may bestow life on all men through him.

∼ PSALM 34   Benedict

The speaker of Psalm 34 has had deep personal experience of what was stated in the previous psalm, "The eye of the Lord is upon those who fear him" (Ps 33:18), and he speaks warmly of this experience to his companions. Several word links also join the psalm to the previous one: "praise" (noun), "be glad," "name," "together/completely," "rescue," "look on," "save," "happy," "hunger," "life," "love" (verb), "eye(s)," "just," "earth," "heart," "spirit," "many (much)," and above all, "fear" of the Lord, found twice in Psalm 33 and four times in Psalm 34. "Fear of the Lord" appears here as the fundamental attitude of the "poor," who "take refuge" in him and "search for" him and can be called the "just."

The psalmist wants his "blessing" and "praise" of the Lord to be continual (v. 2; cf. Eph 5:20). His "boasting in the Lord" will be heard by the "poor," who recognize their need for God, and will be a cause of gladness for them (v. 3, consonance of *yišmĕʿû . . . wĕyiśmāḥû*). He calls on these poor to proclaim God's greatness with him (lit. "magnify" him), to "exalt his name together" (v. 4). The comradely sharing in the praise of the Lord is never so clearly expressed in the Psalms. The psalmist will insert a statement of his own experience before concluding his exhortation to his companions. When he "searched for" the Lord he was answered by a rescue from all his terrors (v. 5). His companions, too, can "look to the Lord and be radiant" in his light, their faces not brought to confusion (v. 6). One may think of the poor Christ (2 Cor 8:9) entering the Father's light and inviting his brothers to accompany him.

For the "poor man" in verse 7 is the psalmist, who "called and the Lord heard" (cf. Pss 31:33, 28:2, 6, 27:7) and from all his distresses saved him. No further details of this rescue are given; instead, the speaker draws a lesson for his hearers. A man who "fears the Lord" (cf. on Ps 25:12, 14) has an "angel" encamped around him to deliver him (v. 8). In telling his listeners to "taste and see that the Lord is good" (v. 9) is the speaker inviting them to partake of a thanksgiving sacrifice that he has offered in the temple? If so, the verse is an adumbration of the Eucharist. The word "taste" is responsible for the use of the word (in noun form) in the Hebrew notation at the beginning of the psalm (v. 1), which speaks of David's pretense of not having "perception" (lit. "taste") at the court of the Philistine King Achish (1 Sam 21:14). The psalmist finishes the line with a beatitude (cf. Pss 33:12, 32:1): happy the man who takes refuge in the Lord. If the "holy ones" who are being addressed fear the Lord and search for him, they will lack nothing (cf. Ps 23:1), even though young lions themselves are destitute and go "hungry" (vv. 10–11; cf. Ps 33:19, Luke 1:53).

The speaker now enters in earnest on his instruction, telling the hearers, whom he calls "sons" (cf. Prov 4:1, 5:7, 7:24, 8:32) to approach and listen so that he may "teach" them this fear of the Lord so essential for the fulfilled life (v. 12; see connection between "teaching" and the "poor" in Ps 25:4, 5, 9, the alphabetical psalm that began the collection that ends with our psalm). Like a good teacher he first awakens a desire for the subject to be taught, asking, "Who is the man who delights in life and loves days to see good things?" (v. 13; cf. Ps 24:12). In the Prologue to his *Rule* for monks Saint Benedict imagines Christ addressing this question to potential disciples. Life and its good things are what we seek;

one who can guarantee them deserves to be heeded, no matter what the cost. The speaker's first instruction is a negative imperative and somewhat unexpected: keep the tongue from evil and the lips from speaking "deceit" (v. 14; cf. Pss 5:7, 24:4). If fear of the Lord means being intent on pleasing him, one will immediately experience the need to restrain wrongful speech that can rise almost spontaneously to our lips (Prov 4:24, Jas 1:26, 3:2–12, Eph 4:29, 31). The awareness of God's loving presence is the best brake on inappropriate use of the tongue. From restraint of speech comes restraint of deed: "turn away from evil" with its positive complement, "do good" (v. 15). Finally the psalmist moves to the realm of thought: "seek peace and pursue it." This peace is the right relationship of a man with his brothers and all men, with God, with himself, and with his world. It is the harmony we are made for. Seeking and actively pursuing it is the noblest vocation of man. Subsequent verses develop the fruits of such an attitude.

The Lord's eyes are on these "just" (v. 16; cf. Pss 33:18, 32:8), his ears open to their "cry for help" (cf. Pss 22:25, 28:2, 30:3, 31:23), whereas his face is turned against those who do evil to cut off their memory from the earth (v. 17). When men cry out, God "hears and from all their distresses [cf. v. 7] rescues" them (cf. v. 5), as the speaker knows from his own experience (v. 18). Paradoxically it is when the human heart is "broken," aware of its own sinful drive to autonomy, that God is "near"; he saves those whose spirit is crushed (v. 19). Many are the evils of (= suffered by) the just man (v. 20), but from all of them the Lord "rescues" (cf. vv. 5, 18) him, not letting one of his bones be "broken" (v. 21, in contrast with v. 19; cf. John 19:36). The wicked man's evil brings him death, and the one who hates the just man will be guilty (v. 22). But the Lord "ransoms" (cf. Ps 25:22) the souls of his "servants" (now a synonym for the poor), and they are not guilty (cf. v. 22) who take refuge in him (v. 23; cf. v. 9).

Human brokenness can be healed by the Lord when it is brought to him, but self-sufficiency blocks him out. It is the "poor in spirit" that enter his kingdom (Matt 5:3).

Synonymous parallelism of a more subtle kind than in the previous psalm prevails here: the second colon generally reinforces the first but with a different syntax or from a different point of view (e.g., vv. 9, 10, 15, 19, 21, 22, 23). Verses 11 and 20 offer examples of antithetic parallelism.

Other verses display synthetic or climactic parallelism, in which the second colon completes the thought of the first (e.g., vv. 7, 8, 12, 13).

The psalm was a favorite of Saint Benedict, who quoted or alluded to nearly half of it in the Prologue to his *Rule* where he sees it as outlining the monk's program of seeking God. Its themes of fear of the Lord, humility, praise of God, obedience, and union with God were at the heart of his monastic vision.

∿ Psalm 35   betrayal

The psalmist speaks out of bitter betrayal: he is mocked by the persons he helped. Each of the psalm's three movements, however, ends in praise. In contrast to immediately preceding psalms the name of the Lord is sparsely used, three times in the first movement, three in the third, and not at all in the long lament of the second (it is found sixteen times in Ps 34, thirteen in Ps 33). Until the end the psalmist has trouble looking beyond his own grief.

Although the opening cry (v. 1) asks the Lord to judge opponents in a legal dispute (see also vv. 11, 19, 21, 23), the psalmist is less interested in exoneration than in the elimination of the unjust attitude of his persecutors. Already in the first verse he leaves the legal language to take up military metaphors. "Fight those who fight me" expresses his acute sense of justice. He asks God to take up defensive weapons (small and large shields) to help him (v. 2) and to wield offensive weapons (sword and javelin) against his pursuers (v. 3). His soul asks from the Lord an assurance, "I am your salvation" (cf. Pss 34:7, 19, 33:16, 17). In the course of the psalm the speaker will cite words of the Lord, of himself, of his enemies, and of his companions, a sign of how important personal relations are to him. In a pattern that will be imitated in later psalms, he asks that they be "shamed" and "confounded" who "seek" his "soul," that they "retreat" and "be brought to confusion" who plan evil against him (v. 4). If the enemies' plans are unjust, it is important that they not prevail. Frenzied, disconnected petitions follow: may the enemies be like chaff before the wind (cf. Ps 1:4; Isa 17:13), may God's "angel" (cf. Ps 34:8, 2 Kgs 19:35) knock them down (v. 5), may their way be dark and slippery (cf. Jer 23:12), may God's angel "pursue" (cf. v. 3) them (v. 6). In verse 7 the enemy become hunters laying their nets in a grave (cf. Pss 9:16, 10:9, 25:15, 31:5) that they dig for his "soul"—all of this "without cause." May "annihilation" (*šô'â*) fall on the enemy (now singular) unawares, may the "net he has laid catch" him (cf. Jer 18:22), may he fall to his annihilation in it (v. 8).

To this jumble of petitions mingled with lament succeed brief expressions of trust and praise. The psalmist's "soul" (cf. vv. 3, 4, 7) will rejoice ecstatically in the Lord (v. 9) and rejoice in his "salvation" (cf. v. 3; Luke 1:46–47). All his "bones" (cf. Pss 31:11, 32:3, 34:21) will say, "Lord, who is like you, rescuing [cf. Ps 34:5, 18, 20] the poor man [cf. Ps 34:7, Jer 20:13] from the one stronger than he, the poor and needy [cf. Jer 22:16] from the one robbing [cf. Jer 21:12] him?" (v. 10). Neither the tone nor the vocabulary of verse 10 matches the earlier petitions; parallels between verses 7–10 and the language of Jeremiah may indicate that these verses are a later addition to the original psalm.

The speaker now plunges into a long lament that forms the center of the prayer. "Violent witnesses arise" (cf. v. 2, Exod 23:1, Deut 19:16), questioning him about things he knows nothing about (v. 11). They repay him evil for good he has done, bereavement for his soul (v. 12). When they were sick, his clothing was sackcloth and he humbled his "soul" in fasting (v. 13)—now he retracts his former prayer (lit. may it "return to [his] bosom"). As if for his friend or his brother he walked about; as if mourning a mother, grieving he was bowed down (v. 14). Here we are at the heart of the betrayal: the ones whose grief he deeply shared "were glad" at his "tripping," gathering even with strangers to "tear" him (like garments, cf. 2 Sam 13:31, Joel 2:13) and not keep still (v. 15). They deride him (Hebrew of 16a is obscure), "gnashing their teeth" against him (v. 16b), a phrase that suggests the "tearing" of the previous verse is verbal. How long will the Master see [without acting]? "Restore my soul from their annihilation [cf. v. 8], my aloneness [cf. Ps 22:21] from the young lions" (v. 17; cf. Ps 34:11). The hunters of verse 7 have turned into wild beasts who tear the flesh of the psalmist with their lying accusations. But the psalmist's petition has given him the assurance that he will "thank" God (cf. Pss 30:5, 13, 33:2) in the "great assembly" (cf. Ps 22:23, 26) and "praise" him in the vast throng (v. 18). His isolation will be taken up into the great communion of those who worship God. Christ in his desertion by his friends will become the leader of many in the heavenly liturgy (Heb 2:10–12).

Resuming his lament yet a third time, the speaker asks that his lying enemies not "be glad" (cf. v. 15) over him, that those who "hate" him "without cause" (cf. v. 7, 1 Sam 19:5) not wink knowingly at each other (v. 19; cf. Prov 6:13). By citing the phrase "hated me without cause" in his Last Supper discourse (John 15:25, the only verse of the discourse that cites an Old Testament passage), Jesus invites us to see in himself the persecuted victim of the whole psalm. Two further verses of lament follow, depicting the cruelty of the accusers. They speak not of peace, but against the tranquility of the land they plan (cf. v. 4) deceitful matters (v. 20). Opening wide their mouths (cf. Isa 57:4), they testify: "Aha, aha! [cf. Ezek 25:3, 26:2, 36:2] Our eyes have seen" (v. 21). But in fact it is the Lord who "sees," whom the psalmist calls on not to be "deaf" or "far" (cf. Ps 22:12, 20) from him (v. 22). Three imperatives follow: "Rouse yourself, awake for judgment" of the psalmist's "cause" (v. 23; cf. v. 1), "judge justly" (v. 24) so that the enemies not "be glad" over him (cf. vv. 15, 19). May they not say in their hearts, "Aha! Our souls [triumph]!," nor say, "We have swallowed him up" (v. 25; cf. wild animal motif of vv. 15–17; cf. also Lam 2:16, Prov 1:12). Adopting the pattern of verse 4, the speaker asks that they be "shamed and brought to confusion" together, who were "glad" (cf. vv. 15, 19, 24) over his evil (misfortune); that they be "clothed" (cf. v. 13) in shame and disgrace, who made themselves "great" over him (v. 26). Petition shades into praise as the psalmist plays on key words of the psalm (v. 27): "May they shout for joy and be glad [cf. v. 26], those who delight in my justice; may they always [cf. Ps 34:2] say [cf. vv. 3, 10, 21, 25], 'Great is the Lord [cf. v. 26] who delights in the peace [cf. v. 20] of his servant' [cf. Ps 34:23]." Yahweh will assert his lordship over the false accusers by recognizing justice and bestowing the peace they could not give. The psalmist's tongue (v. 28) will murmur (cf. Ps 1:2) his justice (cf. v. 24) and all day long his praise (cf. v. 18).

The word links with Psalm 34 in the final four verses may indicate a redactional addition when the two psalms were placed next to each other in the final assembly of Book One.

Through the urgent petitions of the first movement, the dark lament of the middle, and the petitions/laments of the final movement the psalmist has led us to a resurrection where his vindicated life becomes a liturgy. The betrayal he suffered has been turned into union with God and his friends.

∼ PSALM 36   feast

If the speaker of Psalm 35 was solitary against a group of enemies, in Psalm 36 it is the wicked man who is alone and the psalmist who is part of a community enjoying God. The wicked man's sphere is confined to a dark room, the psalmist's is as big as the universe. The psalmist is more interested in exploring this difference than in seeking help against the wicked. The psalm combines aspects of the wisdom and prophetic traditions, the hymn, and the individual lament.

A literal reading of the opening verse (v. 2) gives the following: "Rebellion speaks to the wicked man in the depth of my heart: 'There is no terror of God before his eyes.'" In his own heart the speaker experiences sin's attempt to persuade the wicked man that there is no need for fear of the Lord, that is, for taking account of God in one's life (cf. Hossfeld and Zenger, *Die Psalmen,* 1:225–226). "Terror of the Lord" is a synonym of "fear of the Lord" in 2 Chronicles 19:7–9, which uses the two terms interchangeably. The following verses describe the cramped confines of the sinner's world, which the psalmist himself has experienced as a temptation. As in earlier psalms (cf. Pss 10:4, 13:1) the removal of God from the mind means his replacement by self-will: the self becomes one's god. The sinner has so much flattered himself that he cannot detect or hate his "iniquity" (v. 3). As for the words of his mouth (cf. Ps 33:21), they are injustice and deceit (cf. Ps 33:20); he has ceased to understand how to do good (v. 4). Injustice he plans on his bed (v. 5a; cf. Mic 2:1). He takes his stand on a way that is not good; evil he does not reject (v. 5bc, chiasmus with "good" and "evil" at the center and verbs on the outside).

As for the Lord, in the heavens is the Lord's covenant love, his faithfulness is to the clouds (v. 6, chiasmus), his justice is like mighty mountains, his judgments are a great abyss (v. 7). The extremities of the world are encompassed by these attributes of Israel's God. As the wicked man plots destruction, the Lord "saves" man and beast, for the key activity of his *ḥesed* is "saving" (cf. Pss 6:5, 17:7, 18:51, 31:17). The psalmist praises God for this love, which is so "precious" (v. 8) because the children of men can "take refuge" in the "shadow of [his] wings" (cf. Ps 17:8). The psalmist might well have in mind the wings of the cherubs extended above the ark, for in the next verse these sons of men are in the temple. They feast on the rich food of God's "house" (cf. Jer 31:14), from the channel of his "raptures" (*ʿădānêkā,* hapax in the Psalms, cognate of Eden) God gives them drink (v. 9, chiasmus with change of subject). While communing in the temple sacrifices, the worshippers drink in God's generous love itself. For with him is the fountain of life (cf. Jer 2:13, 17:13), and in his light (cf. Ps 27:1, 4) men see true light (v. 10). Putting the images together, one may say men feast on the Lord's light, drinking in with Crashaw's Saint Teresa "large draughts of intellectual day" ("The Flaming Heart"). The light is Jesus (John 8:12, 12:46), the temple is Jesus (John 2:21), the water of life is Jesus (John 4:10, 14, 7:37–38, Rev 21:6).

In the light of the foregoing the psalmist has two requests. First, may God continue his love (cf. v. 6) for those who know him and his justice (cf. v. 7) for the upright of heart (v. 11). Second, recalling his own temptation to wickedness (cf. v. 2), he asks that the foot of pride, that is, of the man who has not placed God before his eyes (cf. Pss 10:2, 31:19, 24), not approach him nor the hand of the wicked put him to flight (v. 12). Finally he envisions, "There the doers of evil have fallen; they are knocked down [cf. Ps 35:5] and will not be able to rise" (v. 13; Jer 23:12 has "knocked down" and "fall").

Norbert Lohfink draws together the threads of the psalm as follows: "To the look into the heart [i.e., vv. 2–5] and outward to the universe [vv. 6–7] is added the experience of cultic space [vv. 8–10], which lies somewhere in between. . . . The all-encompassing God, in order to be a God of nearness, must have a cultic place where contact is possible" (*In the Shadow,* 106–107). It is the Lord Jesus who as high priest has become our "cultic place" (Heb 10:19–22).

⮑ PSALM 37   patience

A wise man counsels the individual to hold fast to justice even when the wicked seem to flourish since the just will "inherit the land" while the wicked are "cut off"—both verbs are used five times in the psalm. The psalm is alphabetical with two verses per letter (one for *daleth, ki,* and *qoph*) as in Psalm 9-10. Certain words are repeated in different contexts, and words from neighboring psalms are artfully woven in to give an impression of unity in variety. The tone of the psalm is calm, persuasive, even genial, a complement to the anguish of Psalms 35 and 38. Undergirding the psalm is a theological assurance of the inevitability of divine justice, which in other psalms is a subject of urgent pleading (e.g., Pss 7,

35, 58, etc.). The psalmist interweaves counsels of "trust" and "waiting" with descriptions of the inevitable fates of "just" (used nine times) and "wicked" (used thirteen times). The psalm is post-exilic, reflecting the influence of the wisdom literature and Second Isaiah.

The two verses of letter *aleph* illustrate these two modes of discourse, theological and hortatory: an exhortation not to "fly into a passion at wrongdoers or be jealous" (= Prov 24:19) of the workers of perversity (v. 1), followed by the reason for this advice (introduced by conjunction "for"), namely that like grass they quickly fade and like a fresh green plant they wither (v. 2). The letter *beth* gives positive advice—"Trust in the Lord and do good . . . and enjoy him" (cf. Job 27:10, Isa 58:14)—with the consequences of dwelling in the land, "grazing" on faithfulness, and receiving the requests of one's "heart" (vv. 3–4; cf. Ps 36:2, 11). *Ghimel* follows the same pattern: "Roll onto the Lord your way [in life] [cf. Ps 22:9] and trust in him," for he will act and make your "justice" (cf. Ps 35:27) break out like "light" (cf. Ps 36:10) and your judgment like noon (vv. 5–6). *Daleth* counsels stillness before the Lord and "hoping" in him, not flying into a passion (cf. v. 1) at the prosperous "way" of the man who makes schemes (v. 7). Such anger and passion should be dropped and abandoned as only leading to evil (v. 8, *he*). Verse 9 summarizes the psalm's teaching on the two fates: "For the wrongdoers will be cut off, while those who wait [cf. Ps 25:3, 5] for the Lord will inherit the land" (cf. Isa 57:13, 60:21).

Beginning with verse 10, imperatives are suspended as the psalmist focuses solely on the two destinies. In only a little while the "wicked" (first mention in psalm) will not be there; if you try to discern him in his place, he's not there (v. 10, *waw*), while the "poor" (cf. Pss 34:3, 7, 35:10) will inherit the land (v. 11) and "enjoy" (cf. v. 4) the abundance of "peace" (cf. Ps 35:20, 27). In *zain* the plotting of the wicked against the "just" (first mention in psalm) and his "gnashing his teeth" (cf. Ps 35:16) are described, only to be followed by the Master's "laughing" because he "sees" that the wicked man's day is over (vv. 12–13). In the long verse 14 (*heth*) the hostile actions of the wicked are vividly depicted—sword drawn and bow bent to bring down the "poor and the needy" (cf. Ps 35:10) and to slaughter those whose "way" is upright. The companion verse 15 again gives the consequences: their sword enters their own heart and their bows are broken (cf. Ps 7:16–17). *Tob* uses chiasmus to show the double fates: good is the little of the just man, more than the superabundance of many wicked (v. 16; cf. Prov 16:8, Tob 12:8), for the arms of the latter will be "broken" (like the bows in v. 15) while the Lord upholds the just (v. 17). *Yod* is dedicated entirely to the fate of the just, first in positive, then in negative terms. The Lord "knows" (cf. Ps 1:6) the days of the blameless, and their inheritance lasts forever (v. 18); they will not be shamed (cf. Ps 35:4, 26) in time of evil, and in days of famine (cognate of "hunger" in Pss 33:19, 34:11) they will be sated (v. 19, chiasmus; cf. Deut 8:10). Verse 20 (*kaph*) gives the corresponding fate of the wicked: they will vanish, and the Lord's enemies like the beauty of the pasturage will be consumed; in smoke they will be consumed. The Hebrew of this verse is remarkable for its sound correspondences: *kî rĕšā'îm yō'bēdû wĕ'ōyĕbê yhwh kîqar kārîm kālû be'āšān kālû.*

Even in the present the wicked man can borrow but not repay while the just man is generous and giving (v. 21), for the Lord's "blessed" will inherit the land while the cursed will be cut off (v. 22; these two verses of *lamed* arranged chiastically). By the Lord (*mem*) are the steps of a man made firm (cf. Prov 20:24), and in his way the Lord delights (v. 23; cf. Ps 35:27). When this man "falls" (cf. v. 14, Ps 36:13) he will not be thrown down, for the Lord "upholds" (cf. v. 17) his hand (v. 24). The psalmist evokes his life experience (*nun*): he was young and now he is old but has never seen the just man abandoned or his offspring seeking bread (v. 25). On the contrary every day he is generous and lends (cf. v. 21), and his offspring become a blessing (v. 26).

With *samech* there is a return to the imperative of advice. "Turn away from evil and do good [cf. Ps 34:15], that you may dwell [cf. v. 3] forever" (v. 27), for the Lord loves judgment and will not "abandon" (cf. vv. 8, 25) his devoted one (v. 28), who will be guarded forever while the offspring of the wicked will be cut off. The just will inherit the land and "dwell" (cf. vv. 3, 27) in it forever (v. 29). (The latter part of verse 28 and verse 29 may belong to the missing letter *ayin.*) *Pe* details a just man's behavior: his mouth "murmurs" (cf. Pss 1:2, 35:28) wisdom (cf. Prov 10:31), and his tongue speaks judgment (v. 30). Because the law of his God is in his heart his footsteps will not waver (v. 31). The wicked man, on the other hand (*sade*), watches for the just and seeks to murder him (v. 32), but the Lord will not "abandon" (cf. vv. 8, 25, 28) him to the murderer's hand or let him be condemned when he is judged (v. 33). A man must "wait for" (*qoph*) the Lord and guard his "way" (cf. vv. 5, 7, 14, 23); then the Lord will exalt him to inherit the land and "see" (cf. vv. 13, 25) the wicked "cut off" (v. 34). Reverting to his own experience (*resh*), the psalmist has "seen" (cf. v. 34) the wicked domineering, towering (Hebrew word uncertain) like a flourishing cedar (v. 35), but he passed away and was not there, and the psalmist sought him but he was not found (v. 36; cf. v. 10).

Shin gives the final exhortations: "Observe the blameless man, see [cf. vv. 13, 25, 34, 35] the upright" (v. 37), for his "destiny" (cf. Prov 23:18) is peace (cf. v. 11), while the rebellious are exterminated and their destiny is "cut off" (v. 38). The final letter *tau* is taken up entirely with God's saving of the just. He is their fortress in time of distress (v. 39), he will help them and bring them to safety, bring them to safety from the wicked and save them, for they take refuge in him (v. 40).

The psalm seems through its word links to be directed at the speakers of neighboring Psalms 35 and 38 in their times of severe trial. It demonstrates that the reward of justice and upright behavior is certain. The poor man who takes refuge in the Lord, trusts and hopes in him, waits for him, observes his law, is the one who will dwell securely in his own inherited land (cf. Matt 5:5) where he will enjoy peace, while the wicked will be cut off from existence. Similarly Jesus consoled the apostles that their suffering would be only for a time (John 16:22); through their faith they were firmly rooted in him (John 15:5–7) and beneficiaries of an eternal inheritance (cf. 1 Pet 1:4–6, Eph 1:14), while the house of the wicked would collapse in utter ruin (Matt 7:26–27). Adherence to Jesus is life, rejection of him is extinction (John 12:48).

∼ PSALM 38   pain

Psalm 38 is the third penitential psalm and also the central psalm in the fourth subsection (Pss 35–41) of Book One. Unlike the central psalms in the previous collections, Psalms 8, 19, and 29, it is not a hymn but an individual lament expressing unrelieved pain. While the other central psalms seemed to radiate light and joy to the darker psalms around them, here the central psalm is dark and needs illumination from its neighbors. On its own the psalm is a Passion with little sign of a resurrection. Did the compiler of the collection have a premonition that such great suffering would be a key part of man's redemption?

The opening verse (v. 2) is a replica of the opening verse of Psalm 6 with a different word (used only twice in the psalter, cf. Ps 102:11) for "anger" in the first colon. The psalmist calls on the Lord not to reprove or chastise him further (cf. same two verbs in Job 5:17), since the Lord's "arrows" (metaphor for afflictions sent by God, cf. Deut 32:23–24, Lam 3:12, Job 6:4, 16:13) have penetrated him (medieval illustrated psalters graphically depicted the man struck with arrows from above) and his hand presses him down (v. 3). There is no "soundness" (cf. Isa 1:6) in the man's flesh, no peace in his bones, but the former situation is ascribed to God's indignation and the latter to the psalmist's sin (v. 4). The psalmist has merited the divine anger by in some way rejecting God, and now he experiences the inevitable consequences of this rejection, which can be ascribed to God's inability to condone sin (cf. Rom 1:18, 28–30, 2:5–8, Eph 2:3, Rev 19:15). The speaker feels that his "iniquities" have risen above his head (cf. Ezra 9:6) like a burden too heavy to bear (v. 5); the Lord's heavy "hand" is thus really the psalmist's lack of harmony with God's will. "They stink, putrefy, my wounds," he says, because of his folly (v. 6); the rare vocabulary here and elsewhere in the psalm is a sign of the extremity of the sufferings. He is extremely bent and bowed down (v. 7) and goes about all day "mourning" (cf. Ps 35:14). His loins are full of burning (v. 8), and he repeats there is no soundness in his flesh (cf. v. 4). He feels numb and crushed beyond endurance, "roaring" (cf. Ps 32:3) from the churning of his heart (v. 9).

Finally the suppliant manages to call on his "Master," who knows all his "longing," from whom his "groaning" (cf. Pss 6:7, 31:11) is not hidden (v. 10), but then he continues the catalog of pain. His heart beats violently, his power has "abandoned" him (cf. Ps 37:33), even the light (cf. Pss 37:6, 36:10) of his eyes is not with him (v. 11). To physical pain is added social ostracism: those who love him and his friends stand apart from his scourge, his nearest kin stand afar off (v. 12; cf. Luke 23:49). Those who seek his soul try to snare him (as the scribes and Pharisees did Jesus, Luke 11:54), those who search out his harm speak of ruin, "murmuring [cf. Pss 37:30, 35:28] deceit" (cf. Pss 35:20, 36:4) all day long (v. 13). Like a deaf man he does not hear, like a dumb man he does not open his mouth (v. 14). In the following verse (15) he repeats the same idea, adding only that he utters no reproofs.

For the first time since the opening cry the psalmist invokes the Lord by name: "In you, Lord, I hope [cf. Pss 37:7, 33:18, 22, 31:25]; you will answer, my Master, my God" (v. 16). His petition is oblique (v. 17): "lest they be glad over me [cf. Ps 35:19, 24], in the tottering of my foot make themselves great over me" (cf. Ps 35:26). For he is on the verge of "tripping" (cf. Ps 35:15), and his "pain" (cf. Exod 3:7, Isa 53:3, 4, Jer 30:15, Lam 1:12, 18, Qoh 2:23) is always before him (v. 18). Again (v. 19) he exposes his own "iniquity" (cf. v. 5), is anxious over his "sin" (cf. v. 4). Therefore it is surprising that as he approaches the end of his prayer he attributes his suffering to "enemies" who are alive and powerful (v. 20), and many who hate him without reason (lit. "with lies," cf. Ps 35:19), who have repaid him evil for good (cf. Ps 35:12), accuse him for pursuing the good (v. 21).

Only now does the psalmist state his petition (v. 22): "Do not abandon me, Lord, my God [cf. v. 11, Pss 37:8, 25, 28, 33, 22:2], do not be far from me [cf. Pss 22:2, 12, 20, 35:22]. Hasten to my help [cf. Pss 37:40, 35:2], my Master, my salvation!" (cf. Pss 37:39–40, 36:7, 35:3, 9). The many word links with the previous three psalms show how intricately woven together are the psalms of this mini-collection and invite us to read the psalms in the light of one another. The same will be true of the remaining three psalms in the collection. Nonetheless, each psalm retains its individuality, as is clear from the frequency of rare words and images in Psalm 38.

The speaker's torment is so acute, his awareness of sin so heavy that he almost neglects to pray, a common experience in sickness. But it is remarkable that in all his suffering he shows no anger toward God, toward other people, or toward himself. He bears his suffering humbly, as merited, even though it overwhelms him. In this he is akin to the lamb led to the slaughter, silent, not opening his mouth (Isa 53:7), the lamb of God who by bearing our iniquities (Isa 53:5) on the cross takes away the sin of the world (John 1:29, 1 Pet 2:21–24), who by shedding his blood has saved us from the anger of God (Rom 5:9).

∽ PSALM 39   silence

The speaker is a wise man. He has recognized the need to guard his ways lest he sin with his tongue; he would guard his mouth with a "muzzle" (only here in Old Testament) while the wicked man was before him (v. 2). He remained dumb (cf. Ps 38:14) and in stillness, keeping silent "from good [speech]" (or "separated from good [i.e., happiness]" or "without success" or "in the presence of prosperity" or simply "very"), and pain (cf. Ps 38:18) held him down (v. 3). His heart was hot within, and the fire of his meditation burned (v. 4). When his "tongue" finally spoke, it was to ask the Lord to know his end and what was the measure of his days; he would know how fleeting he was (v. 5). He answers the question himself, calling his days "handbreadths" (only here in Old Testament), his lifetime "as nothing" in the Lord's sight, for only "vanity" (Qoh 1:2) is every man standing (v. 6). There is bitterness in his speech, a sense of "why bother?" if the wicked man poses a threat, since life is short anyway.

Yet (after the notation "pause" [*selah*]) the speaker continues his melancholy meditation. Only in shadows does man walk, mere "vanity" (cf. v. 6) is his churning, he piles up [riches] without knowing who will gather them (v. 7; cf. Qoh 2:18–22, 6:2, Luke 12:16–21). The threefold statement matches that of the previous verse. Again he addresses the Lord, this time calling him "Master" (as frequently in this section of the psalter, cf. Pss 35:17, 22, 23, 37:13, 38:10, 16, 23), asking what he can "wait for" now (cf. Ps 37:9, 34), since he has "hoped" in the Lord (v. 8; cf. Ps 38:16). He makes his first petition, namely to be "rescued" (cf. Pss 35:10, 34:5, 18, 20) from all his own "rebellions" (cf. Pss 32:1, 5, 36:2), and not to be made the reproach of the "fool" (v. 9). As in verse 2, he shows his affinity with the wisdom tradition (cf. vv. 6–7): he is aware of his own sin and equally aware of the harm caused by fools. Although he again vows to remain dumb (cf. v. 3), not opening his mouth since the Lord has acted (v. 10; cf. Ps 22:32), he makes another plea (v. 11): "Take away your scourge [cf. Ps 38:12] from me; I am consumed by the blow [word of uncertain meaning used only here in Old Testament] of your hand" (cf. Pss 32:4, 38:3). He recognizes that the Lord "with reproofs [cf. Ps 38:15] for iniquity chastises a man" (cf. Ps 38:2) and makes melt like a moth what he has coveted, for only "vanity" is every man (repeated from v. 6)—another three-part statement (v. 12).

At this point, marked by another *selah*, our psalmist is in a conflicted state. He is aware of man's sin, using all three of the main Hebrew words for it (vv. 2, 9, 12; cf. Ps 32:1–2), aware also of man's short life and the folly of amassing riches, even, perhaps, unlawfully. But twice the effort to accept his fate in silence has been overcome by stronger feelings of protest (cf. vv. 5 and 11). In the remaining two verses he will once again call for help, this time using the Lord's name as in verse 5. Verse 13 has five cola, the first three parallel to each other: a plea for the "hearing of [his] prayer" (a cry not heard since Ps 4:2—indeed the plea "hear" has not been uttered since Pss 30:11 and 28:2; along with the infrequency of the divine name in Pss 35–41, its absence is a sign of the preoccupation of the psalmist with his own sufferings in this group: there is little light from above); a plea for the turning of God's ear to his cry; a request that God not be "deaf" (cf. Ps 38:14) to his tears (cf. Ps 6:7). For the psalmist is but a sojourner before God (cf. Lev 25:23, 1 Chr 29:15, Heb 11:13), a temporary resident like all his fathers. He would like to escape God's gaze (v. 14; cf. Job 7:19, 14:6) in order to have a little cheer (cf. Job 10:20–21) before he moves on and is no more (Ps 37:10, 36).

The tension in the psalm remains unresolved. The speaker knows the right answers from the wisdom tradition, but he personally rebels against them; they do not satisfy him or assuage his painful experience of the human condition. No other lament combines such acute pain with so much wisdom material. The psalmist turns to his Lord for help but can only pray for the hastening of his own extinction. Perhaps this too is part of our suffering, a sense that hope is futile. Perhaps at the moment we feel this revulsion, without the calmness of the wisdom teacher of Psalm 37 or the patience of the humble sufferer of Psalm 38, we are most faithful to our human condition before God, for we can only leave the resolution of the dilemma to him whose thoughts are beyond our thoughts (cf. Isa 55:8–9). For even the Savior himself, who kept silent before his interrogators (Matt 26:63, 27:12, 14), protested his fate in the Garden (Matt 26:39, 42, 44) and on the Cross (Matt 27:46).

An ancient commentator sees the psalm as spoken by the Church, which, "rebuking the avaricious, sighs amid its tribulations on its earthly pilgrimage" (Salmon, Les "Tituli Psalmorum," 102).

∼ PSALM 40   obedience

With Psalm 40 we are back in familiar territory. The suffering speaker of the two previous psalms seemed to have lost sight of God's attributes, his abiding love and faithfulness, his wonders, and also of the virtues of hope and trust. In extolling obedience as a sacrifice pleasing to God the author of Psalm 40 places the earlier psalms into a meaningful context.

He finds himself suffering from his own sin and from enemies, but as in earlier psalms in Book One he is able to petition God for help with the confidence of being heard and the promise of praising him.

The opening of the psalm (v. 2) is almost a response to the speaker of Psalm 39: the speaker waited and waited (cf. Ps 39:8) for the Lord, who leaned down to him and "heard" his "cry" (cf. Ps 39:13). The images for God's help are graphic (v. 3): he drew the man up from the pit of desolation, from muddy clay (like Jeremiah being raised from the cistern, Jer 38:6, 13), placing his foot on a rock (cf. Ps 27:5), making his footsteps firm. The two parts of verse 3 each illustrate the 3 + 2 *qinah* or lament meter, which prevails in the psalm. Suitable for thanking God for this event is a "new song" (cf. Ps 33:3), inspired by the Lord himself, "praise for our God"; when the "many" fellow worshippers see what God has done for him, they will "fear" God (cf. Ps 34:7, 9, 12; Hebrew often puns on the words "see" (*rā'āh*) and "fear" (*yārē'*, cf. Isa 41:5) and will "trust" in the Lord (v. 4). The psalmist will be evidence that the Lord truly hears prayer in accordance with his attributes of love and faithfulness (see on v. 11 below). He generalizes from his experience: happy is the man who has made the Lord his trust and has not turned aside to men who are arrogant or entangled in falsehood (v. 5; most recent beatitudes were Pss 32:1, 2, 33:12, 34:9).

The speaker now addresses the Lord directly in a long verse (v. 6), perhaps singing the "new song" of verse 4: "Many things you have done, you, Lord our God—wonders [cf. Ps 26:7] and designs [cf. Ps 33:11] on our behalf; none can compare with you; when I declare and speak of them, they are too numerous to be counted." He would offer a communion sacrifice (cf. Lev 3:1) or oblation (cf. Lev 2:1) but knows the Lord does not delight in these but instead has given (lit. "dug") him "ears" to listen with (v. 7; cf. Isa 50:4–5); nor does the Lord ask holocaust (cf. Lev 1:3) or sin-offering (cf. Lev 4:8, 1 Sam 15:22). Then he quotes what he has said (cf. the self-quoting in Pss 39:2, 38:17, 32:5): "Behold I come" (v. 8), as if to say he himself is the offering he will make. He believes that in the scroll of the book (cf. Jeremiah's scroll, Jer 36:4, 32), it is written of him (or if the translation is "on" him, the text would be parallel to that describing the new covenant written on men's hearts, Jer 31:33): "In doing your pleasure, God, I have taken delight, and your law is deep in my entrails" (v. 9). Like the speaker of Psalm 1 he "delights" in the law of

God with its account of God's "wonders" and the way to life that it shows (cf. Ps 1:2). Such a delight is the explanation of the obedience of the saints: one who knows that the divine will is love can brook no delay in carrying out that will.

But how does the speaker become his own sacrifice in this liturgical setting? By proclaiming the Lord's attributes and not concealing them. Here the link between worship and obedience becomes clear. Each is a matter of placing God over self, of proclaiming his lordship, of putting him first, of averring his supremacy. Having been saved by the Lord, the psalmist now lives to assert what the Lord has done for him (cf. Mark 5:19–20). He becomes an "evangelizer," announcing justice in the "great assembly" (cf. Ps 35:18). He does not "withhold" his lips, as the Lord knows (v. 10). In verse 11 the Lord's attributes flow from these lips: "Your justice I did not cover in the depth of my heart, your faithfulness [ʾĕmûnātkā] and your salvation I have told; I did not conceal your love and faithfulness [ʾămitkā] in the great assembly." With only one difference the catalog of four attributes is the same as that in Psalm 36:6–7, the companion psalm to Psalm 40 in this subsection of which Psalm 38 is the center. The great pain of Psalm 38 is then to be seen in the framework of God's precious saving love, his faithfulness, and his justice. The obedience that our speaker gives to God thus includes both fidelity to the Lord's will even to death and the proclaiming of his love in the world. Just as he does not withhold (cf. v. 10) his lips from praise, he knows that the Lord will not "withhold" his compassion from him; rather the Lord's love and faithfulness will always protect him (v. 12).

Having praised the Lord's readiness to help, suddenly in verse 13 the psalmist has occasion to invoke it anew, for evils encompass him "beyond counting" (cf. v. 6). His "iniquities" (cf. Pss 39:12, 38:5, 19, 36:3) have overtaken him and he can no longer see; they are more numerous than (cf. v. 6) the hairs of his head, and his "heart [cf. v. 11, Pss 39:4, 38:9, 11, 37:4, 31, 36:2, 11—an entire theology of the heart could begin with these texts] abandons" him (cf. Pss 38:11, 22, 37:8, 25, 28, 33). It now appears that verse 13 is a transition to an individual lament that is nearly a duplicate of Psalm 70. "Be pleased [cf. noun in v. 9], Lord, to rescue me [cf. Ps 39:9]; Lord, to my help hasten" (cf. Ps 38:23); the cry (v. 14) is in chiastic form with verbs at beginning and end. Petitions follow (v. 15) in the pattern of Psalm 35:4 for the shaming and bringing to confusion of the enemy who seek to "snatch away" his soul; let them retreat and be confounded, those who delight (changed from "plan" of Ps 35:4 to match verb used in vv. 7, 9) in his harm. Another verse of petition (v. 16) is patterned on the previous one: "Let them be desolate on account of their shame, those who say to me, 'Aha, aha!'" (cf. Ps 35:21, 25). Then comes a positive petition in the same form (v. 17): "Let them rejoice and be glad [cf. Pss 35:15, 19, 24, 26, 27, 38:17] in you, all who seek you (cf. v. 15); let them always say, 'The Lord is great' [cf. Ps 35:27], who love your salvation" (cf. v. 11). Both enemies and friends have their quotations. A concluding verse (v. 18) combines lament, trust, and a final poignant petition: "For I am poor and needy [cf. Pss 37:14, 35:10], but the Master considers me [verb form of noun in v. 6; cf. Ps 36:4, 20]; my helper [cf. v. 14] and the one who brings me to safety are you; God, do not delay" (cf. "hasten" in v. 14).

The psalm moves from past to present to future. The psalmist is grateful for his rescue by the Lord from unspecified suffering, commits himself to this gracious God in obedience and praise, then begs help in a new crisis. Thanksgiving and praise, trust, lament, and petition are all present but in reverse of the normal order.

The Letter to the Hebrews applies the psalm directly to Christ, who in offering not holocaust but his own body in obedience to his Father's will "offered one sacrifice for sins and took his seat forever at the right hand of God" (Heb 10:5–12). "By one offering he has forever perfected those who are being sanctified" (Heb 10:14). To "do his Father's will" was his food and drink (John 4:34, 14:31). He now continues to proclaim the Father's praise in the great assembly of the redeemed (cf. Heb 2:11–12).

∼ Psalm 41   Judas

The final psalm of Book One, like Psalm 1, begins with a beatitude (cf. also Ps 40:5): "Happy the man who understands about the weak" (v. 2a). In this affirmation of "understanding" we have another evidence of the wisdom tradition so evident in the foregoing psalms (see esp. Pss 36, 37, 39). What the happy man understands is that the Lord frees the weak man in time of evil (v. 2b). The Lord guards him and gives him life, makes him happy in the land (cf. Ps 37:3), does not hand him over (second person verb) to his enemies (v. 3) and supports him on his couch of misery (v. 4a; cf. Ps 6:7). At this point the speaker addresses the Lord directly, "All his sickbed you have changed" (v. 4b).

The psalmist must now apply this lesson to himself. His story, told mostly in long lines of 4 + 4 meter, will illustrate the truths outlined in his introduction. He recalls what he once "said" (cf. Pss 40:8, 39:2, 38:17): "Lord, have mercy on me [cf. Pss 6:3, 25:16, etc.]; heal [cf. Ps 6:3] my soul, for I have sinned against you" (v. 5). In this prayer he attributes his sickness to his own sin, a true judgment if we see the speaker as mankind, suffering bodily and spiritual ills, which God did not intend but which man brought on himself by refusing God (cf. Gen 3:17–19). Insofar as each man participates in the sin of Adam he is the cause of his own suffering (Rom 5:12, 19) and needs both healing and mercy from the Lord. The speaker then cites what evil his enemies speak against him: "When will he die and his name vanish?" (v. 6). He gives a vivid account of one particular visitor who speaks worthless things, whose heart gathers injustice into itself, and who then goes outside and talks (v. 7). The whole group of those who hate him "whisper" (cf. only other use of this verb in this conjugation in 2 Sam 12:19) over him, planning (cf. Pss 40:18, 36:5, 35:4, 20) evil against him (v. 8). They say that some vile thing has sunk into him so that from the place where he lies he will never rise (v. 9). Worst of all another individual, a close trusted friend (cf. Jer 20:10, 38:22, Obad 7) who "ate my bread," has turned a powerful heel against him (v. 10).

One could hardly imagine a better summary of the psalms of Book One. This man alludes to all the major kinds of suffering we have seen: physical sickness, sin, the hostility of enemies and even friends, isolation, betrayal, the need for divine mercy. But as in most of the laments the speaker trusts enough to make the prayer (v. 11): "But you, O Lord, have mercy on me [inclusion with beginning of speech, v. 5]; make me rise up [against v. 9] and I will repay them." He will know that the Lord "delights" in him (cf. Ps 40:9, 15) when his enemy does not utter the jubilant cry (cf. Ps 33:3) over him (v. 12). In his "perfection" (cf. Ps 26:1, 11) the Lord has grasped him and will stand him before his face forever (v. 13). Here again we encounter themes from Book One: sinlessness, standing firm, the Lord's face. It is an appropriate place for the doxology that concludes the book (v. 14): "Blessed be the Lord, the God of Israel, from the ages to the ages. Amen. Amen."

While echoing many themes of Book One the psalm has its uniqueness, particularly in the evocation of the gloating of former friends over the psalmist's illness. When Jesus applied to himself the graphic detail of a man betrayed by one to whom he had given his own bread (John 13:18), he might have been inviting us to see him in all the psalms of Book One with their confused and turbulent pattern of distress, liberation, and joy. In the verse just after the account of his friend's treachery, the psalmist expresses conviction that the Lord will "raise" him (v. 11), as the Father raised his betrayed and crucified Son. It is not the enemies of the Lord who will raise the "jubilant cry" of praise but the risen Son in company with those he has redeemed.

∼ PSALM 42   deer

A new voice is heard in the first psalm of Book Two (Pss 42–72). The writing is more concise than that of the later psalms of Book One, and the author has a gift for striking images. While the psalmist in Book One has a deep personal experience of God in the temple, the author of the psalms in the first part of Book Two has this too but with a more developed theological understanding of the role of the temple in geography and history. This is true of Psalms 42–49 as also of Psalms 84–85 and 87–88, altogether twelve psalms that are attributed in their titles to the "sons of Korah." Notable also is the much more restricted use of the divine name, a characteristic of Psalms 42–83, a group referred to as the Elohist Psalter because of its preference for Elohim over Yahweh in speaking of or to God.

Psalms 42 and 43 compose a single prayer in three short movements, each ending with the same refrain. "Like the deer panting for stream-channels of water," so the psalmist's soul is panting for God (v. 2; feminine verb shows that the female deer is meant). In the only other use of this word for "pant" in the Old Testament it is beasts who are panting for God in a desert where the streams have dried up (Joel 1:20). The gracefulness and beauty of the solitary animal come to mind along with the poignancy of its need (cf. Cant 2:9, 17, 8:14). Its whole being is stretched toward the water that gives it life. This is a more self-conscious artistry than we have seen in the psalter. It conveys the truth that man cannot live without God, that God is refreshing and life-giving; his absence diminishes one's whole being. As Pope John Paul writes of this verse, "[T]he body and soul of the person praying are absorbed by the primary, spontaneous and substantial desire for God" (*Psalms and Canticles*, 97). The opening verse, which can be read as two lines in 2 + 2 meter, is followed by a verse in the lament (*qinah*) meter 3 + 2, which develops the application of the image. Athirst is the psalmist's soul for God, the living God; he wonders when he will enter to "appear before" (= Hebrew, often corrected to "see") the face of God (v. 3). The word "enter" indicates that the speaker is thinking of God's presence in the temple in Jerusalem; later verses will show that the speaker is far away from this compass point of his soul. Perhaps he remembers "drinking from the river" of the Lord's delights in the temple (cf. Ps 36:10). The only "bread" (cf. Ps 41:10) that gives him sustenance is the tears (cf. Ps 39:13) he sheds over this absence (v. 4), especially since every day (or "all day long") he hears the taunt "Where is your God?" (cf. Joel 2:17). As he "pours out his soul" to himself, he has only the memory of former times when he would pass as leader of a throng (translation of these two words disputed) into the house of God amid joyful shouts and thanksgiving as part of the festal crowd (v. 5).

In the rich refrain (v. 6) the psalmist begins by questioning his soul, "Why do you melt away [LXX: *perilypos ei*, "are you extremely sorrowful, cast down"] and churn within me?" The word for "churn" is often used to describe the chaotic waters (cf. Ps 46:4, Jer 5:22, Isa 17:12), suggesting that in his distress the chaos of the underworld has broken into the speaker's soul. He then admonishes himself, "Hope in God" (cf. Pss 38:16, 39:8, Mic 7:7), expressing certainty that he will still give thanks to him who is "the salvation of my face and my God" (emended to agree with v. 12 and Ps 43:5; Hebrew has "his face" and puts "my God" with the following verse).

The second movement picks up a word from the refrain to introduce precisions about the psalmist's whereabouts and condition. His soul "melts away" (cf. v. 6; here LXX has *etarachthē*, "be troubled") within him as he remembers God from the land of the Jordan and Mount Hermon at the northernmost limit of Israel, the hill of Mizar (v. 7). The watery abysses (cataracts at the head of the Jordan?) seem to call to each other threatening to engulf him (v. 8). He sees these as "God's" breakers and waves "passing over" him (same word as "passing into" the temple, v. 5), since even the chaotic waters of the primitive abyss are ruled by God (cf. Gen 1:2, 6–7, 9, Ps 24:2, 29:3, 10; second half of v. 8 quoted verbatim in Jonah 2:4). Since "by day the Lord commands his love and also by night" (cf. v. 4), the psalmist's song within him is a prayer to "the God of my life" (a variation of the expression in v. 3) (v. 9). He quotes this prayer to God his "rock" (v. 10): "Why have you forgotten me, why do I go mourning (cf. Ps 38:7) in torment from my enemies?" In the decaying of his bones his foes scorn him (v. 11), all day long asking, "Where is your God?" (cf. v. 4). The several echoes of the first movement tie the movements together even as the psalmist adds new information; this will be true also of the third movement (Ps 43). The movement concludes with the refrain. In these two sections the psalmist has fluctuated imperceptibly between addressing God (vv. 2, 8, 10) and addressing his soul (vv. 3, 5, 6, 7, 9, 12).

Christian iconography has taken the deer as a symbol of the soul drinking from the life-giving waters that flow from Christ. In the great apse mosaic of San Clemente in Rome, stags (not the female of the psalm!) slake their thirst from the four streams of water (the four rivers of Paradise, Gen 2:10–14) flowing beneath the cross. Christ himself is the fountain of living water (John 4:14, 7:37–39, 19:34, Rev 21:6, 22:17) for whom in this land of exile we "thirst" and "hope" (Ps 42:3, 6, 12; cf. John 4:15). Paradoxically he is also the one whose "soul" was "cast down" (*perilypos,* cf. v. 6) within him in the Garden (Mark 14:34) and "troubled" (*tetaraktai,* cf. v. 7) in Saint John's equivalent of the Agony in the Garden (John 12:27). The psalm thus rejoins the psalms of the suffering individual at the end of Book One.

∼ PSALM 43   (continuation of Psalm 42)

It is now time for petition. In chiastic form the opening verse places verbs at the beginning and the end: "Judge me, God, and defend my cause from a nation that is not holy; from the man of deceit [cf. Pss 35:20, 36:4, 38:13] and perversity bring me to safety" (v. 1). The speaker asks why the "God of [his] fortress" (cf. Ps 42:10) has "rejected" him (v. 2), a stronger verb than the "forgotten" of Psalm 42:10a and one that will become a hallmark of the community lament (cf. Ps 44:10). Then follows a repetition of Psalm 42:10b. This and the following verse are clear examples of the *qinah* meter. A final petition (v. 3) asks God to "send" both that "light" of his that is associated with the temple (cf. Pss 27:1, 36:10) and his "faithfulness," for these personified attributes will "lead" him and bring him to God's "holy mountain" (Pss 2:6, 3:5, 15:1, 24:3) and to his "dwellings" (a favorite word of the sons of Korah). He envisions "coming" (cf. Ps 42:3) to the altar of God, to the God of "the gladness of my joy" (v. 4), where he will thank him with the harp, now addressing him as "God, my God." When the refrain sounds a third time we feel its more hopeful side and find the theme of "thanks" strengthened from its appearance in verse 4.

As a whole the three movements of Psalm 42-43 deal respectively with the psalmist's past, present, and future in relation to the temple in Jerusalem. This temple, the dwelling place of God from which the psalmist is presently far removed, is his one anchor, the source of memories, longings, and joy. Further songs of the sons of Korah will celebrate the joy of actually being in the temple (cf. Pss 46, 48, 84, 87). In our exile we Christians long for the sight of Christ (Phil 1:23, 3:14) our light (John 8:12) "sent" by the Father (John 3:17, 8:26, 1 John 4:14) and with him already thank the Father with anticipated joy (1 Pet 1:6–9).

∼ PSALM 44   slaughter

A new genre appears in Psalm 44: the community lament. Although a single voice, perhaps the king, speaks in verses 5, 7, and 16–17, the remainder of the psalm is spoken by the people, who are aware of their heritage and covenant and feel that God has rejected them without cause. We see in the psalm some of the self-conscious artistry noted in the previous psalm. The suffering depicted is not as immediate as in earlier psalms but has been well crafted into poetic language. The 3 + 3 meter is fairly strictly adhered to.

The author looks back at Israel's history from a higher vantage point than we have seen thus far: only in Psalm 22:5 were the "fathers" mentioned as an example of trust; in Psalm 44 they are the mediators of the people's history, who communicated the actions God (the name Yahweh will not be used in the entire psalm) had done in the "days of long ago" (v. 2; cf. Mic 7:20). The "backward glance" over history is parallel to the previous speaker's glance back at his own past. The key historical event for this speaker was the dispossession of the nations of Canaan (cf. Deut 9:3–5) and the "planting" of Israel, the defeat of the races and the growth of Israel (v. 3). It was not by their sword (Jos 24:12) that they "inherited the land" (cf. Deut 9:3–5, Jos 23:5), nor was it their own "arm" that saved them, but God's right hand and arm (Deut 7:19) and the light of his face (cf. Pss 43:3, 42:3), for he took pleasure in them (v. 4).

The individual speaker comes forth to confess, "You are he, my king, God; command the salvation of Jacob" (v. 5). He or the people confess that in God they will thrust down their oppressors, in his name tread down their attackers (v. 6). The individual replicates the nation's ancient experience, "for not in my bow do I trust, and my sword [cf. v. 4] does not save me" (v. 7, the weapons are in parallelism but in different grammatical positions). God saved them from their oppressors; those who hated them he put to shame (v. 8, chiasmus). All day the people praised God, and they will thank his name (cf. v. 6) forever (v. 9).

Suddenly God has "rejected" (cf. Ps 43:2) and confounded them and no longer accompanies their hosts (v. 10). He has made them turn back from the oppressor, and those who hated them despoiled them (v. 11, parallelism with change of subject). God has given them "like sheep to be eaten" and scattered them among the nations (v. 12), exactly reversing his former actions. The psalm refers to any of the deportations that took place in the later monarchy, from the late eighth to early sixth century BCE. From the sheep image the speaker turns to money: God sells the people for no prosperity, not making any profit (v. 13). He has made them the reproach (cf. Ps 42:11) of their neighbors, the derision and ridicule of those around (v. 14), a "proverb" to the nations, a reason for shaking the head among the races (v. 15). In verse 16 the individual comes forward to embody the feeling of the people: all day long his disgrace is before him, shame covers his face at the voice of the scorner and reviler, at the sight of the enemy and avenger (v. 17). Even in translation one can feel the inexorable 3 + 3 rhythm.

But the heart of the lament is still to come. All these things have happened without the people "forgetting" God (v. 18), without their being false to the "covenant" (thus far only encountered in Ps 25:10, 14). Their heart has not retreated, their footsteps have not declined from God's path (v. 19). Yet God has "crushed" them (cf. Ps 38:9) in a place of jackals (cf. Isa 34:13, 35:7, Jer 9:10, 10:22), and covered them in the "shadow of death" (v. 20; cf. Ps 23:4). If they had forgotten the name (cf. vv. 6, 9) of their God or stretched out their palms to a foreign god (v. 21; cf. Job 11:13, Isa 1:15), would not God have scrutinized these things since he knows the secrets of the heart (v. 22)? For the psalmist the only answer (v. 23) is that for God's sake (cf. Jer 15:15) the people are killed "all day long" (cf. v. 16) and considered as "sheep [cf. v. 12] for the slaughter" (cf. Isa 53:7). He enlightens us no further before launching into the final petitions.

Did the psalmist have a dim intuition that the suffering of the people had a purpose in the divine plan? When Saint Paul cites verse 23 (Rom 8:36–37) it is in the context of Christ's victory over suffering, the victory of divine love. Our suffering does not disappear, but because Christ has entered it and transformed it into glory, and because we share in that suffering and glory (Rom 8:17), our suffering is linked to his redemptive suffering. Saint Paul in a later epistle will claim to "fill up in [his] own flesh what is lacking in the sufferings of Christ for the sake of his body, the church" (Col 1:24). Saint Peter too teaches that suffering for doing right is part of our following of Christ (1 Pet 2:19–21), the lamb whose precious blood redeemed us (1 Pet 1:18–19). Our suffering joined with Christ's has a sacrificial meaning, which the inspired Old Testament author wrote of without knowing it.

Paul Claudel captured this mystery of Christian suffering in his paraphrase of Christ's words, "I came not to destroy but to [ful]fill" (Matt 5:17): "I did not come to explain, to dissipate doubts with an explanation, but to *fill,* that is, to replace with my presence the very need for an explanation." He continued, "The Son of God did not come to destroy suffering, but to suffer with us. He did not come to destroy the Cross, but to be stretched upon it" (*Positions et Propositions,* 245; my translation).

Whatever purpose the people's suffering has in the mind of God, the speakers of the prayer want it to end. They cannot see how it harmonizes with the favor God showed to Jacob (their term for Israel) at the origins. The last four verses consist of two outer verses of petition and two inner verses of lament grounding the petitions. The speaker asks the Master to "rouse" himself (cf. Pss 7:7, 35:23) as if he "slept" like the god Baal (1 Kgs 18:27), to "awake" (cf. Pss 3:6, 35:23), and not to reject (cf. v. 10) forever (v. 24). Why has he hidden his face (v. 25) and forgotten (cf. vv. 18, 21, 42:10) their affliction (cf. Exod 3:7) and torment (Ps 42:10, Exod 3:9, Deut 26:7)? Their soul melts away (cf. Ps 43:5) to the dust, their belly clings to the ground (v. 26). Three final petitions match those of verse 24: "Arise, help us, and ransom us for the sake of your love" (v. 27; cf. Ps 42:9).

∿ PSALM 45 wedding

Psalm 45 extols the grandeur and power of the Davidic king and then addresses his bride and recounts their wedding procession.

The speaker is proud of the "good word" that has "surged up" from his heart, that is, the poem he plans to speak before the king, his tongue the "stylus" (cf. Job 19:24, Jer 8:8, 17:1) of a diligent scribe (v. 2). The four-beat lines will be characteristic of the psalm as will the arrangement of ideas in tricola. The speaker will refer to himself again in the final verse, promising to acknowledge the king's name (through his song) to future generations so that the peoples will "thank" the king forever (v. 18).

The king excels other men in beauty, and graciousness streams from his lips; these gifts from God win (are a sign of?) God's everlasting blessing (v. 3). The poet envisions the king as a "champion" (v. 4), calling on him to put his sword on his thigh in "majesty and splendor" (attributes of Yahweh himself in Pss 96:6, 104:1), to be victorious, to ride out for the cause of faithfulness, poverty (cf. the royal psalm, Ps 72:2–4, 12–13), and justice, and to let his right hand instruct him in fearsome deeds (v. 5). The speaker already sees the "peoples" succumbing to the king's sharp arrows, which fall into the heart of his enemies (v. 6). His "throne," that is, his rule over these enemy peoples, is forever and ever—in fact it is a share in God's own rule so that the poet can address the king as "God" by participation (v. 7; cf. Pss 2:7, 110:3, 89:28). The throne of Israel's earthly king is actually the "sovereign throne of Yahweh" himself over Israel (1 Chr 28:5, 29:23). The "scepter" of his kingship is one of "evenness" (uprightness) since he "loves justice" (v. 8; cf. Ps 11:7) and hates wickedness (cf. v. 5). His mission on earth is to extend over the peoples the righteousness of God. For this reason God, his God, has anointed him with the "oil of rejoicing" (cf. Isa 61:3) above his companions. His "robes" exude the scents of spices: myrrh, aloes, cassia (cf. Cant 4:14); string music from the ivory "palace" (word normally designating the temple or more exactly, the "Holy Place") gladdens him (v. 9)—the poet appeals to several senses to surround the king with an aura of splendor. Finally the king is attended by a harem (cf. 1 Kgs 11:3, Cant 6:8) that includes the daughters of foreign kings, among whom is his "favorite" who stands at his right hand in a robe decorated with fine gold from Ophir (v. 10; cf. 1 Kgs 9:28, 22:49). The accoutrements of the king—sword, arrows, throne, scepter, spiced robes, even his harem—can be viewed as the manifestation of his royal sovereignty over the peoples.

It is time now to address the spouse (v. 11). The poet, addressing her as "daughter," calls on her to listen and see and turn her ear; she must "forget" her people and the house of her father; since the king desires her beauty, he has become her master (cf. Ps 44:24 where the term applies to God) and she must prostrate herself before him (v. 12). As in the first section the imperatives are followed by descriptions of the court scene. The "daughter of Tyre," Israel's close and wealthy neighbor, brings offerings; the richest of the people hope for the spouse's favor (v. 13). She herself, a king's daughter, is "glorious within" (sometimes emended to "her treasure is corals / pearls?"), gold "brocade" is her clothing (v. 14; cf. Exod 28:11). In colored robes she is conducted to the king (v. 15), maidens following her and her friends brought to him (like the queens coming to Jerusalem, Isa 49:23). Conducted with gladness (cf. v. 9) and joy, they enter the palace (cf. v. 9) of the king (v. 16).

Returning then to the king, the poet promises him sons in place of his fathers (cf. Isa 54:1); these sons he will install as princes over all the earth (v. 17).

If it is easy to see Christ as the messianic king of the psalm, loving truth and justice, subduing pagan nations, reigning in splendor, who is the beloved spouse? According to Saint Paul, "as Christ is head of the church and saves the whole body, so is a husband the head of his wife; and as the church submits to Christ so should wives to their husbands in everything. Husbands should love their wives just as Christ loved the Church and sacrificed himself for her . . ." (Eph 5:23–25). The spouse of the king is his messianic people (cf. also Rev 21:2, 9–10, Mark 2:18–19). This is already suggested in our psalm. In referring to the spouse as "daughter," the psalmist may be thinking of Daughter Zion (Zeph 3:14–17; see Hossfeld and Zenger, *Die Psalmen*, 1:279, 283), a title of Jerusalem considered as God's chosen people. Like Israel, she is summoned to "listen" (Deut 6:4) to her lord, to love him exclusively. She had to leave her "father's house" as Abraham left his fatherland (Gen 12:1, Ezek 16:3, 45) to become the beginning of the new people of God. She "prostrates" before the king in worship and in her turn receives gifts from the pagans (cf. Ps 72:10, Isa 60:5) arrayed in splendor. She celebrates her union with her lord in gladness and joy. As an early Christian title puts it, the psalm shows that "the fairest in beauty among the sons of men blesses and anoints the Church which the Father has joined to him" (Salmon, Les "Tituli Psalmorum," 141).

From the fruitful union of Christ and his Church come new children of God, born through baptism. It thus appears that in our psalm the bride is the spouse both of the messianic king and of God himself who had promised to become his people's "husband" (Isa 54:4–5, 62:4–5). The Letter to the Hebrews will apply verse 7 of the psalm to Christ, the messianic king who can be called "God" in a more real sense than any other son of David (cf. Heb 1:8–9). If the spouse in the psalm is "Daughter Zion," then Psalm 45 could be seen as an important link between the psalms on either side of it: it could be a response to the lament about Israel's suffering (Ps 44) and a preparation for the three psalms glorifying God's rule over Zion (Pss 46–48).

∼ PSALM 46   city

If the spouse of Psalm 45 is in fact Daughter Zion, the city of Jerusalem as God's messianic people, then Psalm 46 is well placed since it gives center stage to this city that has God within. The long, fairly regular four-beat lines give the psalm a solemn weight.

The community confesses that God is for them a refuge (cf. Ps 14:6, Isa 25:4) and strength (cf. Ps 28:8), a helper (cf. Pss 27:9, 40:18, 44:27) in distress, "readily found" (v. 2; cf. Isa 65:1). Therefore they will not fear if the earth should rock or mountains totter in the heart of the seas (v. 3), if they churn, they foam, their waters; they quake, the mountains, in their "pride" (v. 4; cf. Isa 24:18–19). The most durable parts of earth can be swamped by chaotic waters (cf. Pss 29:3, 32:6), but behind this earth God remains a stable refuge.

There is a river—its channels (cf. Ps 1:3) gladden (cf. Ps 45:9, 16) the city of God, the holy dwelling of the Most High (v. 5; cf. Isa 66:10–12). Because Jerusalem houses the temple of God, it must be a place of life-giving waters—such is the logic of the poet. Such a river was an essential feature of the garden where God created man and settled him (Gen 2:6, 10, 15). If Jerusalem was not located near a river, it nonetheless had a ceaseless flow of life-giving blessings from the presence of its God (cf. Ps 36:9–10), and these might be called a river. Such a river might be seen to be realized in the spring Gihon at the foot of Mount Zion (cf. Gen

2:13!), the only water supply for the city. Furthermore, with God within it (cf. Zeph 3:17), the city could not "totter" (v. 6), whatever the mountains might do (cf. v. 3, Ps 15:5); God will "help" it (cf. v. 2) as morning appears, the privileged time of God's assistance (cf. Pss 5:4, 30:6). Nations "churned" (like the sea, cf. v. 4), kingdoms "tottered" (like the mountains, cf. vv. 3, 6); God gave his voice, the earth "dissolves" (v. 7, tenses as in Hebrew; cf. Amos 9:5–6, Nah 1:5, Exod 15:15, Jos 2:9, 24). Whether chaos threatens through nature or through society, it is God who has the disposition of earthly affairs.

For the first time since Psalm 42 the divine name appears (v. 8), introducing a profession of faith that sums up what the psalm has said so far and that will reappear at the end as a refrain. "The Lord of hosts is with us; a high refuge [cf. Pss 9:10, 18:3] for us is the God of Jacob" (v. 8, chiasmus). It is Israel's covenant God, Jacob's God, who dwells within the city, not simply "God" or "the Most High," that is, generic terms for the deity. The "Lord of hosts" is the name of the covenant God who was seated above the ark in the Holy of Holies (1 Sam 1:3, 4:4, 2 Sam 6:2, Ps 24:10, Isa 6:3, 25:6). He is the one who is "with us" (*'immānû*), for it is his plan to dwell in the midst of his people, as indicated by the prophetic name "Emmanuel" announced by Isaiah (Isa 7:14). The full meaning of this expression, "God with us," would be revealed in Jesus, God dwelling among us as man (John 1:14). The "God with us" announced to Joseph at the beginning of Matthew's Gospel (Matt 1:21–23) is the one who at the end of the same Gospel promises to be "with" his disciples till the end of time (Matt 28:20). The goal of history is the city where God lives among men (Rev 21:3), and the last words of the Christian Bible are a promise, "I shall indeed be with you soon," and a prayer, "May the grace of the Lord Jesus be with you" (Rev 22:20–21). One could make a case for identifying the preposition "with" as a single-word summary of the entire message of Scripture.

The parallel half of the refrain translates the theme of the first half into a metaphor like the one opening the psalm: God is a "high refuge" or fortified place. It is not the temple or city that is the tower but God himself who makes himself present in these places. In the same way the sacraments are outward signs that make present the power of God. God is mediated to us through material things: he is not identified with them, but in the Christian dispensation he cannot reach us without them. The chief sacrament is the Body of Christ, the temple where God dwells substantially, and we who believe in him are the extension of that body on earth. The Lord of hosts is with us in the Church as a tower of strength.

The psalmist invites the peoples to go and "gaze on" the acts of the Lord, the sheer terror he has inflicted on the earth (v. 9). For he stops battles to the end of the earth (cf. Isa 2:3–4, Hos 2:20); the bow he breaks, and he cuts in pieces the lance, chariots he smelts in fire (v. 10). God not only abides when the earth crumbles (vv. 3–4, 7), he actively eliminates the forces hostile to him and to his people. This God now addresses any hostile powers (v. 11; cf. "his voice" in v. 7), telling them to "desist" and know that he is God, exalted over the nations (cf. v. 7), exalted over the earth (cf. vv. 2–3). Not only all human activity but the environment itself is completely subject to his rule. This is the supreme God who is "with us," the God revealed to Israel as a high refuge (v. 12 = v. 8): what could they possibly fear (cf. v. 3)?

The psalm is remarkable for its lack of connectives: only in three places are the clauses linked with "and." This device (asyndeton) gives the psalm a direct almost "telegraphic" force (see esp. vv. 4, 6, 7, 8, 10, 11).

If the temple and city of God are the church of Christ, then the "river" that "gladdens" the city is the Holy Spirit, the "living water" flowing from the belly of Christ (John 7:37–39, 19:34), the "river of the water of life, bright as crystal, flowing from the throne of God and of the Lamb down the middle of the city street" (Rev 22:1–2). This Spirit "poured on all mankind" (Joel 3:1–2, Acts 2:17–18) makes them members of the Body of Christ (1 Cor 12:12–13, Titus 3:4–6), which abides forever, victorious over the powers of evil.

It is to the sons of Korah that we owe the fullest development of the theology of Zion as the dwelling place of God on earth. These psalms (42–49, 84–85, 87–88) spell out what is meant in other psalms by references to the "house of God," God's "holy mountain," the holy place as "refuge" and "stronghold." The Temple vision of the sons of Korah fills out the meaning of these phrases in other psalms and can be kept in mind as the background and framework of all the psalms. All our prayer ascends to the Father through the Church, which is the fullness of the Body of Christ (Eph 1:22–23), the temple where God is worshipped.

～ Psalm 47   clap

The short psalm is quite complex. It consists of two hymns placed together, the first beginning with the invitation to praise in verse 2 followed by the reason for praise in verses 3–6, the second beginning with another invitation in verse 7 followed by the reason for praise in verses 8–10. Both parts have received additions. Verses 4 and 5, which proclaim the subjugation of the peoples to Israel, are not likely to have been part of a hymn inviting the peoples to praise God. Similarly verse 10, which describes an element of the earthly liturgy, does not flow naturally from the previous verses, which envision God seated on his heavenly throne. The original hymns would have consisted of verses 2, 3, and 6 and verses 7–9. The first of these could be called an "acclamation" at the Lord's ascension, the second a "proclamation" of his kingship over the nations. If verses 3b and 8b are also regarded as later additions not fitting well in their contexts, the result is two hymns in the same pattern: an invitation to praise of two lines, and a reason for praise of three lines (see Hossfeld and Zenger, *Die Psalmen*, 1:289–290). Once the underlying structure of the psalm is recognized, one can see how the added verses and phrases complement the original. The psalm follows a fairly strict 3 + 3 meter.

To call on all peoples to "clap the palm" is to assume a visionary as opposed to a literal stance. The speaker is envisioning an action that is to happen in a world behind this visible world, a superterrestrial reality with implications for the earth. Along with the gesture of clapping, the peoples are to "cry jubilantly" (cf. Pss 27:6, 33:3) with joyful shout to God, acclaiming his supremacy (v. 2). The transitional "For" introduces the reason for praise, and that is that the Lord (Yahweh) is the Most High God, fearsome (v. 3a). Since "Most High" was a title of the Canaanite high god El and the word "fearsome" an epithet of the storm god Baal, our psalm is identifying Yahweh as the true bearer of these divine attributes. Yahweh has replaced the Canaanite gods as supreme deity. The ancient hymn is here supplemented by the addition of comments referring more to God's earthly kingship (v. 3b) and his subjugation of the peoples and races to Israel (v. 4; cf. Ps 18:48), whose inheritance God has chosen for them (cf. Deut 33:2–5), the "pride of Jacob whom he has loved" (v. 5). The original hymn concludes with two more lines celebrating

God's "ascension": "God has gone up to the jubilant cry [noun form of the verb used in v. 2b, here applied to the heavenly court], the Lord to the blast of the ram's horn" (v. 6). These heavenly happenings can be called eschatological since they take place above the confines of time but are eventually to be realized on earth. In this way the subjugation of the nations to Israel is a consequence of the ascension to supremacy of Israel's God in the heavens.

Four calls to "make music" (cf. Ps 9:12) to God "our king" introduce the second hymn (v. 7). "For" (cf. v. 3) God is king of all the earth (v. 8a). A fifth "make music" is added with the adverbial phrase "with understanding" (v. 8b). Verse 9 specifies that God "has become king" over the nations, that he sits on his holy throne, the goal of his "ascension" (cf. v. 6). A later hand added the earthly enactment of this rule over the nations: "nobles of the peoples" gather with the "people of the God of Abraham" (who was himself called from a pagan nation, Jos 24:1–3), for to God belong the "shields" (leaders now become Israel's defenders) of the earth, God who is highly raised (v. 10; cf. Jer 16:19–21, Isa 66:23, Zech 14:16).

Catholic liturgy applies the psalm to Christ ascending to his heavenly throne after his resurrection. God has asserted his worldwide rule by raising his incarnate Son to sit with him on his throne (Rev 22:1, 3), from where he will rule all nations (Rev 1:5, 19:16), receiving their joyful tribute.

∼ Psalm 48   castles

Like Psalm 46, Psalm 48 celebrates Zion as the dwelling place of God on earth; the two psalms form a frame for Psalm 47 with its praise of the God enthroned above the nations. The psalm is a presentation of Zion's place among the nations; into this setting, like a jewel has been inserted a meditation of the worshipping community in the temple (vv. 10–12). Beginning with four-beat lines, the psalm quickly settles into the 3 + 2 qinah meter.

The first verse brings together Yahweh and his city (v. 2): Great (cf. Ps 47:3) is Yahweh and "to be praised highly" in the "city of our God, his holy mountain." Epitome of beauty, exultation of all the earth (cf. Lam 2:15!)—this is Mount Zion in the "far north," the town of the lofty king (v. 3). Like the two previous psalms, Psalm 48 has affinities with Canaanite poetry, which speaks of the mountain of Baal as located in the "north." This Canaanite "Olympus" is probably Mons Casius north of the Orontes River. The term became so closely associated with the dwelling of God that when Israel came to understand Zion as the mountain of God, it was natural for her to call it a mountain "in the north" (cf. Isa 14:13), as if to say "divine mountain" (a similar transfer from pagan myth was made with respect to the "river" in Ps 46). God was in the "castles" of this city where he was manifested as a "high refuge" (v. 4; cf. Ps 46:8, 12). The following verses will give a mythic vision of enemy nations coming to grief against the city fortified by God's presence, the "Emmanuel-city" (cf. Ezek 48:35) in the phrase of John Paul II (*Psalms and Canticles*, 61).

Introducing his vision with the words, "For behold," the poet describes the kings assembling, advancing together (v. 5). Seeing the city, they are amazed, terrified; they hurry away (v. 6). Trembling has seized them there, pangs of a woman giving birth (v. 7). With an east wind the Lord breaks (cf. Ps 46:10) even the strong ships of Tarshish (v. 8). The community that had "heard" of these things now claims to have "seen" them in the "city of the Lord of hosts, the city of our God," which God has firmly established forever (v. 9). The poet's recounting of the "myth" has made the vision real for the first-person speakers.

Turning to address God directly, these worshippers in the midst of the temple contemplate God's *ḥesed,* his unshakable love for his people (v. 10). They see that his "name" is spread to the ends of the earth and evokes a corresponding praise (v. 11). Since his right hand is full of "justice," the judgments he gives are a cause of gladness and joy for Mount Zion and the daughters (towns) of Judah (v. 12). This temple meditation on God's blessings to the community is set in the midst of descriptions of Zion's effect on the nations. For the imperatives that follow are addressed probably to the pagan kings (cf. v. 5), inviting them to walk round the city walls counting its towers (v. 13), taking to heart the bulwarks, examining the castles (v. 14; cf. v. 4), so as to be able to tell to coming generations: "This is God, our God, forever and always, who will urge us along forever" (v. 15). The pagan kings would thus unite with the Zion community in exalting the God who dwells there as shepherd of both Israel and the nations together.

The psalm is a festive celebration of the Church as the Body of Christ. Evil cannot harm it since it is the "pillar and bulwark of the truth" (1 Tim 3:15) through the God dwelling within. It is the locus of the manifold blessings of Christian life: the contemplation of God's love, praise of his name, righteousness, gladness and joy, fellowship. It incorporates all nations and peoples into itself to reconcile them to God (Eph 2:13–22). Its "castles" are the members of the Body of Christ, the "living stones" built on him into a spiritual house where are offered the "spiritual sacrifices which Jesus Christ has made acceptable to God" (1 Pet 2:4–5).

∿ PSALM 49   riches

The last song in this group of the sons of Korah is quite different from its predecessors. It is a wisdom meditation on death, spoken by an individual. It makes no reference to worship, to Zion, or to the community. It is addressed to the peoples of the earth (v. 2), inviting them to explore the "riddle" (v. 5) that no matter how great a man's riches are, he cannot purchase life (v. 8). The psalm only hints at a solution, suggesting that the God of Israel can rescue a soul from the underworld (v. 16).

All peoples, all dwellers in creation, highborn and low, rich and needy are summoned to hear the psalmist's message (vv. 2–3). His mouth will speak wisdom, and the meditation of his heart discernment (v. 4, synonymous parallelism with syntactic variation). He will "turn [his] ear to" a proverb, perhaps the truths expressed in verses 11–15, opening his "riddle" to the accompaniment of the harp (v. 5). Like the speaker of Psalm 45 the author is conscious of the artistry of his poem, which except in the middle section follows a fairly strict 3 + 3 meter.

The body of the psalm begins with a question: "Why should I fear in evil days when the iniquity of my steps surrounds me?" (v. 6). If the Hebrew text is correct, this line is not likely to be spoken by the "wise and insightful" psalmist but must be the citation of a wicked man's words, one who fears no repercussions for his evil behavior (cf. Sir 5:1–8). Such men "trust" (cf. Isa 31:1) in their wealth and "boast" of the abundance of their "riches" (v. 7; cf. Jer 9:22). Alas, one cannot ransom a man or give God a price for himself (v. 8), no matter how many riches he has. Too costly is the ransom of the soul, which ceases forever (v. 9). Does one live on forever and never "see the grave"? (v. 10; cf. Ps 16:10).

What a man eventually comes to "see" is the truth of the proverb that wise men die and the foolish and stupid vanish along with them, leaving their wealth to their successors (v. 11; cf. Ps 39:7, Qoh 2:18–19, 6:2). Neither wisdom nor wealth count for anything; the only eternal homes of those who enjoy these blessings, their lasting dwellings are their tombs (cf. Qoh 12:5, Tob 3:6), even while their names continue to be spoken respectfully on earth (v. 12; cf. Sir 39:9–11). Man in his "preciousness" does not abide; he is like the cattle that are mute (v. 13; cf. Qoh 3:18–22; this verse represents a return to the 3 + 3 meter after two longer verses and will reappear as a refrain at the end of the psalm). This is the way of those whose confidence is in themselves, though their successors take pleasure in what their mouths had spoken (v. 14). Like sheep they are placed in Sheol where death pastures them (v. 15a); the upright will rule over them in the morning (the time of judgment), and their "rock" (title of God) will be there to wipe out Sheol from his mansion. Such is the literal translation of the problematic and metrically overloaded verse 15b. Whereas neither wisdom nor wealth avail in the afterlife, the righteous attain some kind of authority over others after death; in fact their God will destroy the underworld. Such a reading of the verse would prepare well for verse 16.

With verse 16 the 3 + 3 meter returns. The psalmist has had a revelation: while he cannot buy his own ransom (cf. vv. 8–9), "Surely God will ransom my soul from the hand of Sheol [cf. v. 15] and take me up." "Take up" is the verb used when God takes Enoch (Gen 5:24, Sir 44:16, 49:14) and Elijah (2 Kgs 2:3, 5, 9, 10, Sir 48:9) into intimacy with himself (cf. Ps 73:24). The speaker no longer meditates on the melancholy fate of man but has understood how God can destroy death's power. He now counsels an individual not to fear when a man "grows rich" (cf. v. 7), when he increases the glory of his "house" (v. 17; cf. v. 12), as if this man's earthly wealth guaranteed him lasting happiness. For a man "takes" (cf. v. 16) nothing with him into death; his glory will not go down after him (v. 18), even if he thought his "soul" (cf. v. 16) blessed during life and worthy of praise because he had prospered (v. 19; cf. v. 7). He will join the generation of his fathers; they will never see light (v. 20). The refrain is repeated with a slight change: "Man in his preciousness lacks discernment; he is like the cattle that are mute" (v. 21).

Riches blind a man to true life (cf. Mark 10:23–25). They do not accompany him in death but are passed on to those still living (cf. Luke 12:20). The psalm can be read as a "rebuke to the rich who descend to the underworld when they die; the voice of the Church about Lazarus and the rich man who lived in purple" (Salmon, Les "Tituli Psalmorum," 62;

Luke 16:19–31). Death is the absence of light and enjoyment. The only "treasure" that will abide is righteous living according to the law of Israel's God. The soul of a righteous man will be "taken up" by God. The speaker opens to the "nations" the possibility of redemption from death by the God of Israel. He points to a possibility that will become reality in the raising of the righteous Jesus from the dead. Through this act death has been slain (cf. 1 Cor 15:54–55) and eternal life been given (1 Cor 15:20–22). The universal lordship of the God of Israel celebrated in the songs of the sons of Korah has as its aim the ransom from death of each man who renounces confidence in worldly riches. The psalmist's God is truly "the living God" (Ps 42:3), the "God of my life" (Ps 42:9) of the first Korah psalm, who ransoms "my soul" (cf. Ps 42:2, 3, 6, 7, 12) from the underworld.

∼ Psalm 50   covenant

The sons of Korah (Pss 42–49) have said much about the lordship of Israel's God but little about Israel's obligation to God. Man's moral duty to the covenant God is the subject of Psalm 50, a psalm attributed, like Psalms 73–83, to Asaph. Appearing in a theophany, God rebukes Israel for two faults of worship: overconfidence in external rituals and the separation of rite from obedience to the commandments. The psalm is crafted in a fairly regular 3 + 3 rhythm.

The God of gods, Yahweh (the only appearance of the divine name in the psalm), has addressed the earth in a thundering speech that reaches from eastern to western horizons (v. 1). It is from Mount Zion, "perfection of beauty" (cf. Ps 48:3), that he shines out (v. 2); as Israel's God he "comes and does not remain deaf," a devouring fire before him and around him a swirling tempest (v. 3). The psalmist is evoking the Lord's appearance on Sinai at the making of the covenant (Deut 5:23–26, 4:12, 24, Exod 24:17; for tempest see Nah 1:3). God calls to heaven above and to earth for "giving judgment on behalf of his people" (v. 4; cf. Ps 135:14, Deut 32:36). He addresses his "devoted ones" directly, those who make a covenant with him by sacrifice (v. 5; cf. Exod 24:4–8). Meanwhile the heavens manifest his justice, because he is the divine judge (v. 6).

The solemn beginning of the Lord's speech echoes the *Šĕmaʿ Yiśrāʾēl* (Hear [O] Israel) of Deuteronomy 6:4. Israel's own God (cf. Exod 20:2) is going to witness before his people (v. 7). Not for their sacrifices does he reprove them, their holocausts always before him (v. 8); he will not take a bull from their house or goats from their pens (v. 9; cf. Isa 1:11), since already his are all the beasts of the forest, the thousand cattle on the hills (v. 10). He knows all the birds on the mountains, and the creatures of the fields are with him (v. 11, chiasmus). If he were hungry, he would not tell his people since his is the world and what fills it (v. 12). Does he eat bull's flesh, or goat's blood does he drink (v. 13, chiasmus)? All he wants of his people is the *tôdāh*, the thanksgiving sacrifice offered in recognition of divine help. An Israelite making a petition would promise the offering of such a sacrifice when his petition was heard: he must pay these vows to the Most High (v. 14). Then when he "calls" on the Lord (cf. vv. 1, 4) in his distress, the Lord will deliver him, and he will glorify the Lord (v. 15). Such a sacrifice emerging from a grateful heart is more pleasing to God than the official and elaborate sacrifices of the temple liturgy.

In a second speech the Lord addresses the wicked man on a more serious issue: why does he recite the Lord's "statutes" and take his "covenant" (cf. v. 5) in his mouth (v. 16; the two words paired also in 1 Kgs 11:11, 2 Kgs 17:15; cf. Isa 29:13, Rom 2:17–24) while actually "hating discipline" (cf. Prov 5:12) and throwing God's words behind him (v. 17). If he sees a thief he runs along with him, and with adulterers is his portion (v. 18). He uses his mouth for evil and his tongue frames deceit (v. 19); he sits and maligns his brother, against his own mother's son spreading filth (v. 20). Though the wicked man committed these violations of the sixth, seventh, and eighth commandments (cf. Exod 20:14–16, Job 24:14–16), God kept quiet (cf. v. 3). The man seemed to think that God was on his level. God will reprove (cf. v. 8) him and lay the case before his eyes (v. 21).

Those forgetful of God must now discern these things (v. 22) lest he tear them to pieces (like a lion, usually applied to the psalmist's enemy; cf. Ps 22:14, but see Hos 5:14) with no rescue. The threatening call of God is a gracious offer of life: God is asking for that conformity to his will that will make it possible for him to give his people salvation. One who offers a thanksgiving sacrifice (cf. v. 14) honors God (cf. v. 15), and one who places [God's] way [in his heart; for the idiom see Job 24:12] will be shown the "salvation" of God (v. 23). This final verse is an apt summary of the two parts of the psalm.

Jesus, too, placed fraternal reconciliation as a prerequisite for sacrifice (Matt 5:23–24) and condemned the Pharisaic show of righteousness that covered up vainglory (Matt 23:5–7), extortion and self-indulgence (Matt 23:25), hypocrisy and lawlessness (Matt 23:28). It would be his own thanksgiving sacrifice (Mark 14:22–24, Heb 9:13–14), expressing his own perfect obedience (Heb 5:8–9, 10:9–10), that would win for men the salvation of God and give glory to the Father (John 13:31). This sacrifice would establish the new covenant in which man in Christ gives due service to the living God (Heb 9:14, 10:16–17).

~ PSALM 51   repentance

As an individual lament, Psalm 51 is doubly unique: no other psalm focuses so relentlessly on the psalmist's own sin, and the elements of trust, lament, and praise are completely subordinated to the driving petitions. The petitions call for the removal of sin (vv. 3–11) and its replacement by a renewed heart and spirit (vv. 12–19); the clear two-part division is reminiscent of the previous psalm and is found in a number of other psalms (e.g., Pss 18, 27, 45, 62, 66). There is no mention in the psalm of enemies or of the absence of God. The psalmist never turns aside from direct address to God, although he never uses the divine name.

The opening cry for mercy, found over twenty times in the psalter (most recently, Ps 41:5, 11), has given the psalm its name, "The Miserere." The psalmist appeals to God's "covenant love" (ḥesed) as the source of this mercy (v. 3). Parallel to ḥesed is God's "abundant compassion," according to which may he "blot out" (cf. Isa 43:25, 44:22) the psalmist's "rebellion." Modifying the metaphor, the psalmist asks that God "abundantly [cf. v. 3] cleanse" him from his "iniquity," and "purify" him from his "sin" (v. 4). The three principal terms for moral evil have now been introduced (cf. on Ps 32:1–2): "rebellion" and "iniquity" will each occur three times in the psalm, and "sin" with its cognates, seven times.

With the conjunction "For," the psalmist in synonymous parallelism confesses that he is fully aware of his "rebellions" and that his "sin" is continually before him (v. 5). Against God alone has he sinned, and what is evil in God's eyes he has done; therefore God is just in his sentence, correct in his judgment (v. 6; cf. Dan 9:7). With the word "Behold" the psalmist even calls attention to his sinfulness as an abiding condition since birth and conception (v. 7). Another "Behold" shows his awareness of God's "delight" in faithfulness in a man's inner depths, where God makes wisdom known (v. 8).

Having emphasized his profound awareness of guilt, the psalmist renews his petitions. Verse 9 joins metaphors from ritual and nature: "Cancel my sin with hyssop [cf. Exod 12:22, Lev 14:51], and I will be purified; cleanse me [cf. v. 4], and whiter than snow will I be" (cf. Isa 1:18). Such cleansing would make him "hear" rejoicing and gladness; the very "bones" that were crushed (by his opposition to God) would rejoice ecstatically (v. 10): removal of sin would affect his whole person. God is finally asked to "hide [his] face" from the speaker's sin, as if to lose the awareness of it (v. 11); then would the iniquities be truly "blotted out" (inclusion with v. 3; see also note on Ps 90:7–9).

With a new address to "God" and a line in 4 + 4 rhythm (v. 12) the psalmist begins the second half of his prayer, this time for a spiritual regeneration. God is asked to "create a pure heart" in the speaker, as he once created the heavens and the earth from nothing (Gen 1:1, 2:4, Isa 40:28, 42:5). Parallel to the creation of a pure heart is the "making new" of a steady spirit within the speaker. "Whereas 'heart' in the Old Testament signifies simply the center of human existence as the *place* of all feeling, thinking, and willing, 'spirit' refers to the active *power* that animates all feeling, thinking, and willing and that emanates from Yahweh" (Kraus, *Psalmen*, 1:389; see also Ezek 36:26). God must give both the organ and the dynamism for a renewed morality. If God hides his face from the psalmist's sin (v. 11), this does not mean he should cast the psalmist himself from his face (v. 13) or take away from him God's "holy spirit" (cf. v. 12; these are the only negative petitions in the psalm). The "rejoicing" of his bones requested in verse 10 is to be a restoration of the "rejoicing of [God's] salvation," accompanied with a "willing [same word as "noble"] spirit" with which God will uphold him (v. 14).

The psalmist envisages the future effects of his interior renewal: he will teach rebels the ways of God so that sinners will return to him (v. 15). If God, the God of his salvation (v. 16) rescues him from blood-guilt, his tongue will joyfully sing God's justice. If the Lord opens his lips, his mouth will proclaim God's praise (v. 17). The result of God's transforming action must be both praise and public witness for the benefit of others: this is the pattern of the thanksgiving psalms (e.g., Pss 30:2–6, 34:2–5, 12–15). For God does not delight in sacrifice (otherwise the psalmist would offer it), nor is he pleased with holocausts (v. 18; cf. Pss 40:7, 50:13). "God's sacrifices are a spirit broken"; "a heart broken and crushed" God will not despise (v. 19). The spirit and heart are broken when the psalmist recognizes his sin as a defiance of God, which has brought disorder into his life; such a broken spirit and heart are already the beginning of the regenerated heart and renewed spirit that he asked for at the beginning of this second section (cf. v. 12). The two verses form an inclusion in chiastic order: heart–spirit–spirit–heart, corresponding to the inclusion in the first section formed by the word "blot out" in verses 3 and 11. Paradoxically the heart whose pride is broken by awareness and confession of sin is the one that is strong: it becomes the organ strengthened by the love (*hesed*, v. 3) of God. "Since repentance is our only method of resistance against every assault of temptation, the one who has achieved this in himself becomes a constant conqueror of the one who is always wrestling with him," that is, the devil (Gregory of Nyssa, *On the Inscriptions of the Psalms* II.177). The liturgical sacrifice so often promised in the individual laments is here replaced with the sacrifice of the heart in its humble acknowledgement of the justice of God, for which the other sacrifices are a preparation and a sign.

Jesus looked for this repentant attitude, which was already exemplified by King David when the prophet Nathan came to him (2 Sam 12:13), the episode alluded to in the title of our psalm (vv. 1–2). His first command in the Gospel of Mark is "Repent," that is, "Judge your life in the light of the God who comes to save you: acknowledge your need for a savior" (Mark 1:15). The tax-collector who humbly prayed, "God, have mercy on me, a sinner," was the one whose prayer was heard (Luke 18:13–14); the proud heart God could do nothing for. Though sinless himself, Jesus humbly assumed the condition of sinful man, "tempted in every way that we are" (Heb 4:15, 5:7). In this way he can be identified with the one praying our psalm as well as with the one to whom it is prayed.

Psalm 32, the second penitential psalm, had already emphasized the importance of the confession of sin. This fourth penitential psalm shows how profoundly the awareness of sin must be rooted in the heart, or in the rare expression of verse 8, in the darkest inner depths. Those who truly "mourn" their sin will laugh (Luke 6:21).

After the Exile, there was added to the psalm a prayer more favorable to temple sacrifice. God was asked through his favor to do good to Zion and rebuild the walls of Jerusalem (v. 20). Then he would delight (cf. v. 18) in the right kind of sacrifices, holocausts and whole-offerings; then bulls would go up on his altar (v. 21). Such sacrifices would be entirely appropriate when they were accompanied by, or were the expression of, a contrite heart and spirit.

Besides the critique of merely external sacrifice, Psalm 51 has other ties with Psalm 50: cf. the word links "justice/be justified" (50:6, 51:6, 16, 21); "salvation" (50:23, 51:14, 16); Zion (50:2, 51:20); "holocaust" (50:8, 51:18, 21); "bull(s)" (50:9, 51:21). The psalms are of almost the same length and each is in two parts. In one psalm God speaks to man, in the other man to God. Both psalms promote a spiritual attitude that takes God seriously, that is, acknowledges God's justice and one's dependence on him. Such an attitude is manifested in concern for God's will, sorrow for one's sin, prayer for help in trouble, thanksgiving when help is received. This first psalm in the second Davidic collection (Pss 51–65, 68–70) is matched by the final psalm of Book Two, Psalm 72, attributed to Solomon, the offspring of David by Bathsheba with whom he had sinned. Out of David's sin and repentance God brings forth Israel's ideal king.

∾ PSALM 52   olive

An indignant psalmist addresses the treacherous man from the outset, denouncing his behavior, contrasting his fate with that of the psalmist, and turning to God in prayer only in the final verse.

The "champion" addressed by the speaker has been "boasting" (cf. Jer 9:22) of his evil; with the rhetorical "Why?" (v. 3a), the psalmist exposes the folly of such boasting, since "God's love lasts all day long" (v. 3b; omitted by LXX and the Grail; the implication is that evil is powerless against the divine *ḥesed*; cf. Ps 36:5–6). The evil man's tongue plans ruin, like a sharpened razor, causing deception (v. 4). Two verses beginning "You love . . ." characterize the man's preferences: evil more than good (cf. Mic 3:2), lies more than speaking justly (v. 5), words of "devouring" (v. 6). These descriptions addressed to the "tongue of deceit" denounce evil behavior in the language of the prophets (cf. Jer 4:22, 9:4).

The conjunction "Yet" introduces God's reaction to the deceitful man, expressed in four strong verbs: God will pull him down forever, take him away, tear him out from his tent, uproot him from the land of the living (v. 7; cf. Ps 27:13). Rejection or manipulation of the truth has no future in the eyes of God who created man to enjoy life by averring truth. When the just see the evil man's fate, they will both "fear" (cf. Ps 40:4 for Hebrew pun on "see" and "fear") and "laugh" (cf. Pss 2:4, 37:13) at the execution of divine justice (v. 8). They will taunt the man for not making God his "fortress" (cf. Pss 27:1, 28:8, 31:5), for trusting in the "abundance of his riches" (cf. Ps 49:7, Prov 11:28), and for resorting to ruin[ous plots] (v. 9; cf. v. 4). The man who builds his confidence on creatures rather than the Creator is building on sand.

To the annihilation of the man of deceit the psalmist opposes his own flourishing, like an olive tree (cf. Ps 1:3, Jer 17:8), in the house of God; his "trust" has been placed not in ephemeral riches (cf. v. 9) but in the *ḥesed* (cf. v. 3) of God forever (v. 10), the *ḥesed* available to man in God's house (cf. Ps 48:10), which for Christians is the Body of Christ, from which man draws life like branches from a vine (John 15:4–5). After expressing his utter confidence the speaker vows to praise the God who has "done" these things; he will wait on God's name—for it is good—in the presence of God's devout ones (v. 11)—again a reference to the divine name without that name being used in the psalm (cf. Pss 44, 45).

The psalm cannot be classified as a lament in spite of the description of the man of deceit (vv. 3–6), since there is no petition for deliverance. Like a wisdom psalm it teaches the outcome of dishonest behavior, yet it also expresses the psalmist's trust in God and his personal thanksgiving for God's support of the just and his foiling of the deceitful. It can be best described as the confident reproach of the just man to the man of deceit.

∾ Psalm 53   fool

The psalm is a duplicate of Psalm 14 with minor changes. The four occurrences of "Yahweh" in Psalm 14 are replaced by "God" in Psalm 53, and verse 6 reads differently in the two psalms. In its position after Psalm 52, the psalm highlights the origin of sinful actions in the foolish rejection of God (vv. 2, 5c; cf. Ps 52:9). The "no God" is reflected in the "not one who does good" (vv. 2, 4). While the speaker of Psalm 14 promised that the Lord would be a refuge for the poor just man, the speaker of Psalm 53 focuses on the punishment to be meted out to evildoers: they dread with a terror such as has never been, for "God will scatter the bones of those who encamp against you [their victim]; you will put them to shame for

God has rejected them," (v. 6) just as God removed and uprooted the man of deceit in Psalm 52:7.

∼ Psalm 54   attributes

In this short model of an individual lament the speaker invokes divine attributes to support his call for help. The speaker asks to be "saved" by the divine "name" (v. 3), which he in turn will "thank . . . for it is good" (v. 8; cf. Ps 52:11). He asks that he be given judgment through God's "might." May God hear his prayer (cf. Pss 39:13, 17:1, 6:10, 4:2) and listen to the words of his mouth (v. 4). These petitions are explained by the lament in verse 5: "proud men" (corrected from Hebrew "strangers" in accordance with identical verse in Ps 86:14) have risen against the psalmist, and "ruthless" men (cf. Ezek 28:7, 30:11, 31:12, 32:12) "seek [his] soul" (cf. Pss 35:4, 38:13, 40:15; the same expression in 1 Sam 23:15 explains the attribution of this psalm to David's sojourn among the Ziphites, 1 Sam 23:19 [v. 2]). As in the two preceding psalms the root of criminal behavior is the failure to set God before oneself (cf. Pss 52:9, 53:5). But God is the psalmist's helper, the Master who is with those who "uphold" (cf. Pss 3:6, 37:17, 24) the "soul" (v. 6) that the violent seek (cf. v. 5). May God turn the evil against the adversaries, in his "faithfulness" silence them (v. 7). With a voluntary offering the speaker will sacrifice to the Lord, thanking his name (v. 8). For from all distress the Lord (third person) will have rescued him, and over his enemies his eye will gloat (v. 9; cf. Pss 37:34, 112:8).

The thought of the psalmist pierces like an arrow from a frank portrayal of proud and violent foes to the strong and faithful helper who upholds his life and overturns the attackers. The rescue of the psalmist culminates in a thanksgiving sacrifice (cf. Ps 50:14, 23). So Christ at the Supper gave thanks to the Father (Luke 22:17–20, 1 Cor 11:23–25) for the victory over violent men to be obtained on the cross, offering himself as a voluntary sacrifice (Heb 9:14, 10:12, John 10:18) for the destruction of sin (Heb 9:26–28). His prayer was heard because of his unflinching adherence to God (Heb 5:7), which led him to "disregard the shamefulness" of the cross in his ascent to the Father's right hand (Heb 12:2). Christians pray this psalm with Christ and at the same time pray to him as the forerunner whose path through death to life we follow (cf. Heb 12:2–4).

Light variations in meter give energy to the psalm. While the first colon of each verse has three beats, verses 3 and 7 have two beats in the second colon, verses 4, 6, and 9 have three, and verse 8 has four. Verse 5 has three cola of three beats each.

∼ PSALM 55   dove

Like the speaker of Psalm 35, the psalmist has been betrayed by friends; people with whom he once worshipped have turned against him (vv. 13–15, 21). He sees iniquity everywhere in the city (vv. 7–9) and expresses a poignant wish to escape (vv. 10–12). The psalm contains several words used only once in the psalter (nine words†) or once in the Old Testament (eight words*). While several verses fall into the 3 + 2 meter, verses in other meters are also found. These features, together with a fluctuation between singular and plural in speaking of the oppressor(s) and unexplained switches in verb tenses, give the psalm a feeling of nervous disorder.

The opening cry, "Give ear, God, to my prayer," echoes Psalm 54:4; it is matched by a negative imperative: "and do not remain secret [cf. Ps 10:1] at my plea" (v. 2). After asking God to attend to him and answer (v. 3a), the speaker launches into his lament: he "roams about" (translation uncertain), moaning in complaint (v. 3b) at the voice of an enemy, at the wicked man's pressure*; people encumber him with injustice and in anger harbor animosity† against him (v. 4). As a result, his heart "writhes" (cf. Jer 4:19) "within" him, and horrors of death fall on him (v. 5). Fear and trembling† come upon him, and shuddering† covers him (v. 6; cf. Ezek 7:18).

The speaker asked who would give him (cf. same formula in Ps 53:7) pinions† like a dove so that he could fly away and rest (v. 7). The metaphor suggests helplessness and vulnerability, perhaps also innocence. He would flee far away (as another psalmist was advised to do, cf. Ps 11:1) and "spend the night in the desert" (v. 8; cf. Jer 9:1), hastening to find safety* "from wind" of slander* and "from storm" (v. 9; cf. Ezek 1:4, 13:11, 13). He would have the Master "swallow [them] up" and "split their tongues" (v. 10a). Moving out from his subjective pain, he sees "violence" and dispute in the city (v. 10b; cf. Jer 6:7), day and night encircling it on the walls (v. 11); injustice (cf. v. 4) and toil (same pair in Ps 10:7) are "within" it (cf. v. 5), ruin (cf. Ps 52:4) too is "within it" (v. 12), and from its public square (cf. Jer 5:1) do not depart† "oppression [cf. Ps 10:7] and fraud" (Jer 9:5). In the last three verses the vices are paired; their presence in the Jerusalem before the Exile is noted in the preaching of Jeremiah.

But the deepest pain of the psalmist is that it is not an enemy who has scorned him or one who hates him who has dominated him—the former he could bear, and the latter he could hide from (v. 13). "But you, a man like my counterpart, my confidant and acquaintance [v. 14], who joined me in companionship [lit. "we made sweet† the circle together"] as we walked in the house of God among the throng*!" (v. 15). From this pain arises a single verse of petition (v. 16): may death catch them by surprise†, may they descend to Sheol alive (cf. Num 16:30, 33) because of the evils in the chambers* "within" them (cf. vv. 5, 11, 12). The psalmist has passed from the turmoil within himself through the disorder within the city to the evils within the traitors themselves, and wishes the evils to be obliterated. It is for this that he calls to God (v. 17), for the Lord will save him. Three times a day—evening, morning, and noon—he ponders and churns, and the Lord heard his voice (v. 18, tense change in Hebrew), ransoming his soul in peace from war, although many were against him (v. 19).

But the peace is short-lived: the psalmist is not yet rid of his antagonists and must ask that God hear (cf. v. 18) and humble them (v. 20), including the "dweller in the east" (Babylonian captors?; the phrase is sometimes translated "he who is enthroned from of old," referring to God). These folk do not change nor do they fear God (cf. Ps 52:8). The speaker is haunted by the thought of the former companion, who has thrust his hand against his "peace-mates" and profaned his covenant with them (v. 21). Smooth were the buttery* things, but war (cf. v. 19) was in his heart; his words were gentler† than oil but were open blades* (v. 22; cf. the flattering hypocrisy of the scribes and lawyers, Luke 20:20–21). Verse 23 presents an example of such words: "Cast on the Lord your burden* and he will take care of you; he will never allow the just man to totter." Only a determined act of trust in God can resolve the psalmist's torment: the final verse (24) opens with a "But you" parallel to the one that opened the address to the friend/enemy in verse 14: "But you, God, will bring them down" (cf. v. 16) to the pit of the grave. "Men of blood" (cf. Ezek 22:1–12) and "deceit" (cf. v. 12) will not have half† their days. The psalmist's part is not to seek escape but simply to "trust" in God (cf. Ps

52:10) in the midst of oppression. He in fact does what the adversaries hypocritically advised him to do. This trust is the true confounding of the foes because it enables God's "salvation" (cf. v. 16) to be brought into play. It is through adherence to Christ that personal and social evil are overcome.

~ PSALM 56   tears

The psalmist's distress is overshadowed by his trust in God, expressed in similar language near the beginning (vv. 4–5) and near the end (vv. 10–12) of the psalm. Verses of lament precede the expressions of trust, and the psalm ends with vows of praise (vv. 13–14). The 3 + 3 meter predominates with extra beats in verses 2, 7–10, and 13.

Like the first psalm in this second Davidic collection, the prayer begins with the plea for mercy (v. 2; cf. Ps 51:3), although the psalm makes no mention of the need for forgiveness of sin; "mercy" is here understood in the sense of "take pity on me in my distress." The word provides the root of the noun translated "plea" (e.g., for mercy or help) at the beginning of the previous psalm (55:2), and thus a link is formed between the psalms. The speaker addresses his plea to "God" ("Yahweh" will be used once in the psalm, v. 11) and immediately describes his situation: men "hound" him (cf. Ezek 36:3); all day long they do battle, they "press" him (cf. Exod 3:9, Deut 26:7, Judg 6:9, 10:12). In verse 3 he repeats several words of verse 2: his adversaries "hound" him "all day long"; many "battle" against him proudly (or from on high, i.e., to bring him down). The terms allude to typical comparisons of enemies to devouring animals and to armies. But "on the day" when he "fears," he tells God he trusts in him (v. 4). The statement is amplified in verse 5, which speaks of God in the third person: "In God, whose word I praise, in God I trust and do not fear [cf. v. 4]; what can flesh [= man, cf. Jer 17:5] do against me?" The verse is a tricolon with three beats per colon. The ground of the speaker's trust is the word of God, which he celebrates in worship, the word by which God pledged himself to Israel. The speaker may have in mind texts like Second Isaiah with their frequent admonitions not to fear (e.g., Isa 41:10, 14, 43:1, 5, 44:2, 54:4).

A second movement returns to the lament and carries it further: "All day long" (cf. v. 3) they hurt him with words; all their designs are for evil

(v. 6). They lurk and "spy" (cf. Ps 10:8), observing his tracks (like hunters) as they wait for his "soul" (i.e., to take his life; v. 7). But this brief evocation of the enemies' murderous intent gives way to new expressions of confidence and two petitions. The psalmist asks, "In their injustice can there be any safety for them?," implying that evil cannot lead to good. This expression of confidence is matched by the petition: "in anger bring down the peoples, O God" (v. 8). The blurring of the psalmist's enemies with the enemies of Israel was found in Psalms 7 and 9-10. In attacking the psalmist the enemies are no better than pagans who do not know Israel's God. The Christian too is attacked by "many" (cf. v. 3) enemies: a godless culture, the faults of others, his own negative thoughts, evil spirits who inhabit "the air" (cf. Eph 2:2); whether he calls them "peoples" or "armies" or "adversaries" or "lurkers," he confidently asks God to "bring them down" (cf. Ps 55:16, 24) to the underworld. Verse 9 follows the same pattern of confidence followed by petition. Since God has taken account of his "wandering," the psalmist asks, "Place my tears [cf. Ps 42:4] in your leather bottle; are they not in your book?" The image implies that God cares about every suffering of the one who trusts him and calls for help; as verse 10a puts it, surely the psalmist's enemies will turn back.

It is time to restate the expression of confidence of verses 4–5 with some changes. Verse 10b speaks of God in the third person: "On the day I call, this I know, that God is for me." After repeating the initial phrase of verse 5, verse 11 adds, "In Yahweh whose word I praise," and verse 12 repeats the second part of verse 5, substituting "man" for "flesh." The similar statements of confidence are two pillars that provide the framework of the psalm.

The speaker directly addresses God: "Your vows are on me" (v. 13); he will pay these by offering the thanksgiving sacrifice (cf. Ps 50:14, 23). For God rescued his "soul" (cf. v. 7) from death; did he not [rescue] his feet from stumbling so that he might walk before God in the light of the living (v. 14)? Stumbling and wandering have turned into walking, the threat of death into life, the presence of enemies into the presence of God, and the obscurity of fear into light. In the light of the risen Christ the demons are scattered, fear is dispelled, life triumphs over death.

∼ PSALM 57   dawn

As confidence overshadowed lament in Psalm 56, praise eclipses both confidence and lament in Psalm 57. The psalmist is beset by "lions" whose teeth are "swords," but his confidence in the Lord's love and faithfulness (*ḥesed* and *'ĕmet*, vv. 4, 11) inspires an exuberant morning song of praise.

The cry for mercy (cf. Ps 56:2) is here doubled, creating a sense of urgency (v. 2). In his comment on this opening cry Saint Augustine provides a terse summary of the double role of Christ in the psalms: "He who, together with the Father, has mercy on you is crying out in you, 'Have mercy on me.'" (*Enarrationes in Psalmos* 56.5). The psalmist's "soul" (cf. Ps 56:7, 14) "takes refuge" in God—the first appearance of this verb in Book Two (cf. noun in Ps 46:2). The verb is repeated in the second half of the verse: the speaker takes refuge in the shadow of God's wings (cf. Pss 17:8, 36:8) until ruin (cf. Pss 52:4, 9, 55:12; half the occurrences of this word in the psalter occur in these three psalms) passes by. He calls to God (*'ēl*) Most High (*'elyôn*), to the God (*'ĕlōhîm*) who has ended [evil] for him (v. 3); although three different designations for God are used in the verse, the divine name is conspicuous by its absence. The note of intimacy may be missing, but the august transcendence of the divine "refuge" is emphasized. The speaker confidently expects (or asks—the imperfect tense can have both meanings) that God will send from heaven and "save" him (cf. Pss 54:3, 55:17); the one who "hounds" him (cf. Ps 56:2–3) scorns, or as some render the obscure text, God will revile the one who hounds the speaker (v. 4). In any case, the verse repeats the verb "send," now adding an object: God will send his love and faithfulness, his two principal and often-paired attributes that frequently accompany the use of his name (cf. Pss 40:12, 36:6, 26:2–3, 25:10, Exod 34:6).

From these expressions of confidence and, to a lesser extent, petition, the psalmist moves into his lament. He finds his "soul" (cf. v. 2) lying down (suggesting night?) in the midst of devouring lions (v. 5), that is, men whose teeth are like spears and arrows, whose tongue is a sharp sword (the Hebrew uses consonance: *šinnêhem ḥănît wĕḥiṣṣîm ûlĕšônām ḥereb ḥaddāh*). As in other psalms in this second Davidic collection, the enemies' chief weapons are cruel and murderous words (cf. Pss 52:4–6, 55:22, 59:8, 13, 64:4). But the lament has scarcely begun when it is interrupted by praise: "Be exalted above the heavens, God; over all the earth be your glory" (v. 6, chiasmus). It is God's asserting of his lordship over the world that will end the abuse of the foes. The next verse (v. 7) in 3 + 2 meter shows the defeat of the enemy: a net they readied for the speaker's steps, pressed down his "soul" (cf. vv. 2, 5); they dug in front of him a pitfall, but they fell into it (cf. Pss 7:16, 35:8). In two verses (5 and 7) the full gamut of images for enemies—wild beasts, armies, and hunters—is represented.

The remainder of the psalm is praise. The speaker's heart is poised (same verb as "readied" in v. 7), he tells God (v. 8), his heart is poised to "sing and make music" (same verb pair in Ps 33:2–3). He calls on his own strength (lit. "glory," cf. vv. 6, 12!) to rouse itself (reflexive), and on harp and lyre (cf. this pair in Ps 33:2, 1 Kgs 10:12) to rouse themselves; with these he will rouse (transitive) the dawn itself (v. 9). He will thank the Master among the "peoples" (cf. Ps 56:8), make music to him among the races (v. 10, 3 + 2 meter). The grounds for praise (as in a mini-hymn) is given in verse 11, a near repetition of Psalm 36:6: "For great to the skies is your love, and to the clouds your faithfulness." The placing of these two divine attributes near the beginning and end of the psalm recalls the similar structure in the previous psalm (cf. Ps 56:4–5, 10–12). The combination of "dawn," "waking," "be exalted," and "heavens" naturally evokes the image of God as the sun, whose rays will scatter sinister plotters, and reminds us both of the "light of the living" with which the previous psalm ended and of Saint Paul's hymn in Ephesians: "Wake up from your sleep, rise from the dead, and Christ will shine on you" (Eph 5:14). The psalm is thus appropriate for the Church's Morning Prayer.

The prayer ends with a repetition of the praise verse that interrupted the lament in verse 6: "Be exalted above the heavens, God; over all the earth be your glory" (v. 12).

∾ PSALM 58   snake

The strangeness and violence of its images have earned this psalm exclusion from the Roman Liturgy of the Hours, along with Psalms 83 and 109. Communities who recite the whole psalter need to find a way to pray the psalm comfortably as Christians. It is a strong plea for justice on earth and for the definitive elimination of the injustice that has been and is so much a part of human history. Vehement and earthy language is not inappropriate if we apply our petition to the destruction of injustice in the human heart and the conversion of the unjust. What is at stake is whether "there is a God who does justice on earth" (v. 12). The weighty 4 + 4 meter with mostly synonymous parallelism governs the psalm.

As in Psalm 52 the psalmist begins with a question to perpetrators of evil, here the "gods," that is, earthly judges with divinely ordained power: "Do you truly speak justice? Do you judge uprightly the sons of men?" (v. 2). He answers his own question: "In fact in your heart you produce perversity; on earth for the violence [cf. Ps 55:10] of your hands you make a smooth path" (v. 3). Switching to third person, he declares how the wicked have erred from the womb (v. 4); the speakers of falsehood have gone astray from the [mother's] belly. They have a history of perversity in thought, word, and deed. In two ways they are like snakes (v. 5): they have a destructive venom, and like a deaf asp they stop their ears. Verse 6 explains the latter image: they do not listen to the voice of charmers (same root as the "whisperers" of Ps 41:8), of the skilled conjurer of spells (4 + 3 meter): the result of their deafness to the truth is the poisoning of people's lives.[5]

The psalmist now calls on "God" in petition: first that he demolish the teeth in their mouths (cf. Ps 3:8), then, in a new image, that the jaws of the "young lions" (v. 7, different word in Ps 57:5) he break (v. 7, chiasmus); the verse ends with the name "Yahweh" to balance "God" at the beginning—the only use of the divine name in the psalm. The wicked are then likened to four things that vanish quickly: running water (v. 8), the grass one treads on (correction of a corrupt text), a snail that disintegrates as it goes (v. 9), a woman's miscarriage that doesn't gaze on the sun (cf. Qoh 6:3–5). The petition concludes with a difficult verse (10) that seems to mean: "Before your cauldrons [for eating the helpless, cf. Mic 3:3] are aware of the thornbush [fuel with which they are stoked], may he sweep them away in a storm [cf. Ps 50:3, Job 27:21, Dan 11:40],

---

5. Saint Augustine applies the verse to the persecutors of Stephen who "stopped their ears" from hearing the "charmer" (*incantatorem*) with hearts "harder than the stones with which they stoned" him (*Enarrationes in Psalmos* 57.8; cf. Acts 7:57–58).

like a living one, like wrath." The verse matches verse 7: the two violent petitions enclose the four images of disintegration.

Sure that his prayer will be answered, the speaker envisions the "just man" (cf. v. 2) being glad when he "gazes on" (cf. v. 9) vengeance (v. 11) and, in a lurid image, washes his feet (lit. "steps") in the blood of the "wicked" (cf. v. 4; cf. also 1 Kgs 22:38). At this point men will say, "Indeed there is a reward for the just [cf. v. 11]; truly there is a God who judges on earth" (v. 12). The words "judge" and "earth" link the final verse to the opening verses (2–3): the justice of God has replaced the injustice of man on earth.

The cloak of Christ, rider of the white horse, the Word of God, a "judge with integrity, a warrior for justice" is stained with the blood of those whose evil he has destroyed (Rev 19:11–16).

∾ PSALM 59   dogs

The psalmist is beset by attackers whom he vividly compares to dogs roaming the city at night, howling and searching for food. But as in Psalms 56 and 57 he is reassured by the knowledge of a God of love who will not permit evil to prevail.

Two verses, each beginning with the same verb and each in chiastic form, introduce the prayer: "Rescue me from my enemies, God; from my attackers set me on high. Rescue me from those who do evil, and from men of blood [cf. Ps 55:24] save me" (vv. 2–3). The second half of verse 2 introduces the theme of God as a high place of refuge (cf. vv. 10, 18), while the second half of verse 3 hints at the savagery of the enemies, which will be developed with the image of the wild dogs (cf. vv. 7–8, 15–16). The enemies "lie in ambush" (cf. Ps 10:9) for the speaker's soul; against him gather powerful men though he is guilty of no "rebellion," "sin" (v. 4), or "iniquity" (v. 5)—the three main words for transgression in the psalter (see on Ps 32:2–3; see also Ps 51:3–4). At the end of verse 4 the psalmist addresses the Lord by name as if to claim a special intimacy with him. After a brief reference to the enemy "running" and drawing themselves up, he erupts in mid-verse into petition: "Rouse yourself [cf. Ps 7:7] to meet me and see" (v. 5). He calls on Yahweh, God of hosts, the God of Israel, "Awake" (the verb accompanies "rouse yourself" also in Pss 35:23 and 44:24) for calling the "nations" to account and having no mercy on all who unjustly break faith (v. 6). Once again the faithless Israelites are no better than pagan nations (cf. Ps 56:8), and behind both is a God of justice.

The speaker's attention is drawn back to the attackers (v. 7), who return in the evening, churn like dogs (cf. Ps 22:17) and prowl around the city (2 + 2 + 2 meter). They surround the city like besiegers but are kept out by the city walls, while in Psalm 54:10–12 it is the city itself that is full of violence and strife, wickedness and evil, oppression and deceit. The speaker imagines how the animals slaver (lit. "bubble forth") at the mouth, with "swords" behind their lips, for they assume no one can hear them (v. 8). The terse description combines images from war and the world of wild animals to connote the deadly words that spew from the attackers' mouths (cf. Pss 52:4, 55:22, 57:5). But again the speaker's eyes are raised above the dark scene (v. 9): "But you, Lord, will laugh [cf. Pss 2:4, 37:13, 52:8] at them; you deride all the nations" (cf. v. 6). Whether the attackers be Israelites or foreigners, their murderous cruelty is powerless against those whom God protects. Accordingly the first half of the psalm ends with a prayer of confidence: "O my strength, toward you I keep guard, for God is my high refuge" (v. 10).

The psalmist begins and ends the second half of his prayer with the expression "The God who loves me" (lit. "the God of my love," vv. 11 and 18). This God will go before him and make him gloat (cf. Ps 54:9) over his adversaries (v. 11). The psalmist asks God not to kill them lest his people forget, but in his vigor to make them wander and bring them down (v. 12); he addresses God as "our shield, my Master." This petition makes sense if the speaker is thinking of the enemies as pagan nations: he asks that they be not killed but brought low and scattered as a constant reminder of God's victory. The petition in the following verse has more in mind the false accusers of the psalmist: for the "sin" (cf. v. 4) of their "mouth" (cf. v. 8) and the word of their "lips" (cf. v. 8) may they be caught in their pride, as well as for the curses (cf. Ps 10:7) and untruthfulness they utter (v. 13). The psalmist prays, in contrast to the petition of verse 12, "Finish them off in fury, finish them off until there is nothing left of them"; may they know that God is ruler in Jacob and to the ends of the earth (v. 14). Again the enemy is seen as transcending the limits of the city and including pagan nations (cf. on Ps 56:8): in this way the psalm achieves both specific detail and universal application.

Before the final expression of confidence the image of the howling and roaming dogs (cf. v. 7) is repeated (v. 15) with an addition: they prowl for food but will not be sated; they "spend the night" (cf. Ps 55:8 for less sinister use of this verb). But the psalmist will sing of God's "strength" (cf. v. 10) and shout with joy of God's *hesed* in the "morning" when the perils of the previous night will evaporate (v. 16). For the Lord is his high refuge and a secure place on the day of his distress (v. 17). The psalm ends with a near repetition of verse 10: "My strength, to you I make music, for God is my high refuge, the God of my love" (v. 18).

Of the last four psalms, three have ended with allusions to light: "the light of the living" (Ps 56:14), ". . . awake the dawn . . . arise above the heavens" (Ps 57:9, 12), ". . . each morning acclaim your love" (Ps 59:17). God is the light who dispels the darkness of human treachery. The resurrection of Christ scatters the demonic forces. The note of confidence predominates in these four psalms, just as lament predominated in the previous four (Pss 52–55). The psalms within the two groups are also connected by shared titles or superscriptions: *maśkîl,* "wisdom song," in Psalms 52–55; *miktām,* "letter [to God?]," in Psalms 56–59. The final line of Psalm 55, "O Lord, I will trust in you," is both a resolution of the problems posed in the foregoing laments and an announcement of the dominant mood and theme of the psalms that follow.

∼ Psalm 60   Edom

A heartfelt community lament follows on the succession of individual laments. Three verbs express Israel's experience that God has "rejected" (cf. Ps 44:10, 23), "broken down" and "been angry with" them; a fourth verb in the imperative calls on him to "return" to them (v. 3). It is not just a matter of defeat in battle: God has made the earth itself "quake" and has split it; the corresponding petition is that he "heal" it, for it is tottering (v. 4). The two verbs of verse 5 present a different image: God has made his people see hardships and drink a wine that made them stagger (v. 5; cf. Jer 25:15, Isa 51:17, 22). The rout by the enemy has disrupted the stability of Israel's world. Verse 6 can be read as a petition: "Give those who fear you a banner [rallying point] for fleeing from the enemy's bow." An individual speaker asks that in order that God's "beloved" be delivered, God "save" with his right hand and "answer" him

(v. 7). The three designations of Israel in verses 4–6 together define her particular status: loved by God, honoring his lordship, constituting his people. This communion of God and people is the heart of Old Testament faith.

God's answer comes immediately as he speaks from his "holy place" (v. 8). The oracle expresses God's control over both Israel (vv. 8–9) and the neighboring nations (v. 10). In this it is similar to the expressions of confidence in Psalms 56:10–12, 58:11–12, 59:9, 11. Like a conqueror God will "exult" (v. 8) as he divides up Shechem and measures out the Valley of Succoth (places identified with Jacob, father of the Israelites; cf. Gen 33:17–18). To him belongs Gilead, to him Manasseh, while Ephraim is the defense of his head and Judah his scepter (v. 9; together the tribes of Ephraim and Manasseh composed a major part of the northern kingdom, and part of Manasseh inhabited Gilead across the Jordan). Leadership is ascribed to the southern kingdom of Judah. The surrounding nations are allotted subservient roles by God: Moab will be a bowl for his washing, he will appropriate Edom by casting his sandal on its land, he summons Philistia to honor him with the jubilant cry (v. 10). These specific places are symbols of all geographical areas that are to be brought under the sway of Christ (cf. Rev 19:15–16, 21:24–26).

If this world rule is God's plan, the individual speaker, who appears to be a military leader, wishes to know who will bring him to the fortified city of the enemy and lead him to Edom (v. 11), the country that administered the defeat described in the title of the psalm (vv. 1–2). For has not God rejected (cf. v. 3) his people, no longer accompanying its hosts (v. 12)? The speaker must ask God to give the people help in their distress, since worthless is the salvation that comes from man (v. 13). A confident verse in 3 + 3 meter concludes the psalm: "In God we will do powerfully, and he will tread down [cf. Ps 44:6] our oppressors" (v. 14).

The oracle in verses 8–10 can be seen as grounding the petitions for God's victory over the nations in Psalms 56:8 and 59:6, 9, 14. The psalm shares with Psalms 56–59 the title *miktām* (cf. v. 1).

ᔛ Psalm 61   tower

The Son who dwells in the bosom of the Father (John 1:18) prays with longing that the members of his body share in the same inseparable unity he enjoys with the Father. In his risen humanity he already dwells in the Father's tent (presence) forever, yet in his members on earth he does not yet fully enjoy that presence. He asks God to hear his lamentation, to attend to his prayer (v. 2; cf. Ps 17:1), calling from the end of the earth when his heart is faint (v. 3a).[6] He asks God to "lead" (cf. Ps 60:11) him to the rock too high for him (v. 3b), for God has been his "refuge," his "tower of strength" (cf. Prov 18:10 where it is the "name" of Yahweh that is the tower of strength; see vv. 6 and 9 of our psalm) in the face of the enemy (v. 4). The images of rock, tower, and refuge already connote the security of the temple, an association that becomes more explicit in the following verse (5) with the mention of God's "tent" (cf. Ps 27:5) where the psalmist is sure of sojourning forever and where he will "take refuge" (cf. v. 4) in the hiding place of his "wings" (cf. Pss 17:8, 36:8, 57:2). For God has "heard" (inclusion with v. 2) the psalmist's vows (v. 6); he has given the inheritance of those who "fear [cf. Ps 60:6] [his] name" (cf. Ps 86:11). The Christ who is one with the Father longs to share this unity with his people.

Not content to pray for his own dwelling in the temple of God, the speaker asks for God's blessing on the reigning king, whose task it is to ensure that the temple remain the place where God and man can meet. In praying the psalm Christ thus prays that this union be brought about through the messiah, that is, himself. If God adds days to the king's days and makes his years last for generations (v. 7), the king will become the permanent means by which God and people are united. In this way the images of temple and king coalesce: Christ is the temple where God and man are joined and he is the king who makes his people one in himself.

---

6. Reading the plural "ends" of the earth with the LXX, Augustine sees the single person of Christ calling to the Father in his Body spread over the earth:

> The psalm speaks as though one single person is praying; but it is not a lone individual, it is a unity, speaking as one. In Christ we all form one human person, whose head is in heaven and whose limbs are toiling on earth. . . . How can a single individual call from the ends of the earth? One person can, though, because what is shouting is the heritage promised to the Son in another psalm: *Ask of me, and I will give you the nations as your heritage, and the ends of the earth for your possession* (Ps 2:8). This possession of Christ, this heritage of Christ, this body of Christ, this one Church of Christ, this unity that we are–this is what shouts from the ends of the earth. (*Enarrationes in Psalmos* 60.1–2)

A similar merging of the two images is found in the Letter to the Hebrews: "Christ was faithful as a son, and as the master in the house. And we are his house as long as we cling to our hope with the confidence that we glory in" (Heb 3:6). The psalmist asks that the king will sit (cf. Matt 25:31, Mark 16:19, Heb 1:3, Rev 3:21) "forever" (cf. v. 5) in the presence of God (v. 8), as does Jesus the eternal king (1 Tim 6:14–16). May God appoint his supreme attributes, covenant love and faithfulness (*ḥesed* and *ʾĕmet*; cf. Pss 57:11, 40:12), to protect the king.

Christians reign in Christ; inserted in him, they enjoy the same relationship he has with the Father: "The personal relation of the Son to the Father is something that man cannot conceive of nor the angelic powers even dimly see: and yet, the Spirit of the Son grants a participation in that very relation to us who believe that Jesus is the Christ and that we are born of God" (*Catechism of the Catholic Church* 2780). In terms of our psalm, it is the king who ensures the dwelling of the psalmist in God. For this reason the speaker will "make music" (cf. Ps 57:8, 10) to God's "name" (cf. v. 6) forever, paying his "vows" (cf. v. 6, Ps 56:13) "day by day" (v. 9; cf. v. 7). It is in Christ that we dwell in God's temple, praising the Father eternally.

The verses illustrate several different meters: 3 + 2 (v. 2), 2 + 2 + 2 + 4 (v. 3), 3 + 3 (vv. 4 and 5), 4 + 4 (vv. 6 and 8), 4 + 3 (vv. 7 and 9). The tight unity of the psalm is achieved by the several word repetitions.

∾ Psalm 62   only

Trust prevails in the psalm, the speaker communing first with himself (vv. 2–3, 5–8) with a brief interruption to address his attackers (v. 4), then giving advice to his people (vv. 9–13).

"Only in God is there stillness for my soul; from him is my salvation" (v. 2). Man's soul, that is, man as "emotional, combative, vulnerable, hungry for life" (Hossfeld and Zenger, *Die Psalmen*, 2:375), is restless: his "only" rest is in God. The opening word will be a leitmotif for the psalm: Only God is man's recourse, dishonest men plan only to destroy, earthly resources are only emptiness, salvation is from God alone. "Only" he (v. 3) is the psalmist's "rock" (cf. Pss 18:3, 28:1, 31:3), his "salvation" (cf. Pss 27:1, 35:3, 38:23), his "high refuge" (cf. Pss 18:3, 59:10, 17, 18). The three epithets move from concrete to abstract to an image that combines the two. With God offering this security the psalmist will not greatly "totter" (cf. Pss 16:8, 55:23, 60:4).

The speaker then turns to a group who are threatening him, asking how long they will overwhelm a man with disaster, all seeking to murder him, treating him like a leaning rampart, a knocked over stone wall (v. 4). The images contrast starkly with the security expressed in the earlier verses. The speaker now reflects on these same attackers in the third person: they take counsel only to bring him down from his elevated position (v. 5; cf. similar image in Ps 61:3); they take pleasure in falsehood (cf. Ps 58:4): with their mouth they bless but within they curse (cf. same idea in Ps 55:22). Returning to himself, the psalmist varies his opening line, telling his soul to be still only in God (v. 6) since from him is his hope. Verse 3 is now repeated without the final word "greatly" (v. 7). A final confession of faith opens and closes with the word "God": "In God is my salvation and my glory, the rock [cf. v. 3] of my strength [cf. Ps 61:4]; my refuge [cf. Ps 61:4] is in God" (v. 8). Since "glory" is the manifestation of the psalmist's dignity among men, the verse provides a neat transition to the teaching section of the psalm.

Fortified by his divine bulwark the psalmist can turn to the "people" (v. 9), exhorting them to trust in God at all times, to pour out before him their hearts, for God is "a refuge for us" (cf. Ps 46:2). He invites his countrymen to make the same experience of God's protection as he has done. The rest of the psalm will adopt the teaching mode we have seen in trust (e.g., Ps 4), thanksgiving (e.g., Ps 34), and wisdom (e.g., Ps 36) psalms. In exhorting his hearers to "pour out [their] hearts" before God, the speaker is thinking of what occurs in most of the lament psalms: a sincere depiction of personal trials with an urgent and confident plea to the God of Israel for help. For, the teacher explains, "Only vanity" (cf. Ps 39:6, 12, Qoh 6:12, 7:15, 8:10) are the sons of men, falsehood (cf. v. 5) important persons; they are placed in the scales to rise, the sum of them nothing but vanity (v. 10, same word at beginning and end). The unusual (for the Psalms) image of the scales (cf. Isa 40:15) matches the singular image of the tottering walls in verse 4. The speaker specifies what his people should *not* trust in, namely, exploitation, nor should they engage in empty robbery (v. 11); when wealth abounds they should not put their hearts (cf. v. 9) in it (cf. Matt 6:19–21).

The psalm ends in the style of the wise man, first speaking of God and then addressing him: one thing God has said, two the psalmist has heard; "for strength belongs to God [v. 12] and to you, Master, love, for you repay [cf. Pss 56:13, 61:9] each man according to his works" (v. 13). The conclusion neatly summarizes the assumptions behind the psalm: it is God's love that makes his divine power available as a refuge; trust in this God leads to salvation, reliance on anything else leads to emptiness. It was the power (Eph 1:19–20) and the love (Eph 2:4–6) of God that raised Jesus from the dead and gave us a place in him. The last line of the psalm, quoted in Romans 2:6 and Revelation 22:12 (cf. also Matt 16:27, Isa 3:11) is the most concise formulation of the principle behind all the psalms that speak of the condemnation of the wicked: God cannot save those who do not acknowledge the lordship of the author of life.

As in other individual trust psalms (e.g., Ps 4), the speaker, after expressing his personal trust in God, takes occasion to recommend this trust to his entourage. The "my refuge" of the first section (v. 8) becomes the "our refuge" at the beginning of the second (v. 9). Thus a "community of trust" is formed (Hossfeld and Zenger, *Die Psalmen*, 2:373). Christ incorporates us into his own absolute trust in the Father (Heb 2:13, 1 Pet 2:23).

∼ PSALM 63   thirsting

Although the psalm is classified as an individual lament, it lacks the element of petition, and the lament is less a portrayal of suffering than a fervent meditation on what God means to the psalmist. God is everything for him: divinity, object of longing, food and drink, life, love, strength, glory, object of praise, joy, protection, meditation, help, intimacy. The psalm is brief, but the psalmist's heart overflows with expressions of the richness he finds in God. Praise is woven into the "lament," which concludes with expressions of trust in God's saving action. The psalm is addressed to God, the words "you" or "your" occurring seventeen times in eight verses. The psalmist's whole being—soul and flesh, sight and hands, lips and mouth—is focused on God, finds its fulfilment "only in God," to use the phrase from the previous psalm.

In identifying God as "my God" (v. 2), the psalmist is making the infinite One his own, establishing a personal relationship with the infinite. He is appropriating the privilege God gave to his chosen people, that he would be their God and they would be his people (Lev 26:12, Exod 6:6, Ezek 36:28, etc.). The psalmist "is on the lookout for" (cf. Isa 26:9; the similarity of the Hebrew verb to the word for "dawn" led Saint Jerome to translate it "de luce vigilo," a translation that accounts for the use of the psalm at Morning Prayer) this God, his soul "thirsts" for him (cf. Ps 42:3, Isa 55:1, John 4:13–14, 7:37, Rev 21:6, 22:17), his flesh pines for him in a land parched and exhausted, without water; without God this world is a desert for him. The "soul" represents man as "a being that stretches out toward life as toward a precious indispensable gift" (Hossfeld and Zenger, *Die Psalmen,* 2:379) while "flesh" underscores man's weakness, his nothingness without God (cf. Job 34:14–15). Only in the temple (v. 3) where God dwells above the ark can the psalmist "gaze on" (cf. Pss 11:7, 27:4) God in order to see, that is, take in, his strength (cf. Pss 59:10, 17, 18, 61:4, 62:8, 12) and glory (cf. Ps 62:8). It is through dwelling in Christ that Christians experience the strength and the glory of God, and particularly his *ḥesed,* that gracious love that is the source of life itself (v. 4; cf. Ps 48:10).

This love is a more precious gift than even life: God's total affirmation of his creature is a richer experience for man than his experience of being alive: he who has the love of God has everything. Once again we encounter the principle everywhere evident in the psalter: man's life has no meaning apart from his relationship with his transcendent Creator. It is those who deny the "God connection" that founder, having separated themselves from the source of life and meaning. But the one who opens himself to the compassionate love of this God cannot hold in his joy: his lips must adore him. The psalmist will therefore use his "life" (cf. v. 4) to bless this God, lifting up his palms (cf. Ps 28:2) in God's name (v. 5), although the divine name itself is not used in the psalm. While the speaker's "soul" is sated as with "fat" and rich food, with lips (cf. v. 4) of joyful shouting his mouth will praise (v. 6). The imagery is appropriate since the word for soul originally means "throat," the organ of hunger. What satisfies the psalmist's hunger is precisely that praise of God for which he was made. In praising God he is fulfilled. For a similar conjunction of the themes of temple and banquet, along with that of *ḥesed,* see Psalms 23:5–6, 36:9; for the themes of banquet and praise see Psalm 22:27; for "beholding" as a "sating" see Psalm 17:15.

The psalmist remembers God even on his pallet, through the night watches murmuring on him (v. 7, chiasmus). Since he has experienced God as his helper (v. 8), he can sing joyfully (verb form of noun used in v. 6) in the "shadow of [God's] wings" (cf. Pss 17:8, 57:2, and esp. Ps 36:8, where "the shadow of your wings" is used in conjunction with God's presence in the temple). The psalmist's "soul" (cf. vv. 2, 6) "clings" (cf. Gen 2:24!, Deut 10:20) to God while God's right hand takes firm hold of him (v. 9; cf. Mark 9:27). This mutual spiritual "clinging" is expressed in gentle physical metaphors that give it substance. The sequel to the Deuteronomy passage just cited (Deut 10:21) forms an interesting parallel to our psalm: "He [Yahweh] is your praise [cf. Ps 63.4–6], he is your God [cf. Ps 63:2], for you he has done these great and terrible things you have seen with your own eyes" (cf. Ps 63:8). The psalmist might be making his own personal application of this exhortation of Moses to the people.

The "soul" that finds such fulfilment in God may be beset by those who seek his "annihilation" (v. 10; cf. Ps 35:8), but he is sure it is these who will go into the depths of the earth, brought down by war ("the edge of the sword") or becoming the share of foxes (v. 11; cf. Lam 5:18). Their power will be neutralized by the God who is the psalmist's strength. As in Psalm 61 the psalmist's relation with God will be guaranteed by the king, who "is glad" in God, enabling those who swear by him to "boast," for under his just reign the mouth of those who speak lies will be stopped up (v. 12). These final verses put the psalmist's intimate personal experience of God in a social context. It is that common relationship with God, both his own and the king's, that ensures the elimination of persecutors (cf. Rom 8:31, 35, 38–39).

For the Christian, the key motifs of the psalm—temple, thirst-quenching water, rich food (cf. John 6:55), glory (cf. 2 Cor 3:18), love, life (cf. John 6:54, 57)—coalesce in Christ, who both feeds on God (cf. John 4:34) and is bread of the hungry (John 6:35).

The psalm is in 3 + 3 meter with longer lines in verses 2, 6, 10, and 12.

∿ PSALM 64   arrows

Psalm 64 shares with the previous few psalms (Pss 56–63) a strong trust element. Although it begins as an individual lament, the speaker relates not his own suffering but a disorder in society in general, in the manner of Psalm 52, only to follow his "lament" with an account of God's thwarting of the plans of the evil. He is convinced that God will act to destroy evil and that men will rejoice in his victory. The "lesson" aspect of the psalm allies it with the wisdom literature. The basic meter is 3 + 3 with four-beat cola in verses 2 and 4. Tricola are found in verses 7b, 10, and 11, each with at least one colon of only two beats.

The psalmist asks God (v. 2) to hear his voice in his "complaining" (cf. Ps 55:3), to protect his life from terror of the enemy, who are described in verse 3 as the "circle [cf. Ps 55:15] of wrongdoers" and "restless evildoers." He wishes to be hidden from them and the turmoil they cause. The next four verses describe the hostile and destructive behavior of these men. As in other psalms in this second Davidic collection (cf. Pss 52:4–6, 55:22, 57:5) the enemies' weapon is the word, uttered with tongue sharpened like a sword, a bitter word aimed like an "arrow" (v. 4). They shoot at the blameless from hiding (cf. Pss 10:8, 9, 17:12), shoot suddenly and without fear (v. 5). They "firm up" their evil affair (v. 6), discuss how to lay "snares" (shift from military to hunting metaphors as in Ps 57:5–7) that none will be able to see. They contrive perverse things, [saying], "We will finish them off! The trick is well contrived; the innermost part of a man, the heart is profound" (v. 7), that is, too deep to be discovered. The Hebrew text of verse 7 makes most sense as the continuation of the evildoers' words, but it is emended by the Jerusalem Bible and the Grail to read as a reference to God as the searcher of hearts (cf. Jer 17:9).

Abruptly the psalmist shows that if an arrow is to be shot it is God who has shot it (cf. vv. 4–5) to strike the enemies with "sudden" (cf. v. 5) wounds (v. 8). The evil that men inflict on others is inflicted on them by God, who "repays each man according to his deeds" (Ps 62:13; cf. Matt 7:1). The destruction of life is a divorcing of oneself from the author of life, at least until one repents. It is the vicious man's own tongue (cf. v. 4) that has made him stumble (v. 9); all who "see" him (cf. v. 6) will shake their heads in mockery. And all men will "fear" (cf. v. 5) and publish the action of the Lord, and his works they will understand (v. 10, chiasmus). In portraying God acting "behind the scenes" the psalmist is both expressing his confidence in God's righteousness and disclosing this righteousness to others. In lieu of a vow of praise he concludes with the assurance that the just man will be glad (cf. Ps 63:12) in the Lord (first mention of the divine name since Ps 59:9) and take refuge (cf. Pss 61:4–5, 62:8–9) in him (v. 11), while all the upright of heart will glory (lit. "boast," cf. Pss 34:3, 63:12).

The psalmist makes deft use of irony by repeating in his account of God's retaliation several words—"tongue," "arrows," "shoot," "sudden," "fear," "see"—used in the description of the enemy's attacks.

The destruction of malicious persecutors is accomplished by the victorious Christ (Rev 19:21) from whose glorious city "everyone of false speech and false life" is excluded (Rev 22:15).

~ PSALM 65   harvest

If Psalm 64 celebrates God's overthrow of malicious evildoers, Psalm 65 is a magnificent hymn to his beneficent activity in the world. He hears prayer, forgives sin, satisfies hunger, works wonders, establishes the mountains, stills the seas, but above all irrigates the earth with abundant rain to provide fertile crops and pastures. Peoples and nature itself respond with shouts of ecstatic acclaim.

The psalm opens in Hebrew with an unusual phrase, "To you stillness is praise." God receives a kind of silent praise from his creation, but "in Zion," where one pays a vow, this praise is articulated (v. 2). To the "hearer of prayer" (v. 3; cf. Pss 54:4, 61:2) "all flesh will come" (cf. Isa 66:23). The burdens of iniquity are too strong for the psalmist; "our rebellions" God purges away (v. 4, asyndeton). Happy the man whom God chooses and allows to approach; he will inhabit God's courts. The psalmist and his companions are "sated" (cf. Ps 63:6) with the blessings of God's house, his holy temple (v. 5). Answering their prayer with fearsome [deeds] of justice, he is the God of their salvation, the trust of the "ends of the earth" (cf. Ps 61:3) and of distant seas (v. 6). He is the one who establishes the mountains in his power, girded with strength (v. 7). He stills the roaring of the seas, the roaring of their waves, and the uproar of the races (cf. Isa 17:12–13), in which the primitive chaos breaks into history (v. 8). Dwellers at the ends [of the earth] (cf. v. 6) will fear (cf. Ps 64:10) these great signs; God makes the emergings of morning and evening shout for joy (v. 9).

The final five verses of the psalm, forty percent of its length, are given over to God's supreme blessing of rain to ensure earth's fertility. The psalmist delights in the spectacle of mud softened by the waters from God's river. God "visits" the earth and waters it, enriching it abundantly from his "channel" (cf. Pss 1:3, 46:5) full of water (v. 10); in this way he prepares grain (cf. Ps 4:8) for man. Verse 11 focuses on four specific moments of the growth process, each in two beats: earth's furrows he drenches, he levels its ridges, with showers he dissolves it, its growth he blesses. The harvest appears in verse 12: God crowns the year with his goodness, his tracks drip with "fatness" (cf. Pss 36:9, 63:6, Isa 55:1–2). The meadows (cf. Ezek 34:14) of the desert (Joel 2:22) drip, and the hills put on joy (v. 13). As in the first section of the psalm, the awed description ends with nature itself expressing its joy: the pasturage clothed with flocks, the valleys decked with wheat cry jubilantly (the *tĕrû'â*, cf. Ps 47:2, 6), even sing (v. 14). Creation expresses its praise of the creator even as it induces joy in man.

The spirit of this last part of the psalm is captured in the title of Hopkins's poem "Hurrahing in Harvest," a poem in which the poet discerns Christ himself in the end-of-summer sky and earth:

> Summer ends now; now, barbarous in beauty, the stooks rise
>   Around; up above, what wind-walks! what lovely behaviour
>   Of silk-sack clouds! has wilder, willful-wavier
> Meal-drift moulded ever and melted across skies?
>
> I walk, I lift up, I lift up heart, eyes,
>   Down all that glory in the heavens to glean our Saviour;
>   And, éyes, heárt, what looks, what lips yet gave you a
> Rapturous love's greeting of realer, of rounder replies?
>
> And the azurous hung hills are his world-wielding shoulder
>   Majestic—as a stallion stalwart, very-violet-sweet!—
> These things, these things were here and but the beholder
>   Wanting; which two when they once meet,
> The heart réars wíngs bold and bolder
>   And hurls for him, O half hurls earth for him off under his feet.

A later Hopkins poem focuses like Psalm 65 on the wet muddy ruts but at a later moment as they are dried by the wind:

Delightfully the bright wind boisterous ' ropes, wrestles,
   beats earth bare
Of yestertempest's creases; ' in pool and rut peel parches
Squandering ooze to squeezed ' dough, crust, dust; stanches,
   starches
Squadroned masks and manmarks ' treadmire toil there
Footfretted in it. Million-fuelèd, ' nature's bonfire burns on.
                    ("That Nature is a Heraclitean Fire and
                       of the Comfort of the Resurrection")

We believe that the physical world will be "freed, like us, from its slavery
to decay, to enjoy the same freedom and glory as the children of God"
(Rom 8:21). The transformed world will be the environment for the risen
bodies of those who gaze on God and sing his praise. Our psalm can be
read as the description of the new creation (cf. Rev 21:5) as the setting
of the risen Christ and his Church. There the earth, watered by "the river
of life rising from the throne of God and of the Lamb" (Rev 22:1) yields
abundant fruit, which is transmuted entirely into ecstatic praise of the
Creator (cf. Rev 22:1–4).

∼ Psalm 66   fire and water

The psalmist calls on all the earth to praise the Lord for his might
shown in Israel, recounts the trials through which God led his people,
and finally emerges as an individual speaker fulfilling his vow of praise
to God.

The whole earth is called on to utter to God the jubilant worship cry
mentioned at the end of the previous psalm (v. 1). All are to make music
to the glory (cf. Pss 29:2, 57:6, 63:3) of his name, to make his glory praised
(v. 2: cf. Ps 65:2). Christ wishes to draw all the world into his praise of the
Father. Men are called on to say how "fearsome" (cf. Ps 65:6) are God's
works (v. 3a) which include everything from creation to the liberation
of mankind from death and sin by the resurrection of Christ. Through
God's abundant strength his enemies cower before him (v. 3b). All the
earth will therefore worship him and make music to him, make music to
his name (v. 4), the name "Jesus" at which all knees bow as every tongue
confesses his lordship (Phil 2:9–11).

The speaker invites men to "come and see" these "acts" (cf. Ps 46:9) of God, "fearsome" (cf. v. 3) doings toward men (v. 5). This they do by coming to the temple to hear a recital of God's exploits in favor of Israel. Chief among them was the changing of the sea into dry land (cf. Exod 14:16, 22, Jos 4:22, Neh 9:11) so that the Israelites could cross the "river" on foot (v. 6); there they were glad in him (cf. Exod 15:1). The "strength" (cf. Ps 65:7) God manifested in that event abides in an eternal rule (v. 7); since his eyes watch the nations, rebels dare not rise against him. Instead the "peoples" are summoned to bless "our God" (v. 8), to make heard their voices in praise (cf. v. 2, Ps 65:2) of him who brought "our souls into life and did not permit our feet [cf. v. 6] to totter" (v. 9). God's purpose is that man "not totter" (cf. Pss 15:5, 16:8, 21:8, 46:6, 62:3, 7) but find a secure foundation in him. The blessing given to Israel is offered to all nations.

Turning to God, the psalmist recalls the pain of the Exodus experience, how God "tested" his people (v. 10), "smelted" them (same pair of verbs in Pss 17:3, 26:2) as silver is smelted (cf. Ps 12:7). He led them to an enemy fortress, he placed misery on their loins (v. 11). He permitted men to ride over their heads (v. 12), made them pass through the "fire" of Egypt's "iron furnace" (cf. Deut 4:20) and through the "waters" of the Red Sea (see the Lord's promise to Israel, Isa 43:2) before bringing them to superabundance (lit. "overflow," cf. Ps 23:5). It was through his Passion that Christ triumphed, and we triumph in him.

After speaking as a representative of Israel, the speaker addresses God as a praying individual. He enters God's house (cf. Ps 65:5) with holocausts; he will pay his vows (v. 13; cf. Ps 65:2, Gen 28:20–22, 2 Sam 15:7–8), which his lips uttered and his mouth spoke in his distress (v. 14). His own personal praise is a continuation of the praise of God's benefits to the nation. In accordance with Leviticus 22:18–21 and Numbers 15:3 he fulfills his vow by offering to God holocausts of fatlings together with the incense of rams (v. 15); he will prepare bulls and goats (cf. Ps 50:9, 13). As often in the psalms of thanksgiving the fulfilment of a vow of praise is the occasion for an instruction to the bystanders. The "Come and see" of verse 5 now becomes "Come and hear," addressed to all who fear God (v. 16), and the speaker will recount what God did for his "soul" (cf. v. 9, Pss 62:2, 63:2, 6, 9, 10). With his mouth (cf. v. 14) he called to God with exaltation "under his tongue," that is, ready to be uttered (v. 17).

If the speaker had seen injustice in his heart, his Master would not have heard (v. 18). Nevertheless, God did hear (v. 19); he attended to the voice of his prayer (cf. Pss 61:2, 65:3). That prayer is heard which springs from a sincere heart, a heart genuinely seeking to conform to the will of the God to whom one prays. The psalmist fittingly concludes with a doxology: "Blessed [cf. v. 8, Ps 65:11] be God who did not remove my prayer [cf. v. 19] or his love from me" (v. 20). The God who worked wonders in Israel is still at work answering the prayers of those who call on him. The Christ who praises the Father for his act of redemption in Christ praises the Father also in each member who personally appropriates his victory.

Several words link Psalm 66 with the previous psalm: "give the jubilant worship cry," "praise" (noun), "fearsome," "strength," "bless," "house," "fulfill vows," "prayer." Both psalms praise God in the temple, Psalm 65 for his beneficent deeds throughout the earth, Psalm 66 for God's special deeds in Israel. Together they form a fitting climax to the series of lament and trust psalms beginning with Psalm 51.

∾ PSALM 67   Aaron

As in Psalm 66 the speaker envisions the "peoples" worshipping Israel's God. God's blessing on Israel is invoked at the beginning and end of the psalm in the third person, while the central verses (vv. 3–6) are addressed to him in the second person.

The speaker quotes three verbs from the formula of Aaron's blessing over Israel (Num 6:22–27): "May God have mercy on us [cf. Num 6:25b] and bless us [cf. Num 6:24a]; may he let his face shine on us [cf. Num 6:25a]" (v. 2). The purpose of this blessing is to make known God's "way" on earth, and his salvation among all the nations (v. 3). God's "way" is identical with salvation: salvation is the way God acts. Similar terminology is found in the prophet Micah's vision of many nations coming to learn the Lord's "ways" in Jerusalem, submitting to his "judgment," and thus learning peace (Mic 4:1–4; cf. conclusion of the Aaronic blessing, Num 6:26). As a result of their knowledge of God the peoples will thank him (v. 4). The parallelism of verse 4 falls little short of repetition, but the first colon focuses on God, the second on "all" the people: "Let the peoples thank you, God; let all the peoples thank you." The invitation to praise continues in verse 5 and is followed by the reason for praise: the races are to be "glad" (cf. Pss 63:12, 64:11, 66:6) and shout joyfully (Pss

63:6, 8, 65:9), "for" God judges the peoples evenly (cf. Ps 45:7) and leads the races on earth (v. 5). Through God's manifest blessings on Israel, the nations will recognize that he is also their righteous judge and leader: Israel is lesson and witness. After reiterating his desire that the peoples thank God (v. 6),[7] the psalmist returns to third person speech to indicate the form that God's blessing to Israel takes: the earth has given its harvest (v. 7; one is reminded of the images of fertility at the end of Ps 65). The final verse (v. 8) is a précis of the entire psalm: May God bless Israel so that all the ends of the earth may "fear" him (cf. Pss 52:8, 60:6, 61:6, 64:10, 65:9), that is, take him and his "way" into account.

In addition to the words "bless" and "peoples," the psalmist repeats often the word "earth," playing on its different senses. It is first the place of God's revelation (v. 3), next the dwelling place of the peoples (v. 5), third the soil (v. 7), and in the final verse one senses that all three meanings are combined: people dwelling at the remotest ends of the fruitful earth will fear Israel's God whom they have come to recognize as their God.

Christians sing the psalm at Morning Prayer, asking that the light of the risen Christ (John 8:12, 9:5, 12:46, 2 Cor 4:6, Rev 21:23–24, Eph 5:14) shine over our world through his Church, the "light of the world" (Matt 5:14–16). For, in the words of the magnificent opening of *Lumen Gentium,* "Christ is the light of all nations. Hence this most sacred Synod, which has been gathered in the Holy Spirit, eagerly desires to shed on all men that radiance of His which brightens the countenance of the Church. This it will do by proclaiming the gospel to every creature" (*LG* 1).

⮆ PSALM 68   cloud-rider

After two psalms without the attribution to David come three more psalms "of David." This mighty psalm is different from anything else in the psalter. With magnificent sweep it portrays Yahweh as rider of the heavens leading his people from the desert to their own home, trouncing enemies along the way and receiving praise in the land where he has come to dwell. The triumphal procession seems to take place simultaneously in the heavens and on earth. The God who dwells in Zion is the

---

7. This is the last example of several uses of refrain in Book Two (cf. Pss 42-43, 46, 49, 56, 57, 59).

heavenly warrior who showers his people with blessings. The boldness of the images creates a profound awe and excitement.

The psalm is a series of "episodes," each of three to five verses. Views of the divine "march" are interspersed with descriptions of the worshipping community.

As Psalm 67 began with a reference to the blessing of Aaron in Numbers 6, so Psalm 68 begins with a third-person version of the prayer of Moses at the setting forth of the ark, Numbers 10:35, the generic term "God" replacing the name "Yahweh" (v. 2). Immediately we are placed in the context of the desert march. The poet amplifies the theme of the scattering of foes by comparing it to the dissipation (cf. Ps 1:4) of smoke (cf. Ps 36:20) or the melting of wax (cf. Ps 97:5) before fire, and by identifying the enemies as "the wicked," who will vanish (v. 3). The "just," on the other hand, will "be glad" (cf. Ps 67:5) and be joyful in the presence of God, and they will rejoice in gladness (v. 4).

Without specifying an addressee, the psalmist launches imperatives to "sing" to God, to "make music" to his name, to exalt the one who "rides through the desert regions—Yahweh is his name," and to exult before him (v. 5). The Lord is imagined as leading his people on their march through the steppes south and east of the Dead Sea on their way to Canaan. At the same time this father of orphans (cf. Ps 10:18) and defender of widows is in his holy habitation (v. 6), providing a home for those who are alone (cf. Ps 25:16) and leading prisoners into freedom, while rebels (cf. Deut 21:18, 20) must inhabit parched land (v. 7). God's immense might is put entirely at the service of a defenseless Israel (as in Ps 29).

The psalmist turns to God, recalling that as he went forth at the head of his people, marching through the desert (v. 8), the earth quaked and the heavens, too, dropped down rain before God—this was at Sinai in the presence of God, Israel's God (v. 9; the second part of the verse, in the third person, gives the impression of a gloss). An abundant rain God supplied for his exhausted inheritance (v. 10). His family settled there; he established in his goodness [a place] for the "poor" (v. 11). The description of Israel's fruitful land echoes the final verses of Psalm 65.

This peaceful idyll was purchased at the cost of the enemy's blood. The psalmist imagines the "Master" giving a word; a host of women bear the news of the enemy's defeat (v. 12): "The kings of the hosts are fleeing, they flee, and the beautiful one at home divides the spoil" (v. 13; for women enjoying spoils see Judg 5:24, 29–30). While some slackers were "lying [idle] among the sheepfolds" (cf. Judg 5:16), others admired a particular piece of booty: "the wings of a dove plated with silver, its pinions of yellow gold" (v. 14). When Shaddai routed kings (cf. v. 13), it snowed on Black Mountain, the site of the battle (v. 15). The vivid images convey the astonishing might of God at work on Israel's behalf.

What was the goal of the triumphal procession? The mountain where God would make his dwelling. Although the mountain of Bashan north and east of Israel might be a mighty mountain, a high-ridged mountain (v. 16), why does it look with hostility at the mountain God has coveted for his dwelling, where Yahweh will dwell forever (v. 17)? A mountain in the north of Israel is indicated, a place where the ark may have sojourned for a time. The allusion to the Song of Deborah in verse 14 recalls Mount Tabor as a place of worship in the early period of the Judges (see Kraus, *Psalmen,* 1:470–472). The speaker envisions God's chariots in huge numbers, with God in their midst, coming from Mount Sinai to this holy place (v. 18). For a single verse (v. 19) the psalmist addresses God directly: "You have gone up on high, you have captured captives, you have received tribute from men, even rebels to dwell, Lord God." The mighty leader of nations has taken up his dwelling in Israel, whose favored mountain would become Mount Zion. This section can be seen as the center of the psalm, preceded by the account of the procession from Sinai and followed by the account of the Lord's present and future blessings in the midst of his people.

The psalmist prays that God be blessed (cf. Pss 67:2, 7–8 for God's blessing on Israel; both psalms also foretell the praise of God by all peoples) daily for his ongoing bearing (cf. Isa 46:3) of Israel's burdens; he is truly a God of salvation (v. 20). He repeats the idea: "Our God is a God of salvation" (cf. Pss 65:6, 67:3); to the Master Yahweh belong the ways out of death (v. 21). Indeed God will smite the head of his enemies, the hairy crown of the one who parades his guilt (v. 22). The Master declares that from Bashan he will bring back the enemies, bring them back from the depths of the sea (v. 23, chiasmus; cf. Amos 9:2–3 where it is Israel itself he will seek out for punishment) so that Israel's foot might smite (cf. v. 22; LXX has "your foot might wash") in their blood (cf. Ps

58:11), and the tongue of her dogs have their share of the enemies (v. 24; cf. 1 Kgs 21:19, 23, 22:38, 2 Kgs 9:36). The Lord gives Israel a share in his victory over their enemies.

The speaker recounts to God how the people witness the triumphal procession of "my God, my king" to the holy place (v. 25): singers in the lead, string-players following, maidens in between beating tambourines (v. 26; cf. Exod 15:20). The procession of God and his people from Sinai to Canaan is reproduced in the cultic procession to God's earthly dwelling. The speaker tells the assembly to bless God, the Master, from the "fountain of Israel," a term that might be applied to God's dwelling place (cf. Ps 36:10), whence flow all Israel's blessings (v. 27). The princes of four tribes in particular lead the worship (v. 28): first Benjamin, an important tribe in the time of King Saul but "small"; then Judah, a noisy crowd—this tribe perhaps added when the sanctuary had moved from northern Israel to Jerusalem; and finally two tribes, Zebulun and Naphtali, particularly connected with northern Israel, specifically Mount Tabor (see on vv. 16–19 above).

The psalmist now petitions God to continue his mighty work on Israel's behalf. "Command your strength, O God, show your strength, God, as you have done for us" (v. 29). In God's temple (cf. Ps 65:5) over Jerusalem may kings bring him their tribute (v. 30). The ancient psalm relating to a sanctuary in the north has been accommodated for use in Jerusalem, where God is simultaneously *in* the temple and *above* it (cf. Ps 11:4). Even in the additions to the psalm the interplay between heavenly and earthly processes is maintained. God is asked to "rebuke" the beast in the reeds (Egypt), the band of strong ones like young bulls among the peoples (v. 31). The third colon in verse 31 provides textual difficulties—it may refer to the trampling on those who take pleasure in silver; then comes a petition for the dispersal of peoples who delight in wars. Princes of Egypt will come with precious gifts, Ethiopia will hasten with its hands toward God (v. 32; cf. Isa 19:21, 45:14, Zep 3:10).

Finally the psalmist summons the "kingdoms of the earth" to sing to God, to make music to his Master (v. 33), the one who "rides [cf. v. 5] in the heavens, the ancient heavens" (cf. Isa 19:1). Behold, he thunders with his voice, his mighty voice (v. 34; cf. Ps 29:4). They must "give strength" to God (cf. Ps 29:1), whose "pride" is over Israel and whose "strength" (a notable word in nearby psalms, cf. Pss 62:12, 63:3, 66:3b) is in the clouds

(v. 35). Fearsome (cf. Pss 47:3, 66:3) is God in his holy place, the God of Israel who (in his turn!) gives strength (cf. Ps 29:11) and vitality to his people: blessed be God (v. 36). The psalm that began with the seminal events in Israel's history and has celebrated God's abiding and active presence in Israel ends with a look to the future when all nations will praise Israel's God.

The psalm remains focused on God throughout. Nearly every verse contains the word "God" (twenty-six times) or one of several synonyms: El (four times), Yahweh (twice in full form, twice in abbreviated form), Master (seven times), Shaddai (once). But always it is God in relation with Israel, whom he has led in procession from Sinai to his holy mountain, first in the north, then in Jerusalem. Geographical details are important in the psalm because God has made his power known in concrete places on earth: Sinai, the Arabah, Bashan, the tribes of Zebulun and Naphtali, Benjamin and Judah, Israel, Jerusalem, Egypt, Ethiopia. From this it is clear that the presence of God in Jesus, God and man, is a fulfilment of a divine-human relationship that was inherent in Israel's very being. The psalm can be read as celebrating the triumph of the Incarnate God in his victory over man's foes, sin and death, and his ascension to the Father, from whose presence he radiates power to his people. The Church uses the psalm in the liturgies of Ascension time, and Saint Paul uses a version of verse 19 to assert that Christ having ascended to the Father now sends gifts to men in the form of the Holy Spirit (Eph 4:8–10).

Saint Anthony of Egypt, Father of monks, used the opening of the psalm as a prayer against demons besetting him in the desert (Athanasius, *Life of Anthony* 13).

∾ PSALM 69   poison

The speaker views himself as emblematic: he suffers for Yahweh, and what happens to him has repercussions for God's people. The psalm is the last of the great individual laments alluded to in the story of Jesus. While borrowing phrases from Psalms 35 and 38, it adds new dimensions to the theme of the persecuted individual.

The psalmist begins with the cry "Save me, God," for the waters of chaos have come up to his throat (v. 2). It is the cry of Peter sinking beneath the waves (Matt 14:30), the cry of all those who feel overwhelmed

by irresistible forces of destruction. It is the cry that God answers because it implies recognition of both his power and his desire to save (see
on Ps 62:12–13). It is the verb that identifies the nature of Jesus, whose
name means "Yahweh saves." The root of the verb appears 134 times in
the psalter, for it describes God's fundamental activity. Modern man
may claim not to need salvation, but anyone who listens to his heart recognizes there a deep longing for a life that lasts but that he cannot attain
by himself. We need to be saved from death and from the sin that brought
death into the world.

The speaker has sunk into the mud of "the deep" (cf. Ps 68:23) where
there is no foothold (v. 3); he has entered the depths of the waters, and the
torrent has flowed over him. He is worn out (cf. Ps 6:7) with calling,
his throat is burning (hoarse?), his eyes fail from hoping in his God (v. 4).
In verse 5 we learn the psalmist's situation for which his initial descriptions are metaphors: more abundant than the "hairs on his head" (cf.
Ps 40:13, also Ps 68:22) are those who "hate [him] without cause" (cf. Ps
35:19, John 15:25); numerous are those who want to silence him (Hebrew has consonance: 'ṣmû maṣmîtay), those "lying enemies" (cf. Pss
35:19, 38:20) who expect him to return what he never stole (v. 5). In
the malicious hounding of persecutors the primitive chaos is breaking
over him.

Although not guilty of the crime he is accused of, the speaker does
not claim perfect innocence: God knows his folly (cf. Ps 38:6), and his
guilt (cf. Ps 68:22) is not concealed from God (v. 6). But he prays to his
"Master, the Lord of hosts," that those who "wait for" God not be shamed
(cf. Ps 25:3) through God's failure to help him; to the "God of Israel" (cf.
Ps 68:9) he prays that those who "seek" God not be confounded through
his own plight (v. 7). For it is for God that he bears this scorn (cf. Jer
15:15), that disgrace covers his face (v. 8), that he is estranged from his
brothers and an alien to his mother's sons (v. 9; cf. Ps 35:14). For zeal for
God's house has eaten him up (cf. John 2:17); the reproaches of those who
scorn God fall on him (v. 10, applied to Christ by Saint Paul, Rom 15:3).
When he wept while his soul was fasting, this too became a reproach to
him (v. 11); when he made sackcloth his clothing (cf. Ps 35:13), he became to them a joke (lit. "proverb") (v. 12)—two parallel verses in 3 + 3
meter. He ends his lament with a vivid picture of men sitting at the city

gate discussing (lit. "pondering") him and singing taunt-songs (cf. Job 30:9, Lam 3:14) as they drink beer (v. 13).

It is time to make his prayer to Yahweh, time for God to show his favor (v. 14). He relies for an answer on the abundance of God's love (*hesed;* cf. Pss 62:13, 63:4, 66:20), on the faithfulness (reliability) of his "salvation" (cf. v. 2; on connection between love and salvation see Pss 6:5, 17:7, 31:17, 57:4). Terms that designated chaos in the lament of verse 3 are now drawn into petition as the psalmist asks to be rescued from "sinking" in the clay (cf. Ps 40:3, Jer 38:6), from "those who hate" him (cf. v. 5), and from the "depths of the waters" (v. 15). Let the "torrent" of waters not "flow over" him, nor the "deep" swallow him up, nor the pit close its mouth over him (v. 16). A verse in chiastic form (v. 17) appeals again to God's love: "Answer me, Lord, for good [cf. Ps 68:11] is your love; according to the abundance of your compassion turn toward me." The latter prayer is then expressed in negative form (v. 18) in a request that God not hide his face from his "servant," a self-designation we have not seen since Psalm 35:27. The second colon comprises two urgent cries like those of a drowning man: "for I am in distress, answer me quickly." A final verse of petition (v. 19) has three imperatives: "Draw near to my soul, redeem it; because of my enemies ransom me."

But new laments will lead to an even longer list of petitions. God knows the psalmist's "scorn" and shame and "disgrace" (cf. v. 8) and beholds all his oppressors (v. 20). The scorn has broken his heart so that he is incurable; he "waited for" (cf. v. 7) a kindly nod but there was none, for consolers but found none (v. 21). The enemies' perversity culminated in their putting poison in his food and in his thirst giving him vinegar to drink (v. 22). The pernicious detail was fulfilled in the Passion of Jesus as recorded by all four evangelists (cf. Matt 27:34, 48, Mark 15:36, Luke 23:36, John 19:29–30).

Appropriate petitions against the persecutors follow this lament, more aggressive and vengeful than those of verses 14–19. Let their (the persecutors') table before them be a trap, their prosperity a snare (v. 23). May their eyes be darkened so they cannot see, and may their loins always shudder (v. 24). May God pour over them his indignation and the wrath of his anger overtake them (v. 25, chiasmus with change of subject). May their camps become desolate, in their tents let there be no settler (v. 26; Saint Peter in Acts 1:20 applies the Greek version of this verse, which interprets "camps" as "farmstead," to Judas and the field he purchased with blood money). Drastic punishments are in order because it is one struck by God they have persecuted and the pains of one God wounded they recount (v. 27). If the psalmist was in fact undergoing pain for adhering to the divine will (cf. vv. 8–12), then to persecute him is to attack God himself, a foolhardy action of self-annihilation. As frequently in the Psalms, the speaker is asking that this inner dynamic be made visible and actual. He asks God to add iniquity upon their (the persecutors') iniquity; may they not enter his justice (v. 28). May God blot them (cf. Ps 51:3, 11) out of the book of the living (cf. Phil 4:3) and with the just may they not be enrolled (v. 29). The punishments have escalated from external to bodily, from temporal to spiritual.

Parallel to the removal of the enemy will be the rescue of the psalmist, who begins the final section with the Hebrew pun, "But as for me, poor [wa'ănî 'ānî; cf. Pss 25:16, 40:18] and in pain, your salvation [cf. vv. 2, 14], God, will raise me high" (v. 30). He will praise God's name (cf. Ps 68:5) with a song and magnify him with thanksgiving (v. 31), pleasing to Yahweh more than full-grown bulls or bullocks horned and hooved (v. 32). The psalmist has learned the lesson of Psalm 50:9, 14: sacrifices not of bulls or goats but the tôdāh (thanksgiving sacrifice for divine help). The "poor" (cf. v. 30 and Ps 68:11) will see this and those who search out God will "be glad" (cf. Ps 68:4): may their hearts live (v. 33; cf. Ps 22:27, Isa 57:15). For the psalmist is evidence that the Lord hears the needy, and his prisoners (cf. Ps 68:7) he does not despise (v. 34, chiasmus). The speaker invites heaven and earth to join in his praise, the seas and all that teems in them (v. 35), for his own experience proves that God will save (cf. vv. 2, 14, 30) Zion itself and rebuild the cities of Judah (cf. Isa 44:26), that men may dwell there and possess it (v. 36). The offspring of God's "servants" (cf. v. 18) shall inherit it, and those who love the Lord's name will dwell there (v. 37; cf. Isa 65:9). The psalmist has reached out from his own experience to embrace both the universe and the future of his glorified city in his praise of the saving God.

More than other psalms alluded to in the Passion narrative of Jesus, Psalm 69 calls attention to the note of suffering caused by the service of God. The parallels in the psalm to the Book of Jeremiah underline this theme of the persecuted upholder of God's will. While the theme is not so clear in the great passion psalm, Psalm 22, the two psalms end with a similar look to the future when posterity will praise God. That this praise will take place in a "rebuilt" Jerusalem and Judah is a reminder of the catastrophe of the Exile and serves to introduce the theme of the great community laments in Book Three (Pss 73–89) of the psalter.

A third of the verses are in 3 + 3 meter (vv. 8–9, 11–13, 18–19, 24–26, 34–35). Other verses contain cola of two to four beats.

The word links between this and the previous psalm (the unusual word "depth," "God of Israel," "salvation," "good," "poor," "name," "glad," "prisoners") invite us to read the two psalms in relationship. The individual lament of Psalm 69 provides an occasion for the mighty God portrayed in the hymn of Psalm 68 to demonstrate his salvation.

∼ PSALM 70   hasten

The short psalm, a near duplicate of Psalm 40:14–18, is essentially a series of petitions with brief elements of lament, trust, and even praise woven in. The initial call for help (v. 2) is followed by petitions against those who seek the psalmist's evil (vv. 3–4), then petitions on behalf of those who seek God (v. 5), with a final call for help that mirrors the opening.

The opening verse, the prayer that begins each hour of the divine office, is difficult to translate literally. It reads: "God, to rescue me, Lord, to my help hasten," the governing verb not coming until the end (the verse in Ps 40:14 is easier, beginning with the verb, "Be pleased . . ."). The two names for the deity are parallel, but one of the "to" phrases is an infinitive, the other a noun. These differences are obscured in translation— for example, the Latin "Deus in adjutorium meum intende; Domine, ad adjuvandum me festina," or the Grail's "O God, make haste to my rescue; Lord, come to my aid." The word "rescue" is the first of several word links with the previous long lament (cf. Ps 69:15).

The psalmist wishes for his enemies what he himself suffered in the previous psalm: that they be "shamed," "scorned," and "confounded" (= disgraced) (cf. Ps 69:8, 20), with the addition that they "retreat" (v. 3). The verse is a close repetition of Psalm 35:4 and similar to Psalm 35:26. The enemies are characterized as those who "seek" (cf. Ps 69:7) the psalmist's life and delight in his harm. May they turn back (Ps 40:16 has "be desolate") because of their shame (or their shaming of him), those who

say, "Aha! Aha!" (v. 4; cf. Ps 35:21). The scornful laugh epitomizes the
hostile attitude.

The second set of petitions follows the syntactic pattern of the first.
May they rejoice (cf. Ps 68:4) and be glad (cf. Ps 69:33) in the Lord, those
who "seek" the Lord (and not others' harm, cf. v. 3). May they always
"say" (cf. v. 4), "Great [cf. Ps 69:31] is God," who love his salvation (v. 5;
cf. Pss 67:3, 68:20, 69:30).

The conclusion begins with the Hebrew pun of Psalm 69:30: "As
for me, I am poor," adding "needy" in place of "in pain." As in verse 2 the
psalmist calls on God to "hasten" to him ("thinks of" in Ps 40:18), for he
is "my help (cf. v. 2) who brings me to safety" (v. 6). The psalm concludes
with the negative equivalent of "hasten": "Lord, do not delay" (cf. Isa
46:13, Hab 2:3).

The emphasis in the psalm is on that "not delaying." God's judgment on evil must come—it is inevitable, as the Psalms often show. But
there are times when the Christian feels he cannot hold out much longer
or the world cannot bear more suffering, and then he must pray this urgent prayer for the coming of the one who promised: "Surely I am coming soon" (Rev 22:20).

∼ PSALM 71   old

The psalm uses several expressions from the previous two psalms
but focuses on the theme of old age. The psalmist has lived long but still
wishes to maintain his close relationship with the Lord. He asks not to be
abandoned, not to succumb to foes, and to be allowed to praise the Lord
for the rest of his days, the theme to which he constantly returns. The
psalm has a greater percentage of verses dedicated to praise than most
individual laments. It has been suggested that the psalm be read as the
prayer of the aging King David, and that the following psalm, ascribed to
Solomon, would be his prayer for his son, his "royal testament."

The first three verses are very close to Psalm 31:2–4. "Save me" is
added in verse 2; "fortress" (Ps 31:3) becomes "habitation" in verse 3;
the words "where I can always come; you have ordered it" are added after
"habitation"; and the epithet "my rock" is added. The terms "shame," "justice," "rescue," "ransom," and "save" serve as links to Psalm 70. After this
opening cry the speaker asks God to bring him to safety (cf. Ps 70:6) from
the hand of the wicked, from the palm of the wrongdoer and afflicter

(v. 4), but apart from vague references in verses 10–13 we hear no more of these foes; the psalmist is more interested in detailing his lifelong relationship with the Lord. The Master has been his hope, the Lord his trust since his youth (v. 5). By God was he upheld from the "belly" (womb), from his mother's entrails God brought him forth (like a midwife; these two cola recall Ps 22:11), his praise has always been directed to God (v. 6). He may have been a portent (a sign of either blessing or curse) to many (v. 7), but God has been his strong "refuge" (cf. v. 1). His mouth has been filled with God's praise, all day long with his honor (v. 8).

The speaker asks not to be thrown away in the time of his old age (v. 9, chiasmus) nor in the failing of his powers to be "abandoned" (cf. Ps 22:2). For it is precisely God's "abandoning" of him that the enemies, who "observed [his] soul" and took counsel together (v. 10, chiasmus), have noted (v. 11), saying: "God has abandoned him, pursue and overtake him, for there is no rescuer" (cf. v. 2). These two verses of lament are followed by two verses of petition largely borrowed from other psalms. The speaker asks God (v. 12) not to be "far" from him (as in Pss 22:12, 20, 35:22, 38:22) and to "hasten" to his "help" (cf. Pss 22:20, 38:23, 70:2). May they be shamed (cf. Ps 70:3) and fail, those who accuse him; may they be wrapped in "scorn and disgrace" (cf. Pss 69:8, 20, 70:3), those who seek his "harm" (v. 13, same syntactic structure as Ps 70:3, 5, etc.).

After this perfunctory lament enclosed by petitions the speaker is free to return to his main topic: his continual (cf. vv. 3, 6, Ps 70:5) hoping in the Lord and multiplying of his praise (v. 14). His mouth will recount God's "justice" (cf. v. 2) and all day long his "salvation" (cf. Pss 70:5, 69:30), though he knows not their full extent (v. 15). He will "come with the mighty deeds of the Master, the Lord" (v. 16), acknowledging God's singular "justice" (cf. v. 15). God has taught him from his "youth" (v. 17; cf. v. 5, 1 John 2:24, 2 Tim 3:14–16), and till now he proclaims the divine "wonders" (cf. Pss 9:2, 26:7, 40:6; from this point forward the word becomes frequent in the psalter; note how the two cola in this verse represent the divine initiative and man's response). The psalmist's only desire is that even into old age and the time of gray hair (cf. Isa 46:4), his God not abandon him (cf. vv. 9, 11) so that he may proclaim (cf. v. 17) God's "arm" (cf. Ps 44:4) to the next generation, to all who are to come God's "strength" (v. 18, chiasmus; cf. Pss 65:7, 66:7), and his "justice" (cf. vv. 2, 15, 16) to the height, for he has done great things. The litany ends with an amazed, "God, who is like you?" (v. 19).

The speaker has not forgotten his troubles: God has made him see many distresses and evils; may he restore his life and "raise him up" (cf. Pss 30:4, 40:3, Ezek 37:12) again from the "abysses" (cf. Pss 33:7, 42:8) of the earth (v. 20); may he increase his greatness and console him again (v. 21). That will be occasion for even further praise: with stringed instruments the psalmist will thank him for his faithfulness (v. 22), make music on the harp to the Holy One of Israel (favorite title for God in the Book of Isaiah, Isa 1:4, 12:6, 30:15, 41:14, etc.). His lips will shout for joy as he makes music to God (v. 23), along with his soul, which the Lord has "ransomed" (cf. Ps 69:19). Then his tongue "all day long" (cf. vv. 8, 15) will murmur (cf. Pss 1:2, 35:28, 63:7) God's "justice" (fifth mention), for they have truly been "shamed and scorned," those who have sought his harm (v. 24; cf. v. 13, Ps 70:3). A life full of praise will end full of praise, for God's justice has established itself on earth.

Few psalms are cast so consistently in the second person. Every locution is addressed to God. The Christian might see in the psalm a response to Saint Paul's exhortation "always and for everything to give thanks" (Eph 5:20), since this is what we have learned from others to do. "Let the word of Christ dwell in you richly, teach and admonish one another in all wisdom, and sing psalms and hymns and spiritual songs with thankfulness in your hearts to God" (Col 3:16). In verse 20 in particular we praise God for and in the Paschal mystery of his Son (cf. Rom 6:4). The whole meaning of a human life graced by God is to praise his actions and attributes.

∼ PSALM 72   Sheba

Apart from Psalm 45 and incidental references in Psalms 61 and 63, we have heard little of Israel's king in Book Two, but he is the main subject of this final psalm in the book, which can be read as a counterpart of Psalm 2 before the beginning of Book One. The psalm portrays powerfully all the benefits that Israel expected from its king: justice for the poor and helpless, lasting peace in an extended kingdom, tribute from the nations, fruitful land. In short, the king was to be the mediator of the blessings God himself wished to bestow on his people. In the same way Christ is the source of our life, our food, our kingdom, our peace.

What the speaker (King David?, see on Ps 71) asks for the king is a knowledge of God's "judgments" or precepts (cf. Ps 36:7), with which the king was to be conversant (cf. Deut 17:18–19), and for the king's son the administration of God's own "justice" (v. 1; cf. Ps 71:2, 15, 16, 19, 24). May he give just judgment for God's people (v. 2; cf. 2 Sam 8:15) and judgment for his "poor" (cf. Pss 69:30, 70:6). May the very mountains bear peace to the people, and the hills justice (v. 3), so thoroughly will the king's beneficent influence permeate the land. May he judge the "poor" of the people, "save" (normally the prerogative of Yahweh, cf. Pss 68:20–21, 69:2, 30, 36, 71:2, 3) the sons of the "needy" (cf. Ps 70:6), and crush the exploiter (v. 4). May men "fear" God as long as there is a sun and a moon, for all generations (v. 5, 2 + 2 + 2 meter). May the king's influence descend like rain on the mown grass, like "showers" (cf. Ps 65:11) sprinkling the earth (v. 6). May the just man flourish (lit. "sprout") in his days and abundance of "peace" (cf. v. 3) till there is no more moon (v. 7; cf. v. 5). Through the king the divine attributes will become an organic part of Israel's life.

The psalmist prays that the king's rule may extend from sea to sea (Persian Gulf to Mediterranean), and from the River (Euphrates) in the north to the "ends of the earth" (v. 8; cf. Zech 9:9–10). May desert dwellers kneel before him, his enemies lick the dust (v. 9; cf. Isa 49:23, Mic 7:16–17). May kings of Tarshish (in the far west, cf. Ps 48:8) and the islands bring gifts; kings of Sheba (Arabia) and Seba (Africa) offer tribute (v. 10, two bicola in 3 + 2 meter). May they prostrate before him, all kings; may all nations serve him (v. 11, chiasmus). Honors are to be given to the king, which elsewhere are promised to the Lord and his holy city (Isa 60:6, 9–11).

For this place-holder of the Lord will rescue (cf. Pss 69:15, 70:2, 71:2) the "needy" one (cf. v. 4) when he cries for help, and the "poor" man with no one to help him (v. 12). It is this unfailing and divine justice that will convert the nations to Israel's king. May he take pity (cf. Jonah 4:11) on the weak (cf. Ps 41:2, 1 Sam 2:8) and the needy (cf. vv. 4, 12) and the souls of the needy may he save (v. 13, chiasmus). From oppression (cf. Pss 10:7, 55:12) and violence may he redeem their souls, and may their blood be dear in his eyes (v. 14). May he live and give to him (the poor man) the gold of Sheba (cf. v. 10); may he pray for him "always" (cf. Pss 71:6, 70:5) and each day (cf. Ps 71:8, 15, 24) bless him (v. 15; this alternative translation to the Grail keeps the king as subject of the verbs and the poor man as recipient, cf. Hossfeld and Zenger, *Die Psalmen*, 2:415.)

May abundance of grain on the mountaintops of the land, fruitfulness like that of Lebanon, cities populous as the plants of the earth characterize this king's rule (v. 16), while his name lasts forever, as lasting as the sun (cf. v. 5), and all nations "bless themselves by him" (cf. Gen 12:3, 22:18, 28:14) and call him fortunate (v. 17). Israel's king is both the source of divine blessings on earth and the receiver of all men's gifts. He is truly a mediator between Israel's God and mankind. The psalm is fulfilled beyond all expectation in the Incarnation of the Son of God as a son of David. The king is not just a channel of the divine blessings but is himself both God and man, the fountain of blessings for all mankind.

The final verses belong not to the psalm but to the whole of Book Two. Verses 18–19 are the doxology for the book, the longest of the doxologies except for that of Book Five: Blessed be the Lord God (v. 18), the "God of Israel" (cf. Pss 68:8, 36, 69:7) who "alone" (cf. Ps 71:16) works "wonders" (cf. Ps 71:17). Blessed be his glorious "name" forever, and may all the earth be filled with his glory (v. 19). The final phrase is an allusion to Isaiah's vision of the seraphim in the temple (Isa 6:3) and also provides an appropriate echo of Psalm 72: God's glory will fill the earth through the exercise of perfect justice by Israel's king.

The final note of Book Two, verse 20, states that the prayers of David, son of Jesse, are ended. There will be a "third Davidic collection" of psalms (138–145) near the end of Book Five.

∾ PSALM 73   beast

The first eleven psalms of Book Three are ascribed to Asaph, as was Psalm 50. This group of psalms (73–84) shows a special concern for Israel's moral responsibility to the Lord and in particular for her sin and the disasters it has brought. In Psalm 73 the speaker meditates on the temptation to ignore God in one's everyday life when the consequences of doing so are not immediate. It is only when he reflects on the "end" of the wicked that he realizes that lasting happiness is not in this world but in its Maker.

"How good for Israel is God," begins the psalmist (v. 1), but he immediately adds a qualification, "for the clean of heart." "Heart" will be a major word in the psalm: it is in the heart that sin is located, that the psalmist's temptation will be resolved, and that union with God is enjoyed. God is good to Israel, but that goodness is enjoyed only by those who accept his lordship and conform to his saving will. But the psalmist's feet came very close to slipping; like nothing were poured out his footsteps (v. 2), for he was envious of the boasters and saw the prosperity (contrast the true *šālôm* [peace] of the just king's reign in the previous psalm, 72:3, 7) of the wicked (v. 3). The description of these men combines physical and moral characteristics: the former seem the outward sign of the latter. There are no torments for them; hale and well-fed are their bodies (v. 4; cf. Phil 3:19). In the toil of mortals they have no part, and they are not stricken like men (v. 5). So pride (cf. Pss 10:2, 31:19, 24, 36:12) encircles them like a necklace, and the garment they wear is violence (v. 6). Their eye can't see from fat; devices pass through their heart (v. 7). They mock and speak maliciously of exploitation (v. 8; cf. Ps 72:4), speaking "from on high" (cf. Pss 68:19, 71:19). They place in the heavens their mouth while their tongue goes about on the earth (v. 9, chiasmus). A literal translation of the obscure verse 10 gives: "Therefore his people turn here, and waters in full are drained by them," a line that has been corrected in different ways and that perhaps expresses how the common people are taken in by the haughty words of the schemers. As often (see most recently, Pss 59:8, 71:11) the psalmist quotes the arrogant speech of the wicked: "How can God know? Is there knowledge in the Most High?" (v. 11). This completes the psalmist's characterization of the "wicked," who "peacefully" (these two words form an inclusion with v. 3) forever pile up wealth (v. 12). Their chief traits are pride, reckless greed, violence, self-indulgence, rejection of God. When a transcendent reference point for man is denied, man inevitably becomes his own god, dictates to the earth, and violates the rights of others.

But the wicked man's success is a temptation for the speaker. How empty for him to keep his heart correct and wash his palms in innocence (v. 13; cf. Ps 26:6); a similar observation is made by the fearers of God in Malachi 3:14–15. Unlike the wicked the psalmist is "stricken" (cf. v. 5) all day long and reproved morning by morning (v. 14). Then he quotes a prayer he made to God (cf. v. 11): "If I should speak like that, I would be unfaithful to the generation of your sons" (v. 15). He considered how to know these things (v. 16) and found it a great "toil" (cf. v. 5) until he entered the holy "place" ("things"?) of God and discerned the "end" of these wicked (v. 17). We have arrived at the "pulling aside of the veil," so frequent in the psalms, where insoluble dilemmas are put in true perspective by the recognition of a loving, just, and powerful God behind them.

The answer to the psalmist's dilemma comes in prayer, and the rest of the psalm is addressed directly to God. What the psalmist sees in his contemplation is "how" (cf. v. 1) slippery is the ground on which God has placed (cf. v. 9) the wicked, how he makes them fall into delusion (v. 18). How suddenly they are brought to desolation, come to an end, and are finished off by sudden terrors (v. 19). What seemed so substantial will be like a dream after one wakes: "You, Master, on rousing yourself despise it as a phantasm [or idol-image]" (v. 20; Hebrew adds "in the city"). Sooner or later the futility of a life at variance with the Creator will become manifest.

In the final section the psalmist gives his internal reactions to the experience he has had. His heart had been embittered, his kidneys felt stabbed (v. 21). He was stupid and ignorant, a beast was he with God (v. 22). Yet he was precisely always "with" God, who grasped his right hand (v. 23). Into his plan God will lead him and afterwards will "take him up" (cf. Ps 49:16) to glory (v. 24). Who else is there for the psalmist in the heavens? With God (cf. v. 23) he does not delight in the earth (v. 25): the Son has nothing but the Father, his joy (John 17:13) and his glory (John 17:22, 24). At the thought of this destiny the speaker's flesh and heart languish; the rock of his heart and his portion (cf. Ps 16:5) is God forever (v. 26). For those who put God at a distance will vanish (v. 27); God silences all who are unfaithful (lit. "adulterous") to him. But for the psalmist nearness to God is "supreme good" (cf. v. 1, Mark 10:9); he has made his Master the Lord his refuge in order to "recount all your labors" (v. 28; cf. Gen 2:2). Union is perfected in praise (cf. Ps 63:4–6).

The reader has accompanied the psalmist on his painful journey of discovery and by gradual steps has arrived with him at the bliss of union with God before which all comforts pale. In having God he has all things.

∼ PSALM 74   axes

With Psalm 74 the catastrophe of the Exile bursts on the scene. The dramatic and vivid psalm is the first of several community laments in the Songs of Asaph. It portrays the horror of the destruction of Jerusalem's temple and implores the Lord to destroy his adversaries as once he destroyed the monsters of the sea. If the true temple is the Body of Christ on earth, the Christian can think of plenty of ways in which it is ravaged by evil powers. If one thinks of all mankind as destined for membership in this Body, then any abuse of any human being becomes an occasion for heartfelt praying of this lament. The long verses, generally in 4 + 4 meter, give the psalm a weighty solemnity.

The psalm opens with the "Why?" frequent in the laments (cf. Pss 10:1, 22:2, 42:10, 43:2, 44:25). Why has God "rejected" (a frequent word in the community laments, cf. Pss 43:2, 44:10, 60:3, 12) forever, and his anger "smoked" (cf. Exod 19:18) at the "flock of [his] pasture" (v. 1; cf. Pss 79:13, 95:7, 100:3)? The enemy's destruction is an outrage against a people who in a special way belong to God; how can he now reject his own property? Later Asaphite psalms will locate the cause in Israel's own sin (cf. Pss 78, 79), but of that there is yet no trace. God needs to "remember" the congregation (lit. "gathering") he purchased of old (v. 2), the tribe he redeemed to be his inheritance (cf. Pss 28:9, 33:12, 68:10), the mountain of Zion where he has dwelt (cf. Ps 68:17, Zech 2:14, 8:3, Joel 4:17). The psalmist calls on God to lift (lit. "exalt") his steps to these ruins that seem eternal; the enemy has devastated everything in the sanctuary (v. 3). God's foes have "roared" (like lions, cf. Pss 22:14, 104:21) in the midst of God's appointed place, erecting their banners as victory signs (v. 4). It seemed as though one had raised high the axes in a thicket of wood (v. 5). And now all the engravings (cf. 1 Kgs 6:29) they have hacked with axe and crowbars (v. 6; this and preceding verse in 3 + 3 meter). They set fire to God's holy place (cf. Ps 73:17), profaned to the ground the "dwelling of [his] name" (v. 7; cf. Deut 12:11, 1 Kgs 8:17–20). They said (cf. Ps 73:11) in their heart, "Let us subdue them entirely!"; they burned all the appointed places (cf. v. 4) of God in the land (v. 8).

As for the community, they see no signs of their own (cf. v. 4), no longer have a prophet (cf. Lam 2:9), nor with them is anyone who knows how long the situation will last (v. 9). The psalmist ends his lament with a return to questions, asking God how long the oppressor will scorn (v. 10); will the enemy disdain God's name "forever" (cf. v. 1). Why has

God turned his hand and his right hand away? If God is envisioned as hiding his hand in his bosom, the final petition makes sense: "From the fold of your garment finish [them] off!" (v. 11).

At this point the psalmist enters on an extended meditation on God's power manifested in the creation of the world. The Hebrews shared with their Near Eastern neighbors the notion that creation was the result of a battle between God and the turbulent waters of the primitive ocean. In Canaanite and Babylonian myths this ocean was a rival deity whom the creator God overcame by slicing her in two to create a space between the waters where the world could come to be. A reading of Genesis 1:1–11 shows how thoroughly Israel demythologized this story—the primeval ocean is not a god but is completely passive to the Creator's will and action; nevertheless, the trappings of the myth survived in images that could be useful in poetry to stress the divine power over all evil, anti-God forces. The psalmist draws on this imagery to evoke the might of God his "king" (cf. Ps 5:3) from "of old" (cf. v. 2), a worker of salvation in the midst of the earth (v. 12). Seven times in the next five verses he begins clauses with the emphatic pronoun "You" (translated "It was you who . . .") to portray God's mighty deeds at different stages of the creation: "It was you who chased away the sea by your strength, you broke the heads of the sea-monsters [cf. Isa 51:9–10] on the waters [v. 13]. It was you who crushed Leviathan's [Ps 104:26, Job 40:25, Isa 27:1] heads and gave him as food to the people of the wastelands [v. 14]. It was you who split open spring and stream; it was you who dried up ever-flowing rivers [v. 15]. Yours is the day and yours is the night; it was you who fashioned the light and the sun [v. 16]. It was you who stationed the boundaries of earth; summer and winter—it was you who formed them" (v. 17).

The conclusion of the psalm follows like the third statement of a syllogism: since God's people have suffered a horrible reverse and since he is the all-powerful creator, it remains only to ask him to apply this power to defeat the enemy; this the psalmist does in a series of ten petitions. "Remember [cf. v. 2] these things," he begins (v. 18), as if God needed reminding of his creative purpose; "the enemy has scorned the Lord; a people—fools [cf. Ps 14:1]—disdains your name" (cf. v. 10). May God not give to the beast the soul of his "turtledove" (v. 19; cf. Cant 2:12, Jer

8:7), not forget the life (or "band"?) of his "poor ones" (cf. Ps 70:2) forever (cf. vv. 3, 10). He must look at the covenant that bound him to Israel (v. 20), since all the dark corners of the "land" (cf. v. 8) are full of abodes (lit. "meadows") of violence (cf. Ps 73:6). Let not the "oppressed" (cf. Pss 9:10, 10:18) [exiles] return confounded, but let the "poor and needy" (cf. Pss 70:6, 72:4) praise God's name (v. 21). Three imperatives come more quickly: "Arise, God; defend your cause [cf. Ps 43:1]; remember your scorn [cf. vv. 10, 18] from the fool [cf. v. 18] all day long" (v. 22). Finally the complement of the "remember" at the beginning of the psalm and at the beginning and end of its final section: "Do not forget [cf. v. 19] the voice of your foes [cf. v. 4], the uproar [cf. Ps 65:8] of your attackers that ascends continually" (v. 23).

Christians praying the psalm today remind God of the blood of his Son, which redeemed us, the blood of the new and everlasting covenant (cf. v. 20), a blood that pleads more insistently than Abel's (Heb 12:24). It is impossible that God not answer the prayer of his Son, who has promised his poor a kingdom (Luke 6:20).

The psalm is a good illustration of the way in which the psalmist recalls the past to give meaning to the present. The remembrance that occurs in liturgy and prayer becomes a force transforming the present:

> Disconcerted by the present which poses insoluble "whys," unbearable "hows," and "how longs," the faithful are conducted by the liturgy to the recollection of the past actions of God; there they find the solution of the enigma that tortures them: the present takes on meaning; they find there also a guarantee for the future, which the chaotic situation will never disturb and the marvel of which is unfailingly guaranteed by the past. (Monloubou, *L'imaginaire des psalmistes,* 125; my translation)

∼ PSALM 75   horn

The Asaphite writer continues his complaint, this time against arrogant self-promoters in Israel. He remembers (v. 2) a time when "We gave thanks to you, God; we gave thanks" in the Jerusalem temple. Although the temple has been destroyed, God's "name [cf. Pss 72:19, 74:7, 21] is still near" to those who have recounted his "wonders" (cf. Pss

71:17, 72:18).[8] The presence of God that used to be found in the temple can now be found only in the invocation of his name. "In a time without a temple the nearness of God's name nevertheless still mediates the certainty of the divine presence and care as in Psalm 74:10, 18, 21" (Hossfeld and Zenger *Die Psalmen,* 2:429). But now men are forgetting that name and boasting of their own strength (cf. v. 5); they need a reminder of God's judgment. Without introduction the speaker quotes a divine oracle: When God seizes the appointed time (cf. Hab 2:3) he will judge "uprightly" (v. 3; cf. Pss 17:2, 58:2); though the earth and its inhabitants may "dissolve" (cf. Ps 46:7, Amos 9:5, Nah 1:5), it is he who has established (cf. Pss 24:2, 65:7) its pillars (v. 4). As in the preceding psalm (cf. Ps 74:13–17) it is the creator God who will reestablish right order on earth.

The speaker recalls that he once told the "boasters" (cf. Ps 73:3) not to boast (v. 5), and the "wicked" (cf. Ps 73:3, 12) not to exalt their "horn" (symbol of arrogant power). They should not exalt their horns "on high" (cf. Ps 73:8) or speak with a stiff-necked "insolence" (v. 6; cf. Ps 31:19, 1 Sam 2:3). Verse 8 would make a good sequel to this verse, but there intervenes the mysterious verse 7, which has been given various interpretations: "For neither from the emerging or the setting [of the sun], nor from the desert [verb missing] the mountains." Translators often supply the words "comes judgment"; another possibility is that the word translated "mountains" should be rendered "exaltation," with "comes" understood. For it is God who is the judge (v. 8); it is he who brings down and

---

8. Reading the end of verse 2 with the LXX: "I will recount all your wonders," Saint Augustine explains how Christ can at once be the speaker and addressee of the psalm:

> When Christ has begun to dwell in our inmost being through faith, when we have confessed and invoked him, and he has begun to take possession of us, then is formed the whole Christ, head and body, one from the many. . . . Let us listen to this speaker, and in him speak as ourselves. Let us be his members, so that this voice may be ours as well. *I will recount all your wonders,* he says. So Christ is preaching himself, telling the good news of himself even through his members, those who already belong to him. Through them he can attract others, who will be joined to the members through whom his gospel has been spread. One body is to be formed, under one head, living one life in one Spirit. (*Enarrationes in Psalmos* 74.4)

he who "exalts" (as opposed to those who exalt their "horns," vv. 5–6; cf. 1 Sam 2:7, Luke 1:52). It is the "poor" who let themselves be exalted by God; those rich in their own strength deprive themselves of this help from the creator judge: their exaltation of themselves inevitably brings them "low," a theme often met in the Book of Isaiah (cf. Isa 2:17, 5:15, 10:33, 13:11, 25:11–12; cf. also Ps 18:28, Prov 29:23).

There follows a complex image for this judgment of the wicked: the poet sees in the hand of the Lord a cup of wine (cf. Ps 60:5) with a mixture of spices; when he pours from it, all the wicked on the earth must drain it, drink it even to the dregs (v. 9). The cup one must drink is a frequent metaphor in Scripture for one's destiny (cf. Jer 25:15–17, 27–29, Ezek 23:31–34, Hab 2:16–17, Isa 51:17, 22, Matt 20:22–23, Mark 14:36, John 18:11). In this case it is a metaphor for the punishment that comes inevitably on those who have rejected God (cf. God's "cup of anger" in Rev 14:10, 16:19). But the psalmist, for his part (v. 10), will "proclaim forever, will make music to the God of Jacob" (a frequent term for God in the Songs of Asaph).

A final divine oracle both matches that of verses 2–3 and neatly summarizes the psalm's teaching, ending on a positive note: "All the horns [cf. vv. 5–6] of the wicked I will cut down [cf. Isa 10:33, 14:12, Lam 2:3, Jer 48:25]; exalted shall be the horns of the just!" (v. 11, chiasmus; cf. 1 Sam 2:10). Thus in more than one place the psalm shows connections with the Song of Hannah and with the pre-exilic/exilic prophets.

Mary's Magnificat is the best New Testament commentary on the psalm. That God brings down human pride (Luke 1:51) is Good News since it liberates us from the illusion of complete autonomy to open us to the gift of divine life, unattainable by our own striving. For Mary this action of God is the manifestation of his mercy (*eleos*, Greek translation of *ḥesed*; cf. Luke 1:50, 54) promised to Abraham and his posterity forever. She saw in herself the "exaltation of the lowly" that was to be definitively fulfilled in her Son's resurrection from the dead and communicated to us who believe in him (Phil 2:8–11, Eph 2:4–9).

∼ PSALM 76 battle

The psalm presents Zion as a bulwark against hostile powers; weapons and foes are shattered against its firmness. No force in the world can break the bond uniting God and his people in Christ (Rom 8:38–39).

It is in Judah that the creator God is "known," that is, revealed, through his revelation in deed and word (v. 2). He is known to the Hebrew people but also to the surrounding nations who have witnessed his intervention on Israel's behalf. In the second half of verse 2 Israel (northern kingdom) is parallel to Judah (southern kingdom), "great" is parallel to "known," and "his name" (cf. Pss 74:7, 21, 75:2) is parallel to "God." In "Salem" (which tradition has identified as Jerusalem, cf. Gen 14:18) is God's "hut," and his "den" is in Zion (v. 3, chiasmus). The two nouns are normally translated "tent" and "habitation" when they refer to the temple, but they are also used of the abode of the lion (cf. Job 38:40), a more likely reference in a psalm that emphasizes the Lord's terrifying presence rather than his sheltering protection. This interpretation will be strengthened by verse 5. "There" he broke the flashings (i.e., arrows) of the bow, the shield, the sword, and the weapon (lit. "battle," v. 4). Weapons, offensive and defensive, shatter against Zion.

The central section of the psalm is addressed to the Lord, whom the psalmist calls "resplendent" (sometimes corrected to "fearsome" to conform to vv. 8 and 13), "mighty from the mountains of prey" (v. 5), as if God were a lion returning from his victim (sun and lion metaphors were sometimes combined in Near Eastern texts). The strong of heart stand plundered (v. 6), they sleep their slumber (one thinks of the guards "like dead men" at the tomb of Jesus after his victory over death, Matt 28:4); all the "men of vigor" cannot find their strength (lit. "hands"). At the threat of the God of Jacob (cf. Ps 75:10) chariot and horse (cf. Exod 15:21) lie stunned (v. 7). "You, fearsome are you" (cf. Pss 47:3, 66:5, 68:36), states the speaker, "and who can stand before your face, before your anger?" (v. 8). From the heavens God made his verdict known; the earth saw it and was calm (v. 9) when God (third person) rose to judge (cf. Ps 75:3), to save all the poor (cf. Pss 68:11, 69:30, 33, 70:6, 72:2, 4, 12, 74:19, 21) of the earth (v. 10). The poor are those who are open to divine strength; the powerful are closed to it, as the previous psalm made clear (cf. on Ps 75:8). The central section ends with the thanks (cf. Ps 75:2) that will result from the fury of men (v. 11): its survivors (lit. "remnant") will "celebrate" (emended verb) God's feast. Men's anger is the cause of thanksgiving when its attack against the poor is foiled and the poor praise their saving God.

The speaker ends by turning to these worshippers who "surround" God and inviting them to make vows of praise to "the Lord your God" and pay them (v. 12). They will bring gifts in fear. God will humble the spirit of sovereigns, "fearsome" (cf. vv. 5, 8) to the kings of the earth (v. 13). Thus it is the "poor of the earth" (v. 10) who have the advantage over the "kings of the earth."

If the psalm, like Psalm 74, was written at the time of the Exile, it expresses a remarkable faith in the impregnability of God's earthly city, which was then in ruins. Israel was convinced that no ultimate damage could be done to the people among whom God had chosen to dwell. Theirs was a resilient faith, needed precisely when all seemed lost. It is the faith Christians have in the inviolability of the Church (cf. Matt 16:18).

~ PSALM 77   insomnia

While the psalm begins as an individual lament, we soon learn that it is not from some personal trial that the psalmist is suffering but from the disaster that has afflicted his people. He speaks as a representative of the community and feels deeply that the God who helped Israel so spectacularly in the past has changed his "ways." The speaker "remembers" the past and "ponders" the present, suffering from the discrepancy between the two.

The first part of the psalm has parallels in the Book of Lamentations. "Cry out," "day," "night," "without ceasing" (vv. 2–3) are found in Lamentations 2:18–19, and the absence of "consolers" in Lamentations 1:2, 9, 17, 21, although in the psalm it is the psalmist's soul itself that "refused" to be consoled (v. 3). On the day of his distress he "searched out" the Master; at night he extended (Hebrew unclear) his hand without ceasing. When he "remembers" God, he churns within; when he "ponders" his people's crisis (for these two verbs see Ps 55:3, 18), his spirit feels faint (v. 4). God kept his eyelids open; he was upset and could not speak (v. 5). He considered days long past (cf. Ps 74:2), years long ago (v. 6). He "remembered" (cf. v. 4) his ballad (perhaps a hymn celebrating God's deeds) in the night, "pondering" within his heart, and his "spirit" (cf. v. 4) thought up the following questions (v. 7): Has the Master "rejected" (cf. Pss 44:24, 74:1, Lam 3:31) forever? Will he no longer take pleasure (cf. Ps 44:4) [in Israel]? (v. 8). Has his love (ḥesed) come to an end forever; is prophecy at an end for all generations? (v. 9; cf. Ps 74:9). Has God forgotten to "have mercy"? Has he in anger stopped his compassion? (v. 10). It was precisely to God's "love, mercy, and compassion" that Israel owed its existence as a nation (cf. Exod 33:19, 34:6). Now that God seems to have withheld these, the nation has collapsed, experiencing only his anger (cf. Pss 74:1, 76:8).

The speaker sums up his ruminations: his "weakening" (v. 11) stems from the changing of the "right hand" (i.e., beneficent power, cf. Ps 44:4, Exod 15:6, 12) of the Most High (Pss 50:14, 73:11). He "remembers" (cf. vv. 4, 7) the deeds of the Lord as he remembers his ("your") wonders (cf. Exod 15:11) "of old" (cf. v. 6). The second half of verse 12 has slid imperceptibly into direct address to God, which will continue until the end of the psalm. The psalmist "murmurs" (cf. Ps 1:2) all God's actions, and his doings he "ponders" (v. 13, chiasmus; cf. vv. 4, 7); thus the first half of the psalm ends with the verb that has dominated the whole section. These last three verses also provide an introduction to the hymnic material that follows, in which the speaker recites to himself the great deeds of the Lord in the past.

"God, in holiness is your way," he begins: God's actions on earth are rooted in and manifest his transcendence. The question "Who is a great [cf. Ps 76:2] god like God?" (v. 14) is more monotheistic than the equivalent in the Song of Moses, "Who is like you among the gods?" (Exod 15:11). This is a God who works "wonders" (cf. v. 12) and has made "known" (cf. Ps 67:3) among the peoples his strength (v. 15). The principal wonder was, of course, the "redeeming" of his people with strong "arm" at the Red Sea (v. 16; cf. Exod 15:13, 6:6). The people are identified as the "sons of Jacob [cf. Ps 76:7] and Joseph," a phrase suggestive of the northern kingdom settled by the tribes of Ephraim and Manasseh, sons of Joseph (cf. also Pss 80:2, 81:5–6).

The author sees the Exodus event as partaking in the act of creation itself, that is, God's dividing the waters of the primitive chaos in order to make space for the world (cf. Gen 1:2, 6–9, Ps 74:13). Verses 17–19 are cast in the tricolon form of Canaanite poetry, which celebrated the creative triumph of Baal over the turbulent waters (cf. Pss 93:3–4, 29:3, 10, 89:10–11, Isa 51:9–10). The waters saw God, they saw him and writhed, indeed the abysses trembled (v. 17). The "clouds" released their "waters" and gave forth their "voice" of thunder (cf. Hab 3:10), while God's "arrows" (of lightning) went to and fro (v. 18; cf. Ps 18:12–15). The voice of his thunder was in the whirlwind, lightnings lighted up the world (cf. Hab 3:11), the earth trembled and quaked (v. 19). These ingredients of the theophany are presented as accompanying the Exodus, where God made his "way in the sea" (for the union of these two words see Isa 43:16, 51:10, Hab 3:15), his course in the mighty waters, and his tracks were not detected (v. 20). God "led" (cf. Exod 15:13, 32:34, Deut 32:12) his people like a "flock" (cf. Ps 74:1) by the hand of Moses and Aaron (mentioned together in Exod 7:1–2, 6–10, 13). This final verse 21 matches verse 16: in each verse "your people" is found in the first colon and two proper names in the second, representing respectively the people redeemed and their leaders through whom God worked. The last eight verses of the psalm are notable for their combining of traditional Exodus terminology with the language of the theophanies in Psalm 18 and Habakkuk 3.

The psalmist does not return to his dilemma: his recalling of the might of God at the Red Sea has put his anguish to rest and perhaps even sent him to sleep. The God of creation who divided the waters of the Red Sea can certainly defeat the "waters" of the present national disasters (cf. Ps 65:8). As in several other two-part psalms, while the halves are more or less different in tone or point of view, they nonetheless complement each other in their mutual tension (cf. Pss 19, 27, 50, 62, 66, 73).

The earth quaked at the storm on the Sea of Galilee (Matt 8:24), all Jerusalem quaked at the entry of the Lord (Matt 21:10), and earthquakes accompanied his death (Matt 27:51, 54) and resurrection (Matt 28:2) as he overcame the tomb. Christ praises the Father, through whose mercy he himself is the definitive victor over evil and death.

⟿ PSALM 78   faithless

Psalm 78 gives an account of Israel's history from a religious perspective, as a story of God's fidelity and his people's infidelity. While the emphasis is on Israel's failure to trust in the God who constantly worked wonders for them, the psalm ends on a positive note with God's choice of Judah, Zion, and David. While there is no guarantee that this people, too, will not lose faith, David is presented as a virtuous king who can embody on earth God's leadership of his people. The psalm can be read as an explanation for Israel's sufferings: they stem from lack of trust in the God who loved them, but God's fidelity will not in the end be undone by man's disobedience.

The psalm has pride of place as the central psalm in the Asaphite collection (Pss 73–83) and was viewed by the Masoretes as the center of the Book of Psalms. It preserves the truth of a benevolent and just God and lays the responsibility for national disasters squarely on the people's shoulders, leaving open the hope that some day God will obtain the response he seeks.

Over fifty-five of the seventy-two verses of the psalm are in 3 + 3 meter, including long sections like verses 10–19, 57–70, and small corrections to the Hebrew text could account for more. Other meters are represented as follows: 3 + 2 (vv. 7b, 33, 46); 3 + 4 (v. 8b); 4 + 3 (vv. 45, 53); 2 + 2 + 2 (vv. 6a, 20a, 38a, 56); 3 + 3 + 3 (vv. 49, 50, 71); 3 + 3 + 4 (v. 55).

An individual speaker addresses his people, telling them to give ear to his instruction (*tôrâ*), to incline their ears to the speeches of his mouth (v. 1). He will open his mouth in a "parable," "bubble forth a hidden lesson" ("lesson" is the same word as "riddle" in Ps 49:5, cf. Prov 1:5–6) from the past (v. 2). The author is assuming the role of a wisdom teacher uncovering the dynamics of the Yahweh/Israel relationship "from of old" (cf. Pss 74:2, 12, 77:6, 12, 44:2). Moving to the first person plural, he becomes a representative of all Israel's teachers, reporting what they have heard and know, what their fathers told them (v. 3; cf. Ps 44:2), not concealing from their sons, but to the next generation recounting the praises of the Lord and his strength and the wonders he has done (v. 4; cf. Ps 75:2) as well as the testimony and law he gave to Jacob/Israel, to be passed on from fathers to sons (v. 5) and on down the ages (v. 6). What God wanted (v. 7) was that these descendants place their "confidence" (cf. Ps 49:14, Job 31:24) in him, not forget his deeds, and "observe his commands" (cf. Prov 6:20). Verse 8 summarizes the response of Israel's "fathers" to this call: they were a "rebellious and defiant generation" (cf. Deut 21:18, 20), whose heart was not stable and whose spirit was not faithful to God. The reason they could not obey the commands was their failure to trust in God's help. As Augustine succinctly puts it, faith "impetrat quod lex imperat": faith asks for what the law commands (*Enarra-*

tiones in Psalmos 77.8). The introduction thus accurately sets forth the two poles of the psalm, the divine and human partners of the covenant, with their respective characteristics.

Verses 9–11 give a preview of God's judgment on the northern kingdom to be described later in the psalm (vv. 56–67). The "sons of Ephraim," armed archers, proved unreliable on the day of war (v. 9) because they did not keep God's covenant and in his law refused to walk (v. 10, chiasmus; for the parallelism "covenant/law" see Hos 8:1, Isa 24:5). They "forgot" (cf. v. 7) his doings and the "wonders" (cf. v. 4) he had shown them (v. 11). Whatever the specific event referred to, it signified a failure to comply with the revealed will of God. Before "their fathers" (cf. vv. 3, 5, 8) God worked wonders in the land of Egypt, the field of Zoan (v. 12). He split the sea and brought them through, and made the waters stand like a wall (v. 13; cf. Exod 15:8). He led them with a cloud by day and all night by a light of fire (v. 14, chiasmus). He split rocks in the desert and gave them torrents to drink (v. 15). He brought forth brooks from the rock and made waters descend like rivers (v. 16). At the beginning of her history God thwarted Israel's enemies, protected them from destruction and gave them drink in the desert, miracles that should have elicited Israel's trust.

But they continued to sin against God, to defy the Most High in the parched land (v. 17). They tested God in their hearts by asking for food for their souls (v. 18). They doubted whether God could "prepare a table" (cf. Ps 23:5) in the desert (v. 19). He may have struck the rock and made waters flow in overwhelming streams, but could he also give bread and provide meat for his people (v. 20)? God was enraged by this lack of trust: fire (as in Num 11:1) was kindled against Jacob and his anger rose against Israel (v. 21). Verse 22 is a classical expression of the main problem: the people put no faith (cf. v. 8) in God and did not trust in his salvation. It is this lack of faith that is behind Israel's defiance and disobedience. Refusing to "lean on" God (the root meaning of the word for "have faith," cf. Isa 7:9) means depriving oneself of the only true help. Jesus himself was unable to work miracles without the people's faith (cf. Mark 6:5–6), but with faith everything was possible (Mark 9:23): salvation (Mark 5:34, 10:52, Acts 16:31, Rom 10:9, Eph 2:8); justification (Rom 3:22, 25–26, 28, 10:4, 10); eternal life (John 3:15–16, 36, 5:24, 6:40, 47, 11:25, 20:31);

the indwelling of Christ (Eph 3:17); the gift of the Spirit (John 7:39); good works (John 14:12, Gal 5:6). This faith is what Jesus is asking for at the Last Supper when he tells the apostles to "remain" in him and "remain" in his love (John 15:4–9). Faith is the act by which we build our house on God's loving promises in Jesus and in so doing bear the fruit of love.

God did not immediately act on his anger but commanded the clouds above and opened the gateways of heaven (v. 23) to "rain" down on them manna for food and give them grain of "heaven" (v. 24; cf. Exod 16:4). The bread of the strong was eaten by men; provisions he sent to them to sate them (v. 25). After the manna came the quails (reversing the order of Exodus, cf. Exod 15:8, 12–14): he roused the east wind in the heavens and urged on the south wind by his power (v. 26). He rained on them meat like dust, and like the sands of the sea winged fowl (v. 27), making it fall in the midst of their camp all around their dwellings (v. 28). They ate and were utterly sated (cf. v. 25), and what they craved (lit. "their desire") he brought them (v. 29). They had not turned away from their craving (cf. Num 11:33–34), the food was still in their mouths (v. 30) when God's anger rose against them (cf. v. 21) and he killed the fattest among them and brought the elite of Israel to their knees (v. 31).

The author now abstracts from particular instances to describe the overall pattern of Israel's infidelity (vv. 32–37). The section is reminiscent of the Deuteronomist's assessment in the Book of Judges (e.g., Judg 2:11–19). Israel's "sin" is located again in their "not having faith in his wonders" (v. 32; cf. vv. 8, 22). Without that trust God could only finish off their days in vanity, and their years in sudden terror (v. 33)—a pun on *hebel* (nothingness, vanity) and *behālâ* (panic). If he slew them, they would search for him and return and "be on the lookout for" God (v. 34; cf. Ps 63:2). Then they "remembered" (cf. Ps 77:4, 7, 12) God their rock (v. 35), God the Most High their "redeemer" (Pss 74:2, 77:16). But they were fooling him with their mouths and with their tongues were lying to him (v. 36, chiasm; according to the Masora this verse is the exact center of the Book of Psalms). Their conversion was superficial, for "their heart was not firmly with him and they put no faith [cf. vv. 8, 22, 32] in his covenant" (v. 37), which they had promised to obey at Sinai (Exod 24:7–8). The inclusion with verse 32 highlights lack of trust as the root sin. But God maintains his compassion, covers their iniquity and does not ruin them; on multiple occasions he turns aside his anger (cf. vv. 21, 31) and does not rouse all his fury (v. 38). He remembers that these men are flesh, a spirit that passes never to return (v. 39).

The author returns to the desert: "How often they defied him" there (cf. vv. 8, 17) and caused him pain in the wilderness (v. 40). They returned to putting God to the test (cf. v. 18) and the Holy One of Israel they troubled (v. 41, chiasmus). They did not "remember" (unlike God, cf. v. 33) his "hand," the day when he ransomed them from the oppressor (v. 42), when he produced against Egypt his "signs," and his "portents" (see pairing of these nouns in Exod 7:3, Deut 6:22, 26:8) in the field of Zoan (v. 43, chiasmus; cf. v. 12). The author enumerates seven of the plagues of Egypt, following a different order from the Book of Exodus. God changed to blood their Nile branches, and their brooks they could not drink (v. 44, chiasmus; cf. Exod 7:19–21). He sent on them noxious insects to eat them (cf. Exod 8:20) and frogs to bring ruin on them (v. 45; cf. Exod 8:2). He gave to the young locust their produce and their crops to the winged locust (v. 46; cf. Exod 10:12–15). He killed with hail their vines and their fig trees with floods (v. 47; cf. Exod 9:22–25). He handed over to plague (corrected from "hail" in light of Hab 3:5) their cattle and their livestock to pestilence (v. 48, chiasmus as in the two previous verses; cf. Exod 9:3–6). In all these plagues, but especially in the final one to follow, God was sending forth the wrath of his anger (cf. vv. 21, 31, 38), rage, indignation, and distress, a troop of messengers of evils (v. 49). He cleared a path for his anger, did not withhold from death their souls, and their lives to plague he handed over (v. 50). Thus he struck all the firstborn in Egypt, the first of potency in the tents of Ham (v. 51; cf. Exod 12:29).

The immediate sequel to the last plague is the crossing of the Red Sea, already mentioned in verse 13. Here in four verses the author tells of the departure from Egypt and the arrival at Mount Zion. God broke camp for his people like a flock and urged them along (cf. Ps 48:15) like a herd in the desert (v. 52). He "led" them (cf. Exod 15:13) in security and they did not dread, while "the sea covered" (cf. Exod 15:10) their enemies (v. 53). He brought them to his holy territory, the mountain his right hand had acquired (v. 54). And he "drove out before them" (cf. Exod 34:11, 23:29, Deut 33:27) the nations and marked out with a measuring cord their inheritance and made the tribes of Israel dwell in their tents (v. 55).

What was Israel's response to this guidance of "God the Most High"? They put him to the test (cf. vv. 18, 41) and defied him (cf. vv. 8, 17, 40) and did not keep his testimonies (v. 56; cf. Deut 6:17, 2 Kgs 23:3). They were disloyal (cf. Ps 44:19) and faithless (cf. Hos 5:7, 6:7) as their fathers (cf. vv. 3, 5, 8, 12), askew like a deceiving bow (v. 57; cf. Hos 7:16). They grieved him with their high places (cf. Ezek 20:29) and with their idols (cf. Jer 8:19) "made him jealous" (v. 58, chiasmus; cf. Deut 32:16, 21). God "heard and was enraged" (as in v. 21), and he completely rejected Israel (v. 59). He forsook his dwelling in Shiloh, the tent of his dwelling among men (v. 60). He gave his "strength" (i.e., ark) into captivity and his honor into the hand of the oppressor (v. 61; cf. 1 Sam 4:11–22). He handed his people over to the sword (v. 62) and was enraged (cf. v. 59) against his inheritance (cf. v. 55). Fire devoured his young men, and his maidens had no celebrations (v. 63). His priests fell by the sword and his widows did not weep (v. 64).

The northern kingdom paid for its idolatry, but the Master awoke as if from sleep (cf. Ps 44:24, 1 Kgs 18:27), like a champion sobering up after wine (v. 65). He struck his oppressors behind and put them to everlasting scorn (v. 66). He rejected (cf. v. 59) the tent of Joseph, and the tribe of Ephraim he did not choose (v. 67, chiasmus). But he chose the tribe of Judah (v. 68), the mountain of Zion "which he loves" (cf. Ps 47:5). And he built like the [heavenly] heights his holy place, like the earth he founded it forever (v. 69). The construction of the temple in verse 69 is mentioned before the choice of David in the following verse so that the psalm can end with the emergence of one individual whose line would guarantee God's presence on earth, even when temple and monarchy were destroyed. God "chose" David (cf. 2 Sam 6:21, 1 Kgs 8:16) his "servant" (cf. 2 Sam 7:5, 8, Ezek 34:24, 37:25), "taking" him from the pens of the sheep (v. 70; cf. 2 Sam 7:8). He brought him from the care of the ewes to "shepherd" Jacob his "people" (cf. 2 Sam 5:2, Ezek 34:23, 37:24, Jer 30:9) and Israel his inheritance (v. 71; cf. vv. 55, 62). And he shepherded them in the "perfection of his heart" (cf. Gen 20:5–6, 1 Kgs 9:4) and with discerning (skilled) palms he "led" them (v. 72; cf. vv. 14, 53, Ps 77:21).

Thus the psalm ends with the verb that expresses God's guidance of his people: the righteous David is to continue God's "leading" of his people that began at the Exodus (cf. vv. 14, 53). The two themes—the gracious acts of God and Israel's failure to respond—come together in the figure of David, who by behaving "blamelessly" will become the instrument by which God will continue the gracious leading of his people.

The Son of David, Jesus Christ, is both the shepherd of God's people and the one who responds wholeheartedly to the Father's will, atoning for the sins of the "fathers."

~ PSALM 79   blood

Like Psalm 74 the psalm is a poignant lament on the destruction of Jerusalem in 587 BC (recorded in 2 Kgs 25:8–10), but like Psalm 78 it sees the cause of Israel's disasters in her own sin. While Psalm 74 asked for the restoration of the nation, Psalm 79 goes further in asking that God's name be vindicated through his vengeance on the enemies. As these enemies "poured out the blood" of Israel, may God "pour out [his] fury" on them. The Christian prays that hardened hearts throughout the world be toppled lest through them any of God's servants be separated from him (Matt 18:6).

The long opening verse (4 + 3 + 3 meter) summarizes the disaster: "God, the nations have come into your inheritance [cf. Pss 78:55, 62, 71], profaned your holy temple [cf. Lam 1:10], made Jerusalem a heap of rubble" (v. 1). Another tricolon (v. 2, 3 + 3 + 4 meter) describes how they have left the corpses of God's servants as food for the birds of heaven, the flesh of his devoted ones to the beasts of the earth (cf. Jer 7:33). A third verse envisions the slaughter: "They poured out blood like water in the environs of Jerusalem with none to do the burying" (v. 3; cf. Jer 14:16, Tob 1:17–19, 2:4, 7–8, 12:12–14, 13:15; verses 2–3 are applied in 1 Macc 7:17 to the slaughter of the Hasidaeans by Bacchides in 161 BC). The survivors have become the scorn of their neighbors (cf. Ps 31:12), the derision and ridicule of those around them (v. 4; cf. Ps 44:14). This ridicule will become the subject of petitions in the third section of the psalm (vv. 10–12).

The petitions begin in the second section with a solemn question-lament: How long will the Lord be angry—forever? (v. 5). Will his zeal (cf. Ps 69:10) burn like a fire (cf. Ps 78:21)? God is asked to "pour out" (cf. v. 3) his fury (cf. Sir 36:6) on the nations that do not know him and on the kingdoms that do not call on his name (v. 6; cf. Ps 14:4, 1 Thess 4:5), for they have "eaten up" Jacob and his home they have made desolate (v. 7, chiasmus; vv. 6–7 are found almost verbatim in Jer 10:25). The succeeding petitions (in 4 + 3 + 2 meter) ask God not to remember (cf. Ps 25:7) former iniquities but to let his compassion come quickly to meet his people, for they have greatly dwindled (v. 8). The community asks the

"God of our salvation" to help them for the sake of the glory of his "name" (cf. v. 6); may he rescue them and cover over their sins "for the sake of [his] name" (v. 9; cf. Ezek 20:44). The name Yahweh is associated with compassion (cf. v. 8, Exod 34:6): he would not be Yahweh if he did not forgive sins and restore his people's fortunes.

The third section develops this theme of God's vindication of his nature by asking that the nations be made aware of it. Like the previous section it begins with a question: Why should the nations say, "Where is their God?" (cf. Ps 42:11, Joel 2:17). May this God be recognized among the nations before the eyes of his people (cf. Sir 36:1–4) as he exacts vengeance for the blood of his servants that was shed (v. 10; the meter of this verse, 3 + 2 + 3 + 4, is typical of the irregular meter of the psalm). Even the New Testament promises that the blood of the saints will be avenged in God's time (Rev 16:4–6, 6:10), for it is mingled with the precious blood of the lamb without spot (1 Pet 1:19). May the groan of the prisoner come before God; in the greatness of his arm (cf. Ps 77:16) may he spare those condemned to die (v. 11). "Repay seven times over in the breast of our neighbors the scorn [cf. v. 4] with which they scorned you, Master" (v. 12). It is in God's interest as much as in the interest of his people that he act: his reputation among the nations is at stake. How will the nations come to worship him (cf. Pss 66:3–4, 8–9, 67:3–5, 8, 68:32–33) if they do not witness his fidelity to his promises to his chosen people?

The final verse expresses the confident determination of God's people, the flock of his pasture (cf. Pss 74:1, 77:21, 78:52), to thank him forever, to tell his praise forever and ever (v. 13).

The psalm borrows liberally but with discrimination from earlier biblical texts to create a vivid and heartfelt rendering of Israel's worst hour along with an earnest and trusting petition for redress.

∽ Psalm 80　vine

Israel's "specialness" to the Lord is portrayed in the psalm by two strong metaphors: the flock of sheep and the vine. "Shepherd of Israel, give ear; you who drive Joseph along [cf. Ps 78:52] like a flock [cf. Pss 74:1, 77:21, 78:52, 79:13], who sit on the cherubim, shine forth" (v. 2). It is from his throne above the ark that the Lord shepherds his people and lets his "face shine" on them (cf. Num 6:25) with favor. Before the ark found a resting place in Jerusalem it had sojourned at several shrines in the north. The territories allotted to Joseph's sons Ephraim and Manasseh represented much—and after the Assyrian incursions of 732 BC nearly all—of the northern kingdom. God is asked to rouse up his strength specifically on behalf of Ephraim and Manasseh with the addition of the small territory of Benjamin, and to come to save them (v. 3). The main request of the psalm appears in verse 4, which will be used as a refrain (cf. vv. 8, 20): "God, restore us, and let your face shine and we shall be saved." The northern kingdom has been brought down and needs restoration. The psalm, which may have originated in the northern kingdom, could be prayed by inhabitants of the southern kingdom in the years when the union of the two kingdoms was still hoped for (cf. 2 Kgs 23:15–20, Jer 31:1–22).

The speaker begins his lament to "Yahweh God of hosts" with a question (cf. Pss 74:1, 10, 77:8–10, 79:5, 10): how long will he be opaque (like smoke) to the prayer of his people (v. 5)? He makes them eat the bread of tears (cf. Ps 42:4) and drink their measure of tears (v. 6). He makes them the target of their neighbors, and their enemies deride them (v. 7). The refrain appears in verse 8 with the addition of "hosts" after God.

A vine from Egypt God brought; he drove out nations to plant it (v. 9, in 3 + 3 meter). He cleared the ground for it, and it put down its roots (cf. Hos 14:6) and filled the land (v. 10, 2 + 2 + 2 meter). Mountains were covered with its shadow, and its branches were like those of God's cedars (v. 11, 3 + 3 meter). It sent out its boughs to the sea and to the River [Euphrates] its shoots (v. 12; cf. Hos 14:7). The kingdom was prosperous and extensive. Why has God breached its stone walls, and why do they pluck it, all who pass along the way (v. 13)? It is ravaged by the boar of the forest, and the creatures of the field "graze" (verb used for "shepherd" in v. 2) on it (v. 14, chiasmus). Little remains of God's precious vine (cf. Jer 2:21, Hos 10:1, Matt 21:33–34).

The petitions begin with a call to the God of hosts to "return," to look from heaven and see, to visit this vine (v. 15) and to make firm what his right hand has planted and the son he fortified for himself (v. 16; possibly the king as God's adopted son, cf. Ps 2:7). It is burned with fire and cut down; at the rebuke of God's face may they (the ravagers) vanish (v. 17). May God's hand be on the man of his "right hand" (v. 18), the son of man whom God fortified for himself (cf. v. 16). The restoration of the vine will require a strong king who enjoys God's blessing.

Before the final refrain the community vows not to retreat from God. If he gives them life they will call upon his name in worship (v. 19). The name of Yahweh is then added to the refrain in its final appearance (v. 20).

Christ prays for the flourishing of the vine, which is himself, and of us who are the branches inserted in him (John 15:1–5). Ravaged by sin, it is daily renewed by the offering of his sacrifice. He is at once the vine, the lamb, and the shepherd that illumines his people (Rev 7:17).

∾ PSALM 81   honey

The principal speaker in the psalm is God. After the psalmist's invitation to praise, God addresses Israel, encouraging them to honor him so that he may confer on them his richest blessings. The psalm shares with the three preceding psalms (cf. Pss 78, 79, 80) the themes of God's earnest care for his people and the danger of Israel's rejection of this care. God wishes only to give life, but the people must open their hearts to receive it.

The invitation to praise is characteristic of the hymn genre, but here no particular group is addressed. The beginning is ecstatic: "Shout with joy to God our strength, cry jubilantly to the God of Jacob" (v. 2; for Jacob see Pss 75:10, 76:7, 78:5, 71, 79:7). The second verb designates the cry used in Israel's holy battles (Num 10:9, Jos 6:10, 20, 1 Sam 17:20, 52, 2 Chr 13:15), the cry of victory (Ps 41:12), and the cry of worship (Ezra 3:13, Zeph 3:14) before the God seated on the ark (1 Sam 4:5–6, 2 Sam 6:15); the verb was last met in Psalms 65:14 and 66:1. The psalmist calls for the accompaniment of music and the sounding of the tambourine (v. 3), the pleasant harp with the lyre (cf. Pss 33:2, 57:9, 71:22). The blowing of the šôfār (ram's horn) at new moon and full moon is to indicate the celebration of "our feast" (v. 4; no other text mentions two such feast days in conjunction). For that is the statute given to Israel by the God of Jacob (v. 5). Several passages in the Law stipulate certain days for solemn worship of the Lord (cf. Exod 23:14–17 [Elohist]; 34:18–23 [Yahwist]; Deut 16:1–17 [Deuteronomist]; Lev 23 and Num 28–29 [Priestly]).

Where we might expect the body of the hymn, we have instead an oracle introduced by a tricolon (v. 6). The speaker recalls that Yahweh enjoined a testimony on Joseph (cf. Pss 77:16, 78:67, 80:2) when he (the

Lord) went out against the land of Egypt. This "testimony" will be the first of the Ten Commandments, which the speaker introduces with the third part of the tricolon (v. 6c), in which he claims to hear an unknown language: this is the mysterious oracle of God, which will continue to the end of the psalm. God recounts how he freed Israel's shoulder from the harsh burden of servitude in Egypt (cf. Exod 1:11, 2:11, 5:4–5, 6:6–7), how their palms were released from the work-basket (v. 7). In their distress they called and he delivered them; he answered them in the shelter of the thunder (v. 8); the author telescopes the exodus from Egypt and the theophany on Sinai. Following the pattern of verse 6, the third colon of verse 8 announces the passage to follow: God tested the people at the waters of Meribah (without Massah, as in Num 20:13, 24, 27:14).

The opening of God's "speech within a speech" (vv. 9–11) is plangent: "Listen, my people, and I will witness to you; Israel, if only you would listen to me" (v. 9). There is to be for them no foreign god (v. 10; cf. Ps 44:21), and let them not prostrate to an alien god (cf. Deut 32:12). The people's lack of trust in the desert is an apostasy. It was Yahweh their God who brought them up from the land of Egypt (v. 11): if they opened their mouth he would fill it, either with food or with words of praise. But his people did not listen (cf. v. 9, Jer 11:8, 10, Ezek 3:7, 20:8) to his voice, and Israel did not accede to him (v. 12). He had no choice but to leave them in their stubbornness of heart (cf. Deut 29:18, Jer 9:13, 13:10, 16:12) to follow their own counsels (v. 13; cf. Jer 7:24, Mic 6:16). The foreign and alien god is revealed to be their own will, which they have preferred to the will of the saving God.

Yet God's offer is still made: would that his people would listen (cf. vv. 9, 12) to him and Israel walk in his ways (v. 14; cf. Deut 10:12, 11:22). It would take God little to humble their enemies (cf. Deut 9:3) and against their oppressors to turn his hand (v. 15; cf. Deut 32:41). Those who hate the Lord would cower before his people (cf. Pss 18:45, 66:3, Deut 33:29) in a lasting subjection (v. 16). But the Lord would feed his people with finest wheat (cf. Deut 32:14), and from the rock with honey (cf. Deut 32:13) he would sate them (v. 17, chiasmus). Since in the psalms of Asaph God himself has been called Israel's "Rock" (cf. Pss 73:26, 78:35), the psalmist may be suggesting that the taste of God's sweetness is the reward of those who listen to him.

Whether in the Old or New Testament what God wants from his children is such listening (cf. Deut 4:1, 5:1, 6:3, 4, Prov 1:8, 4:1, 10, 8:32, Isa 55:2–3, Jer 7:23, 11:4–7, Mark 9:7). This is not just "overhearing" but a reception of the divine word in mind and heart (cf. Matt 17:5, Jas 1:21–23) with the determination to obey. It is the preference of God to self that undoes the perversion of sin and opens the door to all God's blessings. It is the one who hears the Lord's voice and opens the heart to him that enjoys a banquet with him (Rev 3:20, 22); the one who listens and obeys is the one who endures (Matt 7:24–25); the one who hears the word of God in the soil of a generous and good heart is the one who takes it to himself and bears fruit (Luke 8:15).

⌇ PSALM 82   gods

The psalm discloses that behind the perversion of justice on earth are supernatural powers, which it calls gods. In a heavenly gathering of gods like those envisioned in Near Eastern mythologies (cf. 1 Kgs 22:19), Israel's God stands up; in the midst of the gods he judges (v. 1; for these gods, cf. Deut 32:8–9; for the judgment on them, cf. Isa 41:21–24). God's speech is divided into two parts, separated by a verse of comment by the psalmist. God asks how long (cf. Ps 80:5) will the gods judge wrongly and favor the wicked? (v. 2). They should judge the weak (cf. Ps 72:13) and the orphan (cf. Ps 10:14, 18, Deut 10:18, Isa 1:23, Jer 5:28, Zech 7:10); to the poor (cf. Ps 72:2, 12) and destitute they are to grant justice (v. 3, chiasmus; cf. Lev 19:15). They should bring to safety the weak and the needy (cf. Ps 72:4), and from the hand of the wicked rescue them (v. 4, chiasmus).

But the psalmist observes that the gods are corrupt: they neither know nor discern their duty and walk in darkness. As a result the very foundations of the earth totter: when the divine order of the world which respects every human creature, especially the weak and helpless (cf. Exod 22:20–23, 23:6, Deut 24:17, Prov 14:31, 19:17, 29:7, 31:9, Isa 1:17, 10:1–2, 11:4, Jer 5:28–29, Amos 8:6–7), is violated, the world of human society disintegrates (v. 5).

God resumes his speech and delivers his verdict on the corrupt judges: "I said, 'Gods you are, and sons of the Most High, all of you' [as pagan gods were often conceived to be]. But like men you will die and like one of the princes fall" (v. 7). They lose not only their divinity but their very existence. The psalm shows God's intention to neutralize and pulverize all spiritual powers responsible for the corruption of justice on earth, whether they be pure spirits or human judges under the domination of sin. He will not have a world where evil triumphs definitively.

The speaker or community concludes by asking that God rise and judge the earth, for he is destined to inherit all nations (v. 8). The verse matches the psalmist's comment at the end of the first part of God's speech (cf. v. 5). The justice demanded by the God of Israel is to become the justice of nations hitherto ruled by corrupt powers. The Songs of Asaph have moved from prayer for the restoration of Israel and avowal of her sin to the expectation of an extension of God's reign to the whole world. The theme will be brought to a climax in the following psalm, the last in the Asaph series.

The collapse of the false gods is the work of Christ, who "stripped the Sovereignties and the Powers, and paraded them in public, behind him in his triumphal procession" (Col 2:15; cf. 1 Pet 3:22, Eph 1:20–23, Rev 19:19–21). The kingdom of this God is a reign of justice (Luke 18:7–8, Rev 19:2, 11, 20:14–15).

∼ PSALM 83   Midian

Like Psalm 58 this psalm has been expunged from the Roman Liturgy of the Hours, partly for the strange and unpleasant images, partly for its vengeful tone with respect to the enemies, and partly because of its unfamiliar names of people and places. But the psalm provides a fitting conclusion to the Songs of Asaph (Pss 73–83) with its promise of the overthrow and even conversion of the nations hostile to Israel and her God. The first half of the psalm portrays the threat posed by the nations, the second prays for and foresees Yahweh's victory over these nations and their alliance.

The psalm is in 3 + 3 meter with an extra beat in the first colon of verse 12 and in the second colon of verses 5 and 10. Verse 13 is in 2 + 2 + 2 meter. Removal of "your name" in verse 19 gives a meter of 4 + 3 for that verse; minor deletions in verses 5, 10, and 12 would give 3 + 3 also for those verses (cf. Kraus, *Psalmen*, 2:576).

The psalm opens with an urgent cry: "O God, no silence for you!" (Alter, *Book of Psalms*, 294). "Do not be deaf and do not be calm, God" (v. 2). For behold, the enemies are churning, and those who hate God are lifting their heads [in rebellion] (v. 3). Their hatred for God is manifested in their hatred for his people, against whom they conspire in a circle, taking counsel against God's "sheltered ones" (v. 4; cf. Ps 17:14). Their goal is to efface them from among the nations so that the name of Israel will never be remembered (v. 5). Yes, they take counsel together (cf. v. 4) with a single heart; against Yahweh they have made a covenant (v. 6). Now comes a list of the enemies (v. 7): the tents of Edom and of the Ishmaelites, Moab and the sons of Hagar (= Ishmaelites, cf. Gen 16:7–16, 25:12–18, 1 Chr 5:10, 18–22), Gebal (southeast of the Dead Sea) and Ammon and Amalek, Philistia with the people of Tyre (v. 8). To these nations and tribes to the south, east, and west of Israel is joined the great empire of Assyria, which would invade from the north (v. 9), becoming the "arm" of the "sons of Lot" (Moab and Ammon, cf. Gen 19:30–38).

The bird's-eye view of the enemies reminds the psalmist of God's original victories over enemy incursions under the Judges. The petitions begin by calling on God to repeat these triumphs (v. 10), to treat the enemy like Midian, the tribe expelled by Gideon (Judg 7:23–25), and like Sisera and Jabin, the Canaanite commander and the king defeated under Deborah at the wadi Kishon (cf. Judg 4:15–16, 23–24). According to the psalm the Midianites were exterminated at En-dor (v. 11; Judg 7:1 puts the battle at En-harod); they became like dung on the ground (cf. 2 Kgs 9:37). God is asked to make the enemy nobles like Midianite chieftains Oreb and Zeëb (Judg 7:25), and like Zebah and Zalmunna (cf. Judg 8:5, 12, 21) all their leaders (v. 12, chiasmus). These were men who wanted to take possession of God's "meadows" (v. 13). The next three verses portray the annihilation of the enemies with images from the natural world. May God make them like tumbleweed (cf. Isa 17:13) or stubble before the wind (v. 14; cf. Pss 1:4, 35:5). Like fire burning a forest or a flame devouring mountains (v. 15), may God pursue them with his storm and with his strong wind terrify them (v. 16, chiasmus).

The final three verses express what the psalmist ultimately wants for the nations: may God cover their faces with dishonor so that they seek the name of the Lord (v. 17). May they be permanently shamed and terrified, and may they be brought to confusion and vanish (v. 18). What is to be annihilated is the hostility of the nations while the nations themselves turn to God. Thus would be fulfilled the prophecy of Psalm 81:15–16 and the prayer of Psalm 82:8. The nations who nearly succeeded in destroying Israel (cf. the earlier Asaph psalms) will end by worshipping him as ruler of the world. It is this hope that is expressed by the final petition (v. 19): "Let them know that you alone—your name is the Lord—are the Most High over all the earth." The Elohist Psalter thus ends with the whole world acknowledging Yahweh as the Most High God. The name used so sparingly in Psalms 42–83 ends by conquering the world.

Christians know that the name of God is Jesus, at which every being in heaven, on earth, and in the underworld bends the knee, confessing that Jesus is Lord (Phil 2:9–11). It is the only name by which we can be saved (Acts 4:12), the name to be brought before all pagans and kings (Acts 9:15).

∼ PSALM 84   threshold

The psalmist's love for the temple as the place of encounter with God has been expressed in several psalms—26:8, 42:3–5, 43:3–4, 63:2–3—but never so ardently as in Psalm 84. The psalm is part of the collection attributed to the sons of Korah (Pss 42–49, 84–85, 87–88), in which the centrality of the temple and its holy mountain and city is a major focus. The divine name appears seven times in the psalm, a frequency striking in comparison with the psalms of the Elohist Psalter (Pss 42–83), where it occurs an average of once per psalm.

The psalmist is overcome with the loveliness of the dwellings of the Lord of hosts (v. 2). It is not just an external beauty but the beauty of the infinite God taking up residence among his creatures out of love. The psalmist's soul yearns (cf. Ps 17:12! for the only other use of this verb in the psalter) and languishes (cf. Ps 73:26) for the courts of this Lord; his heart and his flesh shout with joy to the "living God" (v. 3; cf. Ps 42:3). The presence of this living God melts his physical and spiritual being; he feels called into the ecstasy of communion. Visible symbols of the comfort he finds in God's house are the sparrow and swallow that make their nests for their young by the altars of the Lord of hosts, the psalmist's king (cf. Ps 74:12) and God (v. 4). The section ends with the first of three makarisms in the psalm, corresponding to its three sections: Happy those who dwell in his house, continually praising him (v. 5). As in Psalm 63:3–6, the enjoyment of God's presence expresses itself spontaneously in praise, is not complete until it breaks into praise.

A second makarism reveals the joy of the temple spreading out even to those on pilgrimage toward it: happy the man whose strength is precisely in God's dwelling, whose heart is on pilgrimage (v. 6). Passing through the barren "valley of shrubs," pilgrims in their very eagerness transform it into a spring, and rain wraps it with blessings (v. 7). They "go from vigor to vigor" as they approach Mount Zion, where they will "see" (or "be seen by") the God of gods (v. 8; the speaker in this section speaks *about* rather than *to* God): not only joy but strength for the journey emanates from the holy place and from those possessed by the desire to reach it. Those who eagerly seek God make the parched world an oasis.

The celebration of God's presence in the temple is interrupted by two verses of petition, each in chiastic form: "Lord God of hosts, hear my prayer; give ear, God of Jacob" (v. 9); "Our shield see, O God, and look on the face of your anointed one" (v. 10). The first verse is generic, the second asks that God favor the king, as in other psalms where the temple is the focus (cf. Pss 61:7–8, 63:12). Since better is a day in God's courts (cf. v. 3) than a thousand [ordinary days], the psalmist has chosen to lie at the threshold of God's house (switch from second to third person) rather than to stay in the tents (cf. Ps 83:7) of the wicked (v. 11). One who dwells so close to God is inevitably purified by the heat of his rays (cf. Isa 33:14–16)—in fact the following verse calls the Lord God a sun and shield, that is, the source of spiritual healing (cf. Mal 3:20, Isa 60:19–20; in Rev 21:22–23 temple and light images coalesce in God and the Lamb) and a defense against evil, the latter function being shared with the earthly king (cf. v. 10). This Lord dispenses kindness and glory, refusing no good thing to those who walk blamelessly (v. 12). Once again the Psalms proclaim the connection between intimacy with God and moral purity (see on Ps 5): only the pure in heart can see God (Matt 5:8). The final verse of the psalm and its third makarism, addressed to God, declares how this purity is obtained: "Lord of hosts, happy the man who trusts in you" (v. 13). It is through relying on the lordship of Jesus that we obtain the elimination of our sins (cf. Rom 4:5, 24–25, Acts 10:43, 13:38–39, 26:18).

Christ is the temple, Christ with all his members. The believer languishes in his courts, longing for full union with him. When he is possessed by the Lord he becomes a living stone in that temple (1 Pet 2:4–5, 9–10), consumed in praise of the Father with his brothers and sisters in the unity of the Holy Spirit (Eph 5:18–20).

The 3 + 2 meter of the early verses gives way to less obvious meters in the later verses where additions may have been made.

∾ PSALM 85   met

Israel has received the Lord's favor and forgiveness, an end to their captivity and his anger. Yet the people are again experiencing his anger and beseech his mercy and salvation. God answers by promising all they want and more. The 3 + 3 meter prevails in nearly all verses.

The Lord has taken pleasure in his land (cf. Pss 44:4, 77:8, Hag 1:8) and restored the fortunes of Jacob (v. 2). It is not necessary to attach this verse to any specific event, since the Lord's intention throughout sacred history is to make his people prosper against all adversity: it is the constant behind all his works. He has taken away the people's iniquity and covered all their sins (v. 3), the cause of all their hardships. He has put away the rage incurred by these sins, turning back from the wrath of his anger (v. 4).

Yet a new situation makes the people pray, "Restore us, God of our salvation, and eliminate your grievance with us" (v. 5). Can God be forever angry at them, protracting his anger (cf. v. 4) through the generations (v. 6)? Will he not again give them life so that his people might be glad in him (v. 7)? After the two sets of questions, one expecting the answer No, the other Yes, comes another petition to match verse 5: "Make us see, Lord, your love, and your salvation give to us" (v. 8, chiasmus): God's *ḥesed* is his covenant attachment to his people; salvation (cf. v. 5) is the action that proceeds from it.

The psalmist will listen to the response of the Lord God, who speaks peace to his people and his devout ones, who for their part will not return to foolish confidence (v. 9). The speaker summarizes the Lord's message in his own words: God's salvation is near to those who fear him—that is, respect his lordship—so that glory may dwell "in our land" (v. 10; cf. John 1:14). If glory is the radiance of divine beauty, the following verses describe in what it consists. Four fundamental divine attributes/gifts are personified as converging in the land: love and faithfulness have met; justice and peace have kissed (v. 11). Two of the attributes reappear in different imagery: God's faithfulness will be so present that it "sprouts" from the earth (cf. Isa 45:8), while justice looks kindly down from heaven (v. 12). Verse 13 repeats the upward/downward theme in reverse order: The

Lord will bestow good things while the earth gives forth its produce; the latter word includes both fruitful crops and the salvation wrought on earth by God's presence (cf. Ps 67:7). The Lord's gift of rain enables the earth to bring forth and multiply his gifts (cf. Ps 65:10–14). The attribute of "justice" appears one final time, again personified, this time as walking before God, directing his steps on the way (v. 14). When divine love and faithfulness, justice and peace meet in the land, earth becomes a place that produces and reflects the divine goodness.

The words used three or more times in the psalm serve together to convey its meaning: "return/restore" (five times); "land" (four times); "give," "salvation," "people," "justice" (three times each). The genius of the psalm is its giving vivid earthly imagery for divine attributes, showing how the intention of the divine is to become incarnate. In this sense it prepares us, like similar texts in Second Isaiah, for the gospel of the Word made flesh, whose "glory" dwelt among us (John 1:14). The coming of the Son of God and his resurrection from the dead have created a "new heaven and a new earth" (Rev 21:1) where the "fruit of justice is sown in peace" (Jas 3:18).

∼ Psalm 86   forgiving

The psalmist casts himself as a poor man whose salvation depends on the generous mercy of Israel's God, whose servant he is. The center of the psalm glorifies the name of God, to whom the psalmist will give witness among the nations by his life according to the covenant. The psalm thus profiles man and God in their essential natures: one needy, trusting, and reverent; the other full of bountiful and saving love. It portrays how a single human being enjoys the divine "love and faithfulness" featured in the previous psalm. The beginning and end of the psalm are joined by their use of the terms "save" and "servant."

The verses display no consistent meter, but all verses except 3, 7, 12, and 16 contain at least one four-beat colon.

In the first section the verb "call" appears three times, and the verb "answer" twice. God is the one who answers when man calls, a theme that, along with its equivalent "hear/prayer" appears from the very beginning of the psalter (cf. Pss 3:5, 4:2, 17:6, 20:10, 22:3, 27:7, 81:8). The speaker asks the Lord to turn his ear and answer (v. 1), for he is poor and needy (same pun as in Pss 69:30, 70:6). As one of the Lord's devout he asks God to guard his soul and prays: "Save your servant—you are my God—for I trust [cf. Pss 13:6, 25:2, 31:15] in you" (v. 2). The speaker is God's client. He asks his Master to "have mercy" (accompanied with "call/answer" in Pss 4:2, 26:7, with "poor" in Ps 24:16) as he calls on him all day long (v. 3).[9] May God gladden the soul of his servant (v. 4), for to his Master he lifts his soul (cf. Ps 25:1). This Master is good and forgiving (cf. Exod 34:9, Jer 31:34), rich in mercy to all who call on him (v. 5). May the Lord turn his ear to the speaker's prayer and attend to the voice of his pleading (v. 6). On the day of distress he calls, for the Lord hears (v. 7). The distress of the psalmist is generic; minor specifications will be given in the final section, but the business of the opening section is to characterize the relationship that obtains between the two protagonists, that is, humble trust and covenant love.

The center of the psalm focuses on God's glory and wonders and the psalmist's witness to these. No one among the gods is like this God, no works are like his (v. 8). All the nations that he made will come to prostrate themselves before the Master's face and will glorify his name (v. 9) as a great God who works wonders (cf. Ps 78:4) and is the only God (v. 10). The psalmist would be instructed in the Lord's way, which for the

---

9. Just as Augustine regards the psalms as spoken by Christ whose body extends to all the earth (cf. on Ps 61:3), so he views this body as extended through time, commenting on Psalm 86:3:

Have mercy on me, Lord, for I have cried to you all day long. Not just on one day; *all day long* must be understood as throughout time. From the day when Christ's body began to groan in the wine press, until the end of the world when the pressures have passed away, this one person groans and cries out to God, and we, each of us in our measure, add our own contribution to the clamor of the whole body. You have cried out during your days, and your days have expired; someone else took your place and cried out in his days; you here, he there, she somewhere else. The body of Christ cries out all day long, as its members give place to each other and succeed each other. One single person spans the ages to the end of time, and it is still the members of Christ who go on crying out, though some of them are already at rest in him, others are raising their cry now, others will cry out when we have gone to rest, and others again after them. God hears the voice of Christ's entire body saying, *I have cried to you all day long.* But our head is at the Father's right hand to intercede for us; some of his members he welcomes, others he chastises, others he is cleansing, others he consoles, others he is creating, others calling, others recalling, others correcting, others reinstating. (*Enarrationes in Psalmos* 85:5)

Christian is charity (cf. 1 Cor 12:31–13:1), so that he might walk in his faithfulness, that is, rely on God's faithfulness in his daily actions (v. 11a). May God unify his heart to fear the Lord's name (v. 11b; cf. Ps 61:6, Deut 6:2, 13, 10:12, 28:58, Neh 1:11, Mal 3:20): he wishes his heart to be given totally to the God who has revealed himself as savior in Israel. In thanking his Master, his God, with all his heart he will become an eternal witness to the glory of the divine name (v. 12). For he has personally experienced the greatness of the divine love: God has rescued his soul from the depths of the underworld (v. 13).

The final section returns to the urgency of petition. In a near duplicate of Psalm 54:5, the psalmist laments that proud men have risen against him, a gathering of ruthless men seek his "soul" (cf. vv. 2, 4, 13), men who do not place God in front of them (v. 14). In their lack of interest in God's will they are the antithesis of those who "fear the Lord" (cf. v. 11); their attack on the psalmist is what prompts his prayer. He appeals to God (v. 15) in the exact terms of the Lord's self-definition to Moses on Sinai (Exod 34:6): his Master is a "God compassionate and gracious, slow to anger and abundant in love and faithfulness." The psalmist asks this God to turn to him and have mercy on him (cf. v. 3), to give his strength to his servant (cf. vv. 2, 4), and to save the son of his handmaid (v. 16). May God produce for him a sign for good so that those who hate him may see it and be shamed, for the Lord will have helped and consoled him (v. 17).

The psalm is the only song in Book Three attributed to David, coming between pairs of psalms of the sons of Korah. The individual is to benefit from the attributes of God that come to earth in the previous psalm (cf. Ps 85:11). His witness will lead the nations to glorify the name of the God of Israel. The next psalm will portray God as precisely the God of all nations.

The divine *hesed* is shown in God's raising his son Jesus from the dead for the forgiveness of sins (Eph 2:4–6). Through Jesus the nations will come to give glory to God (cf. Rom 15:8–9).

∾ PSALM 87   mother

Several psalms have suggested that the pagan nations are destined to worship the God who dwells in Jerusalem (cf. Pss 2:10–11, 22:28–30, 66:4, 67:4, 6, 8, 68:31–33, 72:10–11, 86:9). Psalm 87 makes this theme explicit, describing how nations in every direction will regard themselves as "born" in Zion. Zion is to become the source of their life, for in her are the "springs" of life.

The foundations of the city are mentioned even before the city is identified: they are on the "holy mountains" (v. 1), the mountain of Zion on which Jerusalem was built. The mountain is holy because God has chosen to dwell there. He loves the gates of Zion more than all the dwellings (favorite word of the sons of Korah, cf. Pss 43:3, 46:5, 49:12, 84:2) in Jacob (v. 2)—gates being both the entrance to the city and the place where judgments were given (cf. Deut 22:15, Prov 22:22, Amos 5:10, 12, 15). Glorious things are told of Jerusalem since it is the "city of God" (v. 3). Glorious things are to be said of the Church of Christ because it is his dwelling on earth.

At the center of the psalm God speaks. He acknowledges Rahab (term for Egypt, cf. Isa 30:7) and Babylon as among those who "know" him, also Philistia and Tyre with Ethiopia (cf. Ps 68:32); nations in all directions acknowledge Yahweh in Zion as their God, who regards them as "born there" (v. 4). They are adopted into the family of God. When we say that the church is "catholic" we mean that the diverse gifts of every people have a place in her and find their fulfilment in her. About Zion it can be said that each man was born in her, and he, the Most High, established her (v. 5). Similarly the Church of Christ, the "Jerusalem above," is "our mother" (Gal 4:26), and we are her freeborn children (Gal 4:31). Yahweh is envisioned as keeping an account of peoples in which is written the name of each person who was "born there" (v. 6; cf. Ps 69:29, Dan 12:1, Luke 10:20, Rev 20:12). We are saved by our membership in Christ, which comes about through faith and baptism, by which we become children of God (cf. John 3:3–8, 15, Titus 3:5, 1 John 3:1–2, 5:1, 4).

A final verse portrays the worshippers, who might be Israelites or foreigners, singing while they dance (for this festive dance see Judg 21:23): "All my springs are in you" (v. 7). As the mountain of God, Zion must have its spiritual rivers like the streams that watered the garden of Eden (Gen 2:6, 10–14, Ezek 47:1–12, Ps 46:5, Rev 22:1–2). Thus the psalms of the sons of Korah bring to completion one of their favorite themes: Zion as the city of God. For Christians the psalm is a celebration of the gathering of all peoples in Christ to the glory of the Father (Matt 8:11, Isa 2:2–3, 25:6–10).

∼ PSALM 88   darkness

Three times in the Garden Christ implored his Father to take away his chalice of suffering (Mark 14:35–41). Three times our psalmist cries out to the Lord from acute pain. The psalm is composed entirely of lament with no petition other than a cry to be heard, no expression of trust, no vow of praise. Even in the lament there is little description of suffering but only a reproach to God, a questioning of how the God of life and mercy can permit his creature to waste away. The lament is in fact an appeal to God to act according to his nature. This last of the psalms of the sons of Korah has little in common with the others in the collection (Pss 42–49, 84–85, 87) with their focus on the temple and the holy city, but the psalm shares some of the spirit of the lament with which the first group opened (Pss 42–44).

A different verb for "cry" is used at the opening of each section (v. 2, "cry out"; v. 10, "call"; v. 14, "cry for help"). The speaker cries out day and night before the Lord, the God of his salvation (v. 2). The image of his prayer coming into God's presence is paralleled by that of God turning his ear toward the lamentation (v. 3; cf. Ps 61:2). Not only sated with evils is his soul, but his life to the underworld is drawing near (v. 4, chiasmus). He is considered to be among those going down to the pit, has become like a man without force (v. 5), homeless among the dead, like the slain lying in the tomb whom God no longer remembers, for they are cut off from his hand (v. 6). God has placed him in a bottomless pit (v. 7), in dark and watery deeps (cf. Pss 68:23, 69:3, 16). Chaos is encroaching on his life and has all but extinguished it. By him was upheld God's fury, as though he bore the full weight of it, and with all his waves God is oppressing him (v. 8, chiasmus)—the abstract "fury" of the first colon is paralleled by the concrete image of waves in the second. God has even distanced the psalmist's acquaintances from him, made him a loathsome thing to them; imprisoned he cannot escape (v. 9).

With his eye wasted with affliction (consonance in Hebrew: ʿênî dāʾăbāh minnî ʿōnî) he "calls on" the Lord all day long, spreading out his palms to him (v. 10). This middle section of the lament is a series of questions: For the dead can God work wonders? Will the shades rise up and thank him (v. 11; cf. Pss 6:6, 30:10)? Will there be recounted in the tomb

God's covenant love, his faithfulness in the realm of the dead (v. 12, chi-asmus)? The twin attributes—God's covenant love and faithfulness—(cf. Pss 85:11, 86:15) make Yahweh a God who gives life, and man's response to the gift is spontaneous praise (cf. Isa 38:17–19, Sir 17:27–28, Luke 7:16). Can there be known in the dark God's wonders (cf. v. 11, Pss 77:12, 15, 78:12) or his justice in the land of oblivion (v. 13, chiasmus)? It is only by giving life that God will be known as the God of life.

Yet a third time the psalmist cries to the Lord for help, envisaging his prayer "going to meet" (cf. v. 3) him in the morning (v. 14). Why does the Lord reject (cf. Pss 43:2, 44:10, 60:3, 12, 74:1) his soul and hide his face from him?—one object referring to the psalmist, the other to the Lord (v. 15). "Poor am I [pun found in Pss 69:30, 70:6, 86:1] and expiring since my youth; I have borne your horrors [cf. Ps 55:5], I am numb" (v. 16). In identifying himself as "poor," the psalmist claims both his helpless-ness and his right to God's help (Pss 12:6, 22:25, 34:7, 35:10, 69:30, 86:1). Over him have passed God's wraths; his terrors (cf. Job 6:4) have silenced him (v. 17, chiasmus). It is no surprise that these onslaughts of God are compared to waters surrounding him all day, engulfing him altogether (v. 18; cf. vv. 7, 8). God has distanced from him the one who loves him and his friend (v. 19; cf. Ps 38:12 for this pair); his acquaintances are darkness (cf. vv. 7, 13).

The pain of the psalmist in the first section was still presented in somewhat objective terms, with a focus on comparisons and surround-ings. In the final section the pain is an interior experience of being over-whelmed by God's hostility to the point of extinction. This pain was ex-perienced by Jesus and overcome in his resurrection from the dead. "If Christ has made himself the speaker of psalms that express the worst misery of the human condition, that corresponds to the kenosis by which God made himself man so that we might become God" (Rondeau, *Les commentaires patristiques*, 394; my translation). Christ's followers experi-ence the same pain,[10] sustained by the faith in that resurrection that is

---

10. An early manuscript tersely defines the psalm as "the voice of Christ and of the Church, the one speaking in his passion, the other in temptations" (Salmon, *Les "Tituli Psalmorum*," 106).

our victory over the world (cf. 1 John 5:4–5, John 16:33). Even in profoundest darkness there remains the conviction that the God of mercy is a God of salvation.

The psalm is generally in 3 + 3 meter, with exceptions in verse 2 (3 + 2 + 2 meter), verses 14–16 (4 + 3 meter) and verse 19 (2 + 2 + 2 meter). Repeated words serve to tie the sections together: "prayer" (vv. 3, 14), "face" (vv. 3, 15), "soul" (vv. 4, 15), "graves" (vv. 6, 12), and by using three words from earlier in the psalm, "distance" and "acquaintances" from verse 9 and "darkness" from verse 7, the final verse provides a tidy summary and conclusion.

∾ PSALM 89   Rahab

Psalm 89 is a vast psalm with three quite different but related sections. It is the final psalm of Book Three and has affinities with the psalms of the sons of Korah and of Asaph, which make up much of Books Two and Three. It is not unlike its predecessor in that it lays before the Lord an earthly situation that belies his faithfulness to his nature and his promises. It is the prayer of the Mystical Body of Christ enjoying God's promise of everlasting fidelity yet experiencing desolation and apparent abandonment. Out of its faith the Body cries out for rehabilitation.

The grand opening line of the psalm in Latin, "Misericordias Domini in aeternum cantabo," appears emerging from the mouth of Saint Teresa of Avila in the portrait painted during her lifetime. The full verse celebrates the two great attributes of the Lord: "The loving deeds [lit. "loves," plural of *ḥesed* and designating acts inspired by God's covenant love, cf. Ps 25:6, Isa 55:3, 63:7] of the Lord forever I will sing; to every generation I will publish your faithfulness with my mouth" (v. 2; the verse exhibits chiasmus as well as a change from third person to second). The psalmist will be a lasting witness to the profoundest of God's attributes. Declaring that love is built forever and God establishes his faithfulness in the heavens (v. 3), he begins with the phrase, "Indeed I say . . . ," indicating that the psalm will involve serious reflection on these two attributes, a reflection that will in fact end in lament. But first and without introduction an oracle of God is cited that prepares for the second section of the psalm: God declares that he has made a covenant with his chosen one, swearing to David his servant (v. 4). This covenant provides the psalm with its backbone (cf. vv. 29, 35, 40): the covenant is firmly in place yet seems to have been spurned. God's solemn promise to David through Nathan (2 Sam 7:8–16) was referred to as a "covenant" only from the time of the Exile (2 Sam 23:5, Isa 55:3, Jer 33:20–21, 2 Chr 13:5, 21:7); in the present psalm the covenant idea is influenced by the covenant with Israel and implies a responsibility on the side of the human partner (cf. Deut 7:9–12). Similarly an "oath" of God is mentioned only in later psalms (cf. Pss 110:4, 132:2, 12). The content of the oath is given in verse 5: For ever God will establish David's descendants (lit. "seed") and will build for generations his throne (cf. 2 Sam 7:13, 16).

Following the short oracle of verses 4–5, the first section of the psalm praises the grandeur of the Lord in heaven and his display of might on earth. The heavens (cf. v. 3) thank him for his wonders (cf. Ps 88:11, 13); his faithfulness too [is praised] in the assembly of the holy ones (i.e., lesser gods in the heavenly court) (v. 6). For who in the clouds can match the Lord or resemble the Lord among the sons of the gods (v. 7; cf. Ps 29:1, Job 1:6)? He is a dread God in the great circle of the holy ones, fearsome (cf. Pss 47:3, 68:36, 76:8, 13) among all who surround him (v. 8). Who is like the Lord God of hosts, a strong God surrounded by his faithfulness (v. 9). The Lord's supremacy is defined in relation to all other spiritual powers, which are subject to him. It extends even to the waters of the primitive chaos: he rules the pride of the sea, the lifting up of its waves he hushes (v. 10, chiasmus; cf. Luke 8:24). He crushed the sea-monster Rahab (cf. Isa 51:9) like a slain victim, with his strong arm scattering his enemies (v. 11) that he might establish the heavens and earth, the inhabited world and what fills it, on a firm foundation (v. 12). Thus he created north and south; Mounts Tabor and Hermon shout joyfully at his name (v. 13), recognizing him as their creator (like the exuberant praise of hills and valleys in Ps 65:13–14).

From deeds of creative prowess the psalmist moves to divine attributes. To God belongs an arm with might; strong his hand, exalted his right hand (v. 14; cf. v. 11 and Pss 44:3–4, 77:11, 16, 25). Justice and judgment are the foundation of his throne; love and faithfulness (cf. vv. 2, 3, Pss 85:11, 86:15, 88:12) attend before his face like courtiers (v. 15): metaphor and personification portray the close connection between the Lord and his attributes. But God's people on earth are not absent from this court: they are happy because they know the jubilant worship cry (cf. Pss 47:2, 65:14, 66:1, 81:2) and walk in the light of his "face" (v. 16;

cf. v. 15, John 11:9), shouting ecstatically every day in his name, exalted in his justice (v. 17; cf. Ps 88:13). In the following verse the transition is made to the "we" of the worshipping community: "For the adornment of their strength is you, and by your favor our horn [cf. Ps 75:6, 11] is exalted" (v. 18): after the verbs of "founding" (vv. 3, 5, 12, 15) come those of "raising" (vv. 14, 17, 18). For to the Lord belongs "our shield" (synonym for the king as in Ps 84:10), and to the holy one of Israel (cf. Pss 71:22, 78:41) [belongs] "our king" (v. 19). The final word of section one thus introduces the theme of section two.

The second section of the psalm is a long oracle of God about the Davidic dynasty. It is addressed not to the king, like the preliminary oracle of verse 5, but to God's devout ones, to whom he spoke in a vision (v. 20). The 3 + 3 meter of the speech, replaces the longer 4 + 4 meter of the first section; in fact the new meter already began in verse 17. God set a crown on a champion; he exalted (cf. vv. 14, 17, 18) one chosen (cf. v. 4) from the people. He found David his servant (cf. v. 4); with his holy oil he anointed him (v. 21, chiasmus; cf. 1 Sam 16:13). God's "hand" (cf. v. 14) will "be established" (cf. vv. 3, 5) for him, and the same arm that scattered sea monsters (cf. v. 11) will fortify him (v. 22). He will not be tricked by the enemy, nor will the perverse man oppress him (v. 23, chiasmus). God will beat down his oppressors before him and those who hate him God will afflict (v. 24, chiasmus). The Lord is here doing for David what he empowered the king himself to do in Psalm 18:33–43. The pair of divine attributes praised earlier in the psalm (cf. vv. 2, 3, 15) are now put at the king's service (v. 25), and in God's name (cf. vv. 13, 17) "his horn will be raised" (cf. v. 18). The king thus partakes in the stability and power of God. The king's "hand" will extend to the sea, and to the River (Euphrates) his right hand (v. 26, chiasmus). He will call God "my father [corresponding to "my son" in Ps 2:7], my God, and the rock of my salvation" (v. 27; cf. Pss 17:3, 88:2); God in turn will make him his firstborn son, highest of the kings of the earth (v. 28).

Forever God will guard his love for David, and his covenant with him is faithful (v. 29; cf. v. 4); it passes on to David's descendants (cf. v. 5), whose throne (cf. v. 5) will be "like the days of heaven" (v. 30). But the covenant has a reciprocal side: the sons of David must not abandon God's law or in his judgments fail to walk (v. 31; cf. Deut 17:18–20). Should they profane his statutes and not keep his commands (v. 32), he will punish their rebellion with a rod, and their iniquity with scourges (v. 33). But his love (cf. v. 29) God will not remove from David, nor will he be false to his faithfulness (v. 34, chiasmus; cf. vv. 2, 3, 6, 9, 25). He will not profane (cf. v. 32) his covenant (cf. v. 29), and what emerges from his lips he will not change (v. 35, chiasmus; cf. Ps 77:11). This same promise is then called an oath which God swore (cf. v. 4) by his holiness; he would never lie to David (v. 36). Verses 37 and 38 repeat the ideas of verse 5, adding the comparison of David's enduring throne to the sun (v. 37) and the moon, the latter a "faithful witness in the skies" (v. 38).

Abruptly reality breaks in (v. 39): "But you have rejected [cf. Ps 88:15], you have spurned, you have been enraged with your anointed one" (cf. v. 21). God has disavowed (cf. Lam 2:7) his covenant (cf. vv. 5, 29, 35) with his servant (cf. vv. 4, 21); he has profaned (cf. v. 35) his crown to the earth (v. 40), breaching all his stone walls, turning his fortifications into rubble (v. 41). All passersby ravage them; he has become the scorn of his neighbors (v. 42). God has exalted the right hand of his oppressors; he has made glad all his enemies (v. 43). God has turned back the blade of his sword and not sustained him in battle (v. 44). He has put an end to his brilliance, and his throne (against vv. 5, 30, 37) to the earth he has hurled (v. 45, chiasmus; this and the previous verse break the pattern of asyndeton in this third section). He has shortened the days of his youth; he has wrapped him in shame (v. 46). The laments lead to a question: "How long, Lord, will you be hidden—forever?—your fury [cf. Ps 88:8] burning like a fire?" (v. 47). The king himself finally speaks, asking God to remember what his lifetime is, of what worthlessness God has created all the sons of men (v. 48). What man lives and will not see death, will free his soul from the grasp of Sheol (v. 49)? Verses 48–49 provide a link with the following psalm on the brevity of life as well as with the previous psalm on the encroachment of death (cf. Ps 88:4, 11).

In the final three verses the psalmist summarizes his lament: where are the former loving deeds of the Master (v. 50), which he swore (cf. vv. 4, 36) to David in his faithfulness (cf. vv. 1, 2, 25, 34)? May the Master remember the scorn (cf. v. 42) of his servants, which the speaker—who now appears to be the king himself—bears in his bosom from all the many peoples (v. 51, translation uncertain). The Lord's enemies are scorning the footprints of his anointed one (v. 52). The final word of the psalm and also of Book Three (apart from the doxology) thus calls attention to

God's representative on earth who at the beginning of the psalter (Ps 2:1–9) and even in the present psalm (vv. 4–5, 20–38) was given such great promises yet seems to have been abandoned by the Lord. The book ends with a giant question mark, which it will be the task of the following book to answer.

The psalms of Book Three have been full of national darkness balanced fairly regularly with passages of light, but for the moment we are at a nadir in Israel's history corresponding to the moment of the Messiah's death on the cross. Nothing is left for Israel but to continue to recite the mercies and faithfulness of the Lord forever, presenting him with the discrepancies between his loving plan and the present sordid reality. The terse doxology of Book Three (v. 53) reflects the grimness of the historical moment.

∼ Psalm 90   years

The psalm is the only one attributed to Moses, who is mentioned several times in Book Four (cf. Pss 99:6, 103:7, 105:26, 106:16, 23, 32; elsewhere in the psalter only Ps 77:21). After the series of psalms in Book Three lamenting the destruction of Jerusalem and the collapse of the Davidic dynasty, the compilers of the Book of Psalms felt the need to reach back to Israel's origins to find the abiding principles that would transcend the current disaster. The covenant with Moses antedated the "covenant" with David by some two and a half centuries. The Davidic king is conspicuously absent from Book Four, while the kingship of Yahweh is strongly asserted (cf. Pss 93, 95–99). While the earthly kings failed to uphold their side of the covenant, God will be faithful to his nature as creator and redeemer of Israel (Pss 103–106). Psalm 90 reaches back even before creation to remind the reader that God alone has eternal being and that man is transient on the earth. The vicissitudes of his life and history can hardly alter the divine plenitude of being.

Israel's "habitation" from one age to another (cf. Deut 32:7) is not even the temple (cf. 26:8) but the Master himself (v. 1; cf. Ps 71:3, Deut 33:27). Before the mountains were born or earth and the inhabited world were "in labor," from eternity to eternity he has been God (v. 2). He turns men back into dust and tells the sons of men (cf. Ps 89:48) to go back (v. 3). A thousand years are in his eyes like yesterday that passes and [like] a watch of the night (v. 4). God ends them, they are but sleep, like grass that in the morning disappears (v. 5). In the morning it sprouts and develops; in the evening it withers and dries up (v. 6).

Impermanent by nature, man is further corrupted by sin by which he makes himself the object of God's anger (cf. on Ps 2:5). Man experiences himself "consumed" in God's anger (v. 7) and in terror at his fury (cf. Pss 88:8, 89:47). God has placed our "iniquities" before him (v. 8), our secrets in the light of his face (cf. Ps 89:16).[11] For all our days pass away in his rage; we have finished off our years like a sigh (v. 9). The two time spans are joined in verse 10: the "days of our years" number seventy years, and with [God-given] might eighty years (but what are these when a thousand years are but a night-watch?, cf. v. 4); their number is but toil and injustice (cf. Ps 55:11), for they pass quickly by and we fly off. Who can know the power of God's anger and his rage that instills fear (v. 11; cf. vv. 7, 9)?

To lament succeeds petition, petition not that God alter man's "share of days" but that he make us know it and that we obtain a wise heart (v. 12), one that does not expect to be satisfied by creatures (cf. Pss 49, 73). The psalmist asks (v. 13) how long before the Lord "return" and "relent" toward his "servants" (cf. Moses context in Exod 32:12–13). Alluding to words used earlier in the psalm, he cries, "Sate us [cf. Pss 17:15, 63:6, 81:17] in the morning [cf. vv. 5, 6] with your love, and we will shout joyfully and be glad all our days" (v. 14; cf. vv. 9, 10, 12). To be sated with God's *hesed*, of which so much was made in the previous psalm (cf. Ps 89:2, 3, 15, 25, 29, 34, 50), is a greater gift than life itself (cf. Ps 63:4) and transmutes one's days into joy. Where God's *hesed* is, in fact there is life (cf. John 3:16, Eph 2:4–5). "Make us glad in the measure of the days when you oppressed us, the years [cf. vv. 9, 10] when we saw misfortune [lit. "evil"; cf. Exod 32:12]" (v. 15). May God's actions be seen by his servants (cf. v. 13), his splendor be over his sons (v. 16). The psalm ends with

---

11. For Gregory of Nyssa these verses imply a petition, which he paraphrases as follows: "Because it is fitting for you to have good things in your sight, but iniquity is not worthy of being seen by you, therefore, make humanity to be such that it may not be unworthy of your inspection, but let our age become worthy of being seen by you, since at present, 'all our days have fainted away.' For not to be in you is not to be at all" (*On the Inscriptions of the Psalms* I.66). God must effect our conversion (cf. "return" in v. 13) if we are to be worthy to be "seen" by his countenance.

petitions in the jussive and the imperative: "May the sweetness [cf. Ps 27:4] of the Master, our God, be over us; and the work of our hands, establish it for us [cf. Pss 89:3, 5, 15, 22], and the work of our hands establish it" (v. 17). Intimacy with the Lord will produce joy and the endurance of our works. In Christ the Christian shares in the divine eternity. As the body of Christ lives forever, so does the work the Spirit has empowered us to do in this life. Only if we know that all our days pass can we place our hope in the Jesus who leads us beyond earthly years.

∼ PSALM 91   pinions

The psalm is dear to those who pray the Church's night prayer. No other psalm gives so extended and complete a portrayal of God's sheltering protection. Here there is neither lament nor petition, neither praise nor thanksgiving, but only fervent exposition. A wise speaker finds as many different metaphors as he can to communicate the manifold care that surrounds the one who trusts in God. His teaching culminates in a citation of God's own promise of salvation.

In two introductory verses the praying psalmist characterizes himself and cites his prayer: "As one who dwells in the shelter of the Most High and in the shadow of Shaddai spends the night [v. 1, chiasmus], I say to the Lord, 'My refuge, my stronghold, my God in whom I trust'" (v. 2). "Shelter" in the Psalms is sometimes the temple (cf. Ps 27:5), sometimes the Lord himself (cf. Pss 32:7, 61:5, 119:114), though generally both referents are present (cf. Ps 31:21); Christians take shelter in the Father through taking shelter in the Temple that is his Son. The title "Shaddai," common in the Book of Job, is found in the psalter only here and in Psalm 68:15. The psalmist has called God his "refuge" in Psalms 61:4, 62:8, 71:7, 73:28, his "stronghold" in Psalms 18:3, 31:4, 71:3, and his declaration of "trust" recalls the use of this verb in several laments of Books One and Two (cf. Pss 13:6, 25:2, 26:1, 27:3, 28:7, 31:7, 15, 52:10, 55:24, 56:5, 12).

Turning to a singular "you," the speaker gives an authoritative lesson about the divine care, either reciting the lesson once taught to him or teaching it to another. It is the Lord who rescues you from the trap of the fowler (v. 3), from the ruinous "thorn" (used in the bird trap). With his pinion he will cover you, and under his wings you will take refuge

(v. 4, note change of subject). The verb "take refuge" (same root as the noun in v. 2) was a recurring motif in Book One (e.g., Pss 5:12, 7:2, 11:1, 16:1, 18:3, 25:20, 31:2, 34:9, 36:8 [with "in the shadow of your wings"], 37:40; see also Pss 57:2, 61:5, 71:1). A third colon in verse 4 makes God's faithfulness a body shield (Pss 5:13, 35:2) and bulwark. As a consequence of this protection you will fear neither terror at night nor the arrow flying by day (v. 5), neither the plague that goes about in the dark nor the sting that lays waste at noon (v. 6). Should one of these bring down a thousand people at your side, myriads at your right, you it will not approach (v. 7; the image recalls Ps 3:6–7). Only look with your eyes, and the repayment of the wicked you will see (v. 8).

An ejaculation similar to the prayer of verse 2, "Truly you, Lord, are my refuge," interrupts the lesson (v. 9), which then continues: you have made the Most High (cf. v. 1) your "habitation" (cf. Ps 90:1). Verse 10 restates the idea of verses 5–7: there will not fall on you any evil (cf. Ps 90:15) nor will any scourge (cf. Pss 38:12, 39:16, 89:33) come near your tent. Not content with protecting the individual from harm, God offers him heavenly companionship: his angels he has commanded for you to guard you in all your ways (v. 11). On their palms they will bear you lest you hurt your foot on a stone (v. 12). Not only will dangers not harm you, but you will take the offensive: with angelic support on the lion-cub and the viper you will tread, trample on the young lion and the serpent (dragon?) (v. 13, chiasmus; cf. Luke 10:19).

God's oracle is a response to the piety of the one who trusts: "For to me he adhered and I will bring him to safety [cf. Pss 17:13, 18:44, 22:5, 9, 31:2, 37:40, 43:1, 71:2, 4, 82:4]; I will set him on high [cf. Pss 20:2, 59:2, 69:30] for he knows my name" (v. 14). To know this name is to commit oneself to the saving love it designates (cf. Pss 9:11, 32:21–22, Exod 34:6). When a person calls, God will answer (v. 15; a frequent pair of verbs in the psalms of David, cf. Pss 3:5, 4:2, 17:6, 20:10, 22:3, 27:7, 86:7; cf. also Ps 81:8, Isa 58:9). He is with the person in distress to deliver him and give him glory (cf. 1 Sam 2:30, Jer 30:19, John 17:1, 22). The climax of God's blessing is the response to Psalm 90 with its lament on the shortness of man's days (cf. Ps 90:9, 10, 12, 15): "With length of days I will sate [cf. Ps 90:14] him, and I will make him see my salvation" (v. 16). The gifts of God in these last three verses are deliverance from all attacks, whether human, pestilential, demonic, or atmospheric; security; the hearing of prayer; glory; and ongoing life that fills one's desire.

It can be seen from the parallel references that the psalm draws on many themes from the first two books of the psalter and from the preceding psalm, yet its weaving of these themes into a coherent, richly imaged lesson is entirely original. It reiterates God's defense and support of the trusting individual in the face of the social and national disintegration portrayed in Book Three. Christ, and the Christian in him, is the one borne by angel's hands beyond the sting of death to be filled with length of days. Ironically, the devil sought to persuade Jesus to use this text as grounds for obtaining an earthly glory instead of relying on the Father for the gift of eternal life (cf. Matt 4:6, Luke 4:10–11).

∼ PSALM 92   palm tree

Through the study of wisdom and his own experience the psalmist knows and declares that praise is the fruit of the strength given by the Lord to the just man.

The prayer begins as a hymn, but instead of inviting a group to praise the Lord, the psalmist states that it is good to give thanks to the Lord, finishing the line by addressing God directly: "and to make music to your name [cf. Ps 91:14], Most High" (v. 2). In particular it is good to proclaim in the morning God's *ḥesed,* and his faithfulness in the nights (v. 3, chiasmus; for the pair of attributes see Pss 85:11, 86:15, 88:12, 89:1, etc.). Song is to be accompanied by the ten-string lyre (Ps 33:2) and the harp and by the murmuring of the lyre (v. 4).

The motive for praise is that the Lord has gladdened the psalmist with his actions; for the works of his hands the speaker shouts for joy (v. 5, chiasmus with change of subject). How great are these works, very deep are the Lord's designs (v. 6). So deep are they that the stupid man does not know them (cf. Ps 73:22) nor can the foolish man discern them (v. 7)— here the psalm shows wisdom influence. What "works" the psalmist has in mind are indicated in verse 8: while wicked men flourish like plants and all evildoers sprout, it is only that they might be forever exterminated. This is because the Lord is eternally on high (v. 9): the wicked cannot prevail because they have rejected the one from whom their life comes (see on Pss 2, 7, etc.). They have made themselves God's "enemies," and the psalmist invites God to witness their inevitable extinction: "For behold your enemies, Lord; for behold your enemies vanish [cf. Pss 1:6, 9:4, 7, 10:16, 37:20, 73:27]; scattered are all evildoers" (v. 10). God has raised the psalmist's "horn" (cf. Pss 75:11, 89:18, 25) like that of oxen; the psalmist is soaked with the freshest oil (v. 11; note change of subject): assertive physical strength and a supple body are God's gifts to the one open to receive them. They enable the speaker's eye to look [fearlessly] on his opponents, the wrongdoers who rise against him, and his ear to hear [their defeat] (v. 12).

In the finale the speaker generalizes from his own experience and, combining the plant metaphor of verse 8 with the strength imagery of verse 11, compares the "just" man (singular) to a palm tree that "flourishes" (cf. v. 8), to a cedar of Lebanon that grows great (v. 13). Such men (plural) are planted in the house of the Lord; "in the courts of our God" they "flourish" (v. 14, chiasmus). The "rootedness" metaphor of Psalm 1:3 reappears and as in Psalm 52:10 is associated with the temple: by rooting oneself in the God who dwells in the temple one becomes vigorous with divine life. Saint Paul too combines the agricultural and architectural metaphors to fill out the understanding of the Church: "You are God's farm, God's building" (1 Cor 3:9); we must be "rooted in [Christ] and built on him" (Col 2:7) or "planted in love and built on love" through the faith in Christ that permits him to live in us (Eph 3:17). These just will still prosper in gray-headedness (cf. Ps 71:18); full of sap and full of leaves they will be (v. 15; the parallelism joins the literal and the metaphorical half-lines). They will spend their time proclaiming that "the Lord is upright— my rock—and there is no perversity in him" (v. 16). We have come full circle from the beginning of the psalm, returning to praise and even, briefly, to the individual speaker, who has presented himself as an icon of the man who allows the Lord to make him vigorous for the praise of God.

If Psalm 90 lamented the passing of days and Psalm 91 expressed confidence in the one who lengthens days, Psalm 92 is the thanksgiving for the gift of vigor, which will continue exultant in the presence of God to an undetermined old age. So Christians praise God eternally in the risen Christ.

∿ PSALM 93   waters

The psalter affirms for the first time: "Yahweh [the Lord] is king" (cf. Ps 47:9, "God is king . . ." and Ps 29:10, "The Lord sits as king . . .").

The statement can be taken as a summary of the Book of Psalms. Every psalm in some way affirms that Yahweh, the God of Israel, is in control of the universe and has subdued or will subdue all hostile powers, all who threaten his people. The New Testament parallel is the sentence "Jesus Christ is Lord" (cf. Phil 2:11, 1 Cor 12:3, Rom 10:9, Acts 2:36); through his resurrection Jesus is constituted Lord of the universe to whom all creation is to be made subject (1 Cor 15:25–28). In Christ, God reigns over the universe. We pray the psalm acknowledging his lordship as well as our share in his victory (Rev 3:21).

God's kingship needs to be envisioned, and first of all through his clothing, about which the psalmist speaks in the third person: he is "clothed with pride" (v. 1), which the parallel phrase interprets as "girt with strength" for battle (cf. Pss 18:33, 40, 65:7). His kingship will be manifest in the defeat of the chaotic waters (vv. 3–4). It is manifest also in the establishment of a world that cannot totter (cf. Pss 46:6, 60:4, 82:5) and of a throne from of old: he (now second person) is eternal (v. 2). Thus without any summons to praise, the Lord is presented in his eternal sovereignty.

But this Lord is attacked (v. 3): the "rivers" (cf. Ps 89:26) of primitive chaos, of anti-God forces, have raised up, have raised up their voices, are raising their pounding (cf. Pss 89:10–11, 65:8; the tricolon in which each colon begins with the same two members but ends differently is a borrowing from Ugaritic poetry, cf. Ps 29:1–2a, 4–5a). But more than the multitudinous waters, mightier than the surgings of the sea, mighty on high is the Lord (v. 4), neutralizing all attack (cf. Ps 29:10). The psalm thus vividly images the truth expressed in the preceding psalm (92:9): "But you are on high [cf. Ps 93:4] forever [cf. Ps 93:2], Lord."

A final verse (v. 5) addressed to the Lord expresses the wonder that this universal kingly power is available to men, first through his Law and next through his temple. "Your testimonies are reliable utterly [cf. Ps 19:8]; to your house [cf. Ps 92:14] belongs holiness, Lord, for length of days [cf. Ps 91:16, cf. also Pss 21:5, 23:6]." As Israel's God was present in word and sanctuary so is he present in the Body of Christ, the temple (John 2:21) that is also the Word Incarnate (John 1:14).

Verse 1a consists of four cola of two beats each, verses 1b and 2 of two lines in 3 + 2 meter, and the remainder of the psalm of three tricola in 3 + 3 + 3 meter.

⟿ PSALM 94   vengeance

The psalm illustrates the working out of God's kingship (cf. Pss 93, 95–99) in his defense of the most vulnerable of his people, a chief task of a king (cf. Pss 72:2–4, 12–14).

Twice addressed as a "God of vengeances" (v. 1; cf. Pss 58:11, 79:10, Deut 32:35, 41), the Lord is called on to "shine forth" (cf. Pss 50:2, 80:2, Deut 33:2), like the sun dispelling the crimes that take place at night (cf. Job 24:14–17, 38:12–15). He is to be "raised up" (cf. Ps 7:7) as judge of the earth, repaying the "haughty" (same root as "pride," Ps 93:1; cf. Isa 2:12, Prov 15:25) for their deeds (v. 2). Pride is the basic sin of replacing God with self, preferring the creature to the Creator, to whom, however, one is oriented by nature. Enthronement of self treats others as useful objects instead of affirming them in being. It diminishes man because it deprives him of his dignity as the image of God who supports in being all his creatures. Having emancipated himself from the God of life, the proud man has cut himself off from his own roots and withers.

Using a question frequent in the Psalms, the psalmist asks "How long" (cf. Pss 6:4, 12:2–3, 79:5) these "wicked" men shall be allowed to "exult" (cf. Pss 28:7, 60:8, 68:5) in their crimes (v. 3). Their pride shows itself first in speech: they bubble forth insolent (cf. Pss 31:19, 75:6) words; the evildoers pride themselves (v. 4). Their words overflow in actions (v. 5): the Lord's people they crush (Isa 3:15, Prov 22:22) and his inheritance (cf. Pss 28:9, 33:12, 68:10, 74:2, 78:62, 71, 79:1) they oppress, targeting in particular the most defenseless (v. 6): the widow and the stranger they kill and orphans they murder (cf. Pss 68:6, 82:3–4). Their behavior is rooted in a faulty assertion about God (v. 7): that Yahweh does not see, and the God of Jacob does not perceive (cf. Pss 10:4, 11, 12:5, 14:1, 59:8, 64:6). The portrait of the wicked exposes the origin of wickedness in the mind's rejection of a transcendent other.

These assertions of the wicked betray a lack of wisdom. Addressing the "stupid" among the people, the psalmist asks the foolish when they will understand (v. 8). Does the creator of the ear not hear or the one who formed the eye not look (v. 9)? God is not only creator of the senses; he is the mind of which all human thought is the image: Will the one who trains nations not reprove, the teacher of men not have knowledge (v. 10)? The Lord knows the designs (cf. Pss 33:10, 11) of man (v. 11)—that they

are vanity (cf. Pss 39:6, 12, 62:10, Qoh 2:15). On the other hand happy
are those who let themselves be trained by the Lord (again addressed directly, cf. vv. 1–6) and taught by his law (v. 12). He provides calmness for
them in evil days while a grave is being dug—perhaps by themselves (cf.
Ps 7:16)—for the wicked (v. 13, antithetic parallelism). For the Lord will
not forsake his people, and his inheritance (cf. v. 5) he will not abandon
(v. 14, chiasmus). He will see to it that to justice will "return" (cf. v. 2)
judgment (the legal process), and all the upright of heart will follow it
(v. 15). The helpless will not continue to be exploited in the Lord's land.

The psalmist now applies this knowledge to his own experience at the
hands of the wicked. Who will rise for him against wrongdoers (v. 16);
who will take a stand for him against the evildoers (cf. 4)? Were not the
Lord a help for him, his soul would soon dwell in silence (v. 17; this and
the following lines in climactic or synthetic parallelism provide variety
after several lines of close synonymous parallelism). When he says his foot
is tottering (cf. Ps 93:1), the Lord's *ḥesed* supports him (v. 18; the subject
of the outer cola in this pair of verses is the Lord; the subject of the inner
cola is the first person speaker). In the swarm of disquieting thoughts
within him, God's consolations (cf. Ps 86:17) caress his soul (v. 19). Can
God be coupled with the ruinous throne (of judicial power; cf. Ps 122:5)
that fashions (cf. v. 9) toil against the prescribed statutes (v. 20)? These
judges band together against the "soul" (cf. vv. 17, 19) of the just man,
and the blood of the innocent they condemn (v. 21, chiasmus). But the
Lord is the speaker's high refuge, his God the rock of his refuge (v. 22; cf.
Ps 91:2). He will repay them (cf. v. 2) for their injustice, and in their evil
he will silence them (v. 23). A final statement makes the psalmist's confession communal: "The Lord our God will silence them."

The kingship to be lauded in the following psalms is made tangible
in the administration of justice for the helpless—so insists Psalm 94.
When Jesus sits on his throne of glory, it will be by their active concern
for the needy that he will judge men, or rather that they will judge themselves (Matt 25:31–46).

∿ PSALM 95 invitatory

The psalm makes starkly clear what has underlain so many previous
psalms: divine worship is a matter of the heart more than of ritual. The
people streaming into the temple to bow down before the divine king are

challenged by this God to listen with the heart so as to know his ways and trust in his saving help. Their worship will consist in reliance on his power and loving promises, a trust based on an understanding of his profound nature, a trust that Israel in the desert failed to manifest.

In the first of two mini-hymns (in 3 + 3 meter), a leader invites his fellow-worshippers: "Go, let us shout joyfully to the Lord; let us cry jubilantly [cf. Pss 46:2, 65:1, 81:2] to the rock of our salvation" (v. 1). The Lord is identified as a rock as in Psalm 94:22 (cf. also Pss 18:3, 32, 47, 28:1, 62:3, 7, 8), the only sure foundation for salvation from evil and death. The people are summoned to "advance into his presence" with thanksgiving, with music to cry jubilantly to him (v. 2, chiasmus). For a great God is the Lord (v. 3), and a "great king over all gods," a title implied in Psalms 82:1, 6–7, 86:8, 89:7, 9 and developed in Psalms 96:4 and 97:7, 9. He is also the proprietor of creation: in his hand are the unexplored depths of earth, and the tops of the mountains are his (v. 4, chiasmus); to him belong the sea, for he made it, and the dry land formed by his hands (v. 5; cf. same two verbs in Isa 44:2). Vertical and horizontal reaches of creation are subject to him; of particular importance is his creation of the sea, which neighboring mythologies saw as a rival god rebellious to the creator (cf. Pss 89:10–11, 93:3–4).

A second mini-hymn, like the first, addresses the worshippers with an imperative followed by three verbs in the first person plural: "Come, let us fall prostrate and bend the knee, let us kneel before the Lord who made us" (v. 6); the emphasis this time is on physical rather than vocal worship. The motive for worship is now Israel's special relationship with the Lord (v. 7a): "For he is our God and we the people [cf. Ps 94:5, 14] of his pasture, the sheep of his hand" (cf. "sheep of your pasture," Ps 74:1). The covenant formula of Leviticus 26:12 is expressed as a credal statement (see also Jer 31:33, Ezek 37:27, the closest among several parallels). In bringing his people out of Egypt the Lord constituted them as his own possession. His covenant cannot be entirely abrogated even by Israel's unfaithfulness: it is fulfilled by the new covenant established in the blood of Jesus (Luke 22:20, Heb 8:6, 8, 10). God had promised to be the God of Abraham and his descendants (Gen 17:7–8, 19) and called Israel his special people at Sinai (Exod 19:5, Lev 20:26), renewing that pledge on the threshold of Canaan (Deut 26:18). The sheep metaphor was introduced by Jeremiah (Jer 23:1–2) and elaborated by Ezekiel (Ezek 34:6–31). The "hand" that grasps the heart of the earth (cf. v. 4) and formed the dry land (cf. v. 5) is the same hand that guides this special flock (cf. Jer 10:16 and esp. John 10:29).

One thing is required of the sheep: they must listen to the shepherd's voice (v. 7b; cf. Deut 27:9–10, John 10:26–28). This was the urgent plea of the Lord through Moses (Deut 6:3–6), Jeremiah (Jer 7:23, 11:4–7), Second Isaiah (Isa 55:2), and the wisdom writer (Prov 1:8, 4:1, 20, 8:32–34). It was what the Father asked of the disciples with respect to the Word made flesh (Mark 9:7). The covenant promise is definitive, but it has to be accepted: the individual must allow himself to be led, or in Pope Benedict XVI's words, be "won over" by him (Message on Easter Monday, 2007). This the Christian does by accepting the gift of Christ's own life and allowing it to become the principle of his activity. This means allowing the charity (*ḥesed*) of the Lord to possess all his faculties and animate them. It is a question not of meriting the Lord's love by keeping his commandments but of allowing the gift of his love to overflow in the keeping of the commandments. What the Israelites failed to do was believe in the saving guidance of the Lord in the trials of the desert (cf. Num 14:11, Ps 78:22): they accepted a false, cheapened idea of God. What is demanded of the Christian is trust, the willingness to rely on the risen Christ for the strength to lead a life pleasing to God. This faith is the acceptance of justification that will show itself in works of love (Gal 5:6). To "listen" to the Lord's voice is nothing less than to accede to his sovereign love.

The obstacle to this loving trust is the hardening of the heart (v. 8; cf. Ezek 3:7, Prov 28:14) as demonstrated at Massah and Meribah (cf. Exod 17:7, Deut 33:8) when the people failed to trust that God would provide drink in the desert. The place names signify the "trying" of God and "quarreling" with him. The fathers "tried" God and "tested" him even though they had seen his action (v. 9; cf. Pss 77:13, 90:16) in the plagues of Egypt, the crossing of the Red Sea, the destruction of Pharaoh's army, the miracle of the manna. They tested the one whose prerogative it was to "test" them (cf. Pss 7:10, 11:4–5, 17:3, 26:2, 66:10, 81:8)! For forty years the Lord was disgusted with "this generation" (v. 10; cf. Mark 8:12), calling them a people whose heart (cf. v. 8, Ps 94:15) was astray and who did not "know" (cf. Ps 94:11) his ways, that is, refused to trust in his identity as saving love. It was impossible for him to give the promised "rest" (cf. Deut 12:9, 1 Kgs 8:56; verb in Exod 33:14, Jos 22:4) in Canaan to those who refused his love. The author expresses this impossibility as an oath sworn by the Lord in anger (v. 11; cf. on Pss 2:5, 6:2). The stark ending forces the reader to consider his own response to the offer of salvation. Is he willing to accept the lordship of the God of love who has in so many ways demonstrated his power to save? On this decision depends his eternal rest (cf. Rev 14:11–13) in the company of God.

The Letter to the Hebrews makes clear that the sin of the desert was lack of faith accompanied by a hardening due to the lure of sin and issuing in disobedience (Heb 3:12–14, 18–19, 4:2). Christians are reminded that they, too, can reach the "rest" that is a share in God's own rest after the work of Creation (Heb 4:3–11; cf. Gen 2:2–3) only by putting their faith in the message they have heard. Such a faith is the obedience God looks for (Rom 1:5, 16:26).

Verses 8–11 constitute the speech of the Lord whose "voice" the people are summoned to listen to at the end of verse 7. The oracle contains within it two mini-speeches in which the Lord quotes himself. These speeches within a speech give the divine oracle a certain depth perspective. The psalm has traditionally been used as the "invitatory" song at the beginning of each day's Divine Office.

∾ PSALM 96   trees

With Psalm 96 the psalmist's perspective rises to a height above Israel from which he views all nations and the whole creation. He sees the world rejoicing as the Lord (the sacred name is used eleven times in the psalm) comes to judge with faithfulness and justice.

The psalm consists of three separate sections or hymns, each containing an invitation to praise and a grounding for praise. The first hymn (vv. 1–6) announces the theme, calling on "all the earth" to "sing to the Lord a new song" (v. 1). "The earth" includes both the foreign nations and the natural world itself. A "new song" is demanded because the Lord is coming to establish definitive justice throughout the world. The phrase was earlier applied to the response of an individual to a saving divine act (cf. Pss 33:3, 40:4); here it is the response of the world to a new intervention of God (as in Isa 42:10; cf. Rev 14:3). While the psalm is made up of bicola, the first two verses imitate the Canaanite tricolon in which each colon begins with the same formula but ends differently (cf. on Ps 29, also Ps 93:3). Verse 2a thus begins like the two cola of verse 1 but ends, "bless his name" (cf. Ps 69:27); the verse concludes, "proclaim [cf. Ps 40:10] from day to day his salvation." The following verse makes clear that it is now Israel who is being addressed, since the summons is to "recount among the nations his glory, among all peoples his wonders" (v. 3). "Glory" and "wonders" (cf. Pss 40:6, 71:17, 78:4, 86:10) are in parallelism: God's wondrous deeds both manifest his glory and augment it. The motive for praise is the greatness (cf. Ps 95:3) of the Lord and his worthiness of praise (v. 4a is a direct citation of Ps 48:2a); he is fearsome (cf. Ps 47:3) above all other gods (v. 4b). Verse 5 gives a new motive for praise (also introduced by the conjunction "for"), specifying that all the gods of the peoples are nothings (cf. Lev 19:4, 26:1, Isa 10:10–11, 31:7), since only Yahweh made the heavens; the verse seems to be a later addition perhaps inspired by Psalm 97:7. "Majesty and splendor" (royal attributes in Pss 21:6, 45:4) are before him, strength (cf. Ps 29:1) and adornment in his holy palace (v. 6).

The invitation to worship of the second hymn (vv. 7–10) cites the Canaanite Psalm 29:1–2, "clans [cf. Ezek 20:32, 21:8] of the peoples" replacing "sons of god" as addressee. This time the worshippers are to give the Lord the glory (cf. v. 3) due his name and to attribute to him the "strength" mentioned at the end of the first section (v. 7; cf. v. 6). Specifically they are to lift up oblations as they enter the temple courts (v. 8b) and to prostrate (cf. Ps 95:6) before the Lord in his holy splendor; indeed "all the earth" (cf. v. 1) should "shake" (cf. Pss 29:8–9, 77:17) before him (v. 9). In place of the customary motive for praise the clans are told (v. 10) to return to their "nations" announcing that "the Lord is king" (cf. Pss 93:1, 95:3); not only did he make the heavens (cf. v. 5) but through him the world is firmly established and will not totter (direct citation of Ps 93:1). A third colon in verse 10 looks to the future and anticipates the final verse of the psalm: God will give upright judgment for the peoples (citations of Pss 7:9, 9:9). Verse 10 thus becomes the pivotal verse of the psalm, praising God for the initial creation (cf. section 1) and the final judgment (cf. section 3).

The invitations of the third hymn (vv. 11–13) are addressed via the third person subjunctive to the physical creation itself. The heavens (cf. v. 5, Isa 49:13) are to be glad and the earth (cf. Isa 55:12) to rejoice ecstatically (v. 11); the sea and what fills it are to "thunder" (cf. Ps 29:3). The open country and all that is in it are to exult; then all the trees of the forest (cf. Isa 44:23) will shout for joy (v. 12) at the presence of the Lord, for he comes (matching the "coming" of the people into the courts, v. 8; cf. Deut 33:2, Hab 3:3); for he comes to judge the earth. The praise of the universe is directed to God's establishment of justice on earth (v. 13): "he will judge [cf. Pss 75:8, 76:10, 82:1, 8] the world with justice and the peoples with faithfulness," that is, according to his promises and his integrity. God's plan will be complete when his justice is mirrored on earth, when all men and women are in conformity with his loving will, freely embracing it with love. When all things are subjected to Christ, God's kingdom will be realized and God will be all in all (1 Cor 15:24, 28).

The psalm celebrates the kingship of Yahweh, drawing on a wide range of texts (in particular Second Isaiah, the Canaanite poem Psalm 29, psalms designating Yahweh as judge, and psalms of the kingship of Yahweh, Pss 47, 48, 93, 95, 97) to present a universal glorification of this kingship. A schematic may convey the richness of the psalm:

Introduction: all the earth summoned to sing a new song to the Lord

	Addressee	*Motive for praise*
First hymn:	Israel	greatness of the creator
Second hymn:	clans of peoples	Yahweh as creator and judge
Third hymn:	natural creation	Yahweh's coming as judge

The central hymn thus looks both backward and forward in praising the past and future actions of the Lord. Repeated words ("earth," " all" [seven times each]; "peoples" [five times]; "glory," "come" [three times each]; "name" [twice]; "in the presence of" [once in each section]) together with a rich vocabulary of synonyms ("proclaim," "recount," "say"; "holy place," "courts"; "fear," "shake"; "earth," "world"; "sentence," "judge"; "right judgment," "justice," "faithfulness"; "be glad," "rejoice ecstatically," "exult," "shout with joy") reinforce major themes while evoking different aspects of those themes. All the words in the final verse fall into one of these two categories so that the psalm's climax is also a summary. In addition, several important theological terms are used once ("new," "bless," "salvation," "wonders," "great," "prostrate," "sea," "justice," "faithfulness"). The richness of the psalm becomes apparent on a slow reading. With reason some commentators consider this and the following two kingship psalms the center of the psalter, its highest worship. The long lines contribute to the poem's solemnity: nine of the verses have at least one four-beat colon; no colon has fewer than three beats.

∼ PSALM 97   fire

The manifestation of a just God in judgment is greeted with joy in Zion because idols and their worshippers are confounded while the just are set free.

"The Lord is king" (v. 1; cf. Pss 93:1, 96:10) expresses the fundamental message of the Psalms, an Old Testament equivalent of "Jesus is Lord" in the New. Those who pray the Psalms are continually making that confession: Nothing can separate us from the love of God; the kingdom of righteousness is being established. The Lord continues to extend his kingship in the world, inwardly turning men's hearts toward him. The present psalm is less interested in the establishment of the Lord's kingship at the beginning of creation (as in Ps 93) than in its ultimate working out on earth. Earth rejoices ecstatically to witness this kingship, the many islands (the edges of the inhabited world) are glad.

The Lord's manifestation is a mixture of darkness and light: cloud and darkness surround him as he sits on his throne that is founded on justice and right (v. 2). Fire goes out from his presence and scorches his oppressors around him (v. 3). His lightnings light up the world (v. 4); the earth (cf. v. 1) sees and shakes (cf. Ps 96:9). Mountains melt like wax (cf. Ps 68:3) before the Lord (v. 5), before the Master of all the earth (a title of Baal applied to Yahweh from the seventh century, cf. Jos 3:11, 13, Mic 4:13, Zech 4:14, 6:5): the one who made the earth firm is also the one who can reshape or dissolve it. The heavens show his justice (cf. v. 2) so that all peoples can see (cf. v. 4) his glory (v. 6). The theophany is less the manifestation of a person than the scalding of a transforming righteousness.

Idol worshippers are shamed, and those who boast of petty gods; all the gods themselves prostrate (cf. Pss 95:6, 96:9) before him (v. 7), surrendering their "divinity." Zion, where the true God is worshipped, hears of his dramatic intervention and is glad, and the daughters (towns) of Judah rejoice ecstatically (cf. v. 1) at the manifestations of the Lord's judgments (v. 8; this and following verse addressed directly to Yahweh). For Yahweh is "most high over all the earth" (= Ps 83:19), a title of the Canaanite high god El. Thus the Lord embodies the attributes of both of the great gods of Canaan: the high god and the storm god; he is raised high above all gods (v. 9).

The psalm ends with a reflection on the impact of these divine judgments on daily lives in the world. Those who love this God (cf. Deut 6:4–5) will hate evil; he in turn guards the souls of his devout ones and from the hand of the wicked will protect them (v. 10). Light "is sown" for the just man, as if it were a seed that will grow, and for the upright of heart there is gladness (v. 11, chiasmus). The just will be glad (cf. vv. 1, 8) in the Lord (v. 12) and will give thanks to his holy revealed name (lit. "memorial," cf. Ps 30:5). The fire and lightning that accompanied the Lord's judgment against evil become the light of joy for those who accept it.

The New Testament, too, proclaims a dissolving of elements in the fire of the Lord's manifestation, while the holy are preserved for lasting joy (cf. 2 Pet 3:7, 10–12, Heb 10:27). For the Lord Jesus will "appear from heaven. . . . He will come in flaming fire to impose the penalty on all who do not acknowledge God and refuse to accept the Good News of our Lord Jesus. . . . They will be lost eternally . . . on that day when he comes to be glorified among his saints and seen in his glory by all who believe in him" (2 Thess 1:7–8, 10). The just who love God and are tried by fire on earth are the entry point for the kingdom of God (see Hossfeld and Zenger, *Die Psalmen*, 2:518).

∼ PSALM 98   arm

Psalm 98 resembles Psalm 96 in its celebration of the kingship of Yahweh and its three-part structure, but it is briefer and profiles more clearly the praise of the world for the wonders God worked for Israel. Since several of the praise expressions come from Second Isaiah, the psalm seems to be praising God for the deliverance of the exiles from Babylon, an event with cosmic repercussions.

After the opening colon, a duplicate of Psalm 96:1, the conjunction "for" introduces six verbs giving the reasons for praise. The Lord's exploits are presented in the language used for his saving deeds in Israel: his working of wonders (cf. Pss 40:6, 72:18, 78:4, 11, 32, 86:10, Exod 3:20), the saving action of his right hand (Pss 44:4, 89:14, Exod 15:6, 12) and holy arm (v. 1; Exod 6:6, 15:16, Deut 4:34, 7:19, 26:8, Isa 52:10). Through these deeds, and particularly through the miraculous return of the exiles, he has made known his salvation and to the eyes of the nations revealed his justice

(v. 2). These deeds are signs that he remembered his truth and love for the house of Israel (cf. Luke 1:54); all the ends of the earth have thus seen the salvation of "our God" (v. 3)—the latter term reveals that the speaker is an Israelite talking to fellow Israelites. God is to be praised by Israel for revealing his lordship through Israel to the whole pagan world.

Now the whole earth is called on to give the jubilant cry to the Lord (v. 4a; cf. Ps 65:1). A series of imperative phrases denote aspects of the worship: be cheerful, shout joyfully, make music (v. 4b; cf. Isa 44:23, 52:9), make music to the Lord with the lyre (cf. Pss 33:2, 81:3, 92:4), on the lyre with the sound of music (v. 5), with trumpets and the sound of the ram's horn (v. 6a). The section concludes with a repetition of the first imperative: give the jubilant cry before the king, the Lord (v. 6b). The expected reasons for praise are replaced by the theme of kingship common to this group, Psalms 96–99. All the earth is to join in the liturgical praise of Israel's God who is king of the whole world.

The final section follows closely the corresponding section of Psalm 96. Verse 7a repeats Psalm 96:11b; verse 7b is identical to Psalm 24:1b. Rivers are to "clap their palms" (cf. Isa 55:12); together the mountains (cf. Isa 44:23, 49:13, 55:12) "shout with joy" (v. 8; cf. Ps 96:12). Verse 9 is identical to Psalm 96:13 with "uprightness" replacing the final "justice" (see also Ps 67:5). The natural world praises the Lord as he comes to establish justice among the nations. The psalm thus moves from Israel's praise of its saving God revealed to the nations, through the joining of the nations in that praise, to the praise of the created world for Yahweh's establishment of righteousness among the nations.

The psalm features prominently in the liturgy at Christmas time, where it expresses the joy of the earth at the coming of its God in flesh to make the world into his kingdom. As the trumpet blast announces in the Book of Revelation: "The kingdom of the world has become the kingdom of our Lord and his Christ, and he will reign for ever and ever" (Rev 11:15).

∼ Psalm 99 holy

In a reminiscence of Isaiah's temple vision (Isa 6:3) the Lord is three times worshipped as "holy," each time at the end of a section of the psalm. Like its predecessors the psalm praises God as king, this time emphasizing God's righteous rule in Zion and the mediation of his law by important figures in Israel's history.

The initial clause repeats the opening clause of Psalm 97 and is here followed by the reaction of the peoples, who "tremble" (cf. Ps 77:17, 19) at the Lord's kingship. In the parallel colon the Lord is presented as seated on the cherubs stretched above the ark and constituting his throne; here it is the earth that reacts by quivering (v. 1). The God who dwells in Jerusalem controls the fate of the world. The following verse (v. 2) expresses this truth explicitly: the Lord in Zion is great; exalted is he above all the peoples. The name "Zion" links this first section with the following section, and the word "exalt" is found in all three sections. The sections are linked also by structure: in each a central statement addressed directly to the Lord is flanked by parts that speak of him in the third person. So verse 3 reads, "They give thanks to your name, great and fearsome [cf. Pss 68:36, 76:8, 13, 89:8, 96:4] one," before returning to third person "Holy is he." The nations praise the one from whom their judgment comes.

Like the first, the second section opens with a statement about kingship. The difficult line can be translated: "The strength of a king is that he loves right judgment" (v. 4a). Then God is addressed directly as one who established uprightness; right judgment and justice in Jacob he made (v. 4b, chiasmus). The land of God's people is again identified as the dwelling of righteousness. Israel is called on to exalt the Lord their God, to prostrate (cf. Pss 95:6, 96:9, 97:7) before his footstool (v. 5), the temple where his presence abides. The section ends with the same phrase that closed the first section.

Synonyms have been used for God's earthly home; now in the third section proper names of great priests are mentioned as the mediators by which his righteousness was made known to Israel. Moses (Exod 32:11–13, Deut 9:26), Aaron (cf. Num 17:11–13, Wis 18:21–23), and Samuel (1 Sam 7:5, 9, 12:18–19, 23) are represented as calling on the Lord's name (cf. v. 3) for help and receiving his answer (v. 6). In the pillar of cloud God spoke (Exod 33:9, Num 12:5); they kept his testimonies and the statute he gave them (v. 7). As the revelation of God's nature and will, the Law disclosed how man could participate in the righteousness or holiness of God. In verse 8 the Lord is praised in direct address for answering the three mediators; he is a God who "bears" for his people while "avenging" (cf. noun in Ps 94:1) their [mis]doings (v. 8). In Yahweh's self-definition in Exodus 34:6–7 it is sins that the Lord bears or takes away; here it is the people itself he bears. Once again the people are called on to exalt the Lord their God (cf. v. 5) and to prostrate before "his holy mountain," Zion (v. 9). The third cry of "Holy" is more formal than the first two: "For holy is the Lord our God." In the light of the whole psalm, holiness here signifies the one who produces holiness on this earth.

The nations recognize that the God who dwells in Zion is the source of right living among his people; Israel sees this right living as both the forgiveness of sins and their punishment. Christ in his sacrifice on the cross both satisfies the requirements of God's justice (Rom 8:3–4) and takes away the sin of the world (John 1:29, Col 2:13, Heb 9:26). His acceptance of the pain involved in turning sinful human nature back to obedience to the Father was the bearing of our punishment that won us forgiveness. For this the Church and all nations will exalt the holiness of our God: "How great and wonderful are all your works, Lord God Almighty; just and true are all your ways, King of nations. Who would not revere and praise your name, O Lord? You alone are holy, and all the pagans will come and adore you for the many acts of justice you have shown" (Rev 15:3–4).

◦∾ PSALM 100   hundredth

All the earth, now integrated into Israel as one people of God, is invited to enter the Lord's presence in joyful thanksgiving, praise, and service.

The psalm has two sections, each comprising a three-line invitation to praise and a three-line reason for praise. The opening imperative is the exultant "cry jubilantly" (Latin *Jubilate*; cf. Pss 66:1, 98:4), addressed not to Israel alone but to "all the earth" (v. 1). All are called to "serve" Israel's God with gladness, coming before his presence in the temple with joy (v. 2). They must know that it is Yahweh who is God, since he made us (all men and women) and we are his, his people and the flock of his pasture (v. 3; cf. Ps 95:7). All humanity is thus drawn into the people with whom God made covenant.

The imperatives of the second section evoke the movement of the procession into the sacred precincts (v. 4): "Come through his gates with thanksgiving, his courts [cf. Ps 96:8] with praise; give thanks to him, bless his name [cf. Ps 96:2]." Voice, movement, and mood are all involved in the action of worship, whose object is the sacred name of Israel's God. The ultimate reason for this praise is the goodness of this Lord (v. 5), specified in his *hesed* and faithfulness, the familiar pair of supreme attributes (cf. most recently Ps 98:3) that can be read as a hendiadys for "faithful covenant love." The two attributes are each praised for their eternal endurance.

This *hesed* is the ultimate reality of the universe, explaining all creation and its movement toward union with the creator. It is the reality that caused God to send his Son with merciful forgiveness into the world (John 3:16, Rom 5:8). It is the source of the Paschal mystery by which earth is united to heaven and all humanity to its loving Father (Eph 2:4–6). It is the principle of the unity of the human race, the brotherhood of sons of God united by his Spirit and mediating his *hesed* to one another in loving charity and service (Rom 5:5, Eph 4:15–16, 5:1–2). It is Jesus Christ, the Incarnation of divine love (Gal 2:20), the bread that nourishes the world (John 6:51). Psalm 100 gives universal praise for the unique universal mystery.

When William Kethe translated the psalm into English to be sung to the famous Louis Bourgeois tune known as "Old Hundredth," he was faced with the problem of rendering the three-line units of the poem into four-line stanzas. The result is a certain redundancy in the English text. But the "grand old Puritan anthem" (Longfellow) has a permanent place in English liturgy.

∿ PSALM 101   loyalty

The psalm is one of only two in Book Four ascribed to David. Coming after Psalm 100 and beginning with the key word from the last verse of that psalm, *hesed*, it delineates the moral justice of the individual inhabitants of the Lord's worldwide kingdom. Unity with the Lord is a matter of conformity to his will.

The psalmist sings *hesed* and judgment, that is, the covenant loyalty that is man's response to God's *hesed* and the judgment that consists in shrewd distinction between right and wrong behavior. The psalmist "sings" these in that his profession and practice of a moral life is an act of praise to the Lord, to whom he "makes music" (v. 1). He acts with understanding in the way of the blameless (cf. Ps 84:12). The interjection of a plea, "When will you come to me?" suggests that the speaker has not yet received the full reward for his allegiance, yet he walks in perfection of heart in the midst of his house, a place where God is obeyed (v. 2). He takes care not to put before his eyes any vile matter; the one who acts deviantly he hates and will not allow to cling (cf. Ps 63:9) to him (v. 3). The man of God derives his principles of conduct from God not men (cf. Pss 1:1, 26:4–5). The perverted (cf. Ps 18:27) heart must keep away from him; evil he refuses to know (v. 4). The man who slanders his friend in secret, this man he will silence (cf. Pss 54:7, 73:27, 94:23); the man haughty of eyes and arrogant (lit. "broad") of heart he will not tolerate (v. 5). His own eyes, on the other hand, will be upon the faithful of the land (i.e., not proud) that they may sit (settle) with him; the one who walks in the way of the blameless (cf. v. 2) will attend on him (v. 6). There will not dwell within his house (cf. v. 2) one who practices deception; one who speaks lies will not be established (v. 7, chiasmus) before his "eyes" (cf. vv. 3, 5, 6). Pride, slander, dishonesty—these are the deviant habits incompatible with union with God. The just man creates a community of goodness around him that will extend beyond his "house": each morning he will "silence" (cf. v. 5) all the wicked in the land, cutting off from the Lord's (cf. v. 1) city all doers of evil (v. 8).

It is Christ who makes righteousness dwell in the heart of God's city (2 Cor 6:15–17) by gathering around him the poor and meek and giving them a share in his righteousness (Heb 2:11–13, 3:6, Mark 3:32–35, 1 Cor 1:30). Those who wish to dwell in the Lord's company, Israelites or foreigners, must learn to live by the Lord's *ḥesed* for all his creatures. Such a life is the definition of the kingdom of God, the place where righteousness dwells.

The dominant meter is 3 + 2.

∽ PSALM 102   days

For the first time in Book Four there is mention of the destruction of Jerusalem, which had been a principal topic of Book Three. The psalms of Book Four have responded to the disaster of the destruction and Exile by stressing the faithfulness of the God who transcends the vicissitudes of history and is king of all the earth. They have looked—and will continue to look—for strength not in the Davidic monarchy but in the promises made to Moses. In this perspective they can now look at the rubble of

Jerusalem and genuinely hope for its restoration. At the same time the psalmist, as a member of the exiled community, can permit himself an individual lament of the type encountered in earlier books. Just as in the preceding psalm an individual represented the moral integrity required for membership in God's worldwide kingdom, so in the present psalm the individual embodies all the pain of the exiled community.

The title (v. 1) identifies the psalm as the prayer of a "poor" man when he is "faint" (cf. Pss 61:3, 77:4) and who before the Lord pours out his complaint. He begins by asking the Lord to hear his prayer (cf. Pss 4:2, 17:1, 39:13, 54:4, 61:2, 65:3, 84:9), and may his cry come (cf. Ps 18:7) to God (v. 2). He asks God (v. 3) not to hide his face from him (cf. Pss 13:1, 27:9, 44:25, 69:18, 88:15) in the day of his distress (cf. Ps 59:17). He asks the Lord to turn his ear to him (cf. Pss 17:6, 31:3, 71:2, 86:1, 88:3) and in the day he "calls" to "answer" him quickly (cf. Pss 4:2, 27:7). Through his language the psalmist is aligning himself with all his predecessors who have cried out to God in their distress.

The lament itself presents more originality. Consumed in smoke (cf. Ps 37:20) are the speaker's days, and his "bones" like a hearth are "burning" (v. 4, chiasmus; cf. Job 30:30). Struck like the plants and dried up is his heart, for he has forgotten to eat his bread (v. 5). From the sound of his groaning, his bones cling (cf. Ps 101:3) to his flesh (v. 6). He has become like an owl in the desert, like a screech owl in the waste places (v. 7). He is emaciated and has become like a bird alone on a roof (v. 8). Other psalms compare the besieged psalmist to a fowl, but none to the unclean birds of abandoned sites; the image conveys the speaker's sense of being excluded from normal society. His enemies scorn him all day long; those who mock him curse by his name (v. 9). For ashes like bread he eats, and his drink with tears he has mixed (v. 10) in the face of God's indignation (cf. Ps 38:4) and displeasure (cf. Ps 38:2); God has lifted him up only to throw him down (v. 11). His days lengthen like a shadow, and "like plants" he "dries up" (v. 12, inclusion with v. 5; cf. Ps 90:6).

But the Lord, in contrast, is forever "seated" (= enthroned, cf. Ps 101:6), remembered in every age (v. 13). He will arise and have pity on Zion, for the time to have mercy on her, the appointed time has come (v. 14). For her servants take pleasure in her stones, and her dust they have mercy on (v. 15, chiasmus). The nations will have cause to fear the Lord's name, and all the kings of the earth his glory (v. 16), for the Lord will have built up Zion, will be seen in his glory (v. 17). He will have turned to the prayer of the naked and not despised their prayer (v. 18), presumably the prayer of verses 1–2. These things should be written down for the next generation so that the people to be created may praise the Lord (v. 19).

The speaker imagines that God "looked down" (cf. Ps 14:2) from his holy place; the Lord from heaven to earth looked (v. 20) to hear the "groan of the captive" (cf. Ps 79:11), to loosen those consigned to death (v. 21). The goal of this liberation is that the name of the Lord (cf. v. 16) be recounted in Zion, his praise in Jerusalem (v. 22) when the peoples are gathered together, and the kingdoms [are gathered] to "serve" (cf. Ps 100:2) the Lord (v. 23). If Zion is rebuilt, it is so that all nations may worship there together with Israel: this is the perspective of Psalm 100.

But the speaker is not there yet: God has humbled his power on the way, shortened his "days" (v. 24; cf. vv. 4, 12). He resolves to ask God not to remove him in the middle of his days, for God's years last from age to age (v. 25). Long ago he founded the earth, and the work of his hands are the heavens (v. 26). Even when they vanish he will abide, and everything like a garment will wear out; like clothing God will change them and they will be changed (v. 27). But God remains the same, and his years have no end (v. 28). The sons of his servants will have a dwelling, and their offspring will "be established" (cf. Ps 101:7) before his face (v. 29; cf. Ps 69:37). The restored community of God's people will partake of his own eternity. In the new Jerusalem the servants of God and of the Lamb "will reign for ever and ever" (Rev 22:5).

The 3 + 3 meter prevails in the psalm (cf. vv. 2, 4, 7, 9–11, 12, 15, 17, 18, 21–23, 26, 29). The 4 + 3 meter is found in verses 5, 13, 14, 16, 19, while the remaining verses display a variety of meters. The outer parts of the psalm address God in the second person, the central section on the restoration of Zion (vv. 16–24) speak of him in the third person. As noted in the commentary, certain words connect the psalm to its immediate predecessors: "cling," "sit," "serve," "be established."

∼ Psalm 103   love

Love is king: this is the message of Psalm 103. The psalms of Yahweh's kingship (Pss 93, 95–99) have established that Israel's God reigns over the whole earth. Psalm 103 reminds us that the essence of this God is *ḥesed,* his covenant love for his chosen people, including the nations who will be joined with them. The passionate commitment to this people is what will lead this God to give his own Son in sacrifice to reconcile them with himself (cf. 2 Cor 5:14–15, 18–19). His *ḥesed* takes away sin, the only obstacle between man and God. In Christ our sins are removed and we become sons of God eternally united with our loving father (Gal 4:4–7). The psalm thus develops the final verse of Psalm 100, praising in detail the breadth and length and height and depth of this love (cf. Eph 3:18–19).

"Bless, my soul, the Lord, and all that is within me his holy name" (v. 1; for "name" cf. Ps 102:16, 22). The psalmist would have every part of his being—body, spirit, mind, emotions—transmuted into praise for the Lord whose being is contained in his sacred name. Repeating the first half of verse 1, he adds a reminder to himself not to forget all the Lord's activities (v. 2), which are enumerated in the participles of the next three verses: forgiving (cf. Pss 25:11, 86:5, Col 1:14) all his iniquities, healing (cf. Pss 6:3, 30:3, 41:5, Matt 9:35, Luke 6:18–19) all his ailments (v. 3), redeeming (cf. Pss 69:19, 77:16, Rom 3:24) his life from the grave, crowning (cf. Ps 5:13, 2 Tim 4:8) him with love and compassion (v. 4), sating (cf. Pss 17:15, 22:27, 63:6, 65:5, 81:17, 91:16, Eph 3:19) him always (Hebrew unclear) with good things so that his youth is renewed (cf. Ps 51:12, Titus 3:5) like an eagle's (v. 5). The Lord removes all blemishes from the one he loves and fortifies him with strength and vigor; in the same way the grace of Christ removes sin and empowers one for the performance of good works (cf. Eph 2:10, Titus 2:14). A final participle and the mention of the divine name conclude the list: "A doer of justice is the Lord, and of judgments for all the exploited" (v. 6); it is the defenseless who are the special beneficiaries of his goodness.

How does the psalmist know these divine behaviors? Because the Lord made known his ways to Moses, to the sons of Israel his doings (v. 7, chiasmus). Here again we encounter the principal historical figure of Book Four, Moses, mediator of Israel's liberation, of the Law, and of desert wonders (cf. Pss 90:1, 99:6, 105:26–27, 106:16, 23, 32). It was on Sinai, in particular, that Yahweh revealed his identity as a God of love, in a passage cited in the next verse of our psalm: "Compassionate and gracious is the Lord, slow to anger and abundant in covenant love" (v. 8; cf. Exod

34:6). The "ways" of the Lord are the way of love (cf. Ps 25:10, 1 Cor 12:31–13:1): he is attached and committed to all his creatures and shows this love in saving deeds. Even should he "dispute" with men because of their sin, it will not be forever; he will not nurse a grudge (v. 9). Not according to their sins does he treat them, and not according to their iniquities does he pay them back (v. 10). For as high as the heavens are above the earth, so strong is his love (cf. Ps 117:2) for those who fear him (v. 11). The Lord does not condone sin but forgives those who know themselves guilty of it. As far as east is from west, so far does he remove from us our rebellions (v. 12). Human sin in its three major aspects (cf. on Pss 32:2–3, 51:3–4) is thus swallowed up in God's merciful love.

From geographical metaphors the psalmist moves to living ones (v. 13): as a father has compassion on his sons, so the Lord has compassion (cf. Ps 102:14) on those who fear him (cf. v. 11). The Lord as a merciful father will be revealed by Jesus as the forgiver of each one's sin (cf. Matt 6:9, 12). He knows what we are made of, remembering that we are dust (v. 14; cf. Ps 102:15, Gen 2:7, 3:19, Qoh 3:20). Man's days are like grass (cf. Ps 90:5); like the blossom of the field he sprouts (v. 15). The wind blows on him and he is no more, and his place recognizes him no more (v. 16). But the love of the Lord is from age to age for those who fear him (cf. vv. 11, 13), and his justice for children's children (v. 17) if they keep his covenant and remember his precepts to do them (v. 18). Man's willingness to be governed by the *ḥesed* revealed in the covenant permits God to give him a share in his own permanence. God can do this because he "in the heavens has established his throne [cf. Pss 10:4, 93:2], and his kingship [cf. Ps 96:10] rules over all" (v. 19). The *ḥesed* that removes sin also bestows an eternal life.

The vision of God's heavenly throne reminds the psalmist of the angels who contemplate him: they are called on to "bless" the Lord (cf. vv. 1–2; cf. also Ps 148:2, Dan 3:58) as powerful champions who carry out his word, listening to the voice of his word (v. 20). Again called to bless the Lord, they are addressed as "all his hosts, who minister to him and do his pleasure" (v. 21). These spirits attend on the Lord, praising him, heeding his instructions, carrying them out in his creation. Next, the Lord's works are summoned to bless him in all the places where he rules (cf. v. 19). Finally the psalmist summons his own soul, as at the beginning, to bless the Lord (v. 22) for his all-encompassing love.

~ PSALM 104   creation

The call at the end of Psalm 103 for Yahweh's "works" to bless him provides a transition to Psalm 104 whose theme is his "works" of creation (cf. vv. 24, 31). Both psalms begin and end with the same self-exhortation to praise, "Bless the Lord, my soul" (which the Grail renders in Ps 103 as "My soul, give thanks to the Lord"), and the two psalms share several common words ("angels," "ministers," "place," "fill," "grass," "dust," "renew," "sin[ner]"), although these are used in quite different contexts. If in Psalm 103 God is blessed for his gracious love, in Psalm 104 he is blessed for the order and harmony of the world he made.

The psalmist follows his initial summons with two statements in direct address (v. 1): "Lord, my God, you are great indeed; you are clothed [cf. Ps 93:1] in majesty and splendor" (cf. Ps 96:6). The Lord himself cannot be seen, but the brilliant light of heaven can be seen as a mantle that enwraps him (cf. 1 Tim 6:16); he stretches out the heavens like a tent cloth (v. 2). The succession "light–heavens" follows the first creation account (Gen 1:3–8). The Lord roofs his upper chambers with waters (the "waters above the heavens," Gen 1:7, Ps 148:4), makes the clouds his chariot (cf. Ps 68:34), and walks on the wings of the wind (v. 3): celestial phenomena are his accoutrements. He uses the winds as his angels/ messengers (cf. Ps 103:20) and flaming fire as his servants (v. 4; cf. Ps 103:21). The six participles describing the Lord's actions in verses 2–4 parallel the six participles of Psalm 103:3–6.

The Lord has founded the earth on its bases; it will not totter (cf. Pss 93:1, 96:10) forever and ever (v. 5). With the abyss as with a piece of clothing he covered it; on the mountains stood the waters (v. 6). At God's "rebuke" they fled (v. 7; cf. Ps 18:16, Nah 1:4, Isa 50:2) and at the voice of his thunder hurried away (like the attackers of Jerusalem, Ps 48:6). The divine rebuke is a vestige of Near Eastern mythology according to which god created the world by rebuking/defeating the sea monster, a rival god (see also on Ps 74:12). Jesus's rebuke of the sea and of the demons it represents (Mark 1:25–27, 4:39) is thus a manifestation of his divine power. As the waters sank away, mountains rose up and valleys were lowered, each to the place (cf. Ps 103:16, 22) God founded for them (v. 8). A boundary he placed, which the waters will not pass (v. 9); they will not return to cover (cf. v. 6) the earth (cf. Prov 8:29, Gen 9:11, Isa 54:9).

Once tamed, the waters become beneficent. God sends springs in the ravines (lit. "streams" or wadis); between the mountains they flow (v. 10). These give drink to all the beasts of the field; wild asses break their thirst (v. 11; the second colon changes the subject of the first, specifies the generic "beasts," and contrasts drink with thirst). By these streams the birds of heaven dwell; from the foliage they give out their song (v. 12). God waters the mountains from his upper chambers (cf. v. 3); with the fruit of his work the earth is sated (v. 13; cf. Ps 103:5). He makes the grass (cf. Ps 103:15) sprout for the cattle and plants (cf. Ps 102:5, 12, Gen 1:12) to serve man, to make bread spring from the earth (v. 14) and wine that gladdens the heart of man, to make his face shine with oil, while bread fortifies (lit. "supports") man's heart (v. 15). The psalmist delights in the feast God has prepared for man through the gift of water.

The trees of the Lord are sated (cf. v. 13), the cedars of Lebanon that he planted (v. 16), where the birds make their nests; the stork in the treetops has her home (v. 17). The lofty mountains are for the wild goats, rocks a refuge for rabbits (v. 18). From the fertility of the third day of creation we move to the fourth day: God made the moon for the appointed times (cf. Gen 1:14); the sun knows where to set (v. 19). God imposes darkness and it is night, when all the beasts of the field teem (v. 20). The young lions, in particular, roar for prey, asking from God their food (v. 21)—we have moved imperceptibly to the sixth day, having already had mention of the birds of the fifth day (cf. vv. 12, 17; for sea creatures see below vv. 25–26). All creatures are dependent on God for sustenance and habitat, and he provides generously for their needs. When the sun rises, the night creatures are gathered in, and in their dens (cf. Ps 76:3) they lie down (v. 22). It is time for man to go out to his activity, to his service (cf. v. 14; Gen 2:15) until evening (v. 23). The psalmist must express his amazement at this harmony of creation, with its meshing of human, animal, plant, mineral, and cosmic dimensions. The world is a product of divine wisdom (cf. Prov 3:19): "How many are your works, Lord; all of them in wisdom you have made; filled is the earth with your possessions" (v. 24). Saint Paul expresses the same enthusiasm before the depth and richness of God's wisdom (Rom 11:33).

But not to be forgotten is the sea, great and broad; it teems (cf. v. 20) with creatures without number, beasts small and large (v. 25). There ships move (cf. vv. 3, 10), and Leviathan, which God formed to play with (v. 26).

God delights in his creatures as much as man does: that may be their principal reason for existence. The hostile monster of Psalm 74:14 is but a tamed pet for the Lord: there is no hint of a primordial battle against chaos. All these creatures of land and sea look expectantly for the Lord to give them their food (cf. v. 21) in its time (v. 27). He gives it to them, they gather it up; he opens his hand, they are sated (cf. vv. 13, 16) with good things (v. 28). God's provision of sustenance for his creatures seems to be the focal point of the psalm.

But the following two verses make clear that the greatest gift is not food but the spirit of life itself. When God hides his face, his creatures are terrified; when he takes back their spirit they expire and return to their dust (v. 29; "dust" links this psalm with its two predecessors, cf. Pss 102:15, 103:14). But he sends forth his spirit (this "sending of the spirit" is applied to the Spirit of God by Jesus in John 14:26 and 15:26 and by Paul in Gal 4:6) and they are created (see Gen 1:1–2 for the association of the spirit of God with creation), and he renews (cf. Ps 103:5; for the connection between the spirit and renewal see Titus 3:5) the face of the earth (v. 30). The theme of a "new creation" is found in Isaiah 65:17, 2 Corinthians 5:17, Galatians 6:15. The image of God revitalizing his creation by sending his spirit was used by Jesus and the early Church to reveal the action of the three persons of God renewing, indeed recreating the human race. This forward look to the new creation is the real climax of the poem, for the second creation of a "new spirit" of righteousness in man (cf. Ezek 36:26) was the whole goal of the first creation.

From this summit the poet descends to some final notations of praise. May the glory of the Lord (which is to be manifested in the restored Zion, cf. Ps 102:16–17) be forever, may the Lord be glad in his works of creation (v. 31). He merely looks at the earth and it is unsettled; he touches the mountains and they smoke (v. 32): the panoply of creation is totally pliant to his action. The psalmist will spend his life singing to the Lord, making music to his God while he exists (v. 33). Just as he wants his meditation to be to the Lord's taste, he himself is glad (cf. v. 31) in the Lord (v. 34). The psalm thus celebrates the mutual delight God and his creation take in each other. Nothing must be allowed to spoil this creation, so the speaker asks that sinners may be eliminated from the earth and the wicked till they are no more (v. 35; cf. Ps 10:15–16). The earth that has been the object of God's work and has been mentioned seven times in the psalm will fulfill its purpose when all mankind turns wholeheartedly to the Lord, delighting in Him as he delights in us. The soul of the psalmist will be eternally consumed in blessing the Lord.

At the end of the psalm the word *halĕlûyāh* makes its first appearance in the psalter; it will become a major motif of Book Five (Pss 107–145).

The psalm shifts between direct address to the Lord and third person speech about him, as if the speaker passes from prayer to meditation and back to prayer. Verses in direct address are 1b, 6–9, 13b, 20, 24–30; verses referring to the Lord in the third person are verses 1a, 3–5, 13a, 16, 19, 21, 31–35. Present participles referring to the Lord but not clearly in second or third person are found in verses 2, 10, 14. The three-beat colon, in pairs or groups of three, dominates the psalm. Exceptions are verse 1 (3 + 4 + 3 meter), verses 8 and 12 (4 + 4 meter), verses 13 and 28 (3 + 4 meter), verse 25 (4 + 4 + 3 meter), and verse 26 (3 + 3 + 2 meter).

ᴘ Psalm 105   Joseph

The psalm takes us on a journey from Canaan to Egypt and back to Canaan. A small number of families with no fixed home but with promises of a land to be inherited are driven by famine to Egypt, where one of their own has stored up food. When they have increased to large numbers, their God overwhelms their oppressors with disasters, liberates his people, and leads them across the desert to inherit the land he had promised. This is Israel's foundational story, not told elsewhere in the psalter at such length.

The story is told in the framework of praise. Ten imperatives call on the congregation to give thanks to the Lord, call upon his name, make known his doings among the peoples (v. 1), sing to him, make music to him, ponder [aloud] all his wonders (v. 2), boast in his holy name with hearts that are glad as they seek the Lord (v. 3), search for the Lord and his strength, seek his face always (v. 4), remember the wonders he has done, the portents and judgments of his mouth (v. 5). Only in verse 6 is the audience specified: it is the "seed of Abraham his servant, the sons of Jacob his chosen one." Israel must praise the Lord who made choice of its ancestors. The epithets "servant" and "chosen one" highlight respectively the human and divine roles in the relationship. Israel's duty of praise is grounded in God's choice of her, by which she can call "our God" (cf. Ps 95:7, Gen 17:7–8, 19, Exod 6:7, Lev 26:12, Deut 26:17) the one whose judgments are in all the earth (v. 7). God has remembered (cf. Lev 26:42) his covenant forever—the word he commanded for a thousand generations (v. 8)—a covenant made with Abraham (cf. Gen 15:18, 17:9–10), and an oath he swore to Isaac (v. 9; cf. Gen 26:2–5). He set it up for Jacob as a statute (cf. Gen 28:13, 35:12), for Israel as an everlasting covenant (v. 10). The content of the promise to these patriarchs is given in verse 11: "To you will I give the land of Canaan, the cord of [marking out] your inheritance." The body of the psalm recounts the fulfilling of this promise.

When these recipients of the promise were few in number, no more than sojourners in the land (v. 12), wandering from nation to nation, from one kingdom to a different people (v. 13), God allowed no one to oppress them (v. 14) and reproved kings on their behalf (cf. Gen 20:2–7). The speaker imagines God addressing the pagan rulers: "Do not touch my anointed ones, and to my prophets do no harm" (v. 15, chiasmus). If Israel is a "kingdom of priests" (cf. Exod 19:6), it can be called anointed; if it witnesses to the true God, its people can be called prophets (cf. Gen 20:7); God's people have a sacred function to fulfill in the world. God began carrying out his promise in a surprising way: he called down a famine on the land (cf. Gen 41:54, 42:1–2); all their bread poles (on which ring-shaped loaves were stacked) he broke (v. 16, chiasmus). To prepare for this disaster he had sent ahead of them a man (v. 17), Joseph, sold (cf. Gen 37:28, 36; 39:1) as a slave (cf. Gen 39:17). They weighed down with fetters his foot; into iron went his soul (v. 18, chiasmus; cf. Gen 39:20 for Joseph's imprisonment) until the time when his word came about; the promise of the Lord proved him true (lit. "smelted") (v. 19; cf. Gen 40:21–22). The king sent and released him; the ruler of peoples loosened him (v. 20; cf. Ps 102:21), making him master of his house and ruler of all his possessions (v. 21; cf. Gen 41:41, 43), to instruct his princes as he pleased and to make his elders wise (v. 22; cf. Gen 41:39; Solomon, too, revealed wisdom to the pagans, cf. 1 Kgs 10:4–8). The psalmist does not state but implies that it was through Joseph that Israel came to Egypt and "Jacob" sojourned (cf. v. 12, inclusion) in the land of Ham (v. 23).

Joseph's ordeal and triumph were ordained by God to benefit both Israel and the "peoples," but Israel was not destined to remain a sojourner. God made his people very fruitful and more numerous than their oppressors (v. 24). He changed the heart of the latter to hate his people, to treat his servants (cf. Pss 90:13, 16, 102:15, 29) with cunning (v. 25).

So he sent another servant (cf. v. 6), Moses, and Aaron whom he chose (v. 26). These men produced signs for the Egyptians and portents (cf. Ps 78:43) in the land of Ham (v. 27), of which the psalmist describes eight. God sent darkness (cf. Exod 10:22) and it was dark, but they did not keep (correction for Hebrew "defy") his word (v. 28). He changed their waters into blood (cf. Exod 7:20) and caused their fish to die (v. 29). Their land swarmed with frogs (cf. Exod 8:2), even in the bedrooms of their kings (v. 30). He spoke and insects came (cf. Exod 8:20), gnats (Exod 8:13) in all their territory (v. 31). He turned their rains into hail (Exod 9:23), a flaming fire in their land (v. 32). With these he struck their vines and fig trees and broke the trees of their territory (v. 33). He spoke and locusts came (Exod 10:14), and creeping locusts without number (v. 34); these ate all the plants in their land and ate the fruit of their soil (v. 35). Then he struck all the firstborn in their land (Exod 12:29), the firstfruits of all their potency (v. 36; cf. Ps 78:51).

The subsequent miracles at the Red Sea and in the desert are described more summarily. God led the people out with silver and gold (cf. Exod 12:35–36), and among their tribes were none who stumbled (v. 37). Egypt was glad when they left, for terror of them had fallen on them (v. 38). God spread a cloud as a covering and fire to give light in the night (v. 39; cf. Exod 13:21–22). When they asked, he brought quails, and with bread from heaven he sated them (v. 40, chiasmus; cf. Exod 16:4, 13–15). He opened the rock and there gushed out waters, which flowed in the parched land like a river (v. 41; cf. Exod 17:6). All these came about because God remembered his holy word to Abraham (cf. vv. 8–9) his servant (v. 42; cf. v. 6).

Three final verses give the climax of the poem. God led out his people with rejoicing, with joyful shout his chosen ones (v. 43, chiasmus), giving them the lands of the nations, and the toil of races they inherited (v. 44, chiasmus), so that they might keep the Lord's statutes and observe his laws (v. 45). God's faithfulness to the covenant comes to fruition in the joyous obedience of the liberated people. Christians have been liberated from the Egypt of sin in order to serve the Father in Christ (cf. Rom 6:18, 22).

The psalm covers a vast stretch of Israel's history by rendering significant moments with original notes of detail. A steady 3 + 3 rhythm is maintained—the only exceptions are verses 1, 11, 25, 44 (4 + 3 meter) and verses 22, 30 (3 + 2 meter). Many common words join the psalm to its predecessor (i.e., "sing," "make music," "meditate," "heart," "be glad," "break," "bread," "send," "possessions," "wisdom," "darkness, "boundary/ territory," "fire," "trees," "plants," "fruit," "soil," "light," "night," "fill," "water") to indicate that praise to the God of creation and praise to the creator of Israel are interwoven.

⁓ PSALM 106   sin

Psalm 106 is similar to Psalm 78: both psalms rehearse Israel's history of sin, both begin with an extended introduction, both recount episodes of Israel's history in a non-chronological order. Psalm 106 is two-thirds the length of Psalm 78 and examines less profoundly than its counterpart the underlying attitudes of sin, but it views historical sin in the context of divine *ḥesed*, a word not found in the former psalm. As the final psalm of Book Four, it acknowledges that Israel is responsible for the exile she suffers, but it knows that God's divine love, like his kingship and strength, justice and holiness, glory and wisdom, is everlasting, a larger context than human sin.

The opening verse will occur again at the beginning of Psalms 107, 118, and 136. It is a mini-hymn composed of an invitation to give thanks to the Lord followed by the motive of thanks introduced by the conjunction "for" (*kî*). In this case there are two motives: "for he is good, for eternal is his love" (v. 1). God is both the good of all his creatures and good in his kindness to them (cf. Pss 25:8, 34:9, 52:11, 54:8, 73:1, 86:5, 100:5). This favorable disposition to man is concretized in the *ḥesed* by which he bound himself to Israel in the covenant. This love is an everlasting love despite the waywardness of those who are its object—such is the theme of our psalm, which can be viewed as a historical commentary on the great psalm of God's covenant love, Psalm 103.

The speaker asks who can express the Lord's mighty acts and make heard all his praise (v. 2): once again the parallel cola highlight God's action and man's response. A surprising third verse seems to answer the "Who?" of the preceding verse with the beatitude, "Happy are they who keep his decree, the one [change to singular] who does justice at all times" (v. 3). The ultimate praise of God is obedience to his commands (cf. Ps 40:4–9, Rom 12:1–2). The speaker asks to be remembered in the Lord's favor for his people (v. 4), to be included in the Lord's "salvation," a word to be used four more times in the psalm. The speaker will then see the good things of God's chosen ones (cf. Ps 105:6), be glad with the gladness of God's nation (v. 5), and boast in his share in God's inheritance (cf. Ps 105:11). Unlike the didactic speaker of Psalm 78, this psalmist is a suppliant wishing to be included in the mercies God showed for his people.

Only with verse 6 does the psalmist announce his theme: "We have sinned along with our fathers, we have done wrong, we have acted wickedly" (cf. same three verbs in 1 Kgs 8:47 and Dan 9:5). He will recount nine episodes showing Israel's forgetfulness of the divine love. When the fathers were in Egypt they showed no understanding of God's wonders (cf. Ps 105:2), did not remember the abundance of his love, defying him by the sea, at the Sea of Reeds (v. 7; cf. Exod 14:11). Yet he saved them on account of his name (cf. Ps 105:1, 3) and made known his might (v. 8; cf. v. 2). He rebuked (cf. Pss 18:16, 76:7, 80:17, 104:7, Isa 50:2, Nah 1:4) the Sea of Reeds and it became dry, and they walked through the abysses (cf. Ps 104:6) as through a desert (v. 9). Thus he saved them from the hand of those who hated them and redeemed them from the hand of the enemy (v. 10). The waters covered their oppressors; not one of them was left (v. 11). Then they had faith (a verb that appears in Ps 78 only in the negative) in his words (v. 12), they sang his praise (cf. v. 2).

Quickly they forgot his works; they did not wait patiently (cf. Ps 33:20) for his plan to unfold (v. 13). Our all-too-natural tendency is to put limits on what the Lord can achieve in desperate situations; our memories are short, our trust short-lived. Thus they desired their craving (lit. "desire") in the desert and tried (cf. Pss 78:18, 41, 95:9) God in the wilderness (v. 14; cf. Num 11:4–6). He gave them their request and sent emaciation into their souls (v. 15; cf. Num 11:18–20, 33–34).

Next they became jealous of Moses in the camp (cf. Num 16:1–3), and of Aaron the holy one of the Lord (v. 16). The earth opened and swallowed up Dathan and covered over the gathering of Abiram (v. 17; cf. Num 16:27–34). Then fire burned up their gathering; a flame blazed against the wicked (v. 18; cf. Num 16:35). As in the previous episode, punishment follows crime without the "happy ending" of the first or fourth episodes.

The psalmist reaches back to the apostasy at Sinai (Horeb) when they built a calf and prostrated before a cast image (v. 19; cf. Exod 32:3–4), thus exchanging their glory for the image of an ox that eats plants (v. 20). They forgot (cf. v. 13) the God who saved (cf. vv. 4, 8, 10) them, doing great things in Egypt (v. 21), wonders (cf. v. 7) in the land of Ham (cf. 105:23, 26), fearsome things (cf. Ps 65:6, Deut 10:21) at the Sea of Reeds (v. 22). And so the Lord said he would exterminate them, had not Moses his chosen one (cf. Aaron in Ps 105:26) stood in the breach before him to turn back his fury from wiping them out (v. 23; cf. Exod 32:11–14). Moses stands between the people and God's wrath, deflecting the latter by his intercession (cf. Ezek 22:30, Ps 99:6).

Now comes the incident that cost the Israelites forty years' wandering in the desert. They rejected (cf. Num 14:31) the desirable land (v. 24; cf. Num 14:1–10), having no faith in his word (cf. v. 12, Num 14:11). They grumbled in their tents, not listening to the voice of the Lord (v. 25). So he raised his hand [in oath; cf. Ezek 20:15, 23] against them to bring them down in the desert (v. 26; cf. Num 14:11, 29–30), to bring down their descendants among the nations, and to scatter them among the lands (v. 27). The punishment of Exile that in Leviticus 26:33 was to be inflicted for Israel's disobedience to the covenant is here attributed to the desert community's lack of faith in the God who would lead them into Canaan. Behind all Israel's sin down the ages the psalmist sees a common lack of trust in their Lord's desire or ability to save.

Forty years later on the threshold of Canaan the people committed themselves to the Baal of Peor (v. 28; cf. Num 25:1–3), eating sacrifices of the dead (i.e., lifeless gods). They grieved God with their deeds and there broke out among them a plague (v. 29). But Phineas stood and executed justice, and the plague (only occurrences of this word for plague in the Psalms) was brought to a standstill (v. 30; cf. Num 25:8–9). This was considered to be justice for him (cf. Gen 15:6) from age to age forever (v. 31; cf. Num 25:13). Phineas's role is analogous to that of Moses in verse 23.

Going back again in time, the speaker recalls the people's angering God at the waters of Meribah (v. 32), where it went badly for Moses because of them (cf. Ps 95:8, Num 20:11–13), for they defied his spirit, and he spoke inappropriately with his lips (v. 33). The account in Numbers identifies this sin precisely as lack of trust.

We now move into Canaan, where Israel did not exterminate (cf. v. 23) the peoples as the Lord had told them to (v. 34; cf. Deut 7:1–2).

Instead they mingled with the nations and learned their works (v. 35), serving their idols, which became for them a snare (v. 36).

The people were deluded by these idols to commit abominable crimes, including sacrificing their sons and daughters to demons (v. 37). Thus they poured out innocent blood, the blood of their sons and daughters, which they sacrificed to the idols of Canaan; the land was defiled with blood (v. 38; the first and last clauses of the verse may have originally referred to murder, the two inner clauses having been added later to relate the verse to the previous verse). In this way they became unclean in their works and were unfaithful (cf. Ps 73:27) in their deeds (v. 39). So the Lord's anger blazed against his people (v. 40) and he came to loathe his inheritance (cf. v. 5). Then he gave them into the hand of the nations (cf. v. 35), and they were ruled by those who hated them (v. 41; cf. v. 10, Ps 105:25); they were oppressed by their enemies and subdued beneath their hand (v. 42). Israel's sin is paid for by loss of freedom and independence.

We are now in a position to see what is meant by a love that is "everlasting," as the psalmist summarizes his message. Though on many occasions God rescued his people, they were defiant in their plan and sank down in their iniquity (v. 43). But he saw their distress when he heard their lamentation (v. 44; cf. Ps 88:3). He remembered his covenant with them and relented in the abundance of his love (v. 45), the *ḥesed* that the covenant guarantees and that was manifested in the compassion shown by all their captors (v. 46; cf. Ezra 9:9).

A final verse of four cola petitions the full restoration of Israel so that God may be properly praised: "Save us, Lord our God, and gather us from among the nations, that we may thank your holy name and adore you with praise" (v. 47). As at the Exodus, the purpose of Israel's liberation is the glorification of God (cf. Exod 7:16, 8:23, etc.). Having won redemption from sin Jesus received the name above all other names and was worshipped by every knee and tongue in the glory of God the Father (Phil 2:9–11). Our praise ascends to the Father through him (1 Pet 4:11, Rom 16:27, Eph 3:21).

There follows the doxology for Book Four, in which the Lord God of Israel is blessed from age to age as the people say *halĕlûyāh* (v. 48; this acclamation has been used at the end of Pss 104 and 105 and at the beginning and end of the present psalm). The psalm is in a consistent 3 + 3 meter. Exceptions are verses 4–6, 12, 17, 43–44, 48.

∼ PSALM 107   thanksgivings

The first psalm of Book Five is a serene meditation, somewhat didactic, on the manifold situations in which Yahweh can save, along with an invitation to give thanks.

The opening verse repeats that of the preceding psalm, linking the first psalm of the new book with the last of the old. While the previous psalm showed God's love overshadowing Israel's sin, the present psalm sees that love operating as an answer to prayer in desperate situations. Thanksgiving is to be uttered by the Lord's "redeemed," whom he redeemed from the hand of the oppressor (v. 2) and gathered from lands east, west, and north and from the sea (v. 3).

A group of people went astray in the desert wilderness; a way to a city to inhabit they did not find (v. 4, chiasmus). Hungry they were and thirsty; their soul was fainting (cf. Ps 77:4) within them (v. 5). But they cried out to the Lord "in their distress" (cf. Ps 106:44, another link with previous psalm); from their hardships (cf. Ps 25:17) he would rescue them (v. 6). Thus he led them on a straight way that they might go to a city to inhabit (v. 7), thus finding food and rest (cf. Heb 12:22). The appropriate response is thanksgiving to the Lord for his love, shown in the wonders he works for men (v. 8), for he satisfies the desiccated soul, and the hungry soul he fills with good things (v. 9, chiasmus). The last two verses follow the normal pattern for a hymn, with the conjunction "for" connecting the exhortation to praise with the motive for praise. The next three sections of the psalm will follow the same pattern: description of specific distress, prayer and immediate rescue of the community, exhortation to thanksgiving and reason for thanks.

A second group were sitting in darkness and the shadow of death (cf. Ps 44:20), prisoners in affliction and iron (v. 10; cf. Ps 105:18). For they defied (cf. Ps 106:33) the utterances of God, and the plan of the Most High they rejected (v. 11, chiasmus). He humbled their heart with toil; they stumbled with no one to help (v. 12). Here their suffering is compounded by their own sin. Again they cried, and this time God "saved" them from their afflictions (v. 13). He brought them out from darkness and the shadow of death and sundered their fetters (v. 14; cf. Ps 2:3). Verse 15 repeats verse 8; this time the motive for praise is that God breaks gateways of bronze, and bars of iron he breaks in pieces (v. 16, chiasmus).

Not only does God provide nourishment and comfort, he shatters imprisoning fetters.

A third group became unwise on their rebellious way (cf. v. 4) and in their iniquities were tormented (v. 17, chiasmus); like the second group their suffering is caused by their own willfulness. Every food their soul loathed, and they approached the gates of death (v. 18). From this distress they made their prayer and were saved (v. 19; cf. v. 13). God sent his word and healed them (cf. Pss 30:3, 103:3) and freed them from [the brink of] the grave (v. 20). After the repetition of verse 8 in verse 21 with its implicit reason for praise (the Lord's "love" and "wonders"), the explicit motive of praise is replaced by a second invitation, this time to offer thanksgiving sacrifices (cf. Ps 50:14, 23) and recount the Lord's works with shouts of joy (v. 22).

The crisis situation of the fourth group is the most developed: men are nearly submerged by the engulfing chaos of the sea. They go down to the sea in ships, doing business on the many waters (v. 23). These men have seen the Lord's works (cf. v. 22), his wonders in the deep (v. 24; cf. Pss 68:23, 69:3, 16, 88:7). Here the works and wonders refer not to the great rescue but to the creation of the peril itself, against which the Lord will display even greater might. He spoke (as at creation, cf. Ps 33:9, Gen 1:3) and roused up a stormy wind (cf. Ps 55:9) and exalted its waves (v. 25; cf. Pss 65:8, 89:10), which rose up to the heavens and sank down to the abysses (cf. Pss 77:17, 106:9), so that their soul dissolved in their harm (v. 26). They staggered and reeled like drunken men, and all their skill (lit. "wisdom") was confused (v. 27). One is reminded of the storms that attacked the ship on which Jonah sailed (Jonah 1:4, 11–13) or Paul's ship on the way to Rome (Acts 27:20). There follows the verse of prayer and rescue (v. 28), the latter expressed by the verb "brought out" (cf. v. 14, Pss 18:20, 66:12). God ordered the storm to be calm, and the waves of the sea became silent (v. 29). The men were glad that they (waves) were hushed (cf. Jonah 1:11–12), and he led them (cf. Pss 77:21, 78:53) to the harbor of their delight (v. 30). The thanksgiving refrain of verses 8, 15, 21 is repeated verbatim (v. 31); as in the third salvation episode it is complemented by a developed exhortation to praise: "Let them exalt him in the assembly of the people, and in the meeting [cf. vv. 4, 7] of the elders let them praise him" (v. 32, chiasmus).

The Lord can save from hunger in the desert, the darkness of prison, the illness consequent on sin, and the upheaval of earthly stability. The remainder of the psalm focuses on his power to change any situation into its opposite. He makes rivers into desert and outlets of water into waterless regions (v. 33), a fruitful land into a salt waste for the evil of those who dwell there (v. 34). He makes the desert into a pool of water and parched land (cf. Ps 105:41) into outlets of water (v. 35, repeating several words from v. 33; vv. 33 and 35 can be seen as an expansion of the idea in Ps 74:15). God settles the hungry there and establishes a city they can inhabit (v. 36, alluding to first salvation episode, vv. 4–9), where they sow fields and plant vineyards that yield a fruitful harvest (v. 37). God blesses them and they increase greatly, and their cattle he does not diminish (v. 38). But they are diminished and stooped from constriction, evil, and sorrow (v. 39), presumably for their own sins as in verse 34. God pours contempt on nobles (v. 40), making them stray in a wasteland without a way (cf. v. 4). But he sets on high the needy from affliction and makes his clans like a flock (v. 41). Thus verses 39–41 repeat the negative/positive sequence of verses 33–38. The reversal of situations reminds us of the Magnificat (Luke 1:52–53). Verse 42 plays the role of the final verse of each of the salvation episodes in expressing men's reaction to God's deeds: "The upright will see and be glad [cf. v. 30], and all perversity will stop its mouth" (v. 42).

The concluding verse reinforces the instructional nature of the psalm: "Who is wise and will keep these things? Such men will discern [the deeds of] the Lord's covenant love" (v. 43). The psalm is notable for its regular 3 + 3 rhythm (exceptions: 4 + 3 in vv. 6, 13, 19, 24, 26, 28, 37, 43; other meters in vv. 3, 23, 25, 35) and its original vocabulary: "desiccated," "unwise," "grave," "drunken," "confused," "stillness," "hushed," "harbor," "waterless region," "salt waste," "constriction," and "wasteland" are used only here in the psalter; the words for "hardships," "sunder," "gateway," "bar," "break in pieces," "stagger," "pool," and "stop" are each found in only one other place in the psalter.

∿ Psalm 108   international

Two pieces of earlier psalms, the second halves of Psalms 57 and 60, have been juxtaposed (with only two minor changes in each section) to form a psalm that begins with a vow of praise and ends with a petition for help against Israel's enemies. Both sections are the prayer of an individual and both suggest Yahweh's lordship over the nations (cf. vv. 4, 10–14). The vow of praise gains from this juxtaposition an "international" significance, and the petition for victory is drawn into the liturgy of celebration. Christians worship the God who has made his Christ the lord of the nations (Rev 11:15–18).

The opening verse eliminates the repetition of the phrase "My heart is poised" found in Psalm 57:8 and substitutes "even my glory" for the phrase "Rouse yourself, my glory" of Psalm 57:9. In verse 10 it is the Lord himself who "cries jubilantly" rather than the Philistines (Ps 60:10), and in verse 11 the word for "fortified" is different from that in Psalm 60:11.

Erich Zenger points out the appropriateness of the position of the psalm near the beginning of Book Five: "With its quotation of 57:8–12 and 60:7, Psalm 108 expresses the theme of the entire composition [Book Five]: the salvation of Israel as proof before all nations of the *ḥesed* and the *ʾĕmet* [love and faithfulness] of Yahweh and hence the revelation of Yahweh's universal reign" ("Composition and Theology," 90).

⁓ Psalm 109   cursing

Christians tend not to pray this psalm, which is one of three (with Pss 59 and 83) entirely omitted from the Roman Breviary. But the psalm displays a theological artistry, which consists in the use of the same words in opposite contexts: "mouth" of wickedness versus "mouth" of praise; the "wicked" calling the innocent "wicked"; the psalmist's "goodness and love" vis-à-vis God's "goodness and love"; the "standing at [one's] right hand" of both the psalmist's accuser and God; the "blotting out" of the psalmist's name but not of his mother's sin; the "remembering" of the psalmist's sins but not of the psalmist himself; "love" for one's fellow man and "love" for cursing; the accuser's refusal to "bless" versus the "blessing" of the Lord; the psalmist's "putting on" curses and the accusers' "putting on" dishonor. Malicious words spoken against others will ultimately hurt their speaker, who by these words is separating himself from the God of *ḥesed* and so choosing the very death he attempts to inflict (cf. v. 16). "He who lives by the sword will die by the sword" (Matt 26:52).

The psalm of curses begins and ends with references to praise (vv. 1, 31). The speaker asks God not to be "deaf" (cf. Pss 28:1, 35:22, 39:13,

83:2), for the mouth of the wicked man and the mouth of deceit (cf. Pss 10:7, 36:4, 52:6) are opened against him; they speak against him with a lying tongue (v. 2). With words of hatred they surround him (v. 3), and they battle against him without cause (cf. Pss 35:19, 69:5). In place of his kindness they accuse him, while he is prayer (v. 4, i.e., totally engaged in prayer, perhaps for his enemies). They repay him evil for good (cf. Pss 35:12, 38:21) and hatred for his kindness (v. 5).

The psalmist now quotes at length these "wicked accusers": Appoint against him a wicked man, and let an accuser stand at his right hand (v. 6). When he is judged let him emerge wicked (i.e., culpable), and let his prayer (cf. v. 4) be taken as sin (v. 7). Let his days be few; let another take his office (v. 8; cf. Acts 1:20). Let his sons be orphans and his wife a widow (v. 9). Let his sons wander and beg and search in their ruins (v. 10). Let the creditor snare all he owns, and let strangers ravage his property (v. 11). Let none extend him any love, and let no one be generous to his orphans (v. 12). Let his posterity fall to destruction (sound word play: ʾaḥărîtô lĕhakrît); in future generations let their name be blotted out (v. 13). Let the iniquity of his fathers be remembered before the Lord and the sin of his mother not be blotted out (v. 14). May they be before the Lord always, and may he cut off their memory from the earth (v. 15).

Many laments call for the destruction of the enemy himself; none so relentlessly seeks the extinction of his family and his destiny. These ten verses are an accurate expression of the depths of human and diabolic malice and cannot be prayed as the words of the psalmist. But in asking that the words be turned against their speaker, the psalmist and the Christian in Christ are asking for the obliteration of that malice from God's creation (as, e.g., in Ps 104:35). Jesus made it clear that the fate of those who bring down the innocent is obliteration (Matt 18:6–7).

The word "remember" is a cue for the psalmist's reflection on the accuser, who "did not remember to show love but pursued the poor and needy man and the broken-hearted to death" (v. 16). He loved cursing, so let it come upon him; and he did not delight in blessing, so let it be far from him (v. 17). And he clothed himself with cursing like his cloak, so let it enter like water inside him and like oil into his bones (v. 18). Let it be like a garment that wraps him and like a loincloth that he always puts on (v. 19). This is the reward of the speaker's accusers from the Lord, and of those who speak evil against his soul (v. 20). The images for the working out of the "immanent nemesis" (see on Ps 7) are particularly graphic.

It is not enough that the cursers suffer their own curses: the victim must be rehabilitated, and so he prays: "And you, Lord, Master, who act for me according to your name, since your love is good, rescue me! [v. 21]. For I am poor and needy, and my heart is pierced within me" (v. 22). Like a lengthening shadow he goes about, he is shaken off like a locust (v. 23). His knees wobble from fasting, and his flesh has become lean without fat (v. 24, "fat" same as "oil" in v. 18). He has become the scorn of others; they see him and shake their heads (v. 25; cf. Ps 22:8).

Lament is followed by petition: "Help me, Lord, my God; save me in your love (v. 26; cf. Pss 6:5, 31:17). Let them know that this is your hand; you, Lord, have done it" (v. 27). The punishment of the wicked by his own sin is part of the natural order ordained by God. A powerful summary of the poem's theology is the following verse 28 (4 + 4 meter, the only verse that does not contain at least one three-beat colon): while the enemies curse, God blesses; they will rise only to be shamed while the Lord's servant is glad (v. 28). The accusers will be clothed in disgrace, and their shame will wrap them like a robe (v. 29). For Saint Paul, too, "Snapping and tearing at each other" (Gal 5:15) destroys the ones who indulge in it.

A mini-hymn concludes this painful lament. The psalmist will thank the Lord much with his mouth and in the midst of many will praise him (v. 30), for the Lord stands at the right hand of the needy to save from those who judge his soul (v. 31).

✎ Psalm 110   footstool

Psalm 110 is the most influential of the messianic psalms and the Old Testament text most often cited in the New. With its summons to the king to sit at the right hand (cf. Ps 109:31) of the Lord, it expresses God's intention to raise a human ruler into the divine presence. The subjugation of enemies foretold in Psalm 2 is here expressed in the stark image of their being made a footstool for the messiah's feet (v. 1). The speaker develops this first oracle of the psalm by adding his own image and summons: "The scepter of your power will the Lord send from Zion; rule [cf. Ps 72:8] in the midst of your enemies" (v. 2). The image recalls Isaiah's vision of the Law going out from Zion and the oracle of the Lord from

Jerusalem to wield authority over the nations, bringing peace (Isa 2:3–4). A mysterious second oracle follows: "Your people are willing on the day of your force [lit. "vigor"]; on the holy mountains [LXX] from the womb of the dawn I begot you [LXX]," to which the Hebrew adds the phrase, "with you is dew" (v. 3). The difficult, often-emended verse suggests that the king's followers willingly join him in battle (cf. Judg 5:9) and that he was fathered by God in a cosmic setting: on (or like) the morning dew he emerged from the earliest dawn on mountains of God. He comes into the world "trailing clouds of glory" (Wordsworth, "Ode on Intimations of Immortality"). The image is suggestive, not yielding to literal analysis.

A third oracle is now introduced with a formula: "The Lord swore an oath and will not change his mind: You are a priest forever according to the order of Melchizedek" (v. 4; for the divine oath, see on Ps 89:4). The utterance continues the mysteriousness of the previous verse, since Melchizedek is otherwise known only from Genesis 14:18–20, where he is both priest and king of the pre-Israelite (Jebusite) Jerusalem. For the Letter to the Hebrews Melchizedek represents a priesthood transcending that of Aaron's descendants since all of Israel in the person of Abraham was blessed by this mysterious figure. The Israelite king occasionally exercised priestly functions (cf. 2 Sam 6:14, 8:18, 1 Kgs 8:63, Zech 6:11–13), but for Christ priesthood enters into the very essence of kingship: it was by offering a pleasing sacrifice to the Father that he became head of an eternal kingdom. "He has offered one single sacrifice for sins, and then taken his place for ever, at the right hand of God, where he is now waiting until his enemies are made into a footstool for him" (Heb 10:12–13). By joining us to his sacrifice he makes us, too, a "kingdom of priests" (Exod 19:6, 1 Pet 2:4–5, 9) to "serve" our God and to "rule" the world (Rev 5:10).

As with the first oracle, the third is "extended" by the speaker's comments to the king. "The Master at your right hand (cf. v. 1) will smite kings in the day of his anger" (v. 5; cf. Pss 2:5, 9, 21:10, 56:8; this is the last attribution of anger [*af*] to God in the psalter). It is now God who is at the right hand of the king, undertaking the destruction of the enemy kings. The God who works at the king's right hand on earth is the God who will raise the king to sit in honor at his own right hand (v. 1). God will give judgment against the nations, filling them with corpses; he will "smite" (cf. v. 5) heads over the wide earth (v. 6). The final verse, unlike the others, is not addressed to the king but spoken about him: from the stream by the wayside he will drink; therefore he will exalt his head (v. 7). Refreshed by his drink the warrior-king will raise his head in victory. The stream may refer to the spring Gihon at the foot of Mount Zion where the anointing of kings took place (cf. 1 Kgs 1:33–35, 38–40). Part of the ritual may have included a drink from the spring, which represented the Lord's gracious gift to Jerusalem (cf. Ps 46:5 and Gen 2:13, where Gihon denotes one of the four paradisal rivers).

The somewhat disjointed statements about the king that make up the psalm convey a powerful impression of Israel's king as a sure instrument in the establishment of God's rule on earth. The most influential of its verses was the first with its three distinct parts: the introduction to the oracle and the first and second halves of the oracle. Jesus, understanding the psalm as spoken by David, sees in the introduction, "The Lord's oracle to my master," a proof that David's son will be of higher rank than he (cf. Matt 22:41–45, Mark 12:35–37, Luke 20:41–44). But it was in the first colon of this first oracle, "Sit at my right," that Jesus, son of David, and after him the whole primitive Church, saw the profoundest prophecy of his own destiny: he would be the human king who would be raised to the divine level itself. It was his application to himself of the Lord's command, "Sit on my right" along with the prophecy of the Son of Man coming on the clouds of heaven in Daniel 7:13, that cost Jesus a sentence of death at his trial (Matt 26:64–66, Mark 14:62–64, Luke 22:69). After his resurrection we are told in the Gospel of Mark that Jesus was installed "at the right hand of God," working with the apostles as they preached everywhere (Mark 16:19–20). On Pentecost morning Saint Peter proclaims Jesus as the only human being summoned to sit in the Lord's presence in heaven (Acts 2:33–35). Stephen sees the Son of Man "standing at the right hand of God," a statement heard by the Sanhedrin as blasphemy and cause for stoning (Acts 7:56–57). Paul often portrays Jesus as standing or sitting at God's right hand, interceding for us (Rom 8:34), sharing in the divine rule (Eph 1:20), the focus of the Christian's eye of faith (Col 3:1). For the Letter to the Hebrews the "right hand of divine Majesty" is the final destination of the Son of God who became man in order to "destroy the defilement of sin" and then take his place in heaven

(Heb 1:3, 12:2), higher even than the angels (Heb 1:13). Later chapters in Hebrews link this place at the right hand with the priest according to the order of Melchizedek (v. 4; cf. Heb 8:1).

As for the second half of the opening oracle, "I will make your enemies a stool for your feet," Hebrews 10:12–13, after applying the first half to Jesus, shows how it too is being fulfilled in Jesus as enemies throughout the world are gradually subjugated to him. This is also Paul's perspective in 1 Corinthians 15, where Christ is depicted as reigning "until he has put all his enemies under his feet"—that is, every "sovereignty, authority and power"—"and the last of the enemies to be destroyed is death" (cf. 1 Cor 15:24–26a). Saint Paul then imperceptibly switches the allusion from Psalm 110 to Psalm 8, stating that not just "enemies" but "all things" are to be placed "under his feet" (1 Cor 15:26b–28 citing Ps 8:6).

So embedded in the Christian's faith is the image of the Lord's being "at the right hand of God" that it has found its way into both the Apostles' and the Nicene Creeds. It expresses the essence of Easter faith, giving a visual equivalent of the doctrine "Jesus is Lord." The enemies to be placed under his feet are not individual nations or armies or kings but the spiritual enemies of mankind, sin, the devil, and death. The created spirit's rebellion against God has been neutralized; it no longer has power to keep men from life.

Saint Benedict's *Rule* for monks makes Psalm 110 the first psalm at Vespers on Sunday, the day of the Lord's resurrection.

∽ PSALM 111   God

God's greatness, power, and compassion are seen in his works, but especially in his covenant and decrees, which provide an eternal security for his people.

The psalmist will thank the Lord with intense interiority ("with all my heart") and at the same time in community ("in the circle of the upright and their gathering"; v. 1). The first object of praise is the Lord's great works, worthy to be searched out by all who delight (cf. Pss 1:2, 40:9, 73:25) in them (v. 2). Majestic and splendid (cf. Pss 96:6, 104:1) is his action, and his justice stands forever (v. 3): God's external actions partake of his splendor and integrity. The "memorial" he made of his "wonders" (cf. Pss 78:11, 96:3, 98:1, 105:5) would be either the written record or the liturgical celebration of his saving deeds. Then follows the single colon that speaks of his person rather than his works (v. 4): "gracious and compassionate" (Pss 86:15, 103:8, Exod 34:6, Joel 2:13, Jonah 4:2) is the Lord. Those who acknowledge his transcendence ("fear" him) receive nourishment, whether natural or supernatural (v. 5); he "remembers his covenant forevermore" (cf. Pss 105:8, 106:45). The power of his works (cf. v. 2) he has shown to his people to give them the inheritance of the nations (v. 6); the goal of God's works is the incorporation of all nations into his people.

Verse 7 combines the two principal manifestations of God, his works and his word: the works of God's hands are stamped with his faithfulness and judgment; reliable (worthy of faith) are all his precepts (v. 7), upheld forever and ever, made in faithfulness and uprightness (v. 8; cf. v. 1). Redemption he has sent to his people (verse quoted in the Benedictus, Luke 1:68); he commanded his covenant (cf. v. 5) forever (v. 9). The divine "name," which sums up his identity and activity, is holy (cf. Luke 1:49); it is like the "memorial" of his deeds (cf. v. 4) and is to be "feared." The only wise stance before such a God is fear of the Lord, understood as a recognition of total dependence on him, a willingness to rely on his help and a concern for his commands; those who do them have good understanding (v. 10ab). Obedience to the commands of God is both the cause and the fruit of knowledge of him (cf. Col 1:9–10, Eph 1:17).

Finally, the "praise" of this God, like his justice (cf. v. 3), stands forever (v. 10c, inclusion with the opening halĕlûyāh).

The risen Christ praises the Father for the "memorial" (cf. v. 4) of his works, which is the Eucharist, a food (cf. v. 5) given in memory (Luke 22:19, 1 Cor 11:24–25) of his great work (v. 2) of deliverance (cf. v. 9). This memorial is a "new and everlasting covenant" (cf. vv. 5, 9) eternally binding God and his people. It is a covenant written on the heart (2 Cor 3:6, 3, Jer 31:31, 33) that enables human beings to carry out the Lord's precepts in justice.

∾ PSALM 112   fear of the Lord

The psalm forms a diptych with Psalm 111. Both are short alphabetic psalms with a single colon of three or four beats beginning with each letter. One colon from Psalm 111 is repeated twice in Psalm 112, and the beginning of the latter psalm picks up the theme of "fear of the Lord" from the end of the previous one. While Psalm 111 treats of God, its sequel treats of the just man, using some of the same concepts. The just man shares attributes of God himself. The individual cola present either qualities of the just man or rewards for his behavior.

After an opening *halĕlûyāh* the man is declared happy who fears the Lord (cf. Ps 111:10). This salutary fear has been encountered several times in the psalms (e.g., Pss 2:11, 5:8, 34:8, 10, 12, 40:4, 67:8). It is an abiding awareness of God as a living reality on whom one's life depends, accompanied by a desire not to separate oneself from him and a reliance on his help. This is filial fear of which St. Thomas speaks: "In filial fear we are not so much afraid that something we hope to obtain through divine help will be lacking to us, but we fear withdrawing ourselves from that help" (*Summa Theologiae* II-IIae.19.9). The opposite of filial fear is servile fear, a cowering before a punishing Master, a fear that both Testaments tell us not to have (e.g., Gen 15:1, Exod 14:13, 20:20, Deut 3:22, 7:21, 31:6, Isa 41:10, 43:1, 5, Hag 2:4–5, Matt 10:26, 28, 31, 14:27, 1 John 4:18). Fear of the Lord leads to happiness because it puts man in the right relation to the Lord. The one who fears the Lord is fully aware of the Lord's goodness and might and trusts in them; he is anxious not to separate himself from this Lord by violating his commands; in fact he "delights" in them greatly (v. 1; cf. Ps 111:2).

Champions in the land will be this man's offspring since he has rooted himself in the divine; the generation of the upright will be blessed (v. 2). Prosperity and riches are in his house, and his justice stands forever (v. 3; cf. Ps 111:3b). Everything about this man suggests fruitfulness. He shines in darkness as a light for the upright (cf. v. 2), gracious, compassionate (cf. Pss 111:4, 86:15), and just (v. 4). His willingness to draw on the power of God makes him a source of blessing for others, in particular the needy. The good man is generous and lending (cf. Luke 6:35); he accomplishes his affairs with judgment (v. 5). For he will never totter; the just man leaves an everlasting memory (v. 6; cf. Ps 111:4). He will not be afraid (with "servile" fear, cf. on v. 1) of a message of disaster; firm is his heart, trusting in the Lord (v. 7). "Upheld" (cf. Ps 111:8) is his heart; he will not fear (cf. v. 7) until he gloats over (lit. "sees on"; note pun on Hebrew words for "fear" and "see" as in Ps 40:4) his oppressors (v. 8). He scattered (cf. Prov 11:24), he gave to the needy (cf. v. 5); here the psalmist repeats verse 3b without the connective "and." These first two cola of verse 9 are cited by Saint Paul in his appeal to the generosity of the Corinthians for the relief of the Christians of Judea (2 Cor 9:9). As a reward for his generosity, the just man's horn (cf. Pss 75:5, 6, 11, 89:18, 25) will be exalted in glory (v. 9). The wicked man will see him and grieve; he will gnash his teeth and melt away (cf. Pss 22:15, 68:3, 97:5); the desire of the wicked vanishes (v. 10).

The man who fears the Lord manifests God's "justice" in all his doings, and by so doing cannot help but endure. Jesus is the "just one" par excellence (Acts 3:14, 7:52, 22:14, Matt 27:19, 1 Pet 3:18, 1 John 2:1), whose endurance is everlasting because he mirrors the "just" one, his Father (cf. John 17:25). Those who are in him share his glory, as he shares his Father's light (v. 4 with Ps 27:1, John 8:12, 9:5, 12:46).

∼ PSALM 113   stoop

Psalm 113 combines ideas from the two previous psalms: the exalted and gracious Lord is the one who makes fruitful the house of the needy. Several words link the psalm with its two predecessors: "blessed," "shine forth," "exalt," "glory," "see," "needy," "house" (all in Ps 112), "name," "nations," "people," "forevermore" (in Ps 111).

Like the two previous psalms, the poem begins with "*halĕlûyāh*" this time immediately followed by a call to the servants of the Lord to praise, to praise the name of the Lord (v. 1). The psalm is the first of the group called the Egyptian Hallel (Pss 113–118), prayed at the celebration of Passover. The speaker himself undertakes the praise he called for: may the name of the Lord be blessed, from now and forevermore (v. 2). From the shining forth of the sun to its setting, praised be the name of the Lord (v. 3). Verses 2–3 are arranged chiastically so that the double praise of the Lord's name encloses references to all time and space. The speaker continues his praise by picturing the Lord exalted above all nations; above the heavens is his glory (v. 4). "Who is like the Lord our God dwelling on high [v. 5], stooping to see the heavens and the earth?" (v. 6). His universal gaze enables him to raise from the dust the weak; from the ash heap he exalts the needy (v. 7, almost identical with 1 Sam 2:8), to make him sit (cf. v. 5) with nobles, with the nobles of his people (v. 8). Similarly he makes the barren one (cf. Gen 11:30, 25:21, 29:31, Judg 13:2, 1 Sam 2:5, Isa 54:1) to dwell in a house, a glad mother of sons (v. 9).

The psalm is about the condescension of the incarnation. God came in person on earth to raise the lowly (Luke 1:48, 52) and make the barren fruitful (Luke 1:34–35). The Church, too, poor in justice of its own, is made fruitful in holiness by Christ (Eph 5:25–27).

~ PSALM 114   skip

The psalm telescopes into a short hymn four events of the Exodus: the crossing of the Red Sea, the miracle of water from the rock, the crossing of the Jordan, and the establishment of God's dwelling in Zion. The name of the Lord is not used, nor is God mentioned until the end, as if to suggest a riddle behind the strange behavior of nature, a riddle answered only in the penultimate verse. The psalm is in regular 3 + 3 meter, except for verse 7a, which begins with a four-beat colon (unless corrected to "Before the Master of all the earth," cf. Kraus, *Psalmen*, 2:778).

In the going out of Israel from Egypt, of the house of Jacob from a people of unintelligible tongue (v. 1), Judah became his (i.e., God's; no antecedent in the Hebrew) holy place, Israel his dominions (v. 2). The first "Israel" designates the twelve tribes, the second either the northern kingdom alone or the twelve tribes. The sea saw and fled (Exod 14:21–22), and forty years later the Jordan turned back on its course (v. 3; Jos 3:16–17). The mountains skipped (cf. Ps 29:6) like rams, the hills like young lambs (v. 4)—a possible reference to the earthquake at Sinai (Exod 19:18; Heb 12:18–21, 26).

The riddle is then posed as the psalmist asks the sea why it fled, Jordan why it turned back (v. 5), the mountains why they skipped like rams, hills like young lambs (v. 6). The answer is given obliquely, in a command to the earth to "writhe" (cf. Pss 29:8, 77:17, 96:9, 97:4) before the face of the Master, before the face of the God of Jacob (v. 7). The reversal of natural phenomena proves that Israel's God is the creator, who can make nature serve his purposes, as he showed also by giving miraculous drink to his people, changing the rock to a pool (cf. Ps 107:35) of water, flint to a spring of water (v. 8; cf. Deut 8:15). Israel's God tames the chaotic waters and provides drink from the earth's bedrock. For a Christian this is a God who destroys the power of death (Rom 6:3–5, Col 2:12–13) and quenches the thirst for life (cf. Rev 21:6, 1 Cor 10:4, John 4:14).

~ PSALM 115   idols

This psalm is joined in the Septuagint with the previous psalm to form a single prayer. At first glance the Hebrew division into two psalms is correct since each psalm has its inner coherence and tone, but in fact the two psalms share a common emphasis on the singular authenticity of Israel's God. The first gives vivid images of his power to change nature; the second expressly states that other gods do not exist.

No other psalm begins with such a resounding "not" (Ps 37 is tame in comparison): "Not to us, Lord, not to us but to your name give glory on account of your love, on account of your faithfulness" (v. 1). The repetition indicates a resolute repudiation of the temptation to seek human glory (cf. John 5:44) and a corresponding pledge to attribute glory (cf. Ps 113:4) to the one who alone deserves it. In the context of the psalm the statement is a rejection of the temptation to worship what our own hands have made. He alone is owed glory who through his covenant love, his faithfulness to his promises, and his creative power can save. While men may not be able to give glory directly to the invisible God, they can proclaim the glory of his "name" (cf. Ps 113:1), which contains all that he is for his people. This is the only verse in Psalms 110–115 addressed directly to God.

The speaker immediately launches into a diatribe against the nations (cf. Ps 113:4). Why should they challenge Israel, "Where is your God?" (v. 2). He answers that "our God" (cf. Ps 113:5) is in the heavens (cf. Ps 113:4), where he can do whatever he delights in (v. 3; cf. Ps 112:1), as was demonstrated in Psalm 114. The psalmist then goes on the offensive, mocking the idols of the pagans, which are nothing but silver and gold, work of human hands (v. 4). Seven ironic statements point out the lifelessness of these idols (see also Isa 44:9–20, 46:5–7, Jer 10:3–16 for more developed taunts): they have mouths but do not speak, they have eyes but do not see (v. 5), they have ears but do not hear, they have a nose but do not smell (v. 6), hands but do not feel, feet but do not walk, they do not murmur with their throat (v. 7). Like them, that is, without life, will be their makers and all who trust in them (v. 8). Only the living one can give life.

By contrast the psalmist reminds his fellow worshippers to trust (cf. v. 8) in the true God, the Lord. He summons first Israel (v. 9), then the sons of Aaron (priests, v. 10), then those who fear the Lord (pagans converting to Judaism, v. 11) to trust in the Lord, following each summons with a third person refrain applied to the group, "Their helper and their shield [cf. Pss 28:7, 33:20, 89:19] is he." In turn the Lord will remember his people and bless: he will bless the house of Israel, he will bless the house of Aaron (v. 12), he will bless those who fear the Lord, the little along with the great (v. 13; cf. 2 Chr 34:30, Esth 1:5, 20, Jer 6:13, 31:34, Jonah 3:5). The psalmist asks that the Lord grant increase to his hearers and to their children (v. 14), who are blessed by the Lord, maker of heaven and earth (v. 15). The consequence of trusting in the creator God is an access of life.

The heaven of heavens belongs to the Lord (cf. Ps 113:6), while the earth he has given to the sons of men (v. 16). He remains untouched in his transcendence yet dispenses life to men and is praised by them. It is not the dead who praise the Lord, nor those who go down to the silence (v. 17); we it is who bless (cf. vv. 12, 13, 15; cf. also Ps 113:2) the Lord, from now and forevermore (v. 18; cf. Ps 113:2). The psalm thus conveys the unique creativity of Israel's God, his gift of life and blessing to his people, their response of praise, and the absurdity and futility of man-made gods.

The psalm demonstrates several points of contact with Psalm 113. Both psalms show a theological concern that dates them to the period after the Exile. The late date is corroborated by the presence of Aramaic expressions.

Jesus, too, praises the Lord "of heaven and earth" (Matt 11:25) while heaven and earth were in fact made "through" himself (Col 1:16) and all things in heaven and on earth were reconciled to the Father through him, as firstborn from the dead (Col 1:18–20). He is the Son who gives glory to the Father (John 7:18, 17:1, 4) while receiving the praise of his people (Rev 5:12).

∼ PSALM 116   helpless

The psalmist was saved from death (cf. Ps 115:17) by calling on the name (cf. Pss 113:1–3, 115:1) of the Lord who is gracious, just, and compassionate (cf. Ps 111:3–4). He gives thanks in the presence of God's people (cf. Pss 111:6, 9, 113:8).

This is the first prayer featuring an individual in distress since Psalm 109. The psalmist tells of his rescue from death and his intention to give thanks. The opening word, "I love," is unusual, but it is followed by conventional language from earlier psalms: "for the Lord has heard the voice of my pleading [v. 1], for he inclined his ear to me, and in my days I will call" (v. 2)—that is, call to the Lord in thanksgiving (cf. vv. 13, 17). Verse 3a is quoted directly from Psalm 18:5 and expanded by two expressions with the verb "find": "the constrictions of Sheol found me; distress and sorrow I find" (v. 3; the verb tenses are problematic). So he calls on the name of the Lord, this time in invocation: "Please, Lord, free [cf. Ps 107:20] my soul" (v. 4). Citing "our God's" attributes from Psalm 111:3–4 (v. 5), he adds that the Lord guards especially the "simple" (v. 6; cf. Ps 19:8); he was brought low, and the Lord saved him. So the speaker's soul can return to his "rest" (cf. Ps 95:11), for the Lord has done good things for him (v. 7). The speaker addresses his prayerful recognition to the Lord in the second person: "Indeed you have delivered my soul from death [cf. v. 3], my eye from tears [cf. Isa 25:8, Jer 31:16], my foot from stumbling" (v. 8). He will walk in the presence of the Lord in the land of the living (v. 9).

With verse 10 the psalmist begins retelling his story, and the Septuagint has seen here the beginning of a new psalm. The tenses are again a problem, as he states: "I was faithful [cf. Ps 106:12, 24], even though I speak, 'I am heavily bowed down [cf. Ps 102:24]' [v. 10]. I said in my haste, 'Every man is a liar'" (v. 11). In his helplessness and simplicity he could rely on no human support but relied on the Lord. The "I was faithful" that begins this second section matches the "I love" that began the first: faith and love are the essential Christian virtues. Trust in the love of God fills our own hearts with that love (cf. Eph 3:17) and stirs up a response of thanksgiving. When the psalmist asks how he can repay the Lord for all his kindness to him (v. 12), the answer comes: "The cup of salvation [cf. v. 6] I will lift and on the name of the Lord I will call" (v. 13; cf. v. 2). His vows to the Lord he will pay before all his people (v. 14). Precious in the eyes of the Lord was the death of his devout ones—too costly for the Lord to allow (v. 15).

The speaker accompanies his sacrifice with words: "Please, Lord [cf. v. 4], I am your servant [cf. Ps 113:1], I am your servant, the son of your handmaid [cf. Ps 86:16; this phrase omitted from the Grail]; you have loosened my fetters [v. 16; cf. Ps 107:14]. To you I sacrifice a sacrifice of thanksgiving [cf. Pss 50:14, 23, 107:22], and on the name of the Lord I call" (v. 17; cf. vv. 2, 13). After repeating his intention to pay his vows

(v. 18 = v. 14), he specifies the locale: "in the courts of the house of the Lord, in your midst, Jerusalem" (v. 19).

The psalm is the clearest expression of the thanksgiving sacrifice offered by an individual in fulfilment of a vow made for help received. The true cup of salvation is the Eucharist, the thanksgiving sacrifice offered by the Lord in the context of his saving death (Luke 22:20, Mark 14:24, Matt 26:27–28) and resurrection. The cup memorializes both the death and the rescue from death, the entry to the land of the living.

∾ PSALM 117   short

The psalm, in classic hymn style, invites universal praise for the God of love.

The two verses are in 3 + 3 meter. The parallelism in verse 1 is strictly synonymous. All nations and all peoples are invited to praise the Lord and adore (cf. Ps 63:4) him. The "nations" shown in recent psalms to be subject to God (cf. Pss 110:6, 111:6, 113:4, 115:2) are now to be integrated into the praise of him. The motive for praise, introduced by the standard "For," is expressed in chiastic form: "For strong over us is his love [cf. Ps 103:11], and the faithfulness of the Lord is forever" (v. 2; cf. Ps 100:5). The praise of this God is both worldwide and everlasting.

Christ invites all mankind to receive the victorious *hesed* of his Father; indeed nothing is stronger than the love that unites the creature to the Creator (Rom 8:35, 38–39). It is the very bond uniting the Father and the Son, by reason of our incorporation into the Son (see *Catechism of the Catholic Church* 2780). This love can be relied on at all times by all people. Its intention is to build up an eternal family in the presence of God. The speaker who celebrates the Lord's strong love "for us" is thinking first of Israel as the Lord's covenant people but no less of the peoples to be assimilated to Israel, for he is their God too (cf. Pss 22:28–30, 100:1–3, Zech 8:22–23, Tob 13:11, Rom 15:9–11, Eph 3:6, Rev 7:9–10, 15:4). The concise psalm is given tight unity by an inclusion: the word "Lord" appears at the beginning and at the end.

∾ PSALM 118   stone

The psalm proclaims the liberation from death worked by the Lord for a leader who trusted in his help. The speaker regards his deliverance as emblematic and invites the whole community to join him in festive thanks. In its length and breadth the psalm is a good match for Psalm 22, with which it shares clear references to the Paschal mystery of Christ, the former psalm focusing on the Passion and the latter on the Resurrection. The prayer shares with Psalm 115 the use of refrain-like repetitions.

Verse 1 repeats verbatim Psalms 106:1 and 107:1 (and cf. Jer 33:11, 2 Chr 20:21): the Lord is to be thanked for his goodness (unless the translation is "for *this* is good") and love. Three groups—Israel (v. 2), the house of Aaron (i.e., priests, v. 3), and those who fear the Lord (v. 4; cf. Ps 115:9–13)—are summoned to say that his love is everlasting, a statement that characterizes the last book of the psalter (see esp. Ps 136). The third group may designate proselytes to Judaism or simply the congregation of worshippers.

The individual emerges in verse 5 to state succinctly his experience: from distress he called to the Lord, the Lord answered him "into broadness" (cf. Pss 18:20, 31:9, 4:2), that is, by giving him freedom. The "call/answer" theme is reminiscent of many previous prayers: Psalms 3:5, 4:2, 17:6, 20:10, 22:3, 27:7, 81:8, 86:7, 91:15, 99:6, 102:3 (and cf. Jonah 2:3). Along with the parallel "hear/prayer" pair it constitutes a fundamental dynamic of the relations between God and man in the psalter. Later verses will amplify the Lord's saving action, but first the psalmist dwells on his bond of unity with the Lord: "The Lord is for me, I do not fear; what can man do to me? [v. 6; cf. Ps 56:5, Heb 13:6]. The Lord is for me as my helper [cf. Ps 54:6], and I shall gloat [cf. Ps 112:8] over those who hate me" (v. 7). These two verses begin with the same confession, but the second shows a progression in intensity. From his experience the speaker draws a lesson for his hearers: it is better to take refuge in the Lord than to trust in man (v. 8), again restating his idea with greater force: it is better to take refuge in the Lord than to trust in nobles (v. 9; cf. Ps 113:7–8).

The speaker recounts his rescue with imagery rather than facts. All the nations surrounded him, but in the name of the Lord he wards them off (v. 10). The nations represent those who do not know or accept Israel's Lord. They surrounded, almost overwhelmed him; in the Lord's name he wards them off (v. 11). They surrounded him like bees, were extinguished (or with LXX: "ablaze") like a fire of thorns, but by calling on the Lord's name he warded them off (v. 12). The formula at the end of these three verses was taken literally by the desert monks, who used the name of Jesus as a weapon against sinful thoughts (see on Ps 20). For a single colon the speaker addresses the Lord directly: "You knocked me down to fall down" (v. 13) implying that his distress was engineered by the Lord with a view to manifesting his help (cf. Christ's words on the death of Lazarus, John 11:4, 15). He cannot forbear bursting into praise in a line found also in Exodus 15:2 and Isaiah 12:2: "My strength and vitality is the Lord, and he was my salvation" (v. 14). He imagines the voice of joyful shouting and salvation coming from the tents of the just who have experienced salvation (v. 15a): three times they acclaim the right hand of the Lord, which has worked with vigor (vv. 15b and 16b), which exalts (v. 16a; LXX adds "me").

The speaker's personal story ended in a victory over death itself. He will not die but live and recount the works of the Lord (v. 17). The Lord may have chastised him but to death he has not given him (v. 18). Saint Paul seems to allude to these two verses in one of his great catalogs of suffering and victory: "as dying and behold we live; as punished and yet not killed" (2 Cor 6:9). Hence the speaker calls on the gates (cf. Ps 24:7, 9) of justice to open before him so that he may enter the temple and thank the Lord (v. 19). This is the gate of the Lord where the just enter (v. 20; cf. Pss 5:5–6, 15:1–5, 24:3–4). For our speaker this "justice" consisted in trusting in the Lord's help rather than in man (cf. vv. 6–12). He summarizes his praise in a final verse: "I will thank you [cf. vv. 1, 19], for you have answered me [cf. v. 5], and you are my salvation" (v. 21; cf. vv. 14–15).

The assembled worshippers now take up the praise, identifying the victorious speaker as a stone rejected by the builders that has become the main cornerstone (v. 22). This is the key verse used by Jesus and the early Church to explain his resurrection from the dead. He was the son of God rejected by Israel's religious authorities only to rise from the dead as the foundation stone of the new people of God (cf. Matt 21:37–39, 42, Mark 12:6–11, Luke 20:13–17, Acts 4:10–11, 1 Pet 2:4–7). Not only does he enter the temple to give thanks, he *is* the temple (John 2:19–22), the place where God dwells in the Spirit. Already at Pentecost Saint Peter applied to Christ the earlier reference to God's "right hand exalting" his suppliant (cf. v. 16; Acts 2:33). From the Lord did this come about, and it is wonderful in the eyes of the congregation (v. 23). This day the Lord made; they will rejoice ecstatically and be glad in it (v. 24). In the midst of the procession into the temple they petition for salvation: "Please, Lord, please save; please, Lord, please prosper" (v. 25). The words "please save" give us the acclamation Hosanna, which from being a petition has become an acclamation of praise. With the following verse it entered into the acclamation of the crowds as Jesus entered Jerusalem before his Passion (Matt 21:9, Mark 11:9, John 12:13) and from there into the Sanctus of the Mass liturgy. Verse 26a underwent a transformation when it passed into the New Testament: from being a blessing "in the name [cf. vv. 10–12] of the Lord on him who comes," that is, on the victorious suppliant of the psalm coming to give thanks in the temple, it became a blessing on the one who "comes in the name of the Lord." Now the one rescued from death becomes God's own envoy, the bearer of his presence. Jesus applied the text in this sense to his own final coming (Matt 23:39, Luke 13:35). From within the house of the Lord a group of priests responds with a blessing for the congregation (v. 26b): it is as if they said, "We wish you the divine happiness of which the sanctuary where we live is the source" (Monloubou, *L'imaginaire des psalmistes,* 69). The participants in turn exclaim, "The Lord is God, and he shines on us" (cf. Pss 27:1, 36:10, 67:2, 80:4, 89:16), summoning each other to "bind the festive dance with bonds [cf. Judg 16:11] even to the horns of the altar" (v. 27). A festive dance involving ropes or woven branches is envisioned.

One last time the protagonist confesses, "You are my God and I thank you [cf. vv. 1, 19, 21]; my God, I exalt you" (v. 28); he exalts the one who has exalted him (cf. v. 16). When the opening verse is repeated at the end (v. 29), its meaning is now filled with the psalmist's experience described in the prayer. While the identity of the speaker remains mysterious, the importance for the community of his victory suggests his role as leader, so that the New Testament was not wrong in calling him a king (cf. Luke 19:38, John 12:13–15, Mark 11:9–10, Matt 21:9). The one who was raised from death is the savior of the community, who praise God along with him.

∿ Psalm 119 Law

There are three principal figures in Psalm 119: God, the psalmist, and the Law, which mediates between them. The Law is the Torah, the first five books of the Bible. It is the revelation of the saving will of Israel's God and of the path that leads to him. It contains both the account of the saving acts by which God made Israel his people and the commandments that this people must follow to remain one with him. For the psalmist the Law is the means, the only means, by which he can enter into communion with this covenant God; hence it is the focus of his life. The Law is mentioned in every verse (except vv. 3, 37, 90, 122; twice in vv. 16, 48, 160, 168, 172) either with the word itself or with one of seven synonyms. The psalmist's rapport with the Law is as multifaceted as his relationship with God himself, and each verse highlights a different aspect or combination of aspects of this relationship. Some verses look to the past, some to the present, some to the future. There are petitions, in the imperative or in the jussive, and statements; negative and positive expressions; verses about God's actions, verses about man's actions. Certain words appear often in the psalm, others only once. The psalmist circles around his theme, with the Law always in the center, gradually revealing a profound network of relationships with the Law and with God through the Law.

For the Christian it is not difficult to see in this Law, of which one of the synonyms is the "word" of God, the Incarnate Word himself, mediator between God and man, the revelation of God and simultaneously the way that leads to God. Jesus is the Word made flesh and the Son of the Father, who by his obedience to the Father's will won eternal life for mankind. The Christian gives all his attention to Christ, the Incarnation of God's will, knowing that in him he shares in eternal life.

The speaker of the psalm is the whole Christ, head and members. The Son speaks to the Father of his total commitment to the divine will. The members speak to the Father and to the Son about the Incarnate Word who mediates life to them. In praying the psalm we allow ourselves to be inserted into the obedience of the Son, permitting the Father to give us the life he has intended us to have.

Each section of the psalm consists of eight verses all beginning with the same letter of the Hebrew alphabet. Each section has at least one word used more than once, giving a loose unity to that section. Adjacent sections also have at least one word in common, usually several; these links weave the parts of the psalm into a close-knit fabric. In the commentary, word links to the immediately preceding section are indicated by verse numbers in italics. Adjacent verses are sometimes paired by structure or vocabulary (e.g., 1/2, 23/24, 81/82, 99/100, 127/128, 145/146). Certain phrases function as refrains, for example, "just decrees," "teach me your statutes" (eight times), "your law [command, etc.] is my delight" (also eight times), "by your word give [you have given] me life." But repeated words are complemented by the over twenty-five words that appear only here in the psalter. Occasional striking images (e.g., vv. 25, 32, 54, 72, 83, 103, 105, 136, 162, 176) provide relief from abstract expressions. The psalmist moves freely between lament and praise, past and future, longing and fulfilment, young and old, just and wicked, turning away and turning toward, positive and negative, love and hate, gradually revealing a rich tapestry of the myriad relationships between man and God through the revealed word.

Further variety in unity is achieved by meter. The 3 + 2 meter prevails (115 verses) but monotony is avoided by the use of other meters: 3 + 3 (twenty-eight verses), 2 + 2, 2 + 3, 2 + 2 + 2, 4 + 3, 4 + 4.

At the beginning of the commentary on each eight-verse section is given a single word meant to characterize some aspect or theme of that section.

Aleph (keep). Conformity to the Law produces happiness: "They are happy whose way is blameless, who walk in the Law of the Lord" (v. 1). Human behavior is viewed as "walking" in a "way" (the latter term will appear thirteen times in the psalm); happiness means not straying from the way and positively remaining in it. Such people "observe" (nine times) the Lord's testimonies because with all their "heart" (fifteen times) they search for him (v. 2); the verse highlights the inner and outer dimensions of moral life as well as the close union between God and his Law. The third general statement, like the first, is expressed in negative, then positive terms: these people have not acted perversely (1 John 3:3–6) but walked in God's ways (v. 3; cf. v. 1). Saint Paul, too, will use the image of walking for the Christian moral life: God created good works for us so that we should walk in them (Eph 2:10). With verse 4 the psalmist turns to the Lord, whom he will address directly for the rest of the psalm (except in v. 115). Since the Lord has commanded his precepts to be "kept" (twenty-two times) thoroughly (v. 4), the psalmist asks that his ways (cf. vv. 1, 3) be firm to keep these statutes (v. 5). Then he will not be shamed (fail of his goal) as he looks on all the Lord's commands (v. 6). Thanksgiving from an upright heart will follow from learning the Lord's just decrees (v. 7; the latter phrase will appear five times in the psalm). The psalmist commits to keeping (cf. vv. 4, 5) these statutes, if only the Lord does not abandon (cf. Ps 22:2) him utterly (v. 8).

Beth (delight). How can a young man keep his path pure (cf. Ps 73:13)?—by keeping (cf. *vv. 4, 5, 8*) God's word (v. 9), for adherence to that preserves from sin. With all his heart (cf. *vv. 2, 7*) the psalmist has searched for (cf. *v. 2*) God; may he not wander from his commands (v. 10, affirmative statement about the past, negative petition for the future). In his heart he has stored up God's promise; it is this that prevents him from sinning (v. 11). The psalmist blesses the Lord and appeals, "Teach me your statutes," a refrain occurring eight times in the psalm (v. 12); worship and the desire to learn overlap. With his lips he has recounted all the decrees of God's mouth (v. 13; matching of body parts), for the Law was something to be "murmured" (cf. Ps 1:2). In the way (cf. *v. 3*) of the Lord's testimonies he rejoiced as over all prosperity (v. 14). On the Lord's precepts he will "ponder" (eight times, cf. Pss 77:4, 7, 13) and will look (cf. *v. 6*) on the Lord's paths (v. 15, chiasmus). In God's statutes he will take delight, not "forgetting" (nine times; cf. Pss 78:7, 11, 103:2) the divine word (v. 16, chiasmus).

Gimel (longing). If God treats kindly (cf. Ps 116:7) his "servant" (twelve times), he will live (sixteen times) and spend his life keeping God's word (v. 17; cf. *v. 9*). If God opens his eyes, he will look (cf. *v. 15*) on the wonders of God's law (v. 18), which include both God's wondrous deeds and the life that comes through observance of the Law (cf. Deut 30:16, 19–20). A sojourner (cf. Ps 39:13) is the psalmist on the earth; if he is to find his true home, God must not hide from him his commandments (v. 19). His soul wastes away in longing for God's decrees at all times (v. 20). God rebukes (cf. Pss 104:7, 106:9) the proud (cf. Ps 86:14), that is, those who do not submit to God, the accursed who wander (cf. *v. 10*) from his commands (v. 21). May God "roll off" from the speaker the scorn and contempt he has earned for allegiance to the Law, for he observes God's statutes (v. 22). Even princes sit speaking against him, while God's servant ponders (cf. *v. 15*) his statutes (v. 23); the psalmist must witness to the Law before hostile officials. God's testimonies are even his enjoyment, the "men" whose plan he follows (v. 24).

Daleth (ways). The psalmist's soul clings to the dust (v. 25a; cf. Ps 44:26) from which he was made (Gen 2:7, 3:19); he exclaims, "Give me life in accordance with your word" (v. 25b). This petition will be a refrain found seven times in the psalm. When the psalmist recounted his ways, the Lord answered him; may the Lord teach him his statutes (v. 26; cf. v. 12). The psalmist wishes to "discern" (ten times) the way of the Lord's precepts; then he will ponder (cf. *v. 23*) the Lord's wonders (v. 27; cf. *v. 18*). His soul (cf. v. 25) pines with anguish (two words used only here in the Psalms); may God raise him according to his word (v. 28; cf. Luke 7:14). The way of lies may God remove from him as he "has mercy on" him with his law (v. 29). The way of faithfulness he has chosen, setting God's decrees before him (v. 30). He has clung (cf. v. 25, Gen 2:24, Deut 10:20, Jos 22:5) to the Lord's testimonies; may God not put him to shame (v. 31; cf. v. 6). The way of the Lord's commands he will run (cf. Heb 12:1, 1 Cor 9:24, 26), for the Lord has widened his heart (v. 32; cf. vv. 10–11). For Saint Benedict this verse describes the monk whose heart, widened by love, carries out the Lord's commandments with alacrity and delight (*RB* Prol. 49).

He (imperatives). Seven consecutive verses begin with imperatives and end with varying constructions. "Instruct me, Lord, in the way [cf. *vv. 27, 32*] of your statutes, and I will observe [cf. v. 22] it to the end [v. 33]. Grant me discernment [cf. *v. 27*] that I may observe your law, keeping it [cf. v. 17] with all my heart [v. 34; cf. *v. 32* and v. 2]. Direct me in the pathway of your commandments, for in it I delight [v. 35; cf. Pss 111:2, 112:1]. Incline my heart [cf. v. 34] to your testimonies and not to profit [v. 36]. Make my eyes pass over the sight of worthless things; in your way [cf. v. 33] give me life [v. 37; cf. *v. 25*]. Carry out for your servant [cf. v. 23] your promise that I might fear [recognize my dependence on] you [v. 38]. Make the scorn [cf. v. 22] I dreaded pass me by [cf. v. 37], for your decrees are good [v. 39; the last word announces theme of Teth section]. Behold I long for [cf. v. 20 for noun] your precepts; in your justice [cf. v. 7] give me life" (v. 40; cf. v. 37).

Waw (witness). Each verse begins with the particle *wĕ* signifying "and." May there come to the psalmist the Lord's *ḥesed* (seven times), manifested in his promised salvation (v. 41). Then he will answer a word to those who scorn (cf. *v. 39*) him, for he trusts in the Lord's word (v. 42). May God not ever snatch from his mouth this trustworthy word, for he hopes in the Lord's decrees (v. 43). These two verses show how closely interwoven are the inner life and outer activity of the psalmist. He will keep (cf. *v. 33*) the Lord's law always, forever and ever (v. 44), walking in broad spaces (cf. Exod 3:8, Neh 9:35), for God's precepts he searches out (v. 45; cf. v. 10). He will speak of the Lord's testimonies before kings (cf. v. 23) and not be ashamed (v. 46; cf. v. 31, Matt 10:18–20, Luke 21:12–15). He will take delight (cf. v. 16) in the Lord's commandments, which he has loved (v. 47), lifting his palms (cf. Ps 63:5) to God's commandments (which he has loved) and pondering (cf. v. 27) his statutes (v. 48).

Zain (remember). May the Lord remember the word by which he made his servant hope (v. 49; cf. *v. 43*). The psalmist's comfort in his affliction is that the Lord's promise gives him life (v. 50; cf. v. 40). Proud men have scoffed (cf. Ps 1:1) at him excessively, but he has not turned aside from God's law (v. 51). The theme of persecution, until now only hinted at (cf. vv. 22, 23, 42), becomes more dominant, to reach a climax in the *Caph* section. Remembering the Lord's decrees from long ago, the psalmist finds comfort (v. 52; cf. v. 50). Raging (cf. Ps 11:6) has seized him at the wicked, who abandon God's law (v. 53); one is reminded of Christ's anger at the Pharisees who preferred their tradition to God's command (Mark 7:9–13). But God's statutes are music for the psalmist in his house of sojourning (v. 54; cf. v. 19). He remembers the name of the Lord at night and keeps (cf. *v. 44*) his law (v. 55). This has been his lifework: the observing (cf. v. 34) of God's precepts (v. 56).

Heth (ḥesed). The psalmist's portion (cf. Ps 16:5) is the Lord; he has promised to keep (cf. *v. 55*) the Lord's words (v. 57): he will adhere to the will of the one who fulfills him. He has "weakened" God's face (sought his favor) with all his heart (cf. v. 34); may God have mercy on him (cf. Ps 86:3, 16) according to his promise (v. 58). He has considered his ways and redirected his feet to the Lord's testimonies (v. 59), hastening and not delaying to keep (cf. vv. 57, *55*) his commands (v. 60). Though cords (cf. Ps 116:3) of the wicked (cf. *v. 53*) encompassed him, the Lord's law he has not forgotten (v. 61; cf. v. 16). At midnight he will rise to thank (cf. v. 7) the Lord for his just decrees (v. 62; cf. v. 7). A companion is he of all who fear (cf. v. 38) the Lord and who keep (cf. v. 60) his precepts (v. 63). Because the Lord's love (cf. v. 41) fills the earth, the psalmist would be taught his statutes (v. 64; cf. v. 26). The section focuses on the strength of the bonds uniting the psalmist with the Law.

Teth (good). "Good things you have done for your servant [cf. v. 49], Lord, through your word [v. 65].[12] Teach me good perception and knowledge, for to your commands I have been faithful" (v. 66; cf. Ps 106:12, 24). Before he was afflicted (cf. Ps 116:10) the psalmist erred, but now he keeps (cf. *v. 60*) the Lord's promise (v. 67). Because the Lord is good (cf. 106:1) and a doer of good, the psalmist would be taught his statutes (v. 68; cf. *v. 64*). Though the proud (cf. v. 51) smear him with lies (cf. v. 29), he with all his heart (cf. *v. 58*) observes (cf. v. 59) the Lord's precepts (v. 69). Unfeeling as fat is their heart, but the psalmist takes delight (cf. v. 47) in God's law (v. 70). Good it was for the psalmist to be afflicted (cf. v. 67), that he might learn the Lord's statutes (v. 71; cf. v. 68). Good for him is the law of the Lord's mouth, more than thousands in gold (cf. Ps 19:11) and silver (v. 72; cf. Prov 2:4, 3:14).

Yod (hands). "Your hands made [same word as "have done" in *v. 65*] me and established me; give me discernment [cf. v. 34] and I will learn [cf. *v. 71*] your commands" (v. 73); note the spanning of past, present, and future, which is observable also in the next verse: "Those who fear you [cf. v. 63] will see me [for "fear/see" pun see Ps 40:4]) and be glad [cf. Ps 107:42], for in your word I have hoped" (v. 74; cf. v. 49). The psalmist

---

12. The only ultimate good is what comes through the word of God:

Many things in this world seem good [lit. "pleasant"] but are not; many seem sweet, many excellent. Dissipation seems good but becomes bitter when its patrimony is exhausted. Lust is sweet while it burns but horrible and execrable when it is indulged. Banquets are sweet while they are being consumed but foul when digested. Many things in this world are esteemed good while we live because they are useful to us, such as money, gold, silver, possessions; the same things can be of no profit to the dead; all are left behind here. Indeed a person dies with greater sorrow since he grieves to be defrauded of this abundance. Therefore there is no true goodness but that which is according to the word of God, through which a person can rejoice at being fortified by the support of good merits and virtues. (Ambrose, *Expositio in Psalmum CXVIII*, IX.6; all translations mine)

has known that the Lord's decrees are just (cf. v. 62), and the Lord has rightly (lit. "in faithfulness") afflicted him (v. 75; cf. *v. 67*); this and the preceding section touch on the therapeutic effect of suffering, for which the Lord's *ḥesed* (cf. v. 64) is invoked to bring comfort (cf. vv. 50, 52) according to his promise to his servant (v. 76; cf. *v. 65*). If the Lord's compassion (cf. Ps 103:4) comes upon him (cf. v. 41) the psalmist will live (cf. v. 50), for the Lord's law is his enjoyment (v. 77; cf. *v. 70*). May the proud (cf. *v. 69*) be shamed for they mislead him with lies (cf. *v. 69*) while he ponders (cf. v. 48) the Lord's precepts (v. 78). Those who fear the Lord (cf. v. 74) will turn to the psalmist along with those who know the Lord's testimonies (v. 79). May his heart be blameless (cf. v. 1) in the Lord's statutes lest he be ashamed (v. 80; cf. v. 6, Ps 25:2).

Caph (languish).   The speaker's experience of affliction and persecution comes to a head. His soul languishes for the Lord's salvation (cf. v. 41); in the Lord's word he hopes (v. 81; cf. *v. 74*). His eyes languish for the Lord's promise as he asks, "When will you comfort me?" (v. 82; cf. *v. 76*). For he is like a wineskin (cf. Ps 56:9) in the smoke, but the Lord's statutes he has not forgotten (v. 83; cf. v. 61). He asks a double question: "How many are the days of your servant [cf. *v. 76*]? When will you execute judgment on my pursuers?" (v. 84). The proud (cf. *v. 78*) have dug for him pitfalls (cf. Ps 57:7), not according to God's law (v. 85). He exclaims in distress, "All your commands are faithfulness [i.e., reliable, cf. *v. 75*], but I am pursued [cf. v. 84] with lies [cf. *v. 78*]—help me!" (v. 86). The nadir of his experience comes as the psalm approaches the halfway mark: "They almost finished me off on earth, but I have not abandoned your precepts" (v. 87). If God, according to his *ḥesed* (cf. *v. 76*), gives him life (cf. *v. 77*), he will keep (cf. v. 67) the testimonies of God's mouth (v. 88). Throughout the psalm life is God's gift and is manifested in obedience to his express will (cf. v. 17). Through Jesus Christ, God in his mercy gives obedience.

Lamed (everlasting).   From near extinction the psalmist recalls that behind the vicissitudes of life God's word and world abide. "Forever, Lord, is your word, standing in the heavens [v. 89]. From age to age is your faithfulness [cf. *v. 86*]; you have founded the earth and it stands [v. 90] For your decrees they [heaven and earth] stand today, for all are your servants" (v. 91). These three "global" statements at the beginning of the second half of the psalm match those of the first half (vv. 1–3). From this perspective of eternity the psalmist looks back on his rescue: if the Lord's law had not been his enjoyment (cf. v. 77), then he would have vanished in his affliction (v. 92; cf. v. 75). Only a delight in the eternal, a passion like that of the psalmist, can fortify man against the trials and persecutions of life. Never will he forget God's precepts, for in them God gives him life (v. 93; cf. *v. 88*). Even now he must ask for rescue: "I belong to you; save me [cf. *v. 81*], for your precepts I have searched out" (v. 94; cf. vv. 2, 10, 45). The wicked (cf. v. 61) waited for him to destroy him; he discerns the Lord's testimonies (v. 95). He fortifies himself in persecution by meditating on the law (cf. v. 23). For all perfection (meaning uncertain) he has seen an end, but very broad (cf. v. 45) is God's command (v. 96).

Mem (more).   The psalmist reaches the height of his enthusiasm for the Law. "How I have loved [cf. v. 47] your law; the whole day it is my pondering" (v. 97; cf. v. 78); pleasure in the Law makes him want to keep it constantly in mind, as in Psalm 1:2. God's command makes the psalmist wiser than his enemies, for he has made it his "forever" (v. 98; cf. *vv. 89, 93*). He has more understanding than all his teachers (cf. 1 John 2:27), for God's testimonies are his pondering (v. 99; cf. v. 97). He discerns (cf. *v. 95*) more profoundly than the old, for he has observed the Lord's precepts (v. 100); obedience deepens one's knowledge of God (cf. Phil 1:9, Col 1:10). From every evil path the psalmist has kept back his foot in order to keep (cf. v. 88) God's word (v. 101). He has not departed from the Lord's decrees, for the Lord has personally instructed him (v. 102; cf. v. 33, John 6:45). How smooth to his palate is the Lord's promise, more than honey in the mouth (v. 103; cf. Ps 19:11). From God's precepts he gains discernment (cf. v. 100) and so hates every lying (cf. v. 86) path (v. 104; cf. v. 101).

Nun (pledge).   A lamp to his feet (cf. *v. 101*) is God's word and a light on his pathway (v. 105; cf. John 12:35). He has sworn and determined to keep (cf. *v. 101*) God's just decrees (v. 106; cf. v. 62). But he is still deeply afflicted (cf. v. 92) and calls on the Lord to give him life according to his word (v. 107; cf. 25, 93). "With the voluntary offerings [cf. Ps 54:8] of my mouth be pleased, O Lord, and teach me [cf. *v. 99*] your decrees" (v. 108).

Though the speaker's soul is always in his palm (i.e., at risk), he never forgets (cf. v. 93) God's law (v. 109). Though the wicked (cf. v. 61) have set a trap (cf. Ps 91:3) for him, from God's precepts he does not stray (v. 110). He has inherited the Lord's testimonies forever (cf. *v. 98*), for they are the rejoicing of his heart (v. 111; cf. v. 80). He has inclined his heart to the carrying out of God's statutes forever, to the end (v. 112; in last two verses "forever" and "heart" appear in chiastic order).

Samech (separation). Men who are inwardly divided (cf. Matt 5:8, 6:24, 22:37, 1 Pet 1:22) the psalmist hates (cf. v. 104), while God's law he loves (v. 113, antithetic parallelism; cf. v. 97). His shelter (cf. Ps 32:7) and shield (cf. Pss 3:4, 28:7) is the Lord; he has hoped in (cf. v. 81) the Lord's word (v. 114). Wrongdoers must depart from him (cf. Ps 6:9), while he observes (cf. v. 100) the commands of his God (v. 115). He prays, in a verse used by monks to profess their vows, "Uphold me according to your promise and I will live [cf. *v. 107*]; let me not be shamed [cf. vv. 31, 80] in my expectation" (v. 116). If God supports him he will be saved (cf. v. 94) and have regard for his statutes always (v. 117; cf. *v. 109*). Only the support of the Lord and reliance on that support can sustain a lifetime commitment to the service of God. God treats as worthless all who wander (cf. v. 21) from his statutes, for lying (or "in vain," translation uncertain) is their deceitfulness (v. 118). Like dross God has put an end to all the wicked (cf. *v. 110*) of the earth; therefore the psalmist has loved (cf. v. 113) his testimonies (v. 119). His flesh has shuddered in terror (cf. Ps 36:2) before the Lord, whose decrees he has feared (v. 120; latter phrase found only here in the Psalms, cf. Prov 13:13).

Ayin (servant). The psalmist has acted with just judgment; may the Lord not leave him behind to those who exploit him (v. 121). May God stand surety for his servant (cf. Job 17:3, Isa 38:14) for his good, lest the proud (cf. v. 85) exploit him (v. 122; cf. v. 121). His eyes languish for the Lord's salvation (cf. *v. 117*) and the promise of his justice (v. 123; cf. v. 121). The next plea goes to the heart of the psalmist's prayer: "Act [cf. v. 121] with your servant according to your love [*ḥesed*, cf. v. 88] and teach me your statutes" (v. 124; cf. v. 68); God shows his love by teaching his servants how they may please him and so have life: his teaching is a gracious teaching. If God grants his servant discernment (cf. v. 104), he will know the Lord's testimonies (v. 125). It is time for the Lord to act (cf. vv. 121, 124); men have violated his law (v. 126). For this reason the psalmist loves (cf. *v. 119*) God's commands more than gold (cf. v. 72) and pure gold (v. 127; cf. Pss19:11, 21:4). For this reason all God's precepts he keeps precisely, hating every lying (cf. *v. 118*) path (v. 128; cf. v. 104).

Pe (body). Wonderful (cf. v. 18) the Lord's testimonies; for this reason (cf. *vv. 127, 128*) the psalmist's soul observes them (v. 129; cf. v. 100). The manifestation of God's word sheds light (cf. v. 105), giving discernment (cf. *v. 125*) to the simple (v. 130; cf. v. 116:6). The psalmist has opened wide his mouth (cf. v. 108) and panted (same verb as "hound" in Pss 56:2–3, 57:4) in longing for God's commands (v. 131). "Turn toward me and have mercy on me [cf. v. 58] in accordance with the decree for those who love [cf. *v. 127*] your name [v. 132; cf. v. 55]. Make my steps firm in your promise, and let no injustice gain power over me" (v. 133). If God ransoms him from man's exploitation (cf. *vv. 121, 122*), he will keep (cf. v. 106) God's precepts (v. 134). May God's face shine (cf. v. 130, Ps 67:2) on his servant (cf. *vv. 122, 124, 125*), and may God teach him his statutes (v. 135; cf. *v. 124*). Channels of water have run down from his eyes, since men have not kept (cf. v. 134) God's law (v. 136).

Sade (just). The section focuses on the Lord and his attributes. Just (cf. v. 123) is the Lord and upright his decrees (v. 137). He has commanded the justice of his testimonies in complete faithfulness (v. 138; cf. v. 90). The psalmist's zeal (cf. Pss 69:10, 79:5) has silenced him, for his oppressors have forgotten (cf. v. 109) God's words (v. 139). Smelted (cf. Ps 18:31) is God's promise, which the psalmist loves (v. 140; cf. *v. 132*). Little he may be and despised, but God's precepts he has not forgotten (v. 141; cf. v. 139). God's justice is justice forever, and his law is faithfulness (v. 142; cf. v. 86). Distress and hardship may have found the psalmist (strong consonance in the Hebrew: *ṣar ûmāṣôq mĕṣāʾûnî*); God's commands (the asyndeton is striking) are his enjoyment (v. 143; cf. v. 92). Just are God's testimonies forever (cf. v. 142); if he gives discernment (cf. *v. 130*) the psalmist will live (v. 144; cf. v. 116).

Qoph (call). The psalmist has called with all his heart (cf. v. 69)— may the Lord answer him; he will observe (cf. v. 129) the Lord's statutes

(v. 145). "I have called on you, Lord; save me [cf. v. 94], and I will keep [cf. v. 136] your testimonies" (v. 146; these two verses follow the same pattern: past action of the psalmist, petition in the present, pledge for the future, all directed to the Lord; cf. vv. 73–74). He anticipated the morning twilight and cried for help; he hoped in the Lord's word (v. 147; cf. v. 114). His eyes anticipated the night-watches (cf. Ps 63:7) in order to ponder (cf. v. 78) the Lord's promise (v. 148). "Hear my voice in accordance with your love [cf. v. 124], Lord; according to your decrees give me life" (v. 149; cf. vv. 107, *144*). They have drawn near, those who pursue him (cf. v. 86) with plots (cf. Ps 26:10); from God's law they are far (v. 150, chiasmus). But near (cf. v. 150) is the Lord, all of whose commands are faithfulness (v. 151; cf. *v. 142*). Long has he known of the testimonies, which the Lord has founded forever (v. 152). Prayer to the transcendent Lord is the psalmist's recourse in continuing attacks.

Resh (life). Confident ardor characterizes the psalmist as he nears the end of his prayer. "See my affliction [cf. vv. 50, 92] and deliver me, for your law I have not forgotten [v. 153; cf. v. 141]. Plead my cause [cf. Ps 35:1] and redeem me; by your promise give me life [v. 154; cf. *v. 149*]. Far [cf. *v. 150*] from the wicked [cf. v. 119] is salvation, for your statutes they do not search out [v. 155; cf. v. 94]. Your compassionate deeds are many, Lord; in accordance with your decrees give me life [v. 156; cf. *v. 149*]. Many [cf. v. 156] are my pursuers [cf. *v. 150*] and oppressors [cf. v. 139], but from your testimonies I have not turned aside [v. 157; cf. v. 51].[13]

---

13. Persecutors can be within and without:

In interior persecutions be faithful and strong so that in outward persecutions you may be proved. Even in the most interior persecutions there are kings and presiders, judges terrible in power. You have an example in the temptation, which the Lord endured; all kingdoms were shown to him and he was told, "I will give you all these if falling down you adore me" (Matt 4:9). And we read elsewhere: "Let not sin reign in your mortal body" (Rom 6:12). Do you see, O man, before which kings you are placed, before which presiders of evil, if sin reigns? However many the sins, how many the vices, so many are the kings. And before these we are led, and before these we stand. These kings even have their tribunal in the minds of many, but if anyone confesses Christ, at once he makes that king a captive, hurling him down from the throne of his mind. How could the devil's tribunal remain in one in whom the tribunal of Christ is raised?

I have seen the faithless [cf. Ps 25:3] and loathed [cf. Ps 139:21] them, who do not keep [cf. *v. 146*] your promise [v. 158]. See that I have loved [cf. v. 140] your precepts; Lord, according to your love give me life [v. 159; cf. vv. 88, *149*]. The essence of your word is faithfulness [cf. *v. 151*], and forever your every just decree" (v. 160; cf. v. 106). Links with the previous section are numerous.

Shin (peace). Exhilaration at his triumph through the word characterizes the penultimate section. Princes (cf. v. 23) have pursued (cf. *v. 157*) the psalmist without cause, but his heart (cf. v. 145) felt dread at God's word (v. 161). He rejoices (cf. v. 14) at God's promise like one who finds much (cf. *vv. 156, 157*) booty (v. 162). Lies he has hated (cf. v. 128) and abhorred; God's law he has loved (v. 163; cf. *v. 159*). Seven times a day he has "praised" God (introducing the verb that gives the keynote of the final section and is the dominant motif in Book Five) for his just decrees (v. 164; cf. *v. 160*). Much (cf. v. 162) peace there is for those who love (cf. v. 163) God's law, and for them there is no obstacle (v. 165). The psalmist has looked expectantly (cf. Ps 104:27) for the Lord's salvation (cf. *v. 155*) and carried out his commands (v. 166). His soul has kept (cf. *v. 158*) the Lord's testimonies and loved (cf. v. 163) them exceedingly (v. 167). He has kept (cf. v. 167) the Lord's precepts and testimonies, for all his ways (word not seen since v. 59) are before the Lord (v. 168).

Tau (praise). The final section recapitulates the major themes of the psalm in the mode of praise. It begins with two pairs of similar verses.

"Many are my pursuers and oppressors." Perhaps even Christ says this, and says it in the voices of each individual; indeed it is he whom the adversary persecutes in us. If you decline the fight, you abjure Christ, who allowed himself to be tempted that he might triumph. Wherever the devil sees him, there he lays ambushes, there he devises stratagems of temptation, there he weaves plots, so that he might, if possible, drive out Christ. But where the devil does battle, there Christ stands to assist. Where the devil besieges, their Christ is within, there he defends the enclosure of the spiritual walls. And so anyone who flees from the persecutor rejects also the defender. But when you hear, "Many are my pursuers and oppressors," do not be afraid, for you can say, "If God is for us, who can be against us" (Rom 8:31). But this is what he says who does not turn aside from the testimonies of the Lord by any deviation of vice. (Ambrose, *Expositio in Psalmum CXVIII,* XX.50–51)

"May my lamentation [cf. Ps 88:3] come near [cf. v. 150] to your face, Lord; according to your word give me discernment [v. 169; cf. v. 144]. May my plea come before your face; according to your promise rescue me [v. 170]. My lips [cf. v. 13] will bubble forth [cf. Pss 19:3, 145:7] praise, for you teach me your statutes [v. 171; cf. v. 135]. My tongue will chant your promise, for all your commands are just [v. 172; cf. *v. 164*]. Your hand [cf. v. 73] will be there to help me [cf. v. 86], for I have chosen [cf. v. 30] your precepts [v. 173]. I have longed [cf. v. 40] for your salvation [cf. *v. 166*], Lord, and your law is my enjoyment [v. 174; cf. vv. 77, 143]. My soul shall live [cf. v. 144] and praise [cf. *v. 164*] you, and your decrees will help me [v. 175; cf. v. 173]. I have strayed [cf. v. 110] like a vanished sheep; seek your servant [cf. v. 125], for your commands I have not forgotten" (v. 176; cf. v. 153). The Christian can only praise God by being a sheep that has strayed and has been sought (cf. Matt 18:12) by the good shepherd, who came to "seek and save what was lost" (Luke 19:10), who is both lamb and shepherd (Rev 7:17).

Through the Spirit the Son in his Body the Church pledges wholehearted obedience to the Father. The psalm is an elaboration of the third petition of the Our Father, "Thy will be done" (Matt 6:10), the prayer of Jesus himself in the Garden (Matt 26:42). It is through this obedience even to death (Phil 2:8, Rom 5:19, Heb 5:8–9) that we are saved. May the obedient one, firstborn of the new creation (Col 1:18), teach his brothers (Rom 8:29, Heb 2:11) his obedience and reproduce it in them.

∼ Psalm 120   Meshech

The great psalm on the Law (Ps 119) was preceded by the group known as the Egyptian Hallel (Pss 113–118). It is followed by a group of fifteen psalms each of which carries the title "Song of Ascents" (Pss 120–134), which itself will be followed by another "Hallel" group consisting of Psalms 135–136. The Songs of Ascents can be regarded as psalms sung in connection with a pilgrimage to Jerusalem for one of the great feasts.

The psalmist is poised between help received from the Lord and ongoing attacks from deceitful and belligerent men. To the Lord in his distress he called and the Lord answered him (v. 1; for verb pair, see Pss 86:7, 91:15, 99:6, 102:3, 118:5, 119:145). After citing his prayer, "Lord, rescue [cf. Ps 119:170] my soul from lying [cf. Ps 119:163] lips, from the deceiving tongue" (v. 2), he confronts the deceiving tongue directly (cf. Ps 4:3–6), asking him what he expects the Lord will give him, what do more to him (see the cursing formula in 1 Sam 3:17, 14:44, etc.) for his slanders (v. 3). He answers his own question: the sharpened arrows (cf. Ps 64:8) of a champion with the glowing charcoal (cf. Ps 18:9, 13) of the broom shrub (v. 4; or "arrows sharpened in the charcoal . . ."?).

Despite his conviction, he remains beleaguered, lamenting his sojourn in Meshech, a region near the Black Sea (cf. Ezek 32:26, 38:2–3, 39:1), and his dwelling among the tents of Kedar, a nomadic tribe of the Arabian desert (cf. Jer 49:28, Cant 1:5); the names stand for hostile and alien environments (v. 5). Long has his soul dwelt there with haters of peace (v. 6). He stands for peace (cf. Ps 119:165), but when he speaks, they are for battle (v. 7).

Christ in his members lives among deceitful men (cf. Phil 2:15) but knows that the Father has answered his prayer and will commit the powers of evil to fire (Matt 13:41–42, 50, 25:41). He himself is our peace (Eph 2:14).

In the Songs of Ascents a verse will often repeat a word from the previous verse before carrying the thought further; in the present psalm see "deceiving tongue" (vv. 2/3), "dwell" (vv. 5/6), "peace" (vv. 6/7). This forward and backward look, known as anadiplosis or staircase parallelism, lends both unity and dynamism to the psalm.

∽ Psalm 121   guard

As in Psalm 91 an experienced Israelite assures another of the Lord's constant protection from danger.

A pilgrim, perhaps daunted by an impending trek to Jerusalem, lifts his eyes to the mountains wondering from where will come his help (v. 1). He answers his question, picking up on the last word: "My help is from the Lord, who made heaven and earth" (v. 2; the latter clause is one of six refrains of the Songs of Ascents: cf. Pss 124:8, 134:3; cf. also Ps 115:15). The rest of the psalm will give grounds for this assurance.

A wise teacher prays that the one who guards the pilgrim not allow his foot to totter (cf. Ps 66:9), not slumber (v. 3), declaring that Israel's guard neither slumbers (cf. v. 3) nor sleeps (v. 4). The Lord will guard him, the Lord be his shade at his right hand (v. 5). By day the sun will not strike him, nor the moon by night (v. 6, chiasmus; cf. Ps 91:5). The Lord will guard him from all evil, will guard his soul (v. 7). The Lord will guard his going and his coming, now and forever (v. 8; the final phrase is another refrain of the Songs of Ascents, cf. Pss 125:2, 131:3).

Jesus prays that the Father "guard" his disciples from evil (John 17:11, 15; cf. Jude 1) and is himself the "guardian" of our souls (1 Pet 2:25, John 17:12).

∼ Psalm 122   Jerusalem

Compact like all the Songs of Ascents Psalm 122 expresses wonder and praise over Jerusalem and its place in Israel's life and implores lasting peace for its inhabitants. The compact buildings of the city become an image of the unity of its people. Christians too express their unity by comparing it to a temple built of living stones (Eph 2:20–22, 1 Pet 2:5). That temple is the Body of the risen Christ in which all live in mutual love (Eph 4:15–16) and care (Acts 4:32), for he himself is peace (cf. Eph 2:14).

An individual, perhaps the pilgrim of the previous psalm contemplating his impending journey, was glad among people who said to him, "Let us go to the house of the Lord" (v. 1). "Standing were our feet at your gates, Jerusalem," exclaims the psalmist (v. 2). For him Jerusalem is "built like a city joined closely together" (v. 3), the parts firmly supporting one another. He remembers that "there" went up the tribes, the tribes of the Lord, for it was a precept (lit. "testimony") for Israel to thank the name of the Lord (v. 4; cf. Ps 106:47). "There" also sat the thrones of judgment, thrones of the house of David (v. 5). Jerusalem was the place where Israel both offered praise to God and received and dispensed his judgments through royal mediators. This double role of Jerusalem will be met again in Book Five (cf. Pss 134:1–3, 135:1–2, 19–21).

Inviting his companions to ask for the peace of Jerusalem (with consonance in *ša'ălû šĕlôm yĕrûšālāyim*), the psalmist again (cf. v. 2) addresses the holy city: "May those who love you [cf. Tob 13:15] have peace and quiet" (v. 6). May there be peace within the city's walls (v. 7), ease (cognate of *šālôm*, like verb in preceding verse) in its castles (cf. Ps 48:4, 14). On his part, for the sake of his brothers and friends—fellow Israelites, fellow pilgrims, or residents of Jerusalem—may he speak only of peace for the city (v. 8). For the sake of the house of their God, he will seek good things for her (v. 9). The dwelling of God among his people is the principle of their unity with each other.

The psalm, like the city, is tightly constructed, several repeated words linking the verses to each other: "house," "Jerusalem," "there," "tribes," "thrones," "peace" (and its cognates), and "for the sake of."

◈ PSALM 123   servant

Another compact psalm, Psalm 123 has three movements. An individual "lifts up [his] eyes" in supplication to the Lord who sits in heaven (v. 1). Then he sees himself as part of a group whose eyes, like those of servants on the hand of their masters, like those of a handmaid on the hand of her mistress, are upon the Lord their God until he have mercy on them (v. 2). Finally, verses 3–4 express the group's prayer, which begins with a double plea for mercy—the only place in the psalter where a group, as opposed to an individual, makes this petition—for they have been much sated with contempt (v. 3). Much sated with it is their soul (cf. Ps 88:4), with the derision of the well-off (cf. Isa 32:9, 11, Amos 6:1), with the contempt of the haughty (v. 4). The group of those who look to the Lord for their needs find themselves scorned by those who have no need of him. The poor who cry to the Lord for justice will be heard while the rich and self-satisfied vanish (Luke 12:19–21, 18:7–8, 6:24–26). The servant Christ prays in the midst of his Church suffering persecution.

Verses are linked by the words, "eyes," "hand," "have mercy," "much," "sated," and "contempt."

The speaker has affinities with the persecuted individual of Psalm 120 and the group spokesman of Psalm 122.

◈ PSALM 124   escape

Israel is summoned to acknowledge the Lord's powerful deliverance from foes depicted as army, waters, beasts, and hunters. Frail Israel endures because the Creator is "for" her, while the attackers vanish. The speaker gives the script for Israel's third-person extolling of her deliverer.

"If the Lord had not been for us" (cf. Gen 31:42), Israel is to say (v. 1; the latter phrase is found again in 129:1), and the clause is repeated with the addition of the circumstance, "in the rising against us of men" (v. 2). Three main clauses follow, each introduced with "then": "then they would have swallowed us [cf. Ps 69:16] alive when their anger burned against us [v. 3], then the waters would have overwhelmed us [cf. Ps 69:3, 16]—the gushing stream passed over our soul [v. 4], then would have passed over our soul the torrential waters" (v. 5). The enemy partakes in both the menace of primitive chaos and the savagery of wild beasts (cf. Pss 35:25, 74:13, 77:17, 89:10–11, Job 7:12).

Israel's response is to bless the Lord who did not give her as prey to their teeth (v. 6; cf. Pss 7:3, 17:12, 22:14). "Our soul [cf. vv. 4, 5 and Ps 123:4] like a bird [cf. Pss 11:1, 84:4, 102:8] has been freed from the trap [cf. Pss 91:3, 119:110] of the hunters; the trap has been broken and we have been freed" (v. 7); the most destructive forces are shattered by Israel's God. The theme is expressed without imagery in the final confession: "Our help is in the name of the Lord who made heaven and earth" (v. 8; cf. Pss 115:15, 121:2); the verse, in typical 3 + 3 meter, has become a staple in Christian liturgy.

Christ broke the power of the tomb (Matt 28:2) and liberated us from the waters of death (Rom 6:3–4, Rev 20:13). We and Christ exult in the victory of Christ for mankind. In a sermon on Saint Peter, Saint Leo the Great gives a Christian application of the combined images of chaotic waters, wild beasts, and enemy nations: "You entered this forest of raging beasts [the city of Rome], this ocean of stormy depths, with firmer steps than you walked upon the sea" (Sermon 82, *A Word in Season*, 94). The ministers of the Gospel share in the divine power over chaos.

In addition to the repeated clauses at the beginning, the words "then," "waters," "pass over," "our soul," "trap," and "save" are all used more than once.

∾ PSALM 125   mountains

The forbidding mountains of Psalm 121 are now seen as the protection of Jerusalem's inhabitants.

Those who trust in Israel's Lord are like Mount Zion itself, which, because the Lord dwells there, will not totter (cf. most recently Ps 112:6) and abides forever (v. 1). The image shifts in verse 2, where it is the surrounding mountains that symbolize the Lord's protection of Jerusalem from now and forever (v. 2). This protection is manifested in his not permitting the "scepter of the wicked" to rest over the territory of the just, lest the just should stretch out their hands to perversity (v. 3). As so often in the Psalms, the guarantee of the Lord's presence among men is their moral conformity with him (cf. Pss 5:5–7, 15:1–5, 101:7–8). He will never allow evil to hold such sway that this conformity becomes impossible (cf. 1 Cor 10:13).

From confidence springs petition: the Lord is asked to repay with good those who are good and upright of heart (v. 4; cf. same logic in Ps 18:21, 25–28). But those who totter on twisting courses the Lord will conduct away with evildoers (v. 5). Israel will then know peace—an important theme of the Songs of Ascents (cf. Pss 120:6–7, 122:6–8, 128:6). Where God is living among his faithful ones, there is peace and well-being. Such is the fellowship of the new Jerusalem on Mount Zion (Heb 12:22–24, Rev 21:2–3), where the sons of God are gathered around Jesus, mediator and Emmanuel.

Repeated words: "mountain(s)," "totter," "forever," "surround," "just."

∿ PSALM 126   sheaves

The psalm follows the pattern of its predecessor, recalling God's help in the past and then asking him to repeat his action amid new needs. The joyful shout with which Israel once celebrated its liberation will be heard again when the Lord renews his saving act. This is the classical pattern of the Roman collect, which recalls God's great deeds in the past as a basis for imploring the continuance and completion of his work. See, for example, the ancient collect for Easter Monday: "Deus, qui solemnitate paschali, mundo remedia contulisti: populum tuum, quaesumus, caelesti dono prosequere, ut et perfectam libertatem consequi mereatur et ad vitam proficiat sempiternam."[14]

When the Lord "restored the fortunes of Zion" (traditionally "led back Zion from captivity," cf. Joel 4:1), the people were like dreamers (v. 1). "Zion" may stand for Israel at the liberation from Egypt, or for a specific population of Jerusalem exiles. The peoples' mouth was then filled with laughter (a hapax in the psalter), their tongue with a joyful shout; then the nations gave witness, "The Lord has done great deeds [lit. "done greatly," cf. Joel 2:21] for them" (v. 2). The worshipping community makes the song its own, replacing "them" with "us" and adding how glad they were (v. 3).

---

14. "O God, who by the Easter solemnity conferred healing on the world, we ask you to accompany your people with your heavenly gifts that they may obtain perfect freedom and advance to everlasting life" (*Saint Andrew Daily Missal*, 511–512).

The petition arising out of new calamity uses the same language as the opening account of deliverance, "Restore, Lord, our fortunes like stream-channels in the Negeb" (v. 4), that is, like wadis in the desert south of Judah suddenly filled with rain. The speaker's certainty of God's acting leads him to express a new theological insight with a metaphor: the tearful march into suffering is a sowing of seed that will bear fruit in the joyful harvest of the return (v. 5; cf. Bar 4:23). A positive meaning is thus given to Israel's misery: it becomes a necessary, perhaps purificatory step toward the fulfilment of God's plan of redemption. The suffering of Israel will not be wasted but will bear fruit in joy (cf. John 16:20–22, Ps 30:6). The terse metaphor of verse 5 (four words arranged chiastically: "Those who sow in tears, with joyful shout reap") is amplified in the imagery of verse 6 (eleven words): the one who walks along weeping is, as it were, carrying pouches of seed; he will come back with joyful shout, carrying his sheaves (v. 6).

For Christians the way of penitence is the way to joy (Luke 6:21); the bearing of the cross is the way to life (Matt 16:24–25); the seed must die to yield a rich harvest (John 12:24–25).

In addition to the repeated song of the nations (vv. 2–3), the psalm is deftly held together with word links: "restore fortunes," "then," "joyful shout," "carrying." The juxtaposition of opposites in so short a space— past and future, laughter and tears, joy and weeping, sowing and reaping— gives the psalm a special power. One is reminded of the saying of Jesus, "Sower and reaper rejoice together" (John 4:36).

⁓ PSALM 127   sons

The psalm illustrates a particular feature of the Songs of Ascents. It combines sacral statements about the Lord's protection of Israel and Jerusalem with folk observations from rural society. The latter often do not have a specific religious content but have been given a cultic dimension by being drawn into the experience of Yahweh-believers in Jerusalem. The reflection on the sons of youth being like arrows in the hand of a warrior (vv. 4–5) is such a piece of folk wisdom; it has been tied to the cult of Yahweh by the verse (3) proclaiming that these sons are the gift of the Lord. Similar pieces of folk poetry can be noted in Psalm 125:3 (scepter of the wicked not being allowed to rest over the just) and Psalm 126:5–6 (sowing in tears to reap in joy).

Sacral themes open the psalm. If the Lord does not build the house, worthless is the toil of its builders; if the Lord does not guard the city, worthless is the vigil of one who keeps guard (v. 1). House and city can be generic terms, but in the context of the Psalms of Ascents they allude also to the temple and the holy city (cf. Jer 26:6, 12, 1 Kgs 8:44, 48). The verse gives clear and succinct images for the theology of grace. Any human work undertaken without reliance on Israel's creator has no guarantee of success. "For by grace you have been saved through faith, and not by anything of your own, but by a gift from God; not by anything that you have done, so that nobody can boast" (Eph 2:8–9). It is worthless for men to rise early and delay rest, eating the bread of pain, so much does God give to his beloved in sleep (v. 2; cf. Prov 10:22). In New Testament terms, success depends "not on the one who wills or the one who runs but on the God who gives mercy" (Rom 9:16).

A supreme example of God's initiating goodness is the gift of sons: behold, an inheritance from the Lord is sons (v. 3), a bounty the fruit of the womb (lit. "belly"). The speaker is now ready to apply his country saying to these sons given by God: like arrows in the hand of a champion, so are the sons of youth (v. 4). Happy is the man who fills his quiver with them; they [sons] will not be put to shame when they speak with enemies at the gate, where cases were tried and judged (v. 5; cf. Prov 22:22, 31:23, 31, Zech 8:16). Sons given to a man by God will prevail over both accusers and armies, that is, over enemies within and without the city.

The psalm is the central psalm of the Songs of Ascents. It communicates the profound source of Israel's strength: not human effort but the action of God. The psalms that follow will show how this divine grace produces true human community. The psalm does not address God but moves from meditation to instruction to exultation with implied praise (cf. other makarisms, Pss 1:1–6, 112:1, etc.).

∼ PSALM 128   wife

With its "focus on the family" the psalm is a good sequel to the previous psalm on the gift of sons. Metaphors celebrating domestic life have been drawn into the group of poems celebrating the holy city and temple. Domestic felicity becomes an image of the family of God gathered for feasts.

Happy is every man fearing the Lord (Pss 111:10, 112:1) and walking in his ways (v. 1; cf. Ps 119:1, 3). Just as fruitful progeny was attributed in the previous psalm to the grace of God, here the requisite human attitude for this gift is shown: the one who receives God's gift is the one open to the divine will, fearing to offend him and eager to obey his commands (cf. on Ps 112:1). Turning from third person speech, the psalmist addresses an individual God-fearer: he will eat the fruit of his palms, be happy, and enjoy good things (v. 2), his wife like a fruitful vine in the inmost part of his house, his sons like olive shoots around his table (v. 3). The image of trees growing in a house reminds us of Psalm 92:13–14: it combines richly the themes of vigorous growth, domestic happiness, and the presence of God. The children of the Church are rooted in Christ, who is the presence of God; drawing life from him, they bear abundant fruit (cf. John 15:5, 8, 16).

The psalmist concludes, "Behold how blessed is the man who fears the Lord" (v. 4; cf. v. 1). He then addresses such a man with a prayer: "May the Lord bless you from Zion; may you see the good things of Jerusalem all the days of your life (v. 5), seeing the sons of your sons. May peace be upon Israel" (v. 6; latter phrase another of six "refrains" of the Songs of Ascents, cf. Ps 125:4 and on Ps 121:2, 8).

The psalm is a wisdom felicitation that both teaches a lesson and celebrates the family as God's gift. It is knit together by repetitions of "happy," "fear the Lord," "good things," "sons," "bless," and "see." In addition to the theme of sons, the words "eat" and "house" link the psalm with its predecessor.

∾ PSALM 129   plow

Agricultural metaphors recur, as in Psalms 126 and 128. Israel's enemies are like rootless grass that withers. As in Psalms 125 and 126 the first half of Psalm 129 celebrates past help while the second petitions help for the future. The psalm contains six words* not found elsewhere in the psalter (cf. vv. 3, 6, 7).

Israel is to say (cf. Ps 124:1): "Much have they oppressed me from my youth [v. 1; cf. Ps 127:4]. Much have they oppressed me from my youth, but they did not overcome me" (v. 2). Israel compares herself to a person whose back* is plowed by unspecified plowmen who draw long furrows* (v. 3) in a kind of scourging of the land. But the Lord who is just has cut the bonds of the wicked (v. 4; see just/wicked dualism in Ps 125:3).

May they be shamed and retreat (cf. Ps 70:3), all who hate Zion (v. 5; cf. Ps 128:5). As in Psalms 125 and 127, Zion/Jerusalem (cf. Pss 122:2, 3, 6, 126:1) becomes a concentration of all Israel (cf. Ps 124:1). At this point the rural metaphor is applied to Zion: may her enemies be like roof grass (cf. Isa 37:27), which dries up before* one plucks* it (v. 6; cf. Ps 90:5–6). The reaper (cf. Ps 126:5) does not fill (cf. Pss 126:2, 127:5) his palm with it, nor the gatherer* his bosom* (v. 7). Passersby will not call down the Lord's blessing (cf. Ps 128:4, 5) on these reapers, nor will the latter respond with the customary words: "We bless you in the name of the Lord" (v. 8; cf. Ruth 2:4). The new life promised to Zion in Psalm 126:5–6 and to God-fearers in Psalm 128:1–4 is denied to those who hate Zion. Again one sees the strange mix of rural and urban images characteristic of the Songs of Ascents.

Persecutors of the Church are branches cut off from Christ—they wither (John 15:6, Matt 13:30). The Lord's intention is that they be grafted on to him and live (cf. Rom 11:17, 23–24).

∼ PSALM 130   depths

If one were constructing a theology of salvation from the Songs of Ascents, one would see the theology of grace, God's sovereign initiative, in Psalm 127, the human attitude that is open to that grace in Psalm 128, and now in Psalm 130 the truth that God's salvation is for sinners, the objects of his forgiveness and love. The psalm begins with the experience of an individual who in the end generalizes his experience for all Israel (see the mixing of individual and collective in Pss 122, 123, and 131). The concise and famous psalm is knit tightly together by several repeated words: "Master," "voice," "watch," "iniquity," "with [God]," "wait," "hope," "my soul," "Israel," "redeem."

"Out of the depths" (an expression evoking the waters of chaos, cf. Ps 69:3, 15) the speaker calls to the Lord (v. 1). May the Master "hear" his voice; may the Lord's ear be attentive to "the voice of his pleading" (v. 2; cf. Pss 28:2, 6, 31:23, 116:1). Verse 3 discloses in what the "depths" consist, namely, the iniquity of sin: if the Lord should "guard" this guilt, says the psalmist, "Master, who would stand?" (v. 3; cf. Ps 76:8). For with the Lord is forgiveness (noun only here in the psalter, and cf. Dan 9:9;

verb in Pss 25:11, 103:3, Exod 34:9, Jer 31:34; adjective in Ps 86:5); therefore men must fear him (v. 4), that is, recognize their need for redemption (cf. Ps 128:1, 4). The psalmist has waited for the Lord (third person), his soul has waited (cf. Pss 25:5, 21, 40:2), and in his word he has
hoped (v. 5; cf. Pss 119:74, 81, 114, 147). His soul is toward the Master
more than watchers (lit. "those keeping guard") toward the morning,
watchers toward the morning (v. 6, phrase repeated in Hebrew): the comparison conveys both certainty and eager anticipation. Morning is the
time for God to show his mercy and help (cf. Pss 46:6, 90:14, 143:8).

The psalmist's own "hoping in" the Lord's word (cf. v. 5) is a model
for Israel's hoping in him (v. 7), for with the Lord there is love (only occurrence of this word in the Songs of Ascents; cf. Pss 118:1–4, 29, 103:8)
and with him abundance of redemption (cf. Ps 111:9). He is the one who
will redeem Israel from all its iniquity (v. 8; cf. v. 3). The verse is applied
by Saint Matthew to the son of Mary and Joseph to explain the meaning
of his name, Jesus, for he will "save his people from their sins" (Matt 1:21).
The psalmist could not have expected that God would accomplish his
people's redemption by becoming a human being, even an infant.

Salvation can only be experienced by those who need it, and what we
need saving from is the iniquity of preferring self to God, a condition inherited from our first parent. The essence of Jesus's mission of mercy was
to redeem us from sin (Tit 2:14, Eph 1:7, Col 1:14, Heb 9:15, Matt 26:28,
1 Tim 1:15). Only by allowing ourselves to experience our alienation from
God can we accept him into it so that he can transform it into friendship
and life. The Good News is not that there is no sin but that salvation comes
through the experience of sin. Jesus could do nothing for those who had
no sense of being sinners but thought themselves righteous (Luke 18:9,
11, 14, John 9:40–41). With the psalmist and with Jesus we experience
the depths of our share in mankind's No to God. Psalm 130 belongs with
Psalm 51 as a classic expression of the repentance that leads to redemption, in this case a repentance full of confident hope.

∽ PSALM 131   humility

In its brief compass the psalm exhibits the main characteristics of
the Songs of Ascents: it makes use of a simile drawn from family or rural
life (cf. Pss 123, 124, 126, 127, 128, 129, 130, 133) to illustrate a sacral
theme (cf. Pss 123–130). In addition it shares with other psalms in the

group an individual perspective that then becomes a model for the community (cf. Pss 123, 130). The element added to the overall theology of the group (see on Ps 130) is trust.

The psalmist has recognized the danger of pride and overcome it in himself. His heart is not elevated nor his eyes exalted (cf. Luke 18:13, Prov 6:17), nor has he walked among great things or wonders above him (v. 1; cf. Sir 3:21–23): he is content to let the Lord be a mystery. In a familiar construction ("If I have not . . ." with a self-curse as implied apodosis), he swears that he has soothed and stilled his soul (cf. Ps 130:5–6) like a weaned child by its mother; like a weaned child is his soul with himself (v. 2). The image conveys the contentment of the one who has been filled by the Lord, perhaps after a bout of arrogance (cf. v. 1). Similarly, let Israel hope in the Lord (cf. Ps 130:7) both now and forever (v. 3; cf. Pss 121:8, 125:2; each colon is one of six refrains of the Songs of Ascents). The psalm has moved imperceptibly from addressing the Lord to speaking about him.

"Unless you change and become like little children, you will never enter the kingdom of heaven. And so the one who makes himself as little as this little child is the greatest in the kingdom of heaven" (Matt 18:3–4). The child is at once dependent and trusting. Jesus himself was humble (Phil 2:7–8) and trusting in his Father's care (Luke 23:46).

∼ PSALM 132   ark

Just as near the beginning of the Songs of Ascents is a psalm (Ps 122) celebrating Zion/Jerusalem, so near the end of the group is another psalm with a similar purpose. Psalm 132 celebrates the instrumentality of King David in ensuring the presence of the ark in Jerusalem. Although its presence is implied in many psalms, Psalm 132:8 contains the only specific mention of the ark in the psalter.

The psalmist asks the Lord to be mindful of David and all his humbling of himself (v. 1; cf. 2 Sam 6:9, 20–22, 12:13, 16–17, 15:30, 16:11–12, 19:22–24). He swore to the Lord, vowed to the Strong One of Jacob (v. 2; latter title found only in this psalm and Gen 49:24, Isa 49:26, 60:16) that he would not go to the tent of his house (same construction with apodosis suppressed as in Ps 131:2) or climb to the couch of his pallet (v. 3) or give sleep to his eyes, to his eyelids slumber (v. 4) until he found a place for the Lord, a dwelling for the Strong one of Jacob (v. 5). The people

(David and his men?) are represented as hearing at Ephrathah (a town associated with Bethlehem in Gen 35:16, Ruth 4:11, Mic 5:1) of such a dwelling (v. 6), finding it in the fields of Jaar (Kiriath-jearim?; cf. 1 Sam 7:1). They decide to go to his dwelling, to "prostrate before his foot-stool" (v. 7; cf. Ps 99:5, Lam 2:1); the Lord's "footstool" would be whatever place contained the ark, above which the Lord was seated invisible. Once arrived at the shrine the people call upon the Lord to "rise" to his "rest" (terms associated with the ark, cf. Num 10:35–36), "you and the ark of your strength" (v. 8); Jerusalem is viewed as the ultimate resting place of the ark (1 Chr 28:2). The procession is accompanied by priests clothed in vestments that symbolize the justice that befits the Lord's presence, while God's devout ones shout with joy (v. 9).

Recalling that David was responsible for this finding a home for the ark, the psalmist asks that for the sake of David, God's servant (cf. Pss 18:1, 36:1, 78:70, 89:4, 21, 144:10), may God not turn the face of his anointed one (v. 10), that is, not reject him. Just as David swore to find a place for the Lord (v. 2), so the Lord "swore" (cf. Pss 89:4, 36, 50) to David [an oath] which he will surely not rescind: to place one from the fruit of his body (lit. "belly") on his throne after him (v. 11; cf. 2 Sam 7:12, Ps 89:5, 30, 37–38); if his sons keep God's covenant and the testimonies that he will teach them, then their sons forever will sit on the throne of David (v. 12). "For" it was through David that the Lord "chose" Zion, which he desired for his abode (v. 13).

In an extended oracle the Lord expresses his plan for Zion: "This is my rest[ing place, cf. v. 8] forever [cf. v. 12]; here will I dwell for I have desired it [v. 14, repeating vocabulary from 13b]. Her produce I will greatly bless [cf. Ps 129:8], her needy I will sate with bread [v. 15]. Her priests I will clothe [cf. v. 9] with salvation, and her devoted ones will shout with great joy [v. 16]. There I will make sprout a horn for David [cf. Ps 89:25, Ezek 29:21]; I will prepare a lamp for my anointed [v. 17; cf. v. 10]. His enemies I will clothe [cf. v. 16] with shame, but on him will flourish his diadem" (v. 18; cf. Ps 89:40). The last two verses signal a final return to the theme of David now seen as embedded ("There") in the theme of the holy city. The task of the king, ensuring food for the needy within and overcoming enemies without (cf. Ps 72:4, 9, 12–13, 16), will be carried on through the holy place established by David, the dwelling of God on earth. The continuing of his messianic function, even when the monarchy has ceased, is symbolized by the "lamp," which the Lord will establish in Jerusalem (cf. 2 Sam 21:17, 1 Kgs 11:36, 15:4, 2 Kgs 8:19). It is also possible that the singer envisions a restoration of the Davidic monarchy. The dwelling of God established by David in Jerusalem becomes itself a guarantee of blessings for David's line.

The pilgrims to Zion know that they have come to the place where God has solemnly promised to dwell. David's love for the Lord and the Lord's love for his city ensure that Zion will be a permanent meeting place between man and God, the place to enjoy the fullness of messianic blessings. The true temple is the Body of Christ, the dwelling of God on earth. In it the blessings of God are extended to his people. The city where God dwells enjoys abundant blessings through the presence of its messianic king (Rev 21:2–3).

∼ PSALM 133   community

The Songs of Ascents have celebrated the presence of the Lord in Jerusalem/Zion (cf. Pss 122, 125, 126, 128, 129, 132) where the pilgrims come to worship. The fruit of their common worship is a strengthening of their unity as brothers. As in the sacrifice of the Mass, worship establishes community. With the help of two similes most likely drawn from secular use, this penultimate psalm of the group briefly but eloquently pays tribute to that fraternal unity.

"Behold [cf. Ps 132:6] how good and how pleasant [cf. Ps 16:11] is the dwelling [cf. Ps 132:12, 13, 14] of brothers [cf. Ps 122:8] in unity" (v. 1). It is soothing and comforting "as fine oil on the head running down on the beard" (v. 2a). Oil is a good agent for making parts work together. The psalmist sacralizes the metaphor by identifying the "beard" as Aaron's, on the collar of whose robes the oil drips (v. 2b). For an early writer the psalm shows that Christ "sanctifies us who have been steeped in the oil of the apostles flowing from the head" (Salmon, Les "Tituli Psalmorum," 147); according to this vision the oil is the grace flowing from Christ the head of the Body via the apostles to the members of his Church.

A second metaphor for community is the falling dew of Mount Hermon, soothing and penetrating like oil and refreshing. Again the metaphor is sacralized by being transferred to Mount Zion (cf. Ps 125:1). Since both oil and dew are presented as "descending," we are not surprised that the speaker sees the blessing (cf. Ps 132:15) they represent as commanded in Zion ("there") by the Lord (v. 3). But the blessing is more than a pleasant feeling of camaraderie among pilgrims, it is "life forever." Life and unity cannot be separated. One who has no love for his brother remains dead, but "we have passed out of death and into life, and of this we can be sure because we love our brothers" (1 John 3:14–15; cf. also vv. 23–24). God's purpose in building us into the temple that is his Son is that the parts should work together in unity (Eph 4:12–13, 15–16, John 17:23, Matt 25:40 with 46).

~ PSALM 134   night
The house of the Lord on Zion is the contact point between heaven and earth: it is the place where men bless God and from which blessing flows to men. The theme of blessing that has appeared in the later Songs of Ascents comes here to full flower. The Body of Christ is the sanctuary where men and women continually bless the Father and in which the blessings of eternal life are dispensed to the world (cf. Col 2:2–3, Eph 1:3).

The psalm begins with an unusual "Behold" without an object (cf. Pss 133:1, 132:6), followed by the command, "Bless the Lord, all servants of the Lord." The latter may be cultic officials, "who stand in the house of the Lord during the nights" (v. 1). The psalm is suitable for night prayer where it can evoke the prayer of Jesus during the night (cf. Luke 6:12, 22:41). The LXX has added to this verse the phrase "in the courts of the house of our God" (cf. Ps 135:3). The officials are to accompany their words with gesture, lifting up their hands (cf. Ps 28:2, 1 Tim 2:8) to the holy place as they bless the Lord (v. 2).

The final blessing (v. 3) is delivered by those addressed in the first part of the psalm: they ask that the blessings of the creator God (cf. Pss 121:2, 124:8) be extended "from Zion" (cf. Pss 128:5, 53:7) on the pilgrims who may be leaving the feast at the end of the last day. The image of the Cross comes to mind, with its reach to heaven and its arms extending to the world. The blessing of the Lord by his servants (vv. 1–2) makes possible the Lord's blessing of his people: worship of God brings blessings for men, including the fraternal communion lauded in the previous psalm.

With this psalm the Songs of Ascents comes to an end. It is appropriate that the final verse of the collection should unite two phrases used elsewhere in the group, "May the Lord bless you from Zion," he who "made both heaven and earth" (v. 3).

∼ PSALM 135   possession

This is the first of the two psalms that compose the Great Hallel. Both psalms celebrate the might of the Lord shown particularly in the Exodus event. At the same time the psalm picks up several expressions from the preceding psalm.

The hymn begins with three verses inviting the "servants of the Lord" (cf. Ps 134:1) to praise his name. The two cola of verse 1 begin and end with the same words but with a different middle expression, one indicating a direct object, the other the addressee: "Praise the name of the Lord; praise, servants of the Lord" (v. 1). The first psalm of the Egyptian Hallel (Pss 113–118) begins with the same two expressions but in reverse order, forming a chiasmus with our verse (Ps 113:1). The second verse specifies the locale of the servants: they are standing in the house of the Lord, in the courts of the house of "our God" (v. 2; cf. LXX, Ps 134:1). They are to praise the Lord "for good" (cf. Pss 106:1, 107:1) is the Lord, make music to his name for he ("it"?) is pleasant (v. 3; cf. Ps 133:1). The invitation to praise thus begins and ends with a reference to the holy name.

The conjunction "For" introduces the reasons for praise. Jacob the Lord chose (cf. 132:13) for himself, Israel for his own possession (v. 4; cf. Deut 7:6–7). This "choosing" was the beginning of God's entry into human history; its culmination is the "choosing" of believers in Christ (Eph 1:4) to be holy and spotless, living through love in his presence. The people whom God chose he rescued from sin, washed clean with water, fed with his Body and Blood, sanctified by his Spirit (cf. 1 Pet 1:1–2). All the events of the Exodus become types for the creation of the new people of God in Christ (1 Pet 2:9). The choice of Israel was motivated by pure love (Deut 7:7–9) and is to end in the participation in that love by men of every people and nation (John 17:26).

The remainder of the psalm spells out the implication of God's choice of Israel. The speaker makes a single first person reference in verse 5, as one who "knows" (cf. Pss 20:7, 56:10) that great is the Lord (Pss 48:2, 96:4). This is the attitude that "magnifies" the Lord, that is, makes him great, confesses that he is greater than self, is one's true Lord (see also verbal form "is great" in Ps 70:5). Israel's Master is greater than all gods (v. 5;

cf. Ps 95:3), who will be shown to be powerless human creations. Everything the Lord delights in he does (v. 6a = Ps 115:3b), in heaven and on earth, in the seas and all the abysses (v. 6); even the chaotic waters are subject to him (cf. Gen 1:2). Three manifestations of his power in the heavens are mentioned: he raises fogs from the end of the earth, produces lightning for rain, brings forth wind from his storehouses (v. 7 = Jer 10:13). With that same creative power the Lord struck the firstborn of Egypt from man to beast (v. 8; cf. Exod 12:29, 13:15, Ps 78:51, 105:36). The history of the chosen people thus partakes in the work of creation itself. The psalmist reminds Egypt that the Lord sent signs and portents in their midst (Exod 11:10, Deut 4:34, 6:22, 26:8, Ps 78:43) before Pharaoh and all his servants (v. 9). Similarly he struck down many nations and killed numerous kings (v. 10): Sihon king of the Amorites (cf. Num 21:23–24, Deut 2:33–36) and Og king of Bashan (cf. Num 21:33–35, Deut 3:1–7) and all the Canaanite kingdoms (v. 11; cf. Jos 10:28–43, 11:8–23). He gave their land as an inheritance (Ps 78:55), an inheritance to Israel his people (v. 12; cf. Deut 4:38, 25:19). Israel inherits the gift of land from the Lord.

The reality of Israel's God is reinforced by a mockery of the powerlessness of pagan gods. The section is introduced by a new reference to the divine name (cf. vv. 1, 3) in the only verse of the psalm addressed to the Lord: the Lord's name is everlasting, his "memorial" (cf. Ps 111:4) from age to age (v. 13). For he gives judgment for his people, and on his servants takes pity (v. 14, chiasmus = Deut 32:36; cf. Ps 90:13). The rest of the section (vv. 15–18) repeats Psalm 115:4–6, 8, although verse 17b: "There is not even a breath in their mouths" has a different reading than Psalm 115:6b: "they have a nose but do not smell."

Even the final call for praise echoes Psalm 115:12–13a, although here the three groups (with the addition of the house of Levi) are to bless the Lord rather than be blessed by him (vv. 19–20; cf. Ps 134:1–2). From Zion blessed be the Lord, the one who dwells in Jerusalem (v. 21; cf. Joel 4:17). The Lord's worship ascends from the very place where he dwells.

Despite borrowings from other Old Testament passages (see on vv. 1–3, 6–7, 14–20, to which should be added verses 10–12 with their echo of Ps 136:17–22), the psalm makes a coherent and forceful theological statement, transmuting it into praise.

∼ PSALM 136   litany

Were there any doubt about the Lord's motivation in bringing Israel out of Egypt, it would be resolved by Psalm 136, a litany that recounts one by one the Lord's saving actions and responds to each with the refrain, "For everlasting is his love [*ḥesed*]" (cf. 2 Chr 7:3, 6, 20:21). Every action of the Lord, from creation through liberation to ongoing providence, is motivated by a gratuitous compassion that will never be withdrawn. After three verses have issued a summons to give thanks to the Lord (cf. the three verses calling for praise in Ps 135:1–3), twenty-two phrases describe his major deeds, often beginning with a participial form, with the Exodus event as the center and high point; a final verse reiterates the call to give thanks. The reader can ponder each deed of the Lord as an expression of his eternal love. The name of the Lord occurs only in verse 1, inviting us to see all other verses as manifestations of the identity of this Lord who is love.

Verse 1 is identical with the first verses of Psalms 106, 107, and 118. The Lord is to be given thanks for his goodness and for his eternal love (v. 1). He is to be thanked as God of gods (v. 2; cf. Deut 10:17) and lord of lords (v. 3, lit. "Master of masters"); the latter phrase is applied to God the Father in 1 Timothy 6:15 and to the Lamb in Revelation 17:14.

Thanks is owed to the only one who does great wonders (v. 4), to the one who made the heavens with discernment (v. 5; cf. Prov 3:19, Jer 10:12), who spread out the earth on the waters (v. 6; cf. Ps 24:2), who made the great lights (v. 7), the sun to rule in the day (v. 8), the moon and stars to rule in the night (v. 9; cf. Gen 1:16–18). The last two verses vary the succession of participles by expanding the statement of verse 7. When the participles return they apply to historical events: as in the preceding psalm the salvation of Israel is a continuation of the work of creation. God is to be thanked as the one who struck the firstborn of Egypt (v. 10), who brought Israel out from their midst (v. 11) with a firm hand and outstretched arm (v. 12; cf. Deut 4:34), who cut in pieces the Sea of Reeds (v. 13) and made Israel pass through its midst (v. 14) and shook off Pharaoh and his army into the Sea of Reeds (v. 15; cf. Exod 14:27). The two verses mentioning the Sea of Reeds enclose the verse naming the chief of God's deeds, the bringing of Israel through the sea. For Christians this Exodus event is the baptism that gives us a share in the victory of Christ over death (cf. Rom 6:3–4, Col 2:12). The bath of water gives us a new birth as a people free of sin; it is a saving act of God motivated only by mercy (cf. Titus 3:5).

Thanks continues to the God who conducted his people through the desert (v. 16; cf. Deut 8:2, Jer 2:6, Amos 2:10), who struck (cf. v. 10) great kings (v. 17) and killed mighty kings (v. 18), namely, Sihon, king of the Amorites (v. 19) and Og, king of Bashan (v. 20). Then he gave their land as an inheritance (v. 21; cf. Ps 111:6), an inheritance for Israel his servant (v. 22; Ps 135:12 has "people" for "servant"; vv. 17–22 are found without the refrain in Ps 135:10–12). In their lowness he remembered them (v. 23) and snatched them from their oppressors (v. 24). He is the one who gives food to all flesh (v. 25). The final deeds remind us of certain petitions of the Our Father (cf. Matt 6:11, 13).

Thanks is to be given to God under a new title, God of heaven (v. 26). God's saving deeds on earth redound to his glory in heaven.

Especially in times of trial the Christian needs to recall that God's love is the supreme power in the universe. Nothing, not even death, can withstand his desire to give us life through his Son (cf. Rom 8:38–39).

∿ Psalm 137   Babylon

With compact intensity and strong images the Israelite exile expresses his passionate attachment to the destroyed Jerusalem. He will have his Lord reverse the mockery Israel has suffered at the hands of her destroyers.

The psalm begins and ends with a reference to Babylon. By its rivers, there sat and even wept the exiles as they remembered Zion (v. 1). On the poplars in the midst of it, they hung up their lyres (v. 2), for there their captors asked for the words of a song, their taskmasters for gladness: "Sing to us one of Zion's songs" (v. 3). The victors would mock the Israelites' faith and joy in their ruined city, but how could the latter sing the Lord's song on alien soil? (v. 4). A song of Zion is a song to Zion's God, whom they will not expose to mockery. We are reminded of the Aramaean Naaman's need to transport some soil of Israel to his homeland in order to be able to worship the God of Israel (2 Kgs 5:17).

But Jerusalem is not forgotten. Switching from plural to singular, the psalmist swears his undying allegiance: if he forgets Jerusalem, may his right hand forget [how to function] (v. 5). May his tongue cling to his palate if he does not remember her, if he does not elevate Jerusalem above the chiefest of his gladness (v. 6; the two curses are arranged chiastically, with the protasis of the second doubled). Jerusalem is thus "remembered" (cf. v. 1) in the center of the psalm as the heart of true gladness (cf. v. 4). The silencing of the song has only intensified the ardor of the love, like a heat confined.

The ardor bursts out as an intense prayer to the Lord (cf. v. 4) for the overthrow of the destroyers. As the exiles remember Zion, so may the Lord remember against the sons of Edom the day of Jerusalem's destruction, which these allies of the Babylonians abetted, saying, "Lay it waste, lay it waste to its very foundations" (v. 7; cf. Obad 10–15, Ezek 35:5, 10–15, 36:2, 5), their taunt matching that of the Babylonians in verse 3. With wrath the speaker addresses the evil city directly: "Daughter of Babylon, about to be despoiled, happy the one who repays you the evil you wrought on us [v. 8]; happy the one who seizes and dashes [verb applied to Babylonians nine times in Jer 51:20–23!; cf. also Ps 2:9] your children on the rock" (v. 9). God's plan to dwell among men requires that their enmity to him be annihilated. Smashing babies was a way of insuring the extermination of hostile peoples (e.g., Samaria, Hos 14:1; Israel, 2 Kgs 8:12; Egyptian Thebes, Nah 3:10; Babylon, Isa 13:16, 18). The monastic tradition applies the curse to the beginnings of sinful thoughts, which are to be dashed against the rock that is Christ (*RB* Prol. 28, 4:50; cf. 1 Cor 10:4, 1 Pet 2:4). The vehemence of the curse expresses the urgency of prayer to Christ against the disordered passions.

Christ, too, shed tears over the fate of Jerusalem (Luke 19:41), which he loved. He expressed grief that her citizens would suffer the same fate the psalmist called down on the Babylonians (Luke 19:44a), and for the same reason, namely, that they had set themselves at enmity with God. He does not wish the death of those he loves but their conversion (Rom 2:4, 2 Pet 3:9), their understanding of the things that lead to peace (Luke 19:42), their recognition of the "time of their visitation" by the Son of God (Luke 19:44b). He cannot give life to those who refuse to be part of his kingdom. The Christian who prays the psalm in him desires vehemently that the evil in men's hearts that sets them against God and their own happiness may be pulverized.

∾ PSALM 138   kings

The speaker of Psalm 138 sees his own experience of salvation as emblematic for the nations, whom he imagines thanking God when they hear of him. The speaker must be representative enough of his people that the nations would hear of him; it is thus appropriate that the psalm is the first in the final group of psalms attributed to David (Pss 138–145). The hostility of the nations in the previous psalm is overcome by international praise of Israel's God, who will in fact be praised on "alien" soil (cf. Ps 137:4). The risen Christ praises the Father for his love in raising him from the dead and joins all creation to his praise (cf. Heb 2:10–13, Rev 15:4, Isa 60:3, 6, 66:20).

The psalmist thanks God with all his heart (cf. Pss 9:2, 111:1); in the presence of the gods he makes music to him (v. 1; LXX adds a middle colon: "for you have heard the words of my mouth"; cf. v. 4b); in post-exilic Judaism the term that had earlier denoted the pagan or lesser gods came to be thought of as referring to supernatural powers (LXX has "angels") or even mighty earthly powers. The psalmist has a supernatural audience for his thanksgiving. He prostrates toward the Jerusalem temple ("your holy place"), risen from the ruins lamented in the previous psalm, and thanks the Lord's name because of his love and faithfulness (cf. Pss 115:1, 89:2, 86:15; cf. also Ps 136 for *ḥesed* alone); for he has made his promise even greater than his name (v. 2)—that is, the nations have not only heard about Yahweh but have heard him speak in the deliverance given to the psalmist, which he now recounts in stereotypical terms. In the day he called the Lord answered (cf. Pss 120:1, 119:145, 118:5, 102:3, 86:7, etc.) and increased (as in LXX, Syriac, and Targum) the strength of his soul (v. 3).

The speaker envisions all earth's kings (cf. Pss 135:10, 136:17–18) thanking the Lord, whose name is mentioned for the first time in the psalm (v. 4), when they hear the promises of his mouth (cf. v. 3). They will sing of the Lord's ways: "Indeed great [cf. Ps 135:5] is the glory of the Lord [v. 5]. For exalted is the Lord, and the lowly [cf. Ps 136:23] he sees [cf. Luke 1:48], and the lofty he knows from afar" (v. 6). They recognize that Israel's Lord is on the side of the needy, not of those who exalt themselves.

As often in the Psalms, the speaker, grateful for past saving acts, is still in need of rescue. He confesses that if he walk in the midst of distress, the Lord will give him life; against the anger of his enemies the Lord will send forth his hand; the Lord's right hand will save him (v. 7; cf. Pss 108:7, 98:1, 69:14). The Lord will act on his behalf, the Lord whose love is everlasting (cf. Ps 136); may he not let go of the work of his hands (v. 8).

In Psalm 138 the nations recognize what Israel has always known: the ways of her God are love and salvation and life, exercised particularly on behalf of the needy who call on him and recognize him as their creator. Kings of the earth join the Israelite leader in offering thanks to this God of glory who dwells in Zion.

∼ PSALM 139   knowledge

The psalmist aspires to complete unity with the will of God. He knows that his whole being is exposed to the Lord and always has been. He would have his thoughts and will and actions totally conformed to the plan of God. In the words of Saint John of the Cross, he desires that his will "become a Divine will, being made one with the will of God" (*Ascent of Mount Carmel* III.xvi.3). God "scrutinizes" (vv. 1, 23) the inmost being of the psalmist; when he sees nothing rebellious to the divine will, he can make that soul one with himself.

The whole psalm is addressed to the Lord, whose name is mentioned at the beginning (v. 1) and near the end (v. 21; cf. also v. 4). The Lord has scrutinized the speaker and knows (v. 1). He knows the speaker's sitting down (cf. Isa 37:27–28) and rising; he discerns his thoughts "from afar" (v. 2; cf. Ps 138:6): exterior and interior are both known to the Lord. What was briefly referred to in earlier psalms (e.g., Ps 7:10) receives extended treatment in this. God measures off the speaker's path and his lying down and is familiar with all his ways (v. 3). Not an utterance is on the speaker's tongue, but the Lord knows it all (v. 4). Behind and before God besieges him and places on him his palm (v. 5). Too wonderful is this knowledge for the psalmist, so high that he cannot see to the end of it (v. 6).

The psalmist tries to imagine where he might evade that scrutiny. Where might he go from God's spirit, or where from his face might he flee (v. 7, chiasmus)? Were he to climb the heavens, there would God be, and were he to crouch in Sheol, "behold you" (v. 8). "I will take up the wings of the dawn, I will dwell at the farthest end [same word as "destiny"] of the sea [v. 9]; even there your hand would lead me [cf. Pss 23:3, 27:11, 31:4], your right hand seize me" (v. 10; cf. Pss 138:7, 137:9). He thought surely darkness would overpower (sometimes corrected to "cover") him, and night be the light around him (v. 11); but even darkness is not dark for God, and night shines like the day—darkness and light are the same (v. 12).

Even the psalmist's remote past is well known to the Lord, for it was God who fashioned his kidneys (cf. Ps 7:10), wove him together (cf. Job 10:11) in his mother's belly (v. 13). This awareness evokes from the psalmist a cry of thanksgiving for his fearsome uniqueness; wonderful are God's works (cf. Ps 138:8), and the speaker's soul knows it well (v. 14). His bones were not concealed from God when he was being formed in secret, woven in the depths of earth (v. 15); the womb is like the dark but fertile earth. God's eyes saw the psalmist's embryo; in God's book all were written down, his days formed before one of them existed (v. 16). As at the end of the first section, the psalmist expresses amazement at the divine knowledge: how mysterious to him are God's thoughts (cf. v. 2), how vast their sum (v. 17). Should he count them, they would be more numerous than sand; when he woke (looked up from his counting?) he would still be with the [unfathomable] Lord (v. 18).

Since God knows the innermost parts of a man, it is of utmost importance that those parts be in accord with his will if one is to be united to him. For this reason the final section of the psalm is an ardent prayer that God's human creation, and particularly the psalmist himself, be in conformity with the mind of the Creator. Hence the psalmist prays that God kill the wicked (cf. Ps 137:8–9) and orders men of blood to depart from him (v. 19), men who "rebel" (corrected from Hebrew "speak") against God with schemes, raise themselves "against him" (Hebrew word uncertain) for things of no worth (v. 20). God can corroborate the speaker's alliance with his plan: "Those who hate you, Lord, do I not hate, and those who rise against you do I not loathe?" (v. 21). With a consummate hate he hates them; they are enemies to him (v. 22). Saint Augustine explains this hatred: "The man who lives according to God, and not according to man, ought to be a lover of good, and therefore a hater of evil. And since no one is evil by nature, but whoever is evil is evil by vice, he who lives according to God ought to cherish towards evil men a perfect hatred, so that he shall neither hate the man because of his vice, nor love the vice because of the man, but hate the vice and love the man. For the vice being cursed, all that ought to be loved, and nothing that ought to be hated, will remain" (*City of God* XIV.6). The psalmist concludes by asking for this purity of intention: "Scrutinize me, God, and know my heart; test me, and know my intentions (v. 23; cf. vv. 1–2 and below). See if the way of idolatry is in me, and lead me [cf. v. 10] in the everlasting way," that is, the way that leads to definitive life with God (v. 24). We are reminded of the two ways at the end of Psalm 1 (1:6): the way of the just is "known" by the Lord, while the way of the wicked vanishes.

The psalmist has penetrated to the core of God's will for man: that the human heart be as limpid in its purity as the mind of God himself. This would be the message of Jesus in the Sermon on the Mount: it is the "pure in heart" who see God and are blessed (Matt 5:8; cf. also Matt 5:28, 6:3–6, 17–18, 22–23, Pss 24:4, 73:1). The Lord "tests" the heart (Pss 7:10, 17:3, 26:2) to ensure that it has allowed the dross of sin to be purged away. Such a pure heart, the creation of the Holy Spirit, is the organ of fraternal charity (1 Tim 1:5). The Lord Jesus exults in his perfect communion with the Father and shares it with us through his Passion and Resurrection.

The psalm is notable for some unusual vocabulary: four words are found only here in the Bible and nine more only here in the psalter. Like other psalms in Book Five it is more theological or reasoned than earlier psalms: while some of their vividness of imagery and rawness of passion are missing, a more developed clarity of thought is achieved. See also Psalms 115, 135, 138 for this theological tone.

⌇ Psalm 140   traps

Like other psalms in the third and final Davidic collection, the psalm borrows several expressions from earlier psalms. The speaker knows that the violent will not prevail against the Lord. Pernicious plans, words, and deeds are to have no place in God's kingdom.

"Deliver me, Lord, from the evil man; from the man of violence [a word not seen since Ps 74:20] protect me" (v. 2, chiasmus). These men plan evils in their heart (cf. Pss 138:1, 139:23); every day they gather for battles (v. 3), sharpening their tongues (cf. Ps 64:4) like the snake (cf. Ps 58:5), with poison (cf. Ps 58:5) of viper under their lips (v. 4; cf. Rom 3:13b). Thought, word, and deed are all directed to evil.

The petition/lament pattern of the first three verses is repeated in the next two. "Guard me, Lord, from the hand of the wicked; from the man of violence protect me [repeated from v. 2]; they plan to knock down my steps" (v. 5). The haughty (cf. Pss 94:2, 123:4) have laid a trap for him and cords they have spread in a net; by the side of the track they have set snares for him (v. 6; cf. Pss 9:16, 31:5, 35:7–8, 57:7, 64:6, 119:110). Both of these opening sections end with the notation *selah* or "pause."

Two verses expressing trust form a bridge to the main series of petitions. The psalmist has said to the Lord, "You are my God [cf. Pss 22:11, 63:2, 118:28]; give ear, Lord, to the voice of my pleading [v. 7]. Lord, my Master, the strength of my salvation, you have shielded my head on the day of battle-array" (v. 8). May the Lord not grant the desires of the wicked man (cf. v. 5) nor further his stratagem (v. 9; Hebrew adds "they will be exalted"). The speaker is surrounded by force; may the cruel toil of their lips overwhelm them (v. 10, Hebrew obscure). May burning coals (cf. Ps 120:4) fall on them, bringing them down in fire; from watery depths may they not rise (v. 11). May the "man of tongue" not stand firm on earth; for the man of violence (cf. vv. 2, 5), let it (violence) hunt him down with blows (v. 12). Perpetrators of evil—the evil man, men of violence, the wicked, the proud, plotters, and vicious tongues—must be eliminated from the land of the Lord. This truth is taught up to the very last page of the Christian Bible (cf. Rev 21:8, 27, 22:15). It is the work of Christ to convert all hearts (cf. 1 Cor 6:9–11, Gal 5:19–21). The wickedness of the age is to be redeemed by Christians (Eph 5:16).

The psalm ends with a further expression of trust and the note of praise. The speaker knows that the Lord will give a verdict for the "poor" (*ʿānî*, not seen since Ps 109:22), judgment for the needy (v. 13; cf. Ps 72:2, 4). Then the just will thank the Lord's name (cf. Pss 106:47, 122:4, 138:2), the upright dwell before his face (v. 14; cf. Ps 11:7).

∼ PSALM 141   incense

The psalmist's evening sacrifice is a staunch repudiation of wicked associations and a declaration of adhesion to the just.

The prayer begins with a conventional appeal to be heard: "Lord, I have called [cf. Ps 119:145] to you; hasten [cf. Ps 70:2, 6] to me; turn your ear to my voice when I call to you" (v. 1). The speaker would have his prayer be set up as incense (cf. Ps 66:15, Exod 30:7–8, 2 Chr 2:3, 13:11) before the Lord, the lifting up of his palms (cf. Pss 28:2, 63:5, 119:148) as an evening oblation (v. 2). May the Lord place a guard over his mouth (cf. Pss 39:2, Sir 22:27), a watch at the door of his lips (v. 3); may the Lord not turn the speaker's heart to an evil word or to perpetrating wicked doings with evildoers (trio of thought, word, and deed, cf. Pss 140:2–3); may he not eat their dainties (v. 4). A just man may strike him, a devout man chastise him, but let not the wicked man's oil adorn his head, for his prayer is directed against their evils (v. 5; cf. v. 4; several words in this and the next two verses represent corrections of a corrupt Hebrew text; for the same idea see Qoh 7:5). May they be thrown into the hands of their judges and hear his utterances, for they were pleasant (v. 6). Like a split rock that tears open the earth, may their bones be strewn at the mouth of the underworld (v. 7). This is the same passion for the destruction of evil that was seen in Psalms 137:7–9, 139:19–22, and 140:10–13.

The psalmist is at once distancing himself from evildoers (cf. Ps 26:4–5) and asking for persistence in loyalty. Evil lifestyles are a real temptation, which with God's help he will abjure. After the violent petition he attains a serenity: "For toward you, Lord and Master [cf. Ps 140:8], are my eyes; in you I have taken refuge [verb not seen since Ps 71:1]; do not lay waste my soul [v. 8, same verb as in Ps 137:7]. Guard me from the jaws of the trap [cf. Ps 140:6a] they have set for me, from the snares [cf. Ps 140:6c] of evildoers [v. 9; cf. v. 4]. May the wicked [cf. vv. 4, 5] fall into their own meshes, while I ever pass through" (v. 10).

Again we breathe the psalmist's disquieting vengefulness. Before the psalter attains its pinnacle of praise, its speaker is more acutely aware than ever of the absolute incompatibility of evil with good: the need for the overthrow of evil becomes ever more urgent. The same duality is evident in Jesus's teaching: the division of sheep and goats (Matt 25:32–33); the distinguishing of doers from mere hearers of the word (Matt 7:24–27); the saying, "He who is not with me is against me" (Luke 11:23, Matt 12:30). Jesus was as explicit as the psalmist in portraying the consequences of rejecting God: the punishment inflicted on those who scandalize little ones (Matt 18:6) or betray the Son of Man (Matt 26:24) and the "gnashing and grinding of teeth" reserved for evildoers (Matt 13:41–42, 49–50; see Deut 28:15–46 for the Old Testament statement of the theme). "What companionship have righteousness and iniquity?" asks Saint Paul (2 Cor 6:14), and Saint James echoes: "Do you not know that friendship with the world is enmity with God?" (Jas 4:4). For Saint John, to love the world is to pass away; to do God's will is to abide forever (1 John 2:15–17). The final book of the Bible leaves no doubt about the dual fates of the godly and sinners: the worshippers of the beast "will be tortured in the presence of the holy angels and the Lamb and the smoke of their torture will go up for ever and ever," while the virtuous redeemed "follow the Lamb wherever he goes" (Rev 14:10–11, 3–5). This duality is the theme of Hopkins's great poem "Spelt from Sibyl's Leaves":

>   . . . Lét life, wáned, ah lét life wind
> Off hér once skéined stained véined varíety ' upon, áll on twó spools;
>   párt, pen, páck
> Now her áll in twó flocks, twó folds—black, white; ' right, wrong;
>   reckon but, reck but, mind
> But thése two; wáre of a wórld where bút these ' twó tell, each off
>   the óther; of a rack
> Where, selfwrung, selfstrung, sheathe- and shelterless, ' thóughts
>   agaínst thoughts ín groans gaínd.

∼ PSALM 142   prison

Psalm 142 is the poignant lament of one utterly alone except for God. The prayer has a simple purity in comparison with more turbulent individual laments; even the loaded imagery of a Psalm 88 is abandoned. The speaker is stripped of help but serenely confident.

With his voice (cf. Pss 77:2, 130:2, 141:1) to the Lord (third person) he cries, with his voice to the Lord he pleads for mercy (v. 2; cf. Ps 30:9). He "pours before the Lord his complaint" (cf. Ps 102:1[title]), his distress before the Lord he reveals (v. 3, chiasmus) while his spirit "faints" (cf. Ps 102:1) within him. But the Lord (second person) knows his pathway: in the path where he is to walk, they have laid a trap for him (v. 4; cf. Pss 140:6, 141:10), one of two vague references to enemies. "Look to the right and see: there is no one concerned about me; a place of escape has vanished from me; there is no one caring [lit. "searching"] for my soul" (v. 5).

Repeating the opening verb, the psalmist says he has cried to the Lord, this time in trust, and has said (selecting expressions from previous psalms), "You are my refuge [cf. Pss 71:7, 91:9], my portion [cf. Ps 73:26] in the land of the living [cf. Ps 27:13]" (v. 6). There follow three petitions, the first two grounded in laments, the final one followed by a forecast of praise. May the Lord attend to the speaker's lamentation (cf. Ps 119:169), for he is brought very low (cf. Ps 116:6); may he rescue him from his pursuers, for they are sturdier than he (v. 7; cf. Ps 18:18). He asks, "Bring my soul [cf. v. 5] out of this prison [word found only here in the psalter] so that I may thank your name" (v. 8a; cf. Pss 138:2, 140:14). The just will circle around him, for the Lord has acted kindly toward him (v. 8b; cf. Pss 13:6, 116:7). The final two cola take the form of a mini-hymn with its inviting of a particular group to praise followed by the motive for praise.

The number of borrowings from earlier psalms (at least a dozen are noted above) does not rob the psalm of its spare uniqueness. The Christ who suffers alone and abandoned (cf. Mark 14:50) knows that the Father is with him (cf. John 16:32) and will treat him kindly. Around him crucified and risen, the just who believe in him offer thanks to the Father through him (cf. Heb 13:15, Rev 7:9–10, 14:1–3).

◦ PSALM 143   justification

Like other psalms in the final Davidic collection, this psalm echoes many earlier psalms (e.g., Pss 14, 27, 28, 63, 69, 77, 88, 102, 142). As in music, the author is recapitulating the great themes of the whole psalter to give them a final meaning. An individual profoundly aware of his own unholiness and of hostile personal forces, puts his trust in the God who can guide him on the path of righteousness.

He begins by asking the Lord to hear his prayer (cf. Pss 4:2, 39:13, 65:3, 84:9, 102:2), to give ear to his pleading (cf. Pss 116:1, 140:7), and to answer him in the divine faithfulness and justice (v. 1). These two attributes are singled out because the psalmist is relying on God's fidelity to his promises and on God's ability to justify the unjust. May God not enter into judgment with his servant, "for before you no living being is just" (v. 2; cf. Job 9:2, 15:14). The latter statement is a fresh formulation of the idea found in Psalm 14:3 and will be cited by Saint Paul in his case for the universal need for redemption (Rom 3:20, Gal 2:16). The psalmist's awareness of sinfulness is compounded by a sense of enemies pursuing his soul (cf. Ps 7:6), striking his life to the ground, and finally making him sit in darkness like those long dead (v. 3; cf. Ps 88:7, Lam 3:6). These hostile activities can be literal or metaphorical, denoting perni-

cious cultural influences that others mediate to us without even knowing it: comments that undermine our faith in a good God (cf. Ps 3:3),
temptations to indulge in creatures, advertising that creates false needs
or stirs cupidity, inducements to corrupt paths to wealth and power. A
culture that ignores the transcendent is hostile to the soul that seeks the
living God. In addition, the demons of negativity against which others
are struggling can have their influence on us. In this sense our "enemies"
are the negating, anti-life forces in our own hearts and in the hearts of
those among whom we live. We are tempted to say, "God doesn't love me."
Only divine help, the divine *hesed* can liberate us from these forces. The
psalmist's spirit within him is faint (cf. Pss 77:4, 142:4) from these influences; within him his heart is numb (v. 4; cf. heart/spirit parallelism in Ps
51:12, 19).

Using expressions from Psalm 77:6–7, 12–13, the speaker "remembers" the "days of old," "murmurs" all God's "actions," on the work of
God's hands "ponders" (v. 5). These recollections lead him to stretch out
his own hands to God, his soul like an exhausted land (cf. Ps 63:2) before
God (v. 6).[15] May the Lord quickly answer him (cf. Pss 69:18, 102:3);
his spirit (cf. v. 4) languishes (v. 7; cf. 119:81). May God not hide his face
from him (cf. Pss 27:9, 69:18, 102:3) lest he become like those who go
down to the pit (cf. Pss 28:1, 88:5). Lament and petition are artfully woven
together in these two central verses. When petition continues in verse 8,
"Make me hear in the morning your love" (cf. Pss 90:14, 92:3), it is
grounded in the psalmist's act of trust in the Lord (cf. Ps 125:1), making
explicit the implied trust in verse 5. In addition may God make him know
the way he should walk, for to God he has lifted up his soul (cf. Pss 25:1,
86:4). This "way" is the right behavior that leads to God, the way that is
ultimately Christ (John 14:6) and love (1 Cor 12:31–13:1).

The appeal for God's self-revelation is followed by a petition for rescue from enemies, matching the lament of verse 3, for the psalmist has
"covered [himself?]" in the Lord (v. 9). At last comes the double petition for outward and inward regeneration (v. 10): "Teach me to do your

---

15. An early writer sees in this verse Christ, "fixed on the height of the cross
[where] he raises his hands either to an unbelieving people or to the Father" (Salmon,
Les "Tituli Psalmorum," 148).

pleasure, for you are my God; let your good spirit lead me on even ground" (cf. Pss 26:12, 27:11). The verse is the complement of verse 2: only God can convert the unjust into one who carries out the divine will; only God's spirit can "lead" a man to God (Luke 4:1, John 16:13, Rom 8:14, Gal 5:18). This petition is the ultimate cry of Old Testament man longing for the justification that only Christ could bring (cf. Rom 3:23–25, 4:25, 5:9, 21) and that is applied to us by Christ's sanctifying Spirit (cf. 2 Thess 2:13, 1 Pet 1:2, Rom 8:9–11, 1 Cor 6:11) who makes charity alive in us (cf. Rom 5:5, Gal 5:22). Thus before its final coda of praise, the psalter brings to full consciousness the need for complete moral regeneration by God.

The final two verses comprise four summary petitions. For the sake of his name (cf. Ps 142:8) may the Lord give life (cf. Ps 119:40, 88) to the psalmist and in his justice (cf. v. 1) bring the psalmist's soul out of distress (v. 11). And in his love (cf. v. 8) may God silence the psalmist's enemies (cf. vv. 3, 9) and destroy all those who oppress his soul (cf. vv. 3, 6, 8, 11), for he is the Lord's servant (v. 12; cf. v. 2). In this final petition, which repeats so many words from the psalm, the speaker would have not only justification for himself but the elimination of all forces in the environment that separate him from God.

∼ Psalm 144   daughters

Again a psalm combines old material in fresh ways. Elements of Psalm 18 are transposed from thanksgiving to petition and amplified with references to Psalms 8 and 39. The final section presents new images for a messianic age to come. David is plucked by God from disaster to initiate a reign of prosperity. As the previous psalm showed the need for man's renewal by the Spirit of God, Psalm 144 shows that a new and happy people will owe its existence to God's rescue of the king. It is in raising Jesus to life that God inaugurated his Son's messianic kingdom. The perspectives of the two psalms are nicely combined in Hebrews 13:20–21: "I pray that the God of peace, who brought our Lord Jesus back from the dead to become the great Shepherd of the sheep . . . may make you ready to do his will in any kind of good action and turn us all into whatever is acceptable to himself through Jesus Christ. . . ." Again the purpose of Jesus's sacrifice was to "purify a people so that it could be his very own and would have no ambition except to do good" (Titus 2:14), this people "set apart to sing the praises of God" (1 Pet 2:9).

The opening verse blesses the Lord as "my rock [cf. Ps 18:3] who trains my hands for war, my fingers for battle" (v. 1; cf. Ps 18:35), thus linking the two major sections of the earlier psalm. The appellation "my love" is followed by four epithets and the verbal phrase, "I have taken refuge in him," all cited from Psalm 18:3 though in different order, and the verse ends with a remote echo of 18:48, "who subdues my people under me" (v. 2). These verses of praise are preparation for the lament to follow, in which the king pleads for deliverance from encroaching threats.

The king begins his lament with a variant of Psalm 8:5 (see also Job 7:17, 15:14), asking what importance man has that God should consider him (v. 3). He answers, alluding to Psalm 39:6, that man is like vanity, his days like a passing shadow (v. 4). The Lord must bend the heavens and come down (as he did in Ps 18:10a), touch the mountains so they will smoke (v. 5), as only the creator can do (cf. Ps 104:32b). He must flash lightning and scatter them (the enemies, see following verse), send his arrows and bring panic (v. 6; cf. Ps 18:15); send his hands from on high, draw and rescue the psalmist from the many waters (cf. Ps 18:17), from the hands of aliens (v. 7). Only God's hand can pluck weak man from the forces engulfing him. The mouths of these enemies speak worthless things, and their right hand is a right hand of lying (v. 8), that is, they swear to untruths.

Now citing Psalm 33:2–3, the psalmist looks forward to the new song he will sing to God; on the ten-stringed harp he will make music to him (v. 9) who gives salvation to kings, who sets free David his servant (cf. Ps 18:1 [title], 51, Ps 143:2, 12) from the evil sword (v. 10). After reiterating (v. 11) the petitions of verses 7b–8 (minus the reference to many waters; the Grail changes the imperatives to past tense verbs), the speaker envisions the salvation God will provide for his people. Their sons will be planted (cf. analogous idea in Ps 128:3), made great from their youth (v. 12), their daughters like corner-posts carved as though for a palace (word used for the Jerusalem temple). Their granaries will be full, providing grain of every sort, their sheep producing a thousandfold, ten thousand-fold in their open fields (v. 13), their cattle laden, with no rupture or miscarriage, and with no wailing in their squares (v. 14). Extravagance seems to break through the limitations of words and meter. In these three verses are found six words that appear only here in the psalter, four of them found nowhere else in the Bible. The idyllic picture has affinities with the one found at the beginning of Book Five, Psalm 107:35–38, 41 (see also Amos 9:11–15).

A beatitude concludes the psalm: Happy the people for whom these things are so; happy the people whose God is Yahweh (v. 15). Rescued from death, Jesus, God's servant-king, celebrates with us the abundance of his Paschal banquet (1 Cor 5:7–8).

∼ PSALM 145   kingdom

The last psalm before the final coda of praise (Pss 146–150) is a magisterial alphabetical psalm, which defines with theological precision the relationship between Yahweh and his people. He is the king (v. 1), great (v. 3) and glorious (v. 5); they are his kingdom (vv. 11–13). His kingship is manifested in his loving support of the needy and downtrodden (vv. 14–19). For their part the individual speaker and people down the ages spend their lives in praise of his goodness (vv. 1–2, 4–7, 10–12, 21). The psalm makes explicit the mutual give-and-take between God and his people, which is at the heart of the Book of Psalms. The people of God whose happiness and prosperity were limned at the end of the previous psalm are now seen to be engaged in perpetual thankful recognition of their gracious God and savior. The psalm provides a natural springboard for the five psalms of praise that bring the psalter to completion.

The psalm alternates between direct address of the Lord (vv. 1–2, 4–7, 10–11, 13, 15–16) and third person speech about him (vv. 3, 8–9, 12, 14, 17–21). Those who praise God sometimes turn to each other to speak of his attributes and deeds.

The individual speaker appears at the beginning (vv. 1–2), in vv. 5–6, and at the end of the psalm (v. 21). "I will exalt you [cf. Pss 30:2, 118:28], my God, the king, and I will bless your name forevermore [v. 1]. Every day I will bless you and praise your name forevermore" (v. 2). The second verse repeats words from the first but in different combinations. The object of praise is the Lord's greatness (v. 3a = Pss 48:2a, 96:4a), which is beyond "scrutinizing" (v. 3b, see Ps 139:1 for the opposite use of this root). Age to age will adore (cf. Ps 117:1, here "honor") his works, and his might they will proclaim (v. 4, chiasmus). The splendor of God's glory, his majesty, and his wondrous deeds the speaker will ponder (v. 5; cf. Ps 143:5), and the strength of his fearsome deeds people will tell, and his greatness the psalmist will recount (v. 6; cf. v. 3). The psalmist "weave[s] his own voice of praise with the universal chorus of praise" (Alter, *Book of Psalms*, 501).

A new attribute is God's goodness. The memorial of his abundant goodness they will bubble forth, and over his justice (cf. Ps 143:1, 11) they will shout for joy (v. 7). Gracious and compassionate is the Lord, slow to anger and of great love (v. 8; cf. Exod 34:6, Ps 103:8, etc.). Good (cf. v. 7) is the Lord to all, and his compassion is upon all his works (v. 9; cf. v. 4). They will thank the Lord, all these works, and his devoted ones will bless him (v. 10, chiasmus; cf. vv. 1–2). Patterns of inclusion give the first part of the psalm a well-defined structure.

At the center of the hymn are the three verses that speak of the kingdom. The glory of his kingdom they will tell, and his might they will speak of (v. 11), to make known to the sons of men his mighty deeds (cf. Ps 106:8) and the glorious splendor (cf. v. 5) of his kingdom (v. 12). His kingdom is a kingdom of all ages (cf. Dan 3:33, 4:31), and his rule is from generation to generation (v. 13). The kingdom of God consists in his loving deeds for men and their loving response of praise.

The verses following this core extol the Lord's external activities, which demonstrate the attributes mentioned in the earlier part. Upholding is the Lord for all who fall and upraising those who are bowed down (v. 14). (Before this the LXX supplies the verse corresponding to the letter *Nun*, missing in the Hebrew: "Faithful is the Lord in his words, and holy in all his works," v. 13b; see Ps 111:7 for the combination of word and work). The eyes of all look expectantly to God, and he gives them their food in its time (v. 15; the verse closely parallels Ps 104:27). To the creatures' longing eyes corresponds God's "open hand," which satisfies the pleasure of every living thing (v. 16; cf. Ps 104:28). Just is the Lord in all his ways and devoted in all his works (v. 17).

With verse 18 the psalm begins to indicate the appropriate dispositions of the creature vis-à-vis the goodness of God. Near is the Lord to all who call on him, to all who call upon him in faithfulness (v. 18). It is those who fear him whose pleasure (cf. v. 16) he accomplishes, and their cry he hears and he saves them (v. 19). The Lord guards all who love him, but all the wicked he exterminates (v. 20, chiasmus). Those who expect and ask all from God are filled, while those who trust only themselves lose even what they have (cf. Matt 13:12, 25:29, Luke 8:18). Psalm 33 in a similar way ends with notations about the appropriate human attitude for receiving God's benefits (cf. Ps 33:18–22). As in Psalm 112, the wicked are mentioned only at the end (cf. Ps 112:10).

The final verse unites speaker and all the world in praise of God: "The praise of the Lord my mouth will speak, and all flesh will bless his holy name forevermore" (v. 21, chiasmus; cf. inclusion with vv. 1–2). The verse is a fitting introduction to the last five psalms of the psalter.

A curious feature of the end of the psalm is that verses 19 and 20 contain no fewer than six words that exhibit the consonants *sh (š)* and *m* in that order: *šawʿātām, yišmaʿ weyôšîʿēm, šômēr, hārešāʿîm, yašmîd*. These are the two consonants of the noun *šēm*, "name," which is found in the final verse as also at the beginning. The Lord's name and presence are concealed in his actions in everyday life.

The kingdom of heaven is Christ praising the Father in his Church. In him God has stooped down to his creatures, needy and bowed down, to raise and save them. He reigns over them with love while they praise his deeds of justice (cf. Rev 15:3–4). He is the mediator (1 Tim 2:5, Heb 12:24) in whom heaven and earth are joined. He leads us in worship of his heavenly Father.

∾ Psalm 146   blind

In accordance with the program announced in Psalm 145:21, the final group of psalms (Pss 146–150) begins with the praise of an individual (Ps 146; cf. "my mouth," Ps 145:21a) and will continue with the praise of wider groups (Pss 147–150; cf. "all flesh," Ps 145:21b). The body of the psalm (vv. 6–10) recounts beneficent activities of the Lord in participial form much as Psalm 145:14–16. It is preceded by a warning not to "trust" (last mention of this fundamental theme in the psalter) in creatures that pass away.

Each of the last five psalms begins and ends with "Halleluyah" [*Halĕlûyah*]. In verse 1 the psalmist summons his own soul to praise the Lord (cf. "Bless the Lord, my soul" in Pss 103:1, 104:1). He intends to praise the Lord during his life, making music to his God as long as he exists (v. 2). Since the object of praise is the God who acts in the world, the speaker warns hearers not to rely on other powers. They are not to trust in nobles (cf. Ps 118:9), in mortal men in whom there is no salvation (v. 3). Their spirit goes, returns to their dust (cf. Ps 104:29, Gen 3:19); on that day their thoughts vanish (v. 4). They are happy who have the God of Jacob as their help, whose expectation (cf. Ps 119:116) is for the Lord their God (v. 5). The beatitude is reminiscent of Psalm 144:15, "Happy the people whose God is the Lord."

This God is maker of heaven and earth (cf. Pss 115:15, 121:2, 124:8, 134:3), of the sea and all that is in it; he guards faithfulness forever (v. 6). He produces judgment for the oppressed (cf. Ps 103:6, Qoh 4:1), gives bread to the hungry (cf. Ps 107:9); the Lord sets prisoners free (v. 7; cf. Isa 61:1). The Lord gives sight to the blind (only occurrence of "blind" in the psalter; cf. Isa 35:5, Tob 11:10–14), the Lord upraises those who are bowed down (= Ps 145:14), the Lord loves the just (v. 8). The verse alludes to the previous psalm both in the citation of one colon and in the verb "love": here God loves his people, there they love him (cf. Ps 145:20). The Lord guards (cf. Ps 145:20) strangers; orphan and widow (cf. Deut 24:19–21) he relieves (verb link to following psalm, cf. Ps 147:6), and the way of the wicked (cf. Ps 145:20) he makes crooked (v. 9). In short, the Lord is king (cf. Ps 145:1) forever, "your God, Zion, from generation to generation" (v. 10). If the speaker has been addressing himself (cf. v. 1), it is in the presence of those who worship God in the Jerusalem temple. No other God can accomplish such salvation.

Christ manifested his divinity in giving sight to the blind, for which people praised God (cf. Luke 18:43). At the same time his heart is the vehicle of praise to God for the whole creation (Eph 3:20–21, Heb 13:15, 1 Pet 4:11).

∼ PSALM 147   snow

Zion, mentioned at the end of Psalm 146, is called to praise the Lord in a hymn of three parts, each beginning with an invitation to praise and continuing with motives for praise. The third of the three mini-hymns was treated as a separate psalm by the Septuagint. The psalm is notable for its intermingling of the themes of God's creative power (vv. 4–5, 8–9, 15–18) and his particular beneficence to Israel (vv. 2–3, 13–14, 19–20; verses 6 and 10–11, on the Lord's special relationship to certain groups, seem to fall between these two themes). God's restoration of Zion is part of his creation of the universe. Similarly the Church of Christ is the greatest work of God, the fullness to which all creation tends (cf. Col 1:15–20, Eph 1:10, 22–23).

The opening "*halĕlûyāh*" plays a grammatical role in verse 1 (this is not the case in the other four psalms of this final collection): it is followed by the clause, "for it is good to make music [cf. Ps 146:2] to our God; pleasant and fitting is praise" (v. 1; cf. Pss 145:21, 135:3). The Lord builds up Jerusalem, the dispersed of Israel (cf. Isa 56:8) he gathers (v. 2, chiasmus). He is the one who heals (cf. Ps 103:3) the broken-hearted (cf. Pss 34:19, 51:19, Isa 61:1) and binds up (cf. Ezek 34:16) their wounds (v. 3). He is the same one who counts the number of the stars, calling them all by their names (v. 4). Great is our master and of much power; his discernment is beyond reckoning (v. 5). The Lord relieves (cf. Ps 146:9) the poor (*'ānāwîm*, not seen since Ps 76:10); he brings low the wicked to the earth (v. 6; cf. Luke 1:52). This is the last mention of the wicked in the psalter, which ends with a vision of a creation purged of evil.

The second movement begins with a new summons to praise still to an unspecified group: "Chant [cf. Ps 119:172, Exod 15:21, 32:18, 1 Sam 18:7, Ezra 3:11] to the Lord with thanksgiving; make music [cf. v. 1] to our God with the lyre" (v. 7). Musical instruments will come into their own in the last psalm of the psalter. Here the cosmological theme comes to the fore: God is the one who covers the heavens with clouds, establishes rain for the earth, makes the mountains sprout with grass (v. 8; cf. Ps 104:14), giving their sustenance to the cattle and to young ravens who call on him (v. 9; cf. lions "seeking" their food from God in Ps 104:21). In view of God's might man can only recognize his neediness and dependence (cf. Ps 146:3–4): in the might of the horse (cf. Pss 20:8, 33:17) God has no delight, nor does he take pleasure in a man's thigh-strength (v. 10). Rather the Lord takes pleasure in those who fear him (cf. Pss 34:8, 10, 12, 112:1, 128:1, 4), in those who hope in his love (v. 11; cf. Pss 33:18, 130:7). Only in this last verse of the section is there an oblique reference to Israel.

The final movement calls directly on Jerusalem to adore (cf. Ps 117:1) the Lord, on Zion to praise her God (v. 12). Here the Israel references come at the beginning and end of the section with the cosmological themes in between. For the first time in the psalm the conjunction "for" joins the invitation to the body of praise itself. God has strengthened the bars of Zion's gates, blessed her sons within her (v. 13, consonance in *bĕrak bānayik bĕqirbēk*). He has made her borders peaceful, with fine wheat (cf. Ps 81:17) sated her (v. 14). He has sent forth his promise to the earth; quickly runs his word (v. 15). God's spoken word effects in creation what it commands (cf. Gen 1:3, etc.); similarly Jesus the Word of God (John 1:14, 1 John 1:1–2), sent (John 3:17, 7:28–29) by the Father, accomplishes his will and work on earth (John 4:34, 5:30, 6:38, 8:29). The "sending" of God's "word" to earth is illustrated by his giving snow like wool; in Isaiah 55:10–11 the snow is an image for God's word sent to earth to do his will. Further, God scatters hoar-frost like ashes (v. 16), throws ice in pieces (hail)—who can stand before his cold? (v. 17). He sends forth his word (cf. v. 15) and it makes them melt; he makes his wind (*rûaḥ*) blow; the waters flow (v. 18). The verse is susceptible of Trinitarian interpretation: the Father sends the Word that is his Son and breathes forth his Spirit (*rûaḥ*) to melt man's hardened heart. But in a special way God reveals his word to Jacob, his statutes and decrees (cf. Deut 4:1) to Israel (v. 19). It is through this revealed word of the Law that Israel came to recognize the word active in creation. God has not sent this revelation to all nations, nor made known his decrees to them (v. 20; cf. Deut 4:8).

The verses on winter are unusual in the psalter. Verses 16–18 contain six words used nowhere else in the Book of Psalms. The phenomena of winter complement the rain and growing plants mentioned earlier in the psalm (vv. 8–9, 14): all times reflect God's active word in the world, a word made explicit in the Law and known in Jerusalem (cf. Ps 93:5). The Word made flesh fills his people with finest wheat in the Eucharist.

◇ PSALM 148   universal

Praise widens out from Jerusalem to the whole universe. Several repeated words connect this psalm with its predecessor: "stars," "statute," "snow," "wind," "word," "mountains," "cattle," "praise" (noun). Heavenly, then earthly creatures are summoned to praise the Lord: the variety of addressees predominates over the reasons for praise, in contrast to other hymns of praise.

After the opening "*halĕlûyāh*," seven imperatives summon heavenly beings to praise the Lord. He is to be praised from the heavens, in the heights (v. 1), by all his angels (cf. Ps 103:20), all his host (v. 2), sun and moon, all stars of light (v. 3), the heaven of heavens and the waters above the heavens (v. 4; cf. Gen 1:7). A summarizing verb orders them to praise the name (cf. Ps 145:21) of the Lord, for he commanded and they were created (v. 5), and he made them stand forevermore, giving them a statute, which will not pass (v. 6). It is man who releases the praise in inanimate creatures, recognizing in their being the God who created them. In man creation finds a mouth to glorify its Author.

Next it is earth's turn to praise. This time only one imperative controls the list of addressees, which number twenty-three: sea-beasts (cf. Gen 1:21) and all abysses (v. 7; cf. Prov 3:20), fire and hail, snow (cf. Ps 147:16) and mist, the stormy wind doing his word (v. 8), mountains and all hills, fruit trees and all cedars (v. 9), wild beasts and all cattle, creeping things and winged birds (v. 10), kings of the earth and all races, princes and all judges of the earth (v. 11), young men together with maidens, old men with youths (v. 12; last four categories along with "princes" found together in Lam 5:11–14). The list avoids monotony by using "all" only with the second noun of a pair (cf. vv. 7, 9, 10, 11), by alternating single nouns with longer phrases (cf. vv. 8, 10), and by moving quickly and schematically from sea to air to land to living things and categories of men. Again a summarizing verb commands these elements to praise the name of the Lord (cf. v. 5), for his name alone is supreme; his majesty (cf. Ps 145:5) is above earth and heaven (v. 13). It is this creator God who exalts the horn (cf. Pss 75:11, 89:18, 92:11) of his people; he is the praise of all his devoted ones (cf. Ps 145:10), the sons of Israel, the people close to him (v. 14; cf. Ps 145:18, Deut 4:7). Through this final verse the psalm in its own way links the creative and redemptive activity of the Lord, as other psalms do in their unique ways (cf. Pss 136, 147).

Jesus had an appreciative eye for all creatures, which he used as vehicles for his teaching (e.g., Matt 6:26–30, 10:29, 31, John 4:35–36). His redemption of the world overflows from man to the whole natural world (Rom 8:19–23), which is to become a new heaven and new earth (Rev 21:1, 5) where the Father is praised in and through the Son (Eph 1:5–6).

"We may say that a 'house of praise,' including everything in existence, is the finest edifice to be constructed on earth in the quest to stabilize the whole known cosmos" (Gerstenberger, *Psalms*, 2:452).

∿ Psalm 149 saints

A particular group within Israel, the "devoted ones" (*ḥăsîdîm*), are featured in the penultimate psalm. In a preliminary hymn Israel is called on to praise the Lord in the assembly of the devout. In the second part it is the devout themselves who are called to praise God at the same time as they execute judgment on hostile nations.

The opening colon is identical with Psalms 96:1a and 98:1a; the "new song" is the response to a definitive intervention of God in Israel's favor. A second object of "sing" is "his praise [cf. Pss 145:21, 147:1, 148:14] in the assembly [cf. Pss 22:26, 35:18, 40:10–11] of the devout" (v. 1). Israel is to be glad in its maker, Zion's sons rejoice ecstatically (same two verbs in Pss 96:11, 97:1, 118:24) in their king (v. 2; cf. Pss 95:3, 96:10, 97:1, 98:7, 99:1, 4, 145:1). A third verse focuses on accompaniments of praise: "Praise his name with dancing; with tambourine [cf. Ps 80:3, Exod 15:20, Judg 11:34, 2 Sam 6:5, Jer 31:4] and lyre [cf. Ps 147:7] make music to him" (v. 3; cf. Pss 146:1, 147:1, 7). The reason for praise is that the Lord takes pleasure (cf. Ps 147:10, 11) in his people; he adorns the poor (cf. Ps 147:6) with salvation (v. 4; cf. Pss 18:28, 76:10). God's people are poor in their dependence on him; his favor is expressed in a saving action that ennobles the needy.

The devout are now called to exult in glory, to shout for joy on their beds (v. 5), high praises to God in their throats and a two-edged sword in their hand (v. 6). These devout ones simultaneously enjoy rest, utter joyous praise, and execute judgment: those who share in the victory of Christ rest from their labors (Rev 14:13) while they sing praise (Rev 15:3–4) and extinguish iniquity (Rev 17:14, 18:20; 2 Chr 20:21–22 similarly shows how praise itself is the most potent weapon). The final verses develop this last theme. The devout accomplish vengeance against the nations, punishment on the races (v. 7; cf. Ps 148:11), binding kings in chains and potentates in fetters of iron (v. 8). Kings can truly reign only in subjection to Christ. This judgment is "written" in the sense that God has determined it in his counsel; it is the splendor of all the devout to be the instruments of his reign (v. 9; cf. 1 Cor 6:2, Dan 7:22, 27).

Christians share in the kingship of Christ. This is made apparent in the links between this penultimate psalm and Psalm 2. In the earlier psalm, God confirms his anointed one on Mount Zion (Ps 2:6) as his son (Ps 2:7) who will smash the nations (Ps 2:1, 8) with a rod of iron (Ps 2:9). In Psalm 149 it is Zion's sons (Ps 149:2) who take vengeance on nations and races (Ps 149:7; cf. also Ps 2:1), binding kings (cf. Ps 2:2) and dignitaries in iron (Ps 149:8). It is the subjection of all to Christ that allows them to share in his kingdom (cf. 1 Cor 15:28, Matt 19:28, Rev 3:21, 5:10, 20:4–6). Our task is to permit him through us to neutralize all forces opposing his benign reign.

~ PSALM 150   orchestra

The psalter ends with the jubilant praise of all breathing beings for the mighty God. Only the concourse of musical instruments can fittingly express this praise.

Ten commands to praise match the ten "Halleluyahs" at the beginning and end of the last five psalms. The first two imperatives tell where to praise God, the next two why to praise him, and the last six with what instruments to accompany the praise. Only after these imperatives in a final exhortation to praise are we told who is being addressed: no longer just an individual or the devout or Zion/Jerusalem or Israel or all nations or inanimate creation, or heaven and earth but the totality of beings capable of praise. God is to be praised in his holy place, which signifies the Temple and the mystery it houses, and in his mighty firmament (v. 1; cf. Gen 1:6–8); God is praised in his infinite transcendence and in the earth where he dwells. He is to be praised in his mighty deeds (cf. Ps 145:4, 11, 12) and in the abundance of his greatness (v. 2; cf. Ps 145:3, 6).

Musical instruments have been mentioned as accompanying song in several psalms but never as many as seven instruments have appeared in one psalm (nine psalms mention only one instrument, seven mention two, and Psalms 81 and 98 mention four; five of the seven instruments feature in David's joyful procession with the ark to Jerusalem, 2 Sam 6:5, 15). First (v. 3) comes the blast of the ram's horn (*šôfār*, cf. Ps 98:6), then harp (cf. Pss 33:2, 144:9) and lyre (cf. Pss 33:2, 147:7, 149:3). Percussion enters the ensemble (v. 4) with mention of the drum, which is accompanied by dancing (cf. Ps 149:3 for both); then come strings (only here and Ps 45:9 in the Bible; do they denote different instruments from harp and lyre?) and flute (only here in the Psalms). The finale of the catalog of instruments comes with the double mention of cymbals (v. 5), which often mark a climax in a piece of music: "Praise him with resounding cymbals, praise him with the cymbals of the jubilant cry" (*terû'â;* cf. Ps 47:6), the cry that acclaims Yahweh as King. The praise that began with the mention of the *šôfār* (v. 3a) and passes through all timbres ends with a resounding combination of percussion and exultant acclamation. The final verse

(v. 6) draws every breathing being (cf. Ps 18:16, Gen 2:7, Isa 57:16) into praise of the Lord, whose sacred name ends the psalter before the final Halleluyah shout.

It may not be coincidence that two relatively rare biblical words used in the psalm, "firmament" (v. 1) and "breathing being" (v. 6), allude respectively to the two creation stories in Genesis. The meaning of the created world, animate and inanimate, is fulfilled in praise of the Creator, who is Yahweh, king and redeemer.

Jesus Christ marshals all the forces of creation into the praise of his Father (Eph 1:5–6, 10–12). In that praise we find our profoundest meaning and the fullness of life. It is the Spirit of God who breathes the praise of the Son through us (Rom 8:14–16).

Amen

GLOSSARY OF TERMS

Anadiplosis, or staircase parallelism
Repetition of words in succeeding verses of a psalm so as to create a link between verses. A verse may repeat a word used in the previous line and also introduce a word that will be repeated in the following line, creating a staircase effect. Used in the Songs of Ascents (Pss 120–134).

> Alas, that I abide a stranger in Meshech,
> *Dwell* among the tents of Kedar!
> Long enough have I been *dwelling*
> With those who hate *peace.*
> I am for *peace,* but when I speak,
> They are for fighting.
>   (Ps 120:5–7, Grail translation)

Apodosis . . . protasis
The main and conditional clauses, respectively, in a conditional sentence.

Asyndeton
Absence of conjunction between clauses.

Categories (genres) of psalms
Early in the twentieth century Hermann Gunkel identified several distinct categories of psalms. Following are the generally recognized categories with the number of psalms in each category. Classification is not a rigorous science, and several psalms can be regarded as belonging to "mixed" categories:

individual lament (45 psalms). The prayer of an individual in distress, normally composed of an introductory cry and four parts: lament proper (description of suffering), petition, expression of trust, vow of praise.

individual thanksgiving (14 psalms). Also may be regarded as an expansion of the "vow of praise" of the individual lament.

individual trust (6 psalms). Can be regarded as an expansion of the "trust" element of the individual lament.

community lament (13 psalms)

community thanksgiving (3 psalms)

community trust (3 psalms)

hymn (29 psalms). A song of praise consisting of two parts: the invitation to praise and the reasons for praise. The second part (body of the psalm) is often introduced by the conjunction "For" (*kî*). A subcategory of the hymn is the group celebrating Yahweh as King.

history (3 psalms)

wisdom (11 psalms, including Ps 19b, with Ps 19a classified as a hymn)

royal (10 psalms). Celebrates the human king of Israel.

Zion (5 psalms). Celebrates the temple and holy city.

liturgy (9 psalms). Generally accompanying a liturgical movement, procession, etc.

Chiasmus
Reversing the order of parallel elements in the second half of a verse.

Colon (pl. cola)
A line of a psalm, normally part of a verse consisting of two or more cola. While the bicolon is the most common form of biblical verse, there are tricola and sometimes larger verses.

Conjugations

The Hebrew verb has seven major conjugations. A verb that appears in different conjugations may need to be translated differently for each conjugation (see English Renderings of Selected Hebrew Words).

qal	active or stative
nifal	passive
piel	intensive
pual	intensive passive
hifil	causative
hofal	causative passive
hitpael	intensive reflexive

Crux interpretationis

A passage whose meaning is unclear, often as a result of a corrupted text. Following is a list of the major "cruxes" in the Book of Psalms: 2:12, 4:4, 7:5, 13, 10:10, 16:3, 17:3, 11, 14, 32:9, 35:12, 15–16, 42:5, 45:14, 49:15, 58:8, 10, 64:7, 68:31, 73:10, 110:3, 140:10, 141:5–7.

Hapax legomenon

Word found only once in a given body of literature.

Inclusion

Beginning and ending a passage—e.g., a psalm, section of a psalm, or even a whole book—with the same word or phrase, forming "bookends."

Makarism

Another word for "beatitude," i.e., an expression beginning "Happy is he (are they) who . . . ." There are 26 makarisms in the Psalms. From the Greek *makarios*, "blessed."

Masora

The group of rabbinic scholars who defined the correct text of the Hebrew Bible between the seventh and ninth centuries, the text now known as Masoretic.

Meter

Each colon of biblical verse generally has a definable number of beats, roughly corresponding to each major word in the colon. The meter of a verse is indicated by the number of beats in each colon joined by +. The most common meter of the Psalms is 3 + 3. A frequent meter is the 3 + 2 or *qinah* meter. A longer common meter is 4 + 4. There can be any number of meters depending on the number of beats in each colon and the number of cola in the verse. Other regularly encountered meters: 2 + 2 + 2, 4 + 3, 3 + 4, etc.

Parallelism

The principal feature of biblical poetry. Since the typical Hebrew verse is a bi-colon, there can be an infinite number of ways the two cola of the verse may relate to each other. Often the second colon restates the idea of the first in different language: this is synonymous parallelism. If the second colon expresses an opposite idea, one has antithetic parallelism. If the second colon completes the first or develops it in a new direction, one has synthetic or climactic parallelism. The terms are extremely fluid and only useful if they call attention to the dynamic tension between the parts of the verse. The relation between the cola in a verse ranges from nearly exact repetition to shocking disjunction. The biblical authors were masters at exploiting this interplay. Only a few examples can be highlighted in the commentary.

Penitential psalms

Seven psalms singled out in the medieval Church as specially appropriate for asking pardon for sins. Psalms 6, 32, 38, 51, 102, 130, 143.

Psalter

The Book of Psalms considered as a collection of prayers for (Christian) public use.

Selah

A notation often found in the psalms and seeming to indicate a break between sections. Occasionally the term seems significant; often its purpose is unclear. The term has been largely ignored in this commentary.

Septuagint (LXX)

The Greek translation of the Hebrew Scriptures made in Alexandria in the third century BCE.

Tense

Hebrew has two verb tenses, perfect and imperfect, denoting respectively a finished action (often past) and an ongoing action (present or future). The imperfect tense can function as a volitional or jussive subjunctive; whether this use is operative in a given case is a matter of interpretation based on the context. Interpretations will differ.

Theophany

A manifestation of the divine presence through (or accompanied by) powerful natural phenomena, such as earthquake, volcano, tempest.

Titles (superscriptions) of psalms

Of the 150 Psalms 117 are preceded in Hebrew by a verse (sometimes two verses) giving technical notations about the psalm or its performance. For this reason the numbering of the psalm itself often begins with "verse 2" or even "verse 3." The significance of many of these notations is obscure or disputed. The commentary refers to them only when a given word in the title seems to have some significance in the prayer itself.

ENGLISH RENDERINGS OF SELECTED HEBREW WORDS

As noted in the introduction the attempt has been made to render in translation a Hebrew word by the same English word whenever it occurs. The following table gives the (transliterated) Hebrew equivalent of those words that have near synonyms in the language, for example, "hope" and "wait for," or the many words for "rejoice." Words that do not have such synonyms, such as "sun," "father," "city," are not included, nor are common verbs in frequent use ("come," "give," "put," etc.).

In conformity with the custom of modern English lexicons, verbs are vocalized in the form of the perfect third person singular masculine. Where this form is not attested in the Hebrew Bible, the three consonants of the verb are given unvocalized.

The third column shows the number of times the word occurs in the Book of Psalms. Roman numerals I, II, III identify homonyms. Conjugations are given after the transliterated word, in parenthesis.

	Transliterated Hebrew word(s)	*Number of Occurrences in the Book of Psalms*
abandon	*ʿāzab*	22
accuse	*śṭn*	5
accuser	*śāṭān*	1
acknowledge	*zkr* (hifil)	4
act (n)	*mipʿāl*	2

act wickedly	ršʿ (kal)	2
action	pōʿal	11
	pĕʿulâ	3
adore	šbḥ	5
adornment. *See* honor		
adversary	šôrēr	5
affliction	ʿănî, ʿōnî	10
alien	nēkār	5
	nākrî	1
anger (n)	ʾaf	35
angry, be	ʾnf	4
annihilation	šôʾâ	3
answer (vb)	ʿānāh	38
appointed time/place	môʿēd	5
assembly	qāhāl	9
	maqhēl	2
astray, go. *See* stray		
attend (to)	qšb	8
awake, wake	qyṣ	7
awe, be in	gwr III	2
battle (n)	milḥāmâ	10
bed	miškāb	4
belly	beṭen	10
blameless(ness)	tām	2
	tāmîm	12
boast (vb)	hll (hitpolel)	8
break	šābar	21
break down, out	pāraṣ	4
broad space	merḥāb	3
bring to safety. *See* safety		
bubble forth	nbʿ	6
call (vb)	qārāʾ	56
calm, be	šāqaṭ	3
champion	gibbôr	12
channel	peleg	4

chastise, chasten, train	*ysr*	9
churn	*hmh*	11
circle (of friends)	*sôd*	6
clan	*mišpāḥâ*	3
clean (adj)	*bar*	3
cleanse	*kbs*	2
cling	*dābaq*	8
clothe	*lābaš*	10
clothing, clothes	*lĕbûš*	6
command(ment)	*miṣwâ*	26
companion	*ḥābēr*	2
compassion (n)	*raḥămîm*	11
compassion, have	*rḥm*	5
complaint	*śîaḥ*	5
conceal	*kḥd*	5
condemn	*ršʿ* (hifil)	2
conduct (vb)	*ybl*	6
confidence	*kesel*	2
confound	*klm*	6
confusion, be brought to	*ḥpr*	7
consider. *See also* plan (vb)	*ḥāšab*	18
consumed. *See* languish		
contempt	*bûz*	5
cord	*ḥebel*	8
correct, be correct	*zkh*	3
cot	*miṭṭâ*	1
couch	*ʿereś*	3
counsel (n)	*môʿēṣâ*	2
counsel, take or give	*yāʿaṣ*	6
cover	*ksh*	17
cover over	*kpr*	3
covet	*ḥāmad*	3
cower	*kāḥaš* (piel)	3
crush	*dkʾ*	4
	dkh	5
cry (n)	*šawʿâ*	6
	šewaʿ	1

cry (vb)	*zāʿaq*	5
cry, jubilant. *See* jubilant cry		
cry for help (vb)	*šwʿ*	9
cry jubilantly	*rwʿ*	12
cry out	*ṣāʿaq*	5
cut off	*kārat* (nifal, hifil)	10
deaf, be	*ḥrš* (kal)	6
deceit	*mirmâ*	14
deception	*rĕmîyâ*	6
decree (n). *See* judgment		
deed	*maʿălāl*	5
defy	*mārāh*	10
delight (n)	*ḥēpeṣ*	4
delight in (vb, adj)	*ḥāpēṣ*	23
deliver	*ḥālaṣ*	12
demolish	*hāras*	3
deride	*lʿg*	4
derision	*laʿag*	3
design (n)	*maḥăšābâ*	6
desire (n)	*taʾăwâ*	8
	maʾăwiyyîm	1
desire (vb)	*ʾwh*	4
despise	*bāzāh*	8
destiny	*ʾaḥărît*	5
destitute, be	*rwš*	2
destroy	*ʾbd* (piel, hifil)	5
devoted (one)	*ḥāsîd*	25
discern	*byn* (hifil, hitpolel)	14
discernment	*tebûnâ*	4
disdain (vb)	*nāʾas*	5
disgrace (n)	*kĕlimâ*	7
displeasure	*qeṣef*	2
dissolve	*mwg*	4
distress	*ṣar* I	12
	ṣārâ	24
	mēṣār	2

doing (n)	ʿălîlâ	9
draw	mšk	5
dread (vb)	pḥd	5
drive along. *See* urge		
dry up	yābēš	4
dumb, be, remain	ʾlm	3
dwelling	miškān	11
earth, land	ʾereṣ	190
emerging, outlet	môṣāʾ	6
empty(iness)	rîq	3
end, be at an	gāmar	5
enemy	ʾôyēb	74
enjoy	ʿng	2
enjoyment	šaʿăšûʿîm	5
even(ness)	mîšôr	5
evil, harm (n)	raʿ, rāʿ, rāʿâ	64
evildoers	pōʿălê ʾāwen	18
exalt	rwm	50
expectation	śēber	2
exploit (vb)	ʿāšaq	6
exploitation	ʿōšeq	3
exterminate	šmd	6
exult	ʿlz	7
exultation	māśôś	1
fade	nābēl	3
fail. *See* languish		
faithful, be; have faith	ʾmn	17
faithfulness	ʾĕmet	37
	ʾĕmûnâ	22
falsehood	kāzāb	6
favor (n). *See* pleasure		
fear (n)	yirʾâ	8
fear (vb, adj)	yareʾ	58
fearsome	nôrāʾ	15
fill	mālēʾ	7

finish off	*kālāh* (piel)	6
foe	*ṣôrēr*	4
fool (n)	*nābāl*	5
foolish	*kĕsîl*	3
footstep	*ʾāšur*	6
foreign	*zār*	5
forsake	*nāṭaš*	3
fortify	*ʾāmaṣ* (piel, hifil)	5
fortress	*māʿôz*	9
fountain	*māqôr*	2
free (vb)	*mlṭ*	8
fresh (vegetation)	*dešeʾ*	2
friend	*rēaʿ*	8
fury	*ḥēmâ*	14
garment	*begged*	4
gathering (n)	*ʿēdâ*	10
gaze (vb)	*ḥāzāh*	9
generous	*ḥônēn*	4
gird	*ʾzr*	5
give judgment. *See* judgment		
glad, be	*śāmaḥ*	52
gladness	*śimḥâ*	13
gloat	*rāʿāh* [see] *bĕ*	4
gold	*zāhāb*	8
gold (yellow)	*ḥārûṣ*	1
gold, fine	*ketem*	1
gold, pure	*paz*	3
gracious	*ḥannun*	6
graciousness	*ḥēn*	2
grass	*ḥāṣîr*	6
grave (n)	*šaḥat*	9
	šĕḥît	1
green plant	*yereq*	1
grief, grievance	*kaʿas*	1
grieve	*kāʿas*	3
groan (n)	*ʾănāqâ*	3
groaning	*ʾănāḥâ*	4

guard, keep (law)	*šāmar*	70
guide (vb)	*nhl*	2
guilty, be, declare	*ʾāšam*	3
habitation	*māʿôn*	5
	mĕʿōnâ	2
hand	*yād*	84
hardship	*mĕṣûqâ*	5
harm (n). *See* evil		
harp	*nēbel*	8
haughty	*gēʾeh*	3
	gābēha	1
hear, listen	*šāmaʿ*	79
helpless	*ḥēlkâ*	3
hide	*str*	22
high place	*bāmâ*	2
high refuge	*miśgāb*	14
honor, adornment	*tipʾeret*	4
hope (n)	*tiqwâ*	3
hope (vb)	*yḥl*	20
horror	*ʾēmāh*	2
host (army)	*ṣābāʾ, ṣĕbāʾôt* (pl.)	23
hut	*sōk*	3
	sukâ	2
indignation	*zaʿam*	4
iniquity	*ʿawōn*	31
injustice. *See also* evildoers	*ʾāwen*	13
innocence	*niqqāyôn*	2
innocent	*nāqî*	5
insolence, insolently	*ʿātāq*	3
instruct	*yrh* III	8
joy	*gîl*	3
joy, shout for. *See* shout for (with) joy		
joyful, be	*ʿālaṣ*	4
jubilant cry	*tĕrûʿâ*	5

judge (vb)	*šāfaṭ*	32
judgment, decree	*mišpāṭ*	58
judgment, give	*dîn*	8
justice	*ṣedeq*	49
	ṣĕdāqâ	33
keep (law). *See* guard		
keep precisely	*yāšar*	2
kill	*hārag*	9
knock down	*dḥh*	6
know	*yādaʿ*	94
lamentation	*rinnâ* I	6
land. *See* earth		
languish, fail, be consumed	*kālāh* (qal)	15
laugh (vb)	*ṣāḥaq* (qal)	4
law	*tôrâ*	36
lay (snare, trap)	*ṭmn*	7
lead	*nḥh*	18
learn	*lmd* (qal)	4
lie (n)	*šeqer*	21
lie (speak falsehood)	*kzb*	3
lion	*ʾarēh*	6
	lebeʾ	1
lion, young	*kĕfîr*	6
lion-cub	*šaḥal*	1
listen. *See* hear		
loathe	*tʿb*	6
long for	*tʾb*	2
look (at, on)	*nbṭ*	17
look down	*šqf*	4
look expectantly	*śbr*	3
lookout, be on the	*šḥr*	2
Lord	*yhwh*	683
love (n) (Ps 109:4, 5)	*ʾahăbâ*	2
love (vb)	*ʾāhab*	39
love, covenant	*ḥesed*	123
lyre	*kīnnôr*	14

majesty	*hôd*	8
Master (God)	*ʾādôn, ădônāy*	64
meadow	*nāwâ*	4
melt, make	*msh*	3
melt away	*šyḥ*	4
mercy, have	*ḥānan*	26
might (n)	*gĕbûrâ*	17
mighty. *See* splendid		
murder (n)	*rāṣaḥ*	2
murmur (vb)	*hgh*	10
music, make	*zmr*	42
nations	*gôyim*	59
needy	*ʾebyôn*	23
net	*rešet*	8
noble (n)	*nādîb*	8
numerous. *See* powerful		
observe (obey), protect	*nṣr*	24
oppressed (adj)	*dak*	3
oppression	*tōk*	3
oppressor	*ṣar* II	24
outcry	*ṣĕʿāqâ*	1
outlet. *See* emerging		
pain	*makʾôb*	3
	kĕʾēb	1
pain, be in	*kʾb*	1
pallet	*yāṣûaʿ*	2
palm (of hand)	*kaf*	21
parched land	*ṣiyyâ*	4
pasturage	*kar* II	2
pasture (n)	*marʿît*	4
path	*ʾōraḥ*	15
pathway	*nātîb, nĕtîbâ*	4
pay, repay	*šlm* (piel)	16
people	*ʿam*	117
peoples (Ps 117:1)	*ʾummîm*	1
perfection	*tōm*	7

perversity, perverse	ʿawlâ	7
	ʿôlâ	2
perverted	ʿiqqēš	2
pinion	ʾēber	1
	ʾebrâ	2
pit	bôr	7
	bĕʾēr	2
pitfall	šîḥâ	2
plan (n)	ʿēṣâ	11
plan (vb). *See also* consider	ḥāšab	18
plea (n)	tĕḥinnâ	3
pleading (n)	taḥânûn	8
pleasant	nāʿîm	6
pleasure, take ... in	rāṣāh	13
pleasure (favor)	rāṣôn	13
plot (n)	zimmâ	2
plot (vb), intend	zāmam	3
plunder (vb) (Ps 7:5)	ḥālaṣ (*see* deliver)	
ponder	śyḥ	14
poor	ʿānaw, ʿānawîm	13
	ʿānî, ʿānîyim	28
portent	môfēt	5
portion	ḥêleq	6
pour	šāpak	12
power	kōaḥ	11
powerful, numerous, be	ʿāṣam	6
praise (n)	tĕhillâ	30
praise (vb)	hll (piel, pual)	79
prayer	tĕfillâ	30
precepts	piqqûdîm	24
pride (n)	gaʾăwâ	7
	gēʾût	3
	gāʾôn	2
prince	śar	9
prisoner	ʾāsîr	5
promise (n)	ʾimrâ	26
prosperity	hôn	3
prostrate (oneself), fall	šḥh	17

protect. *See* observe		
proud	*zēd*	8
proverb	*māšāl*	4
pure	*ṭahôr*	3
purify	*ṭāhēr*	2
put on	*ḥgr*	4
quake	*rʿš*	5
quiet, be, keep	*ḥrš* (hifil)	2
races (= people)	*lĕʾummîm*	14
rage	*ʿebĕrâ*	5
ram's horn	*šôfār*	4
ransom (vb)	*pādāh*	14
rebel (n)	*sôrēr*	4
rebellion	*pešaʿ*	14
rebuke (n). *See* threat		
redeem	*gāʾal*	11
refuge	*maḥseh*	12
refuge, high. *See* high refuge		
refuge, take	*ḥāsāh*	11
reject	*māʾas*	8
rejoice	*śwś*	7
rejoice ecstatically	*gyl*	19
rejoicing (n)	*śāśôn*	5
render (good, evil)	*gāmal*	10
repay. *See* pay		
reproach (n). *See* scorn (n)		
reprove	*ykḥ*	7
rescue (vb)	*nṣl*	44
rest (n)	*menûḥâ*	4
	mānôaḥ	1
retreat (vb)	*sûg*	8
riches	*ʿōšer*	3
ridicule (n)	*qeles*	2
ridicule (vb)	*lʿg*	4
river	*nāhār*	15
rock (n)	*ṣûr*	25

	selaʿ	9
rouse (oneself)	ʿwr	11
ruin (n)	hawwâ	8
ruin (vb)	šḥt	3
safety, bring to	plṭ	17
salvation	yĕšûʿâ	44
	tĕšûʿâ	13
	yēšaʿ	20
sate, satisfy	śābaʿ	23
save	yšʿ	57
scheme (n)	mĕzimmâ	5
scoff	lyṣ	2
scorn (vb)	ḥrf	12
scorn, reproach (n)	ḥerpâ	20
scourge (n)	negaʿ	4
scrutinize	ḥqr	3
search out, for	dāraš	24
secret (n). *See* shelter (n)		
secret, secretive, be	ʾlm	3
security, in	beṭaḥ	3
seek	bqš	27
set on high	śgb	7
shake, writhe	ḥîl (kal)	7
shake off	nʿr	2
shame	bōšet	7
shame, be shamed	bwš	34
shelter, secret (n)	sēter	10
shelter, store (vb)	ṣāpan	9
shepherd (vb)	nāhag	4
shield (n)	māgēn	19
shield, large	ṣinâ	3
shout, joyful	rinnâ II	9
shout for (with) joy	rnn	26
shut	sāgar (qal)	6
sign	ʾôt	7
silence (n)	dûmâ	2
	dămî	1

silence (vb)	ṣmt	11
silent, be, keep	ḥšh	3
simple	petî	3
sin (n), sinner	ḥăṭāʾâ, ḥēṭʾ, ḥaṭṭāʾt, ḥaṭṭāʾ	25
sin (vb)	ḥāṭāʾ (qal)	8
smelt	ṣāraf	8
smite	māḥas	5
snare (n)	môqēš	6
snare, try to	nqš	3
	yqš	2
sojourn (vb)	gwr I	6
sorrow	yāgôn	4
splendid, mighty	ʾaddîr	6
splendor	hādār	13
spring (of water)	maʿyān	5
statute	ḥōq	30
step (n)	paʿam	8
still, be, keep	dmm	7
stillness	dûmîyyâ	4
stone wall	gādēr, gĕdērâ	3
store (vb). *See* shelter (vb)		
stratagem, arrogant	zāmām	1
stray	tāʿāh	6
stream (n)	naḥal	7
stream-channel	ʾāppîq	3
strength	ʿōz	44
	ʿĕzûz	2
strike	nkh	13
strong	ʾabbîr	5
strong, be	gābar (kal)	3
stronghold	mĕṣûdâ	7
stumble, wobble	kāšal	7
stupid	baʿar	3
sturdy, be	ʾāmaṣ (kal)	2
support (vb)	sāʿad	6
sweetness	nōʿam	2
take hold of	tmk	4

take up	*lāqaḥ*	13
teach	*lmd* (piel)	22
tear (in pieces)	*ṭārap*	4
tears	*dimʿāh*	8
temple	*hêkāl*	13
terrify	*bhl* (piel)	2
terror (sing.)	*paḥad*	9
terror, be in	*bhl* (nifal)	8
test (vb)	*bḥn*	9
testimony	*ʿēdût*	13
thank, give thanks	*ydh*	62
threat, rebuke (n)	*gĕʿārâ*	4
toil (often evil) (n)	*ʿāmāl*	13
tomb	*qeber*	3
torment (n)	*laḥaṣ*	3
tower	*migdāl*	2
track (n)	*maʿgāl, maʿgālâ*	4
trample	*rāmas*	2
train (vb). *See* chastise		
trap (n)	*paḥ*	9
tread down	*bws*	3
tremble	*rāgaz*	5
trembling (n)	*rĕʿādâ*	2
	raʿad	1
tribe	*šēbeṭ* II	5
tripping (n)	*ṣelaʿ*	2
trumpet	*ḥăṣōṣrâ*	1
trust (n)	*mibṭāḥ*	3
trust (vb)	*bāṭaḥ*	46
try (put on trial)	*nsh*	6
understand	*śākal*	11
underworld	*šĕʾôl*	16
uphold	*sāmak*	11
upright	*yāšār*	25
uprightness, uprightly	*mêšārîm*	7
	yōšer	2
urge (drive) along	*nāhag*	4

vanish	*ʾābad* (qal)	21
vanity	*hebel*	9
verdict	*dîn* (n)	3
vigor. *See* wealth		
vileness	*běliyyaʿal*	3
wait on, for	*qwh*	17
wait patiently	*ḥkh*	2
war	*qěrāb*	5
wash	*rāḥaṣ*	3
watch (for)	*ṣph*	3
waver	*mʿd* (kal)	3
weak	*dal*	5
wealth	*ḥayil*	17
weep	*bākāh*	4
weeping (n)	*běkî*	3
wipe out	*blh* (piel)	1
wither	*mll* I	3
wobble. *See* stumble		
womb	*reḥem*	3
wonder(s) (n)	*niflāʾôt*	28
	peleʾ	7
work (n)	*maʿăśeh*	39
worthless(ness)	*šāwʾ*	14
wrath	*ḥārôn*	6
wrathful, be	*ḥārāh*	5
writhe. *See* shake		
wrong (n)	*ʿawel*	3
wrongdoer(s)	*mēraʿ, merēʿîm*	9
yearn	*ksf*	2
zeal	*qinʾâ*	3

BIBLIOGRAPHY

Alter, Robert. *The Book of Psalms: A Translation with Commentary.* New York: W.W. Norton, 2007.

Ambrose, Saint. *Expositio in Psalmum CXVIII.* Edited by J.-P. Migne. Patrologia Latina 15.

Athanasius, Saint. *The Life of Antony and the Letter to Marcellinus.* Translated by Robert C. Gregg. New York: Paulist Press, 1980.

Augustine, Saint. *Concerning the City of God against the Pagans.* Translated by Henry Bettenson. Harmondsworth: Penguin Classics, 1984.

―――. *Enarrationes in Psalmos.* 3 vols. Corpus Christianorum Series Latina 38–40. Turnhout: Brepols, 1956. *Expositions on the Psalms.* English translation by Maria Boulding. New York: New City Press, 2000–2004.

Benedict XVI. Message on Easter Monday, 2007. *Regina Caeli,* 9 April 2007. http://www.vatican.va/holy_father/benedict_xvi/angelus/2007/documents/hf_ben-xvi_reg_20070409_easter-monday_en.html.

Benedict, Saint. *RB 1980: The Rule of Saint Benedict in Latin and English with Notes.* Edited by Timothy Fry. Collegeville, MN: Liturgical Press, 1981.

Bernard, Saint. *On the Song of Songs.* Translated by Kilian Walsh. Cistercian Fathers Series 4. Spencer, MA: Cistercian Publications, 1971–1980.

Biblia Hebraica. 7th ed. Edited by Rudolf Kittel. Stuttgart: Württembergische Bibelanstalt, 1951.

Byrne, Brendan. *Romans.* Sacra Pagina 6. Collegeville, MN: Liturgical Press, 1996.

Cassian, John. *Conférences.* Translated by E. Pichery. 3 vols. Sources Chrétiennes 42, 54, 64. Paris: Éditions du Cerf, 1955–1959.

Catechism of the Catholic Church. 2nd ed. Vatican: Libreria Editrice Vaticana, 1997.

Claudel, Paul. *Positions et Propositions: Art et Littérature.* Paris: Gallimard, 1928.

Corbon, Jean. *The Wellspring of Worship.* Translated by Matthew J. O'Connell. New York: Paulist Press, 1988.

Crashaw, Richard. *The Verse in English of Richard Crashaw.* New York: Grove Press, 1949.

Crow, Loren D. *The Songs of Ascents (Psalms 120–134): Their Place in Israelite History and Religion.* Atlanta: Scholars Press, 1996.

Donne, John. *Complete Poetry and Selected Prose.* Edited by John Hayward. London: Nonesuch Press, 1945.

The Englishman's Hebrew and Chaldee Concordance of the Old Testament. 5th ed. Grand Rapids: Zondervan, 1970.

Fiedrowicz, Michael. *Psalmus Vox Totius Christi: Studien zu Augustins "Enarrationes in Psalmos."* Freiburg [im Bresgau]: Herder, 1997.

Gaudium et Spes. In *The Documents of Vatican II.* Edited by Walter Abbott. Garden City, NJ: Guild Press, 1966.

General Instruction for the Liturgy of the Hours (GILH). In *The Liturgy of the Hours,* vol. 1, 21–98. Sacred Congregation for Divine Worship. New York: Catholic Book Publishers, 1975.

Gerstenberger, Erhard S. *Psalms.* 2 vols. Grand Rapids: Eerdmans, 1988, 2001.

Gregory of Nyssa. *Gregory of Nyssa's Treatise on the Inscriptions of the Psalms.* Translated by Ronald E. Heine. Oxford: Clarendon Press, 1995.

Holladay, William. *A Concise Hebrew and Aramaic Lexicon of the Old Testament.* Grand Rapids, MI: Eerdmans, 1971.

Hopkins, Gerard Manley. *Poems and Prose of Gerard Manley Hopkins.* London: Penguin Books, 1953.

Hossfeld, Frank-Lothar and Erich Zenger. *Die Psalmen,* vol. 1, *Psalm 1–50*; vol. 2, *Psalm 51–100.* Würzburg: Echter Verlag, 1993, 2003.

The Jerusalem Bible. Edited by Alexander Jones. London: Darton, Longman and Todd, 1966.

The Jewish People and Their Sacred Scriptures in the Christian Bible. Vatican City: Pontifical Biblical Commission, 2002.

John of the Cross, Saint. *The Ascent of Mount Carmel.* Translated by E. Allison Peers. Garden City, NY: Image Books, 1958.

John Paul II. *Psalms and Canticles: Meditations and Catechesis on the Psalms and Canticles of Morning Prayer.* Chicago: Liturgy Training Publications, 2004.

———. *Veritatis Splendor. Origins* 23, no. 18 (October 14, 1993): 297–334.

Kraus, Hans-Joachim. *Psalmen.* 2 vols. Biblischer Kommentar. Neukirchen: Neukirchener Verlag, 1961.

Lohfink, Norbert. *In the Shadow of Your Wings: New Readings of Great Texts from the Bible.* Translated by Linda M. Maloney. Collegeville, MN: Liturgical Press, 2003.

Lohfink, Norbert and Erich Zenger. *The God of Israel and the Nations: Studies in Isaiah and the Psalms.* Translated by Everett R. Kalin. Collegeville, MN: Liturgical Press, 2000.

Lumen Gentium. In *The Documents of Vatican II.* Edited by Walter Abbott. Garden City, NJ: Guild Press, 1966.

Monloubou, Louis. *L'imaginaire des psalmistes: psaumes et symboles.* Paris: Cerf, 1980.

Pius XII. *Mediator Dei.* Translated by Canon G. D. Smith. *Christian Worship: Encyclical Letter of Pope Pius XII, 'Mediator Dei.'* London: Catholic Truth Society, 1947.

The Psalms: A New Translation from the Hebrew Arranged for Singing to the Psalmody of Joseph Gelineau. Copyright by The Grail. New York: Paulist Press, 1963.

Rondeau, Marie-Josephe. *Les commentaires patristiques du Psautier (IIIe–Ve siècles),* vol. 2. Rome: Pontifical Institute of Oriental Studies, 1985.

The Rule of the Master. Translated by Luke Eberle. Kalamazoo, MI: Cistercian Publications, 1977.

Sacrosanctun Concilium. In *The Documents of Vatican II.* Edited by Walter Abbott. Garden City, NJ: Guild Press, 1966.

Saint Andrew Daily Missal. Dom Gaspar Lefebvre, O.S.B. Bruges: Abbey of St. Andrew, 1958.

Salmon, Pierre. *Les "Tituli Psalmorum" des manuscrits latins.* Paris: Cerf, 1959.

The Sayings of the Desert Fathers: The Alphabetical Collection. Translated by Benedicta Ward. Kalamazoo: Cistercian Publications, 1984.

A Word in Season: Monastic Lectionary for the Divine Office, vol. 4. Villanova, PA: Augustinian Press, 1991.

Wordsworth, William. *Selected Poetry.* New York: Random House (The Modern Library), 1950.

Writings from the Philokalia on Prayer of the Heart. Translated by E. Kadloubovsky and G. E. H. Palmer. London: Faber and Faber, 1951. Reprint, 1979.

Zenger, Erich. "Composition and Theology of the Fifth Book of Psalms." *Journal for the Study of the Old Testament* 80 (1998): 90.

INDEX OF BIBLICAL BOOKS OTHER
THAN THE PSALMS

The following index lists biblical books (other than the Psalms) referenced in the
commentary with respect to specific psalms or verses. For example, in discussing
Psalm 8, I refer to Gen 1, in Psalm 51:12, I refer to Gen 1:1.

OLD TESTAMENT

Genesis	*(Psalm)*
1	8
1:1	51:12
1:1–2	104:30
1:1–11	74
1:2	135:6
1:2–6	33:6
1:2, 6–9	29:3, 42:8, 77:16–20
1:3	107:25, 147:15
1:3–8	104:2
1:6–8	150:1
1:7	104:3, 148:4
1:12	104:14
1:14	104:19
1:16–18	136:9
1:21	148:7
1:26–27	1:2
1:28	8:6
2:1	24:10
2:2	73:28
2:2–3	95:11
2:4	51:12
2:6	46:5, 87:7
2:7	103:14, 119:25, 150:6
2:10	46:5
2:10–14	42; 87:7
2:13	46:5, 110:7
2:15	8:6, 46:5, 104:23
2:24	63:9, 119:31
3:5–6	8
3:16–19	6
3:17–19	41:5
3:19	103:14, 119:25, 146:4
4:8	10:8
5:24	49:16
7:1	12:8
9:11	104:9
11:30	113:9
12:1	45:11
12:3	72:17

New Testament

INDEX OF SELECTED TOPICS

The following index indicates where certain topics that appear frequently in the Psalms are discussed in greater detail in this commentary.

LAURENCE KRIEGSHAUSER, O.S.B.,

is a Benedictine monk at St. Louis Abbey,

St. Louis, Missouri.